D0876366

The Study
of Urban History

To
The Urban History Group

The Study
of Urban History

The proceedings of an international round-table conference
of the Urban History Group
at Gilbert Murray Hall, University of Leicester
on 23–26 September 1966

edited by
H. J. Dyos

New York · St. Martin's Press · 1968

© Edward Arnold (Publishers) Ltd. 1968

First published 1968
First published in
the United States of America in 1968
First published in Great Britain by
Edward Arnold (Publishers) Ltd.

Library of Congress Catalog Card Number: 68-29379

Printed in Great Britain by
William Clowes and Sons, Limited, London and Beccles

Foreword

The essays in this book were produced in 1966 for the first conference of British urban historians, reinforced by geographers, sociologists, and 'civic designers', including a number of distinguished scholars from overseas. The essays provide a fascinating glimpse of work in progress. Out of many of them, doubtless, books will eventually emerge.

Conferences on cities have by now become a familiar feature of the international academic scene. They are usually interdisciplinary in character, and either directly or indirectly they usually relate historical evidence and interpretation to contemporary problems and analysis. Just because the contemporary city is a focus of so many problems, it is natural to look back to the past for origins and for parallels. The 'looking back', however, may be either systematic and disciplined or brief and almost a matter of ritual, giving a 'time dimension' to the immediate and the practical. Simple analogies may be 'discovered' which cannot bear sustained examination. When historians gather together on their own— or with invited guests from other disciplines—most of them will be very suspicious of long-term views and neat comparison, which, however ingenious, illuminate the present rather than the past. They may or may not be particularly concerned with the immediate issues of the present— many of the participants at the Leicester Conference said that they were not—but they will find it difficult to study historical problems without being influenced if not by the techniques at least by the pre-occupations of modern inter-disciplinary urban studies.

They may, of course, be influenced even more by recent changes within the study of history itself, which have allowed greater scope for team effort and for more sophisticated modes of analysis. Certainly, the inspiration for historical studies not only of particular cities but of cities as a category and of urban processes in society certainly seems to spring from changes within history itself—the recognition of the need to examine in detail social structure and change in the most meaningful units that historians can discover; the attempt to relate quantitative data to other data, with historical demography as a base; dissatisfaction with 'narrow' economic history and trivial social history; the desire to revise and re-write national histories in the light of fuller knowledge of local relationships and pressures; and the growing interest in the comparative method, carrying with it the need to investigate similar phenomena, of which 'the city' is one of the most obvious, in different societies.

The British historians who met at Leicester were fully representative not only of the present generation of urban historians—a growing number, particularly at the level of postgraduate research—but of historians as a whole. I was sad, for unavoidable reasons, to have to miss the conference myself, where I would like to have taken part in the discussions, and I welcome the publication of this volume which taken as a whole constitutes a progress report as well as a glimpse of current work in hand. The survey by Dr. Dyos of books and articles is one of the most valuable features of the volume, the fullest bibliography that has yet appeared. The range of its contents and the balance of topics covered may be usefully compared with the range and balance of historical output in such other developing fields as labour history and business history. So also may the kinds of arguments and controversies through which discussions of the subject seem to lead— how to define it; how to determine to what extent it should develop by the borrowing of concepts from the social sciences; how to decide in what ways models and theories should be constructed and applied; how to settle whether or not it can encompass 'micro' and 'macro' studies; how to assess its relationship to other branches of history. Certainly developments in urban studies influence other kinds of historical research, and the development of a deeper, a broader, and a more disciplined social history obviously depends on work being carried out by specialised groups of historians like those associated with the pioneer enterprises of the Urban History Group and the *Urban History Newsletter*.

To be a successful historian of the city or of cities the historian not only requires the same gifts as other historians—analytical power, imagination, and a real sense of the past. He must also be a historian of something else besides the city—of families, business, social and political movements, buildings, and of cultures and styles. There are, after all, difficulties in pivoting too much on the city. While there is a sense—elusive to define, difficult to track historically through successive periods—of the 'identity' of the particular city, all sentences beginning 'Birmingham thought' or 'Manchester influenced' must be treated with critical reserve. It may well be that some historians in the past have attributed to cities what is better attributed to economic and social groups within them or have not probed deeply into the social influences of 'class' or religion. Moreover the 'identity' of places as social units can change. The 'images' of British cities and their 'contributions' to national life may often have shifted, at least as much as say the 'images' and 'contributions' of Melbourne and Sydney shifted in Australia, a country with an exceptionally large proportion of city dwellers, between the 1880s and the 1960s. The very conception of 'identity' itself is changing, as cities begin to look increasingly alike and as common norms—national or international—influence so much city activity.

There is a particular urgency behind urban studies in this country just because of the speed of the processes of urban transformation—the obliteration of many of the signs of the past; the destruction of so much of the environment, blighted or beautiful; the break in continuity both of feelings and of policies and of the symbols associated with them. There are obvious links between urban archaeology and industrial archaeology, but there are other links, too, between the understanding of architecture and the history of older cities. The visual dimension of urban studies is so important that it is remarkable how often it has been neglected. There are particular assets in this connection, however, in being an urban historian in Britian, because of the strong sense of identity of particular places, the number of historical layers, and the variety of urban experience. Indeed, the neglect of the visual has probably been less marked among historians in this country than overseas, and in recent years a number of important and interesting books concentrate on the study of the past, medieval as well as modern, through maps, plans, pictures, and photographs. This approach to urban history is represented in this volume alongside more analytical sociological approaches relying on statistical or conceptual analysis.

As the different approaches develop and urban history continues to boom, as I believe it will—with the help of the camera and the computer— it is useful to recall, as many of the contributors to this volume emphasise, how recent both the general and the specialised interest is. When along with Professor Conrad Gill I wrote the *History of Birmingham* in 1952 there were no recent models—only compartmentalised studies of particular aspects of city economy and government. Our history was a belated attempt to produce a centenary volume which had originally been mooted in 1936 when the centenary of Birmingham's incorporation loomed ahead in two years' time. By 1948 the modest 40,000 words on modern Birmingham commissioned from Sir Charles Grant Robertson had not been written, and when I took over my own assignment, there were no clear specifications. It seemed a bold decision at that stage to try to break down the artificial barriers between the separate divisions of history, particularly the barrier between economic and political history, and to try to describe the evolution of the community as a whole. A strictly chronological treatment of the narrative of Birmingham history did not appeal to me, and I was determined to work my way through 'problems' rather than through 'topics'. At the same time I had to establish my chronology and cover my topics. I had in mind during this early period of my work a sentence from Professor Herbert Butterfield which seemed to carry with it valuable advice:

> 'Some people imagine that if a man conducts research on a particular area of historical happening the effect will be that one fact here and another fact there will be corrected; or that the story will be told as before, only it will be told in greater detail, or that the narrative will merely be amended or supplemented at some marginal point. The result is far more radical than this because total reconstructions are often necessary when a certain fact has proved to be pivotal or requires not merely to be added to the other facts but to be followed out in the displacements it produces among the rest. One of the high tests of an historian is the degree to which he possesses the requisite elasticity of mind, so that he is not a mere compiler, adding new facts to old ones, not a mere prisoner of a current framework of study, but a detective determined not to miss the clue that may lead to a fresh reconstruction of the theme and carry the issue to a higher order of thought.'

Often in writing about Birmingham I had the sense of reaching a complete historical reconstruction, even after I had found a series of explanations which seemed to cohere and had, indeed, cohered in the minds of other historians. For instance, in my chapter on 'The Best Governed City in the World'—where I wanted to deal with something bigger than civic administration—I began with what one could call the conventional local interpretation of the 'civic revolution'—that Birmingham blazed the trail until it became, in the words of Sidney Webb, 'a municipal Mecca'. Yet it began to be clear to me after a time, particularly as a result of examining, albeit cursorily, the history of other cities, like Liverpool or Glasgow, that the rapid pace of civic change in Birmingham during the 1870s was dependent to some extent, at last, on its relative backwardness before 1870. Dr. Hennock, one of the essayists in this volume, has subsequently made the same point more firmly on the bais of a deeper investigation of Birmingham, and Professor Geoffrey Best and others have reached the same conclusion in the light of detailed work on other cities.

Writing my own history—and carrying out the arduous but rewarding research which was a requisite preliminary to writing—I came to five conclusions which I set out in a paper which I read to the Ashley Society in Birmingham University when the history was finished: first, that the sources were limitless; second, that there was often, nonetheless, a shortage of basic documentary material, some of it of strategic importance; third, that many other monographs, the existence of which would have been invaluable to me, still needed to be written; fourth, that the history which Professor Gill and I had written was *a* history and not *the* history of Birmingham, and that as new documentation was discovered—say in, business firms or solicitors' offices—as urban studies in general developed, and as there was a change from these post-1945 perspectives—very limited perspectives, as the most recent history of Birmingham has shown —there would be need for alternative histories; and fifth, that the work which I had done needed to be extended in range to encompass other cities, including cities outside Britain, as well as deepened in relation to Birmingham itself. It was out of this last conclusion that I deliberately moved forward first to the study of American urban sociology, particularly the sociology of the still active Chicago School, then to work on urbanisation and cities in other countries besides Britain and during other periods besides the high distinctive nineteenth century, and finally to the writing of *Victorian Cities*.

A study of the essays in this volume convinces me that there is not one valid approach to urban history but many, and that different kinds of historian are needed just as different kinds of technique or insight. There is ample opportunity to learn from each other, and, as has not always been the case in the preparation of earlier international conferences or in the publication of their proceedings, all the essayists represented in the volume are themselves actively and specifically engaged on urban research. Some of the new techniques described here are particularly relevant to further study of quite different contexts, and such is the increasing 'sophistication' of history that much that looks novel when it first appears very quickly and firmly takes its place as an accepted feature in the historian's repertoire. I confess that for myself, however, the kind of urban history which most appeals to me is that which is placed in a bigger and perhaps sturdier historical framework, the kind of social history which ignores neither politics nor ideas and relates forms and styles to facts and figures.

One final point seems to me to be of central importance. There is much to be said for initially approaching the problems both of the history of individual cities and of urbanisation in the terms in which contemporaries approached them—in talking of social categories, for instance, to begin by looking at the categories contemporaries used themselves rather than by superimposing upon them our own more sophisticated categories, and to go on to examine and to evaluate the social argument, with all its limitations, in which contemporaries indulged. This process is the very reverse of seeking 'a time dimension' for our own problems and points of view. Likewise, in bringing to bear quantitative evidence, much of it unknown to contemporaries, it is invaluable to seek to understand what they made or did not make of quantitative evidence. The increasing interest in statistics in the nineteenth century, even when the techniques were not very highly developed, seems to me to be the best lead-in to the use of more developed statistics in relation to nineteenth-century urban history. Through this line of entry which entails total immersion in reports, debates, periodicals, and newspapers, there can be a recovery of the sense of immediacy—at times even of the sense of shock—which is as essential in recreation of the past as the achievement of a sense of perspective. It is valuable also to turn to those past general statements about cities which still retain their sense of immediacy, like Vaughan's comment in the 1840s that

> 'the new and speedy communication which will soon be completed between all great cities in every nation of Europe, will necessarily tend to swell the larger towns into still greater magnitude and to diminish the weight of many smaller places, as well as of the rural population generally in social affairs. Everywhere we trace this disposition to converge upon great points. It avails nothing to complain of this tendency as novel, inconsiderate, hazardous. The pressure toward such an issue is irresistible, nor do we see the slightest prospect of its ceasing to be so.'

Hindsight comes in later, and with it refinement, so that we can see how one reaction was related to another through continuity or through break, or more generally, as G. M. Trevelyan has put it, how the social historian can get 'to know more in some respects than the dweller in the past himself knew about the conditions that enveloped and controlled his life'.

The essayists in this volume are all trying to do this—through the study of the 'smaller places' as much as the 'great cities' and, when relevant, through an effort to understand the often neglected relationships between urban and rural history. It will be interesting to compare their methods and conclusions with those reached at future conferences, when the field will have been cultivated still more and when many of the fascinating projects described in these pages have reached completion.

ASA BRIGGS

University of Sussex,
December 1967

Preface

This volume contains the proceedings of the round-table conference held in the University of Leicester by the Urban History Group between 23 and 26 September 1966. Attendance was by invitation and those present are listed below. It was the first symposium of its kind to be held in Britain and it marked an important step in the development of a rapidly expanding field of historical research.

For that reason it was given a form which would allow for the greatest possible discussion of the questions raised in the papers in an atmosphere of maximum informality. The conference was concerned essentially with two issues; the materials and methods of urban history; the comparative study of British cities. These form the basis of Sections II, III, and IV, and of V and VI, respectively, in this volume. Most of the papers were circulated in advance, and were discussed jointly in a series of long seminars presided over by a separate *rapporteur* in each case. The discussions were taped and synopses prepared from the verbatim transcriptions. The papers and reports of the discussions are given here in the order in which they took place and, except for minor amendments, they remain substantially in the form in which they were taken at the conference. There are just two departures from this: the opening paper has been enlarged to include a short bibliographical treatment of the subject; the two papers on visual evidence are not accompanied here by precisely the same sets of illustrations as those used in delivering them because it has not been possible in every case to make suitable reproductions from the slides.

The Warden and his staff at Gilbert Murray Hall made us exceptionally comfortable and served us much good food. This was as well because discussion went on virtually without a break from breakfast to nearly midnight on each day. I must express the warmest thanks to all who participated for their very ready co-operation during the planning of the conference, and for their indefatigable resolve when it was taking place not to miss a moment of the programme; to the *rapporteurs* for the tasks they all performed with such wit and resolution; to the contributors for accepting the assignments and keeping the deadlines I gave them; to my secretary, Susan Davies, for keeping vigil with the tape-recorder and, with Linda Allen, typing the greater part of the proceedings; and to Marie Forsyth for the speed and care she took in making the index. Professor Asa Briggs, who was to have taken the chair for one of the sessions, was prevented from doing so at a late stage, and it is therefore especially appropriate that he should have contributed the foreword to this volume. I am most grateful to him for agreeing to do so.

HJD

The Participants

MR. W. A. ARMSTRONG	Lecturer in Economic and Social History, University of Nottingham
PROFESSOR W. ASHWORTH	Head of Department of Economic History, University of Bristol
MRS. A. B. M. BAKER	Research Assistant, Department of Economic History, University of Leicester
MRS. S. E. BAKER	Research Scholar, Department of History, Queen's University, Belfast
PROFESSOR T. C. BARKER	Head of Department of Economic History, University of Kent at Canterbury
MR. FRANÇOIS BEDARIDA	Director, Maison Française, Oxford
PROFESSOR G. F. A. BEST	Department of History, University of Edinburgh
MR. H. CARTER	Senior Lecturer in Geography, University College of Wales, Aberystwyth
MR. C. W. CHALKIN	Lecturer in History, University of Reading
DR. W. H. CHALONER	Reader in History, University of Manchester
PROFESSOR S. G. CHECKLAND	Head of Department of Economic History, University of Glasgow
DR. R. A. CHURCH	Lecturer in Economic History, University of Birmingham
PROFESSOR P. A. W. COLLINS	Department of English, University of Leicester
PROFESSOR M. R. G. CONZEN	Department of Geography, University of Newcastle-upon-Tyne
DR. H. J. DYOS	Reader in Economic History, University of Leicester
DR. D. E. C. EVERSLEY	Reader in Population Studies, University of Sussex
DR. H. E. S. FISHER	Lecturer in Economic History, University of Exeter
MR. W. FORSYTH	Lecturer in Economic History, University of Glasgow
MR. JOHN FOSTER	Fellow of St. Catharine's College, University of Cambridge

xiv

The Participants

MR. T. W. FREEMAN	Reader in Geography, University of Manchester
MR. C. HARRIS	Lecturer in Sociology, University College, Swansea
DR. J. R. HARRIS	Director of Social Studies, University of Liverpool
DR. E. P. HENNOCK	Senior Lecturer in History, University of Sussex
PROFESSOR W. G. HOSKINS	Head of Department of English Local History, University of Leicester
MR. F. M. JONES	Director of the Housing Research and Development Group, Liverpool School of Architecture, University of Liverpool
DR. J. R. KELLETT	Senior Lecturer in Economic History, University of Glasgow
PROFESSOR W. KÖLLMANN	Historisches Institut der Rhur-Universität, Bochum
DR. P. H. MANN	Lecturer in Sociology, University of Sheffield
DR. J. D. MARSHALL	Senior Lecturer in the Regional History of Northwest England, University of Lancaster
DR. G. H. MARTIN	Reader in History, University of Leicester
MR. R. J. MORRIS	Research Scholar, Nuffield College, University of Oxford
DR. R. NEWTON	
DR. R. E. PAHL	Lecturer in Sociology, University of Kent at Canterbury
DR. D. A. REEDER	Head of Department of Education, Garnett College, London
PROFESSOR LEO SCHNORE	Department of Sociology, University of Wisconsin
DR. F. H. W. SHEPPARD	Editor, *Survey of London*, County Hall, London
MR. K. M. SPENCER	Research Officer, Housing Research Group, School of Architecture, University of Liverpool
SIR JOHN SUMMERSON	Curator of Sir John Soane's Museum and Slade Professor of Fine Art, University of Cambridge
DR. A. SUTCLIFFE	Research Officer, Department of History, University of Birmingham
MR. D. M. THOMPSON	Research Fellow, Fitzwilliam College, University of Cambridge
DR. P. R. THOMPSON	Lecturer in Sociology, University of Essex
MR. P. M. TILLOTT	Staff Tutor in Local Studies, University of Sheffield
MR. J. WESTERGAARD	Centre for Urban Studies, University College, London

Acknowledgments

The Editor and Publisher wish gratefully to acknowledge permission given by the National Monuments Record to reproduce plates 2, 3, 7, 8, 9, 10, 12, 13, 14, 15, 20, 21, 22, and 23; by the *Essex County Standard* to reproduce plates 5 and 11; by the *Westmorland Gazette* to reproduce plates 17, 18, and 19; by Manchester City Library to reproduce plates 31, 32, 48, and 53; by *Bolton Evening News* to reproduce plate 34; by Ian Paterson, Esq. to reproduce plate 1; by Miss Sylvia McIntyre to reproduce plate 4; by Dr. G. H. Martin to reproduce plates 6, 25, 28, and 29; by Terry Noon, Esq. to reproduce plate 16; by Michael Ricketts, Esq. to reproduce plate 24; by Miss Elaine Dennis to reproduce plate 26; by Tom Sharpe, Esq. to reproduce plate 27; by S. M. Haughton, Esq. to reproduce plates 30 and 54; by J. E. Turner, Esq. to reproduce plates 35, 36, 39, 40, 41, 42D, 43, 44, 45, 46, 47, 49, 50, 51, and 52; by J. Allan Cash, Esq. to reproduce plates 37 and 38; by Rex Wailes, Esq. to reproduce plates 42A, 42B, and 42C; by the University of Wales Press Board for permission to reproduce figures 11 and 13 from *The Towns of Wales, a Study in Urban Geography*, by Harold Carter; by Ordnance Survey to reproduce figures 1, 2, 3, 7, 9, and 14; by the County Archivist, Lancashire County Council, to reproduce figures 4, 5, and 6; by the Editorial Board of *Victorian Studies* to incorporate parts of Dr. Dyos's article on 'The Growth of Cities in the Nineteenth Century' (Vol. IX, No. 3, pp. 225–37) in his paper; and by Leicester University Press to print 'Society and Politics in Exeter, 1837–1914' which is based on their forthcoming publication *Victorian Exeter*, by R. Newton.

Contents

2   xvii

Contents

Illustrations

Maps and Diagrams

Tables

I

Agenda for Urban Historians[1]

H. J. Dyos

Robert Ezra Park, one of the founding fathers of modern urban studies, wrote 50 years ago: 'The city is a state of mind, a body of customs and traditions, and of unorganized attitudes and sentiments that inhere in those customs and are transmitted with this tradition.'[2] As a definition of what a city is, this statement strikes many students of the subject nowadays as dated, ragged, or even mistaken. There has never been an agreed glossary of terms.[3] But as I was thinking about the purpose and possibilities of this conference it struck me that Park's was not such a bad description of urban history as it may be of urbanism! I am, of course, using that

[1] To meet requests made at the conference this paper has been developed bibliographically and now incorporates, in addition to some new material of this kind, parts of my article, 'The growth of cities in the nineteenth century: a review of some recent writing', *Victorian Studies*, ix, No. 3 (March 1966), pp. 225–37.

[2] See 'The city: suggestions for the investigation of human behaviour in the urban environment', *American Journal of Sociology*, xx (1916), pp. 517–612, reprinted in R. E. Park, E. W. Burgess, and R. D. MacKenzie, *The City* (1925), pp. 1–46, and R. E. Park, *Human Communities: The City and Human Ecology* (1952), pp. 13–51.

[3] Among the most interesting attempts in a large literature to make measurements and form concepts of the city and of urbanism are: H. B. Woolston, 'The urban habit of mind', *American Journal of Sociology*, xvii (1911–12), pp. 602–14; Pierre Clerget, 'Urbanism: a historic, geographic and economic study', *The Smithsonian Institution, Annual Report for 1912* (1913), pp. 653–67; Max Weber, *The City* (first published 1921), translated and edited by Don Martindale and Gertrud Neuwirth (1958); N. S. B. Gras, 'The rise of the metropolitan community', in E. W. Burgess (ed.), *The Urban Community* (1926), pp. 183–91; William B. Munro, 'City', in *Encyclopaedia of the Social Sciences* (1930), iii, pp. 474–82; Louis Wirth, 'Urbanism as a way of life', *American Journal of Sociology*, xli (1938), pp. 1–23, reprinted in *On Cities and Social Life*, ed. Albert J. Reiss, Jr. (1964), pp. 60–83, and 'The urban society and civilization', *ibid.*, xlv (1940), pp. 743–55; Charles E. Merriam, 'Urbanism', *ibid.*, pp. 720–30; Hope Tisdale, 'The process of urbanization', *Social Forces*, xx (1941–2), pp. 311–16; V. Gordon Childe, 'The urban revolution', *Town Planning Review*, xxi (1950), pp. 3–17; Kingsley Davis, 'The origin and growth of urbanization in the world', *American Journal of Sociology*, lx (1955), pp. 429–37; N. Anderson, 'Urbanism and urbanization', *American Journal of Sociology*, lxv (1959–60), pp. 68–73. See also W. D. McTaggart, 'The reality of "urbanism"', *Pacific Viewpoint*, vi (1965), pp. 220–4; D. Popenoe, 'On the meaning of "urban" in "urban studies"', *Urban Affairs*, i (1965), pp. 17–34.

term very loosely and being rash enough to include most of the disciplines represented here in this room. Perhaps we shall discover over this long weekend that that was rash indeed.

What *is* urban history? What are its tasks? What are its methods? What is the scope of its literature and its sources? This opening paper cannot give any pat answers. The history of towns has too many faces, and the commentaries that have been made upon their histories have too many controversial aspects, for easy generalisation.[4] Though we would probably all agree that urban history does not comprise everything that happened in towns in the past, we would not agree so easily about what to leave out, nor how to interpret what is put in. If we think about the connections between urban history and other historical issues, such as those between urban concentration and national economic expansion or between suburban development and shifts in political power or between the symbiosis of cultures in the cities and the practice of the arts, then we shall begin to disagree more violently still.

But if we can narrow our attentions for the time being, let me ask whether we want the kind of free-wheeling—some might say mindless—empiricism that gives us shelf upon shelf of encapsulated studies under one Dewey decimal and more or less quantified abstractions of the general experience under another? What should be the connection between histories of individual towns and of urbanisation at large? Are there any

[4] Apart from work noted separately below, see the following, much of which is ostensibly concerned with American historiography but is highly relevant to British urban history: Constance M. Green, 'The value of local history' in Caroline F. Ware (ed.), *The Cultural Approach to History* (1940), pp. 275–86; W. Diamond, 'On the dangers of an urban interpretation of history' in Eric Goldman (ed.), *Historiography and Urbanization* (1941), pp. 67–108; Bayrd Still, 'Patterns of mid-nineteenth century urbanization in the middle west', *Mississippi Valley Historical Review*, xxviii (1941–2), pp. 187–206, 'Local history contributions and techniques in the study of two colonial cities', *Bulletin of the American Association for State and Local History*, ii (1959), pp. 225–50, and 'The history of the city in American life', *The American Review*, ii (1962), pp. 20–34; Blake McKelvey, 'American urban history today', *American Historical Review*, lv (1952), pp. 919–29; W. Stull Holt, 'Some consequences of the urban movement in American history', *Pacific Historical Review*, xxii (1953), pp. 337–51; Richard Wohl, 'Urbanism, urbanity, and the historians', *University of Kansas City Review*, xxii (1955), pp. 53–61, reprinted in part in Charles N. Glaab, *The American City. A Documentary History* (1963), pp. 7–13; Asa Briggs, 'The study of cities', *Confluence*, vii (1958), pp. 107–14, 'Historians and the study of cities', *George Judah Cohen Memorial Lecture* (1960), pp. 3–24, and 'Urban perspectives: a review article', *Urban Studies*, iv (1967), pp. 165–9; Eino Jutikkala, 'The borderland: urban history and urban sociology', *Scandinavian Economic History Review*, iv (1958), pp. 191–5; M. D. Hirsch, 'Reflections on urban history and urban reform, 1865–1915' in D. Sheehan and H. C. Syrett (eds.), *Essays in American Historiography* (1960), pp. 109–137; Eric E. Lampard, 'American historians and the study of urbanization', *American Historical Review*, lxv (1961), pp. 49–61; Charles N. Glaab, 'The historian and the American urban tradition', *Wisconsin Magazine of History*, xlvii (1963), pp. 12–25; A. F. Davis, 'The American historian vs. the city', *Social Studies*, lvi (1965), 91–6 and 127–35.

approaches to the subject that seem exceptionally promising? Is this the stage in the development of the subject when we should be concentrating our efforts on carefully chosen lines of research, or should we simply encourage every original idea and applaud every virtuoso performance?

Frankly, I am not at all sure. I do not feel qualified to provide a complete framework of reference for a field of research that has more mysteries to it than self-evident facts, several scores of thousands of writings with hardly a guide, and an impenetrable jungle of records of which no census has ever been taken. All that I can do in this paper is to ask a few questions that may help us to decide where we think we are going, and to pick out a few of the landmarks that show where others have already been. Such a survey cannot help sparkling with omissions and being, to a large extent, a reflection of personal tastes and interests, but I hope it is wide enough to show not only what has been done but what now needs doing. I would also like to say something about the disorganised condition of this field of research and to kick a little at some of the stumbling blocks in the way of unifying—or at any rate of linking—these investigations. For I think we shall find it difficult even to identify, let alone to make good use of, the field of urban history without having some dialogue between the disciplines involved in and bordering on it: perhaps this explains the chemistry of this conference, as it does the tune that I now want to call to it.

Let me take the most obvious difficulty first. The growth of cities has been taken as one of the most self-evident facts of modern societies for so long that it cannot surprise the historians to find that the history of cities is not being left to them alone. Indeed, there are enough dark images of the city in literature and painting over the last two centuries at least—and fewer smiling ones—to make one think that the historians may be the last to have discovered them. Robert Vaughan's *The Age of Great Cities* appeared as long ago as 1843, but though that was among the very first works to give urban development an historical dimension it was more of a testament of hope in the possibilities of urban progress in an ominous industrial age than it was an account of how that promise was being fulfilled. Historians proper followed long after. Except for the pioneers, they arrived like prospectors late for the first rush. Geographers, sociologists, economists, social psychologists, and civic designers were already out ahead panning the gold. Some of them are now making good strikes; some are turning over the old boundary stones; some are already disputing the methods being used. Among the sociologists, for instance, the argument whether environmental conditions or prevailing cultural values are more fundamental in controlling the cadences of social life in cities, and even their growth, has passed into the second or third generations of its

3

protagonists.[5] Here is the Chicago school, with its background of classical economics and the ideas and language of Darwinistic biology, and the notion that land values and social structure inter-act to produce distinctive neighbourhoods; refuting this allegedly 'one-eyed' analysis is what one historian perched on his empirical peak has called the 'sterile Harvard idea' of adding symbolic values to this theoretical explanation of urban ecology.[6]

Whether or not he makes theories himself, the historian now watches others doing so, or endlessly applying theses developed in one context in a series of others. But he also sees the tendency of sociologists to make a collector's gallery of the aberrations of urban life and to overlook its normal routines, or that of geographers to isolate the purely geographical controls on town growth and to leave aside the more dynamic factors, fading fairly rapidly. What is happening now in the study of the various processes that combine in urbanisation is a positive attempt to grapple as well as possible with the over-spilling problems—as exemplified in Peter Self's *Cities in Flood* (1957)—of organising our own social space to-day. We need to impose more order on the social life of our own cities and to adapt the human personalities of living generations to these environments, and to their cultural opportunities. The literature of town-planning is becoming more sociological,[7] and it is not surprising that the history no less than the present problems of urban society should be recognised more and more as one of the major pre-occupations of the social sciences. Nor should it be surprising that among them there is a widening awareness of the possibility—as Louis Wirth once pointed out to the sociologists[8]—that here, in the study of the way in which urban society has organised itself spatially and structurally and has developed such a variety of social systems, there exists an incomparable arena in which to bring together more explicitly a number of these converging disciplines.

Though the largest part of all this research and policy-making is taking place almost without reference to the historians, one's impression is that the majority of urban historians are conducting their own researches with

5 See Leonard Reissmann, *The Urban Process. Cities in Industrial Societies* (1964), especially Chap. VII on 'The scope of an urban theory'.

6 Eino Jutikkala, 'The borderland: urban history and urban sociology', *Scandinavian Economic History Review*, vi (1958), pp. 191–5.

7 See S. Spielvogel, *A Selected Bibliography in City and Regional Planning* (1951), and Centre for Urban Studies, *Land Use Planning and the Social Sciences: A Selected Bibliography. Literature on Town and Country Planning and related Social Studies in Great Britain, 1930–1963* (1964).

8 'The urban society and civilization', *American Journal of Sociology*, xlv (1940), pp. 743–55.

very little reference to contemporary urban experience.[9] In one sense this is right. The historian ought not to be at the beck and call of every specialist brought in to solve a contemporary problem or he will end by looking at history through the peep-hole of the present. An eminent historian to whom the study of long-term trends is of top priority once asked: 'Must a pre-occupation with a growth of the town and the railway make us ignore the search for the lost village or the road that led (or seems to have led) nowhere?'[10] I am not sure that this means he would have agreed with Oliver Cromwell, whom the chairman has quoted, that the man who went furthest was the man who didn't know where he was going. But it is a warning against being too pre-occupied merely with end-results which we know at first hand. Mr. Carter's paper to this conference contains a more explicit demonstration of this very point. The urban scene is a palimpsest, and we should not ignore the insignificant scratches which our own marks have now all but obliterated.

Just the same, there are other grounds for lingering regret that the study of the urban past and the urban present should stand somewhat apart. Although there are some signs of a change, I think it is still true to say that the study of the problems of urban life and growth in the past is persistently uninformed by the disciplines being applied primarily to contemporary affairs. Of course, the most hackneyed lament of historians is that the reverse is also true. This situation may have arisen because contemporary problems appear to be more complex and to require a multi-disciplinary approach, while those that congeal in the present appear to remain discrete and capable of being approached unilaterally when looked at in the past. A more stubborn reason often is that historical sources are just too meagre or perverse or shut away to give historians the chance of making more of them. Yet one nagging explanation for this sometimes is that historians are more easily embarrassed by riches than most people, and shy away from the vast, undisciplined annals of the very recent past. One of the processes of history secretly beloved of historians must be that of the random, creative destruction of its records.

As a result, one almost has that sense of unreality in reading some urban history that one gets from an historical account of events one has lived through oneself. So that's what it was like, one tells oneself, but cannot help thinking something important has been left out. Take, for example, the sense one has of living in two worlds when one reads the historical account of Birmingham as revealed by the *Victoria County*

---

[9] See Leo F. Schnore and Henry Fagin, *Urban Research and Policy Planning* [*Urban Affairs Annual Reviews*, No. 1.] (1967).

[10] T. S. Ashton, in a review, *Scandinavian Economic History Review*, v (1957), p. 83.

History for Warwickshire and the sense one has of the place from catching crowded buses from New Street into the flat expressionless steppe of Greater Birmingham suburbia.[11] The *V.C.H.* does not enter the suburbs with any purpose, any more than it does one or two other large areas of ordinary life. We get virtually no sense of what it has been like living together and living apart there, nor even how the sheer physicality of the city of Birmingham has evolved, how the million-piece jigsaw has been solved. I want to return to this point later. In any case, it would be unfair to belabour the *V.C.H.*, which is a special kind of historical prisoner, for not breaking recklessly free from these constraints.[12] I wanted simply to illustrate the general sense of unease which is being widely felt, I am sure, by readers of such accounts. Perhaps there is a problem here that can be solved only in terms of a particular historian's interests and abilities and subject. The study of cities clearly cannot be cooped up in one discipline, but just how many disciplines are actually involved in handling the history of a city? How many of these can the individual historian handle himself? How can he collect usable data from non-historians when his own expertise gives out? What are the limits to this kind of collaboration?

The problem is the familiar one of relating to each other researches which bear upon a common historical theme but which are being under-taken under the constraints of disciplines which are at worst totally ignorant, or even cynical, of each other, or which are at best, grudgingly communicative and inclined to be held fast in the purdah of their own jargon. Urban history is the most newly discovered continent and into the scramble for it goes every kind of explorer. What one begins to hope for is some concerted action, not merely to raise the efficiency of the operation but to enhance its value, and its benefits. Hardly anything has yet been done, in Britain at least, to provide this common basis, much less a unified theory, though some such ideas are in embryo. Professor Parry Lewis, for example, who is an economist, is presenting to an urban studies conference in Exeter at this moment some tentative ideas for an urban model by which the present 'hotch-potch of studies of towns' can be organised into a new discipline which he calls *polismetrics*, and which promises to be highly mathematical and, to historians at least, a little arcane. So far as I am aware, no sociologist in this country has propounded anything like that, nor even suggested the points of reference needed in this field.

[11] *The Victoria History of the County of Warwick*, Vol. VII: *The City of Birmingham*, ed. W. B. Stephens (1964).
[12] For a defence of the *V.C.H.* see R. B. Pugh, 'The structure and aims of the *Victoria History of the Counties of England*', *Bulletin of the Institute of Historical Research*, xl (1967), pp. 65–73.

Alone among the historians, Sydney Checkland has begun to work out an approach through the use of four related models which refer to the economic, spatial, social, and policy aspects of city growth in places large enough to display the 'trends typical of urbanisation'. I imagine we shall be hearing how the application of this to the case of Glasgow is working out in practice later in the proceedings. Perhaps it is necessary merely to add here that this is not, strictly speaking, a fully-articulated, dynamic model of city development but rests, if I am not mistaken, on a series of static formulations of the urban economy at 25-year intervals, though there is the possibility that these might be sub-divided later. It depends primarily on the collaboration of economic historians and geographers, though it would seem that sociologists will have to be on hand, too. This is essentially an attempt to identify the crucial phenomena and to divide the labour of investigating them. It is not a theoretical explanation of urban growth itself.

One could wish that urban historians would find themselves getting enmeshed to a greater extent with the new kinds of thinking about these phenomena that are being developed by other disciplines, especially perhaps those concerned with contemporary problems. The reproach that one American economic historian long concerned with the study of urban history levelled at the American Historical Association five years ago could also be aimed, not unfairly, at the majority of British urban historians. We have neglected quite as badly the *social processes* that create cities and persisted as doggedly with the old pre-occupations as our American colleagues have done. The study of urban history must mean not merely the study of individual communities, fixed more or less in time and space —what might be called the urban aspect of local history; but the investigation of altogether broader historical processes and trends that completely transcend the life cycle and range of experience of particular communities. I am not suggesting that among the agenda for urban historians may be the need to abandon 'the historical method' though we could profitably be less precious about it sometimes; but it is refreshing to see younger historians more inclined to get hold of problems just as they are, pursuing them with whatever means seem best, however unfamiliar at first sight, and in whatever company they find themselves. More conspicuously than most, the urban historian cannot remain an historian *pur sang* for long without running the danger of deserting the problem in front of him. Let me, quite unhistorically, give an unintended irony to the remark of a reviewer of Hollingshead and of Mayhew, writing in 1862: 'Our great cities are at once a history and a criticism of our progress, philosophy, and philanthropy.... Day by day they

7

chronicle themselves. . . . Their greatness confronts us everywhere; their littleness and misery only at home.'[13]

Every critic, in fact, points to the necessity of operating on a comparative level and within a multi-disciplinary framework. It may not simply be, as Joan Thirsk has pointed out, that no abiding impression can be held of a town without comparing it with others.[14] It may be that individual urban portraiture itself is almost meaningless without the larger dimension. Consider for a moment Sir Francis Hill's *Georgian Lincoln* which was published this year (1966). This is the third volume in what is already the most remarkable piece of individually sustained research to have been directed at the whole history of a single English town in this century. It describes a situation in which the surrounding farmland helped a decaying cathedral city *qua* market town achieve a kind of economic renaissance that in turn remodelled its social hierarchy, inflected its politics, and altered its very geography. In this little drama the more distant demands for wool, meat, and corn, which made it possible for the town to scramble out of its moribund glory are mere muffled voices off-stage, and Lincoln's achievements rest in a kind of void, without any bench mark but their own beginnings. Yet this is a distinguished work by one of the country's most intrepid amateur historians. It is also a book in which the inter-penetration of Lincoln's agrarian and urban economies utters a silent warning against differentiating between them too sharply— or similar categories elsewhere—by any arbitrary analysis, or supposing that rural-urban differences are morphological playthings of geographers or sociologists alone. Apart from this, Sir Francis' book, like so many other less worthy examples, cannot contribute directly to a more general understanding of the process of social change of which it is an individual product until it has been filtered through a somewhat different set of categories from those he used himself.

It is commonplace already that what we need is some means of relating the work being done on the small scale with that on the large; some comprehensive frame of reference capable of embracing studies, however microscopic, of individual towns or even of single streets or particular houses within them, as well as those macroscopic sweeps which cross centuries of change or cultural divisions within or across political frontiers. But how far can this go? It is all very well to suggest that what we want to be able to make, say, are comparisons in terms of the structure of the labour force and the level of real wages, between London and Singapore

---

13 *Meliora*, iv (1862), p. 297.
14 *Urban History Newsletter*, 6 (June 1966), p. 10.

or Paris and Timbuctoo at the present day,[15] and quite another simply to compare, for example, the occupational structure of Soho and Spitalfields in 1851 or between 1851 and 1951. It strikes me as a little fatuous to attempt too much and, in effect, to take on the whole history of cities at once. At best, that way leads to what historians are bound to regard as rather inchoate studies, like G. A. Wissink's *American Cities in Perspective* (1962), with its sweeping inter-cultural allusions. At worst, it leads rapidly to 'the city in history', to unhistorical and even apocalyptic visions which, like Mumford's, convey all the images and excitement of a fireworks display that fizzles out in chilling caricature of actuality itself! It may simply be that what we want for the time being are one or more unifying themes.

The most that this conference can expect to do is to discern some of the main issues confronting the student of urban history and exercise, however tentatively, one or two of its many techniques. Like the Urban History Group itself, which originated simply from a desire to exchange information on the scope and progress of research and published work, this conference offers itself very modestly indeed as a forum for the expression of views, probably partisan, on the question whether urban history has a definable entity and a distinctive approach to its subject matter; whether it has a true identity among, or conceivably even as a focus for, the disciplines already being applied to it; or whether it is a mere description of a *locale*, the scene of activity rather than the activity itself, a derivative rather than a substantive study. To put it bluntly, are urban historians some of the actors, if not the bit-players, or merely the scene-shifters? Is it too tiresome to ask if the process of urbanisation—whatever that may mean precisely—is an independent or dependent variable in history, or is it conceivably both? Whether dependent or independent, how is the historical study of the city to be related to other major themes such as industrialisation or the growth of the population? How, for that matter, are the data that are being collected on somewhat disconnected planes to be combined satisfactorily if they are not strictly comparable? Is it proper to try to construct a typology of historical experience in the rise and decline of cities, or is it feasible to hypothecate a single multi-stage process of urbanisation? Or is all this system-building just an attempt to round off the corners?

More fundamentally, is this historical study of cities to be classified with the kind of 'idiographic' discipline that history itself is usually taken to be, concerning itself with unique events which may properly be

---

[15] N. Anderson, *American Journal of Sociology*, lxv (1959–60), p. 71.

studied for their intrinsic interest: that is, with actual rather than typical events? Or is it 'nomothetic' and concerned instead with the classification of phenomena and the formulation of general 'laws', with characteristic behaviour and representative data?[16] Or is it, again, capable of being developed in more than one way? On what scale or scales is all this best conducted? By the time we come to the final session of the conference it is to be hoped that we might see these problems of definition and approach a little more clearly.

It would be surprising if these questions were now being asked for the first time. In fact there have been already in the last twelve years several pathfinding conferences of the multi-disciplinary kind, not to mention a series of UNESCO conferences on urbanisation in different parts of the world, and a number of others.[17] Let me refer to three of them quite briefly, for they illustrate the standing opposition of interests between the 'particularisers' and the 'generalisers' that I have just mentioned and which we cannot ignore in the discussions we shall be having. The first conference most relevant to our own purposes was given to 'The Rôle of Cities in Economic Development and Cultural Change', and was sponsored by the United States Social Sciences Research Council and the Research Center on Economic Growth and Cultural Change in the University of Chicago. That was in May 1954.[18] It took some account of the demographic, sociological, economic, cultural, and historical aspects of urbanisation exclusively in relation to economic development, and raised a whole series of theoretical and methodological issues. In particular, it included a long essay by Eric Lampard on 'The history of cities in the economically advanced areas' in which he tried to differentiate historically between the urban and non-urban elements in economic growth. In all this the main emphasis was clearly being laid on a universal process of urbanisation, not on idiosyncratic urban characteristics. The main issue was not one of definition as

16 The terminology is explained by John H. Goldthorpe, 'The relevance of History to Sociology', *Cambridge Opinion*, xxviii (1962).

17 The principal published proceedings apart from those listed below, are: Georges Friedmann (ed.), *Villes et Campagnes: Civilisation Urbaine et Civilisation Rurale en France* (1953); UNESCO, *Social Implications of Industrialization and Urbanization in Africa South of the Sahara* (1956); W. L. Thomas, Jr. (ed.), *Man's Rôle in Changing the Face of the Earth* (1956); P. M. Hauser (ed.), *Urbanization in Asia and the Far East* (1957); C. H. Kraeling and R. M. Adams (eds.), *City Invincible: A Symposium on Urbanization and Cultural Development in the Ancient Near East* (1960); Werner Z. Hirsch (ed.), *Urban Life and Form* (1963); R. L. Stauber (ed.), *Approaches to the Study of Urbanization* (1964).

18 See *Economic Development and Cultural Change*, iii (1954–5), pp. 4–198.

such but an attempt to state a general theory covering urbanisation and economic growth. In this it was defeated, though not without some very fruitful examination of the generative and parasitic effects of different types of cities on their regions, which was recognised as implying extensive historical study of the relationships of cities to their hinterlands. This might be done, it was suggested, by comparing a series of static situations over a long period of time—a method similar to that of Checkland. These papers must still be regarded as required reading for anyone interested in the process of urbanisation at large.

Four years later another inter-disciplinary conference was held, again under the auspices of the Social Science Research Council, with the object of clarifying what it called 'the major frameworks for research on urbanization' in the fields of economics, geography, history, political science, social anthropology, and sociology. From this a high-powered research committee emerged under the chairmanship of Professor Philip Hauser, of the Department of Sociology in the University of Chicago, and this spent six years deliberating on its assignment before reporting last year (1965) in its seminal and provocative volume *The Study of Urbanization*. Rather surprisingly, this report does not seem to have been at all widely noticed over here.[19] The book has in turn formed the subject matter of a conference in July 1965—held after publication—though I know no more about this than the programme itself.[20] However, we are fortunate in having here this weekend the secretary to that Committee on Urbanisation and co-editor of the published findings, Professor Leo Schnore, and we might look to him for elucidation here.

There is scarcely time now to do more than allude to the elaborately comprehensive reports contained in *The Study of Urbanization* on the respective contributions of the social sciences to the study of urbanisation in the United States, nor to comment on the scope they are finding for comparative, especially inter-cultural, research. Some of the directions in which high-powered research is now going over there seem exciting and their early results promising. The study of political and social behaviour is becoming more and more comparative, as one might expect, but the geographers and economists are also catching up. Urban Geography in particular is developing new concepts and producing some tangible, if stylised, findings on the new constellations of cities that are forming and the allocation of space within them; the economic analysis of urban

[19] It has since been reviewed by Asa Briggs, 'Urban perspectives: a review article', *Urban Studies*, iv (1967), pp. 165–9.
[20] I am grateful to Professor R. C. Wade and Professor Norton Ginsburg for enabling me since the conference to read the transcription of the discussions.

II

growth is by contrast in a much more tentative condition, though income differentials and entrepreneurial initiatives are now being studied more explicitly in relation to the structure of cities.

It is worth noticing that, impressive as the results of the research embodied in this volume are, the gaps in the knowledge of the contributors to it, particularly on the antecedents to and the consequences of urbanisation, were confessedly more impressive still. The field of vision of *The Study of Urbanization* was held entirely to the social sciences, though it did not by any means take in all relevant disciplines even there; it overlooked numerous areas of study beyond them, and its basic outlook, if not all its data, was palpably Westernised, not to say Americanised. In its most conscious desire for a *general* understanding of urbanisation its discourse was pitched beyond the normal frequency of historians committed to the same problems; and many of its theses were directed more towards those aspects of the field that could somehow be quantified than at those that could not. There was also a somewhat more pronounced interest in the urbanisation of under-developed countries (and by implication those of Western Europe, say, in the middle ages) than in that of the advanced countries outside North America.

It may be invidious to try to distil anything of value from such a complex book in two or three minutes but at least let me simply suggest that its importance may be in stressing the *major* factors to be investigated, whether or not we agree with the causality assigned to them. First, *population*, not merely to help determine hierarchies but to measure the broadest of all parameters of urban growth and decline and the whole demographic patterns involved. Hope Tisdale's ruthless analytical pruning of the concept of urbanisation 25 years ago to a process simply of population concentration underlies much of the thinking here. Secondly, *technology*, and the opportunities and peculiar demands it makes for and on massed populations, not only in terms of transport systems and local industrial structures but in the organisation of markets of every kind and the implications these have for economic welfare. Thirdly, *environment*, both the topographical disposition of the physical apparatus of urban societies and its geographical basis, a field embracing the whole development of urban estates, urban renewal, and so on. It is possible to conceive that the whole complex covered here may also be studied in terms of its overall organisational framework—the structure of its society and the everyday minutiae of making it all work, including the play of politics. This is, very crudely, what Schnore would call, I believe, the 'ecological complex', though he has been very careful to distinguish the already diverse connotation of that term ecology. Judged as sectors of urban historical research, population, technology, environment, organisation perhaps, make a short but pregnant list, though historians, not to mention architects, political scientists, sociologists, and students of the arts, would not want to be bound by it.

Does all this, however, offer anything more than a three-ring circus for the numerous disciplines now engaging in the study of the urban past? We cannot yet say, but it is certain that historians—no less than the municipal authorities of dozens of riot-prone American cities—will feel it leaves a great deal out. The cultural setting, in its very largest sense, is the most conspicuous absentee, of course, and this includes a range of issues far too wide to be cramped up under 'environment'. One thinks inevitably of the bearing on the cities of Europe, for instance, of their immensely rich artistic heritage. We cannot but rebel against the notion that what we need to know about the history of these cities can all be contained within the categories of the social scientists alone—just as forcibly as one social scientist (T. S. Ashton, I think) once rejected the idea that it was the unseen hand of capitalism that had been the moving spirit in the paintings of El Greco as much as it had been in the evolution of the lounge suit.

There are some aspects of reality which will never fit these categories and are bound to remain hidden unless set forth by a Doré or a Daumier. Could the full dimension of the immigrant cities of the eastern seaboard of the United States have been seen, one wonders, if Oscar Handlin had not broken out of some of the conventional categories in writing his *The Uprooted*? What substitutes can one find, in France, for the social commentaries of a Zola or a Balzac? No one who has read Anselm Strauss's fascinating book, *Images of the American City* (1961)—perhaps one of the most original works to have appeared in this field for the past five years—in which he has conveyed the multiple sense of shock imparted by rapid urbanisation in the nineteenth century by concentrating on what Americans of the time *thought* of their own and other cities, will doubt that social psychology, too, has a large but undefined role to play. Morten and Lucia White's semi-literary and philosophical study of Americans' ambivalence toward urban life, *The Intellectual Versus the City* (1962), comes into the same category. One naturally wonders about any differences that might be discerned in a similar study of Britain, where city life has only been made palatable for so many people by making the urban scene contain so many natural features.

While the American SSRC Committee on Urbanization was at work, the third conference I had in mind and whose findings still have to be digested met five years ago under the auspices of the Joint Center for

Urban Studies of the Massachusetts Institute of Technology and Harvard University. Its findings were published in 1963 in the volume *The Historian and the City*, edited by Oscar Handlin and John Burchard. Despite its containing the most searching and catholic array of ideas on the subject, this volume began with an apology for the lack of definition in urban history—a fuzziness which is not altogether inconsistent, it ought perhaps to be remembered, with the observed facts, and which the participants ended by not regretting. It is a report containing two or three brilliant essays in particular—notably that by Oscar Handlin on 'The Modern City as a Field of Historical Study', which remains one of the best statements of the historian's fundamental problems. But it offers no definition of basic terms or any elucidation of the concepts commonly used, much less an analytical framework which might relate the particular and general aspects of urbanisation. But here, too, was repeated recognition of the need for the comparative study of problems, a readiness to use more rigorous methods of analysis, and the tacit acceptance by most of the contributors at the conference of a viewpoint expressed most clearly by Handlin:

> 'However useful a general theory of the city may be, only the detailed tracing of an immense range of variables, in context, will illuminate the dynamics of the processes here outlined. We can readily enough associate such gross phenomena as the growth of population and the rise of the centralized state, as technological change and the development of modern industry, as the disruption of the traditional household and the decline of corporate life. But *how* these developments unfolded, what was the causal nexus among them, we shall only learn when we make out the interplay among them by focussing upon *a* city specifically in all its uniqueness.'[21]

Is this a valid, even *the*, historical approach? Is it preferable that we should concentrate, after all, not on the *general* pattern of the historical process of urbanisation, but on particular cases? The easy answer would be to say we need both: that the generalisers are likely to outnumber the effective particularisers, so the historians had best 'stick to the facts' and concentrate on individual towns, or study them in twos or threes for comparative purposes. This would not prevent an exchange of benefits between those developing the large hypotheses and those gathering the empirical evidence on which to test them.

Briggs, for one, has been inclined to argue strongly for pegging the

21 Oscar Handlin and John Burchard (eds.), *The Historian and the City* (1963), p. 26.

whole subject down in the study of individual cases, though in such a way that their individual characteristics—could one really use the term personalities?—may be compared and the nature of the general experience of a nation in the process of becoming urbanised emerge from this. 'However much the historian talks of common urban problems,' he warns, 'he will find that his most interesting task is to show in what respects cities differed from each other.'[22] *Victorian Cities* (1963) is his demonstration of how this might be done in relation to one quite specific problem: that of discerning the connections between civic administration and the social structure and political leadership, including the tensions and confusions surrounding them, in just half-a-dozen deliberately-chosen cases. What fascinates him is elemental civic self-consciousness, a topic not easily reducible to conventional categories and difficult to portray deftly. The book cannot be used as a model because it is a work of such singular virtuosity that it could almost certainly not be followed up by anyone else. What he has done, of course, is to illustrate through a restless search for comparisons the subtlety of the inter-play between historical factors which defy precise measurement or standardised catagories, and which have not been authenticated in every case by strict historical tests. What, happily, he has not done is to reduce confusing variety to all-too-easily grasped half-truths; yet we do get a view of a common experience in terms of local diversities. What is likely to come from an over-enthusiastic application of his approach, I fear, is the representation of some local experience as the common form.

If we are to continue to rely mainly on the individual approach and brief encounters only between the disciplines we face two prospects. One is an inordinate proliferation of case studies. One contributor to the conference at the Joint Center wryly remarked that he would 'flinch at the prospect of monographs covering every Camberwell, all arranged like Gilbert's dull M.Ps. in close proximity'![23] Dare I balance for you the prospect of a spectrum of Camberwells against an urban cosmography? The other prospect flows directly from this, namely the improbability of our being able to make real sense of the monographs, even though they look like Gilbert's M.Ps., because they are bound to use heterogeneous terms and definitions. American urban historians have already encountered these difficulties in an acute degree, and this is part of the explanation why the most ambitious attempt so far to write a general historical account of the urbanisation of America—Blake McKelvey's *The Urbanization of America* (1963)—should have failed. If we want to develop more

22 *ibid.*, p. 32.
23 *ibid.*, p. 260. [John Burchard].

sustained comparisons it is vital that we identify the basic variables un-
equivocally and define the standard terms quite precisely. This is partly a
question of agreeing on a standard numerical terminology of the kind
developed by the International Urban Research team at Berkeley and
partly a question of agreeing on what we mean when we use 'urban',
'urbanisation', and so on. This is really the first step in approaching our
subject in a scientific spirit.

Why has it taken so long for such a heavily urbanised country as Britain
to develop such a marked interest in the history of its cities and towns?
Mr. Bédarida has been one of those to express surprise at this neglect,[24]
but I think it will become clear from his paper to the conference that,
although French scholarship has produced some particularly percipient
studies of French towns—the best of them with a clearer sense of urban
space and volume than most British work—urban history has remained
in its chrysalis there also for half-a-century or more. In Germany, where
historical traditions in relation to urban studies tend to be different again,
the activity now going on also seems to have been generated comparatively recently.[25] In the United States alone has urban history already
struck really deep roots. One reason for this, insofar as the stimulus has
come from the historians, may be that the Turner thesis, in its search for
the environmental rather than the hereditary factors in the making of
American society was bound in the end to lead both its champions and its
critics—as it did Frederick Jackson Turner himself—towards the saga of
the frontier town.[26] Local history may in any case be taken as the natural

24 'Un centre d'études urbaines en Angleterre', *Annales*, 15th Year (1960), pp. 767–8.
25 Some early work had a wide influence. Note particularly the approach and techniques used
by Werner Hegemann, *Der Städtebau: nach den Ergebnissen der Allgemeinen Städtebau-
Austellung*, 2 vols. (1911). A good starting point for German urban history is Erik Keyser,
'Neue Veröffentlichungen über deutsche Städtgeschichte', *Blätter für Deutsche Landes-
geschichte*, xcvii (1961), pp. 228–59, and 'Travaux d'histoire urbaine Allemande (1961–3)',
Cahiers Bruxellois, viii (1963), pp. 279–86. Note also J. H. Westergaard, 'Scandinavian urbanism: a study of trends and themes in urban social research in Sweden, Norway, and Denmark',
Acta Sociologica, viii (1965), pp. 304–23. Information on other European countries is scattered,
but see V. G. Davidovich, 'On the patterns and tendencies of urban settlement in the
U.S.S.R.', *Soviet Geography*, vii (1966), pp. 3–31.
26 The best introduction to urban history in the United States is Charles N. Glaab, 'The
historian and the city: a bibliographic survey' in Philip M. Hauser and Leo F. Schnore (eds.),
The Study of Urbanization (1965), pp. 53–80. Professor Glaab is the present editor of the
American Urban History Group *Newsletter*, which has been a stimulus to the subject since it
was started, within the ranks of the American Historical Association, in 1954. See also Eric
Lampard, 'American historians and the study of urbanization', *American Historical Review*,
lxvii (1961), pp. 49–61; A. F. Davis, 'The American historian versus the city', *Social Studies*,
lvi (1965), pp. 91–6, 127–35.

unit of historical study in a country so vast and diverse. This explains to some extent the incredibly voluminous and impressive scale on which urban biography has flowered there. In my opinion, nothing has yet been written in this country, for example, which quite matches those highly percipient, graceful, compassionate volumes of Constance Green's on that multi-dimensional city of Washington.[27] But, more than this, we see in action in the States the much more influential teachings of the Chicago school of sociologists, the true children of the slums, with their heavy emphasis on the ecological and pathological study of the city. It seems very much, when viewed from Britain, that, for a whole variety of reasons which it might be impertinent of me to try and draw out, this tradition has had the dominant voice. I am not referring here to any one of the ecologists' camps in particular but to the enormous stimulus they have given collectively to the study of the city and the challenge this now represents to some of the other disciplines—to history, for example.

Yet when we think about the whole development of urban history, it is not so surprising to realise that none of the studies of any importance to have been written on the modern aspect of urbanism since Patrick Geddes' *Cities in Evolution* (1915) has come from this country as it is to find how few of them there really are. Henri Pirenne,[28] Lewis Mumford,[29] Pierre Lavedan[30] have more recently been joined by Elisabeth Pfeil,[31] Erwin Gutkind,[32] and one or two others.[33] In this country the geographers

[27] Constance McLaughlin Green, *Washington: Village and Capital, 1800–1878* (1962) and *Washington: Capital City, 1879–1950* (1963).

[28] Henri Pirenne, *Medieval Cities. Their Origins and the Revival of Trade* (1925) and *Les Villes et les Institutions Urbaines*, 2 vols., 2nd ed. (1939); but see H. van Werveke, 'The rise of the towns' and A. B. Hibbert, 'The economic policies of towns' in *Cambridge Economic History of Europe*, Vol. III: *Economic Organisation and Policies in the Middle Ages*, ed. M. M. Postan, E. E. Rich, and E. Miller (1963), pp. 3–41, 157–229.

[29] Lewis Mumford, *The Culture of Cities* (1938) and *The City in History. Its Origins, Its Transformations, and Its Prospects* (1961). Two valuable commentaries on Mumford's work are: Sylvia Thrupp, 'The creativity of cities'. A review article', *Comparative Studies in Society and History*, iv (1961–2), pp. 53–64; Asa Briggs, review article in *History and Theory*, ii (1962), pp. 296–301.

[30] Pierre Lavedan, *Histoire de l'Urbanisme*, 3 vols. (1926–52); see, too, his *Qu'est-ce-que l'Urbanisme?* (1926).

[31] Elisabeth Pfeil, *Grossstadtforschung, Fragestellungen, Verfahrensweisen und Ergebnisse einer Wissenschaft die dem Neubau von Stadt und Land von Nutzen sein könnte* (1960).

[32] E. A. Gutkind, *Revolution of Environment* (1946), *The Twilight of Cities* (1962), *Urban Development in Central Europe* (1964), *Urban Development in the Alpine and Scandinavian Countries* (1965), *Urban Development in Southern Europe, Spain and Portugal* (1967).

[33] Among the more important general and regional studies are: Edward C. Kirkland, *Men, Cities and Transportation: A Study in New England History, 1820–1900*, 2 vols. (1948); Carl Bridenbaugh, *Cities in the Wilderness: The First Century of Urban Life in America, 1625–1742* (1938) and *Cities in Revolt: Urban Life in America, 1743–1776* (1950); Pierre George, *La Ville: Le Fait Urbain à Travers le Monde* (1952); Edith Ennen, *Frühgeschichte der Europäischen Stadt*

17

alone have made any attempt to handle urban phenomena in national or regional terms, and in this symposium Mr. Carter's paper is characteristically broader in scope than any of the historians'. It is, however, to the nineteenth century that we must still turn for a classic of incomparable dimensions. The recent re-printing of Adna Ferrin Weber's monumental work, *The Growth of Cities in the Nineteenth Century* (1899)[34] is bound to strike urban historians as a disturbing and challenging event. It was first published in New York and acknowledged at once as a masterpiece of statistical compilation. A number of writers—Legoyt and later Meuriot in France, Gamborg in Sweden, Kuczynski in Germany, and some others[35]—had recently made some attempt to quantify what was coming to be regarded as the most conspicuous social phenomenon of the day. But what Weber did was to pick up a great variety of statistical fragments from the censuses and other official sources of an astonishing range of countries, to supplement these by a pitiably limited number of barely relevant monographs and municipal reports, to address to the whole just the right questions, and to write a work, not of history, but of historical demography. Looked at from our own vantage point, it may seem surprising that Weber should have assembled so large a body of evidence to make incontrovertible a connection that now seems obvious: the relationship between the growth of industrialism and that of the cities that contained it. What he recognised in fact was something we do not perhaps fully seize even to-day, that this process—to which quantified data are sometimes the worst of clues—was no simple reflex action resulting from a single inflexible experience of urban development. The pre-industrial town is no more of a stereotype than the industrial city, and more detailed historical inspection of its types is likely to emphasise their differences rather than their similarities. These are some of the qualitative unknowns,

(1953). Also worth noticing here are W. A. Robson, *Great Cities of the World, Their Government, Politics and Planning*, 2nd ed. (1957), which constitutes an approach through public administration and contains a little historical material; R. E. Dickinson, *The West European City* (1950), an essay in comparative historical geography; A. Korn, *History Builds the Town* (1953), which offers a slight illustrated commentary on urban morphology since the Stone Age; Christopher Tunnard, *The City of Man* (1953), which gives a city-planner's view of urban development. In this connection see also Sigfried Giedion, *Space, Time and Architecture. The Growth of a New Tradition* (1941).

34 Cornell Reprints in Urban Studies, 1963.

35 M. A. Legoyt, *Du Progrès des Agglomérations Urbaines et de l'Emigration Rurale en Europe et particulièrement en France* (1867); Paul Meuriot, *Des Agglomérations Urbaines dans l'Europe Contemporaine. Essai sur les Causes, les Conditions, les Conséquences de leur Developpement* (1897); J. C. Gamborg, *Om Byerne og Landet i deres indbyrdes Forhold med Hensyn til Befolkning og Produktion* (1877); R. R. Kuczynski, *Der Zug nach der Stadt. Statische Studien über Vorgänge der Bevölkerungsbewegung im Deutschen Reiche* (1897). Note also S. Schott, *Die Grossstädtischen Agglomerationen des Deutschen Reiches* (1912).

but there are still yawning gaps in the quantitative material, too, and the most serious reproach of Weber's must be that his is still the only general statistical definition available in comparative terms of the process of urbanisation as it developed in the nineteenth century at least. Within his own Columbia University a whole team of demographers led by Kingsley Davis began probing statistically some years ago for a more refined view of the current pattern of world urbanisation;[36] and this work has been continued more recently by him in the Center for International Population and Urban Research at Berkeley in the University of California.

More generally, as Sydney Checkland showed some years ago, the writing of the histories of British cities and towns has had more parlous than it has had praiseworthy aspects.[37] The brave days of the town boosters of the eighteenth century, when amateur history was all there was and a few men found time to write very readably on their home towns, were brought to a close by that hand-over-fist process of packing Britain's manufacturing towns till they burst and thrusting on them problems for which there were no known answers. What was happening was really a collective act of supreme subtlety which involved a re-ordering of space and time, of authority and freedom, of custom and contract, of work and leisure; and it gave to contemporary urban historians a different set of agenda, which they were not over-ready to accept. One can almost hear the exultant voices of the town boosters—men like William Hutton, paper merchant and bookseller, of Birmingham, or William Barrett, surgeon, of Bristol, who had written their modest panegyrics in less hectic times—drop to a whisper.[38]

[36] See Kingsley Davis and Hilda Hertz, 'The world distribution of urbanization', *Bulletin of the International Statistical Institute*, xxxiii (1951), pp. 227–41; Kingsley Davis and Hilda Hertz Golden, 'Urbanization and the development of pre-industrial areas', *Economic Development and Cultural Change*, iii (1954), pp. 6–26; 'The origin and growth of urbanization in the world', *American Journal of Sociology*, lx (1955), pp. 429–37.
[37] S. G. Checkland, 'English provincial cities', *Economic History Review*, 2nd Series, (1953), pp. 195–203.
[38] William Hutton, *The History of Birmingham* (1781)—it had gone through eight editions by 1840; William Barrett, *The History and Antiquities of the City of Bristol* [1789]. Other examples of this kind are: John Whitaker, *The History of Manchester*, 2 vols. (1771–5); William Enfield, *An Essay towards the History of Leverpool* (1773); John Watson, *The History and Antiquities of the Parish of Halifax* (1775); Charles Parkin, *The History and Antiquities of the City of Norwich* (1783); John Brand, *The History and Antiquities of the Town and County of the Town of Newcastle-upon-Tyne*, 2 vols. (1789); John Brewster, *The Parochial History and Antiquities of Stockton-upon-Tees* (1796); John Tickell, *The History of the Town and County of Kingston-upon-Hull* (1798); Charles Coates, *The History and Antiquities of Reading* (1802); Alexander Jenkins, *The History and Description of the City of Exeter* (1806); William Reader, *The History and Antiquities of the City of Coventry* (1810); William Richards, *The History of*

Industrialism did not at first make good reading, though a few of what became classic industrial histories of the period did embody somewhat anaesthetised accounts of the towns in which industrial history was being made.[39] But the authentic note was quietly struck by Dr. Calvert Holland's painstaking assessment, *The Vital Statistics of Sheffield* (1843), in which he took what stock he could of the activity, amenities, and mortality of the town just as it was and not as he might have supposed it to be.[40] It was an unfamiliar attitude. Perhaps one or two historians of the day were capable of taking it, as John Cleland's *Enumeration of the Inhabitants of Glasgow* (1832) and Charles Wilkins' *History of Merthyr Tydfil* (1867) rather differently suggest. But for a time urban historiography lost ground as publishers turned either to the grim pathological treatises which were being written by medical men like Gaskell, Gavin, Thackrah, Walker, Bell, full as they were of eloquently foreboding social statistics;[41] or to a rich variety of guide-books and directories to the more polite and commercially promising parts of the new industrial society.[42] Grave sermons on the perils of urban life and discomforting commentaries by people who had

Lynn, 2 vols. (1812); John Blackner, *The History of Nottingham* (1815); James Cleland, *Annals of Glasgow: Comprising an Account of the Public Buildings, Charities, and the Rise and Progress of the City*, 2 vols. (1816); William Kennedy, *Annals of Aberdeen*, 2 vols. (1818).

[39] See, for example, Thomas Baines, *History of the Commerce and Town of Liverpool, and of the Rise of Manufacturing Industry* (1852); John James, *History of the Worsted Manufacture in England* (1857)—for Bradford and Halifax; William Felkin, *History of the Machine-Wrought Hosiery and Lace Manufactures* (1867)—for Nottingham and Leicester.

[40] Among his other writings were *An Enquiry into the Moral, Social and Intellectual Condition of the Industrial Classes of Sheffield* (1839) and *The Mortality, Sufferings and Diseases of Grinders*, 3 vols. (1841–2).

[41] Charles Turner Thackrah, *The Effects of the Principal Arts, Trades, and Professions, and of Civic States and Habits of Living, on Health and Longevity with a Particular Reference to the Trades and Manufactures of Leeds* (1831); Peter Gaskell, *The Manufacturing Population of England* (1833), presently revised and enlarged as *Artisans and Machinery: the Moral and Physical Condition of the Manufacturing Population Considered with Reference to Mechanical Substitutes for Labour* (1836); G. A. Walker, *Gatherings from the Graveyards; particularly those of London* (1839); Hector Gavin, *Sanitary Ramblings, Being Sketches and Illustrations of Bethnal Green. A Type of the Condition of the Metropolis and Other Large Towns* (1848); George Bell, *Day and Night in the Wynds of Edinburgh* (1849) and *Blackfriars' Wynd Analyzed* (1850). See, too, J. P. Kay, *The Moral and Physical Condition of the Working Classes employed in the Cotton Manufacture in Manchester* (1832) and H. D. Littlejohn, *Report on the Sanitary Condition of the City of Edinburgh* (1865).

[42] For example: E. Parsons, *The Civil, Ecclesiastical, Literary, Commercial and Miscellaneous History of Leeds, Bradford, Wakefield, Dewsbury, Otley and the District within Ten Miles of Leeds* (1834); B. Love, *Manchester as It is* (1839); John Glyde, *The Moral, Social, and Religious Condition of Ipswich in the Middle of the Nineteenth Century* (1850); Thomas Baines, *Liverpool in 1859. The Port and Town of Liverpool and the Harbour Docks, and Commerce of the Mersey* (1859); C. Capper, *The Port and Trade of London, Historical, Statistical, Local and General* (1862); F. Hooper, *Statistics Relating to the City of Bradford* (1898).

gone out of their way to explore the darkest corners provided some kind of link between the two.[43]

Certainly, this was also a time when civic historical societies began their collections of local curiosa, and a few histories of towns did appear that are useful still,[44] but it was not in general until the last quarter of the nineteenth century that civic history enjoyed any kind of renaissance. The pity of it then was that the earlier tradition of tracing the living history of the provincial towns tended to be thrown over either for a much more antiquarian or a narrowly municipal approach. The general also tended to give way to the particular. I suppose this might be recognised as just one aspect of a new surge of civic consciousness in which a salute to a remote ancestry was practically as important as the erection of a central clock-tower or a new town hall, just as the era hardly closed had been epitomised by the gesture of the corn exchange. 'Where are the Heroes of the Ages past?' ran the first line of a poetic dedication to Glover's and Andrew's *History of Ashton-under-Lyne* (1884), and glum came the reply: 'On their fallen fame . . . Sits grim Forgetfulness.' This was the tone of many of the plush publications that now began to pile on to the shelves of the new municipal libraries to meet the romantic desire felt in such places for a sense of identity and style. Descriptions of local finds from one or other Ice Age, meticulous chronicles of events since the Romans left, verbatim transcriptions of the churchwardens' accounts, and a brisk gallop over the period within living memory—these were the standard components of so many of them.[45] London was big enough to have the

---

[43] See T. Chalmers, *The Christian and Civic Economy of Large Towns*, 3 vols. (1821–6): F. von Raumer, *England in 1835*, 3 vols. (1836); E. Buret, *De la Misère des Classes Laboreuses en Angleterre et en France*, 2 vols. (1840); W. Cooke Taylor, *Notes of a Tour in the Manufacturing Districts of Lancashire* (1842); Léon Faucher, *Manchester in 1844: Its Present Condition and Future Prospects* (1844) and *Etudes sur l'Angleterre*, 2 vols. (1845); [C. Kingsley], *Cheap Clothes and Nasty* (1850)—a Christian Socialist tract about tailors' sweatshops: W. D. Henderson, *J. C. Fischer and his Diary of Industrial England, 1814–1851* (1966) is a useful reprint with commentary.

[44] For example: Archibald Prentice, *Historical Sketches and Personal Recollections of Manchester* (1851), which is a rare example of a local political history; C. Hardwick, *History of the Borough of Preston* (1857); J. Fawcett, *The Rise and Progress of the Town of Bradford* (1859); A. D. Bayne, *A Comprehensive History of Norwich* (1869); J. A. Langford, *A Century of Birmingham Life: or, A Chronicle of Local Events from 1741 to 1841*, 2 vols. (1868) and *Modern Birmingham and its Institutions: A Chronicle of Local Events from 1851 to 1871*, 2 vols. (1873–7); J. A. Picton, *Memorials of Liverpool*, 2 vols. (1873), which gives over half the volume devoted to the history to the nineteenth century, including an account of the development of the Dock Estate; G. Benn, *A History of the Town of Belfast*, 2 vols. (1877–80); H. G. Reid (ed.), *Middlesbrough and Its Jubilee* (1881); J. F. Nicholls and J. Taylor, *Bristol Past and Present*, 3 vols. (1881–2).

[45] The following are representative: Thomas Richmond, *The Local Records of Stockton and the Neighbourhood* (1868); Wm. Alexander Abram, *A History of Blackburn, Town and Parish*

The Study of Urban History

bonus of some sure-handed history relevant to the period, though only
Allen's and Loftie's works[46] stand out to any extent among the general
studies, and a mere handful of others among the metropolitan village
histories.[47] The rest made a vast sorry assortment of relics and annals
which for so many metropolitan, as well as provincial, boroughs must
still keep a dreary and ludicrous vigil.

What did not emerge even from the best of these writings so far was a
realisation that beneath the superficial differences between towns were
more fundamental patterns of life and death, and a number of important
distinctions to be made between the experience even of the manufacturing
towns which apparently generated the same pall of smoke, the same
obscene slums, the same sprawling suburbs.[48] Weber did discern some
vital differences in birth and death rates and of migrational movements—
which have not yet, in fact, been fully exploited by more detailed research[49]—but his view of the city as the spectroscope of society is justifiable, not by reference to his own researches, much less to those of the
urban historians of his time, but to the sociologically inclined students of
actual living conditions. Charles Booth's observations in London,[50]

(1877); Dr. John Doran, *Memories of our Great Towns* (1878); E. A. Freeman, *English Towns
and Districts* (1883); William E. A. Axon, *The Annals of Manchester* (1886); Simeon Rayner,
The History and Antiquities of Pudsey (1887); John Latimer, *The Annals of Bristol in the
Nineteenth Century* (1887) and *The Annals of Bristol in the Eighteenth Century* (1893).

[46] W. J. Loftie, *A History of London*, 2 vols. (1883–4). This is still the best account, but see
also G. L. Gomme, *London in the Reign of Victoria (1837–1897)* (1898) and for municipal
affairs see Charles Welch, *Modern History of the City of London: a Record of Municipal and
Social Progress from 1760 to the Present* (1896) and William Saunders, *History of the first
London County Council* (1892). François Bédarida makes some challenging points about the
neglect of London by historians in his article, 'L'histoire sociale de Londres au XIXe siècle',
Annales, 15th Year (1960), pp. 949–62.

[47] The following are of definite interest: William Robins, *Paddington: Past and Present*
[1853]; Samuel Palmer, *St. Pancras; being Antiquarian, Topographical and Biographical
Memoranda* (1870); W. H. Blanch, *Ye History of Camerwell* (1875); William J. Pinks, *The
History of Clerkenwell*, ed. Edward J. Wood (1880); A. Montgomery Eyre, *Saint John's Wood.
Its History, Its Houses, Its Haunts and Its Celebrities* (1913). Particular houses or districts have
formed a focus for some reputable work, for example: Charles Gordon, *Old Time Aldwych,
Kingsway, and Neighbourhood* (1903); R. Needham and A. Webster, *Somerset House, Past and
Present* (1905).

[48] Two writers who did were: S. J. Low, 'The rise of the suburbs', *Contemporary Review*,
lx (1891), pp. 545–58; F. Tillyard, 'English town development in the nineteenth century',
Economic Journal, xx (1910), pp. 547–60.

[49] See W. Farr (ed. N. A. Humphreys), *Vital Statistics* (1885), E. J. Syson, 'On the comparative mortality in large towns', *Transactions of the Manchester Statistical Society* (1870–1),
pp. 37–47, and T. A. Welton, *England's Recent Progress* (1911). D. V. Glass, 'Some indicators
of differences between urban and rural mortality in England and Wales and Scotland', *Population Studies*, xvii (1964), pp. 263–7 is a demonstration of how difficult it is to discern these
differences.

[50] C. Booth (ed.), *Life and Labour of the People in London*, 17 vols. (1892-1903).

Seebohm Rowntree's in York,[51] and, in less obvious ways, Lady Bell's in Middlesbrough,[52] and Victor Branford's in Westminster and at large,[53] pointed not only to new possibilities but to a distinction between students of urban affairs that is visible still.

The condition of urban history in the period that followed—the first 30 or 40 years of this century—looks stagnant. It was certainly the period in which the writing of the local history of British towns fell behind that of the American. Yet it was also one in which the two dominant characteristics of urban historiography were being firmly established. One of these was economic and industrial; the other political and civic. The reasons why the subject should seem to have been standing still are explicable, I think, in terms of quite general factors. There was plainly a general revulsion from the cultural traditions of the previous century, and this seems to have smothered to some extent the quaintly antiquarian drift of pre-war years. It was deepened by the fact that many of the towns now important enough to have their histories written were handicapped economically by their industrial legacy. What little enthusiasm there might have been for the civic satisfactions of an historical stock-taking could not last long on this basis. Instead, economic historians, a new race, who were to make a more direct contribution to the subject later, got down to their main task of re-shaping basic concepts of the industrial revolution. They might also be regarded now as having been at work on part of the conceptual framework and some of the factual foundations into which more detailed studies of urban communities would later fit. The major industrial towns—London, Manchester, Birmingham, Sheffield, Leeds, among others—were now coming into sharper view, as they have continued to do by dint of this kind of research, though hardly one of these places was being treated biographically, as a complete entity.[54]

[51] B. S. Rowntree, *Poverty. A Study of Town Life* (1901); see, too, A. L. Bowley and A. R. Burnett-Hurst, *Livelihood and Poverty: a Study in the Economic Conditions of Working-Class Households in Northampton, Warrington, Stanley and Reading* (1915).

[52] Lady [Mrs. Hugh] Bell, *At the Works* [1907]. The work was dedicated to Charles Booth.

[53] Mumford comments that Branford's *Our Social Inheritance* (1919) and his own walks around Westminster with him in 1920 made an indelible mark on all his later thinking (*City in History*, p. 585). Branford later became editor of *Sociological Review*.

[54] It would be rash to overlook some quite general studies like J. L. and Barbara Hammonds' *The Age of the Chartists* (1930), or even some of their earlier work; Paul Mantoux, *The Industrial Revolution in the Eighteenth Century* (English translation, 1928) exhibits the formative stage of urbanised industrialism very well; H. D. Fong, *Triumph of Factory System in England* (1930) has useful urban aspects. Representative of work on London's economic development at this time which has not been superseded are the following: George Unwin (ed.), *Finance and Trade under Edward III* (1918); J. G. Broodbank, *History of the Port of London*, 2 vols. (1921); D. H. Smith, *The Industries of Greater London* (1933); F. J. Fisher, 'The development of the London food market, 1540–1640', *Economic History Review*, v (1934–5), pp. 46–69; P. G. Jones

The geography of industrialism was also fastening on questions of location, and since the factors at work here were to be explained at least as frequently by reference to the past as they were to the present, historical geographers began to make their own distinctive contribution to the subject. This has often been of the greatest value, especially in relation to the ecology of the coastline, the structure of urban regions and urban spheres of influence.[55]

and A. V. Judges, 'London population in the late seventeenth century', *ibid.*, vi (1935–6), pp. 45–63. Touching Manchester are: J. Lord, *Capital and Steampower* (1923); D. G. Barnes, *A History of the English Corn Laws* (1930); A. P. Wadsworth and Julia de L. Mann, *The Cotton Trade and Industrial Lancashire, 1600–1780* (1931); G. T. Jones, *Increasing Return* (1933); A. Redford, *Manchester Merchants and Foreign Trade, 1794–1858* (1934); W. D. Henderson, *The Lancashire Cotton Famine, 1861–1865* (1934); J. Jewkes and E. M. Gray, *Wages and Labour in the Lancashire Cotton Industry* (1935). The industrial history of Birmingham and the Black Country is particularly diverse and well-documented. See particularly: H. Hamilton, *The English Brass and Copper Industries to 1800* (1926); G. C. Allen, *The Industrial Development of Birmingham and the Black Country, 1860–1927* (1929); I. A. Williams, *The Firm of Cadbury, 1831–1931* (1931); H. W. Dickinson, *Matthew Boulton* (1936); W. H. B. Court, *The Rise of the Midland Industries, 1600–1838* (1938); R. D. Best, *Brass Chandelier. A Biography of R. A. Best of Birmingham* (1940). The urban history of the West Riding was being laid in books like G. I. H. Lloyd, *The Cutlery Trades* (1913); W. B. Crump, *The Leeds Woollen Industry, 1780–1820* (1931); H. Heaton, *The Yorkshire Woollen and Worsted Industries* (1920); W. B. Crump and G. Ghorbal, *History of the Huddersfield Woollen Industry* (1935); D. L. Burn, *The Economic History of Steelmaking, 1867–1939* (1940). Other work in this vein which is still of importance includes: G. Unwin, *Samuel Oldknow and the Arkwrights. The Industrial Revolution at Stockport and Marple* (1924); C. Gill, *The Rise of the Linen Industry* (1925); G. H. Tupling, *The Economic Development of Rossendale* (1927); F. A. Wells, *The British Hosiery Trade* (1935). Among later work in this tradition the following are some of the most important: F. J. Fisher, 'The development of London as a centre of conspicuous consumption in the sixteenth and seventeenth centuries', *Transactions of the Royal Historical Society*, xxx (1948), pp. 37–50 and 'London's export trade in the early seventeenth century' *Economic History Review*, New Series, iii (1950–1951), pp. 151–61; A. H. John, *The Industrial Revolution in South Wales, 1750–1850* (1950); T. C. Barker, 'Lancashire coal, Cheshire salt, and the rise of Liverpool', *Transactions of the Historic Society of Lancashire and Cheshire*, ciii (1951), pp. 83–101; Charlotte Erickson, *British Industrialists. Steel and Hosiery, 1850–1950* (1958); W. G. Rimmer, *Marshall's of Leeds, Flax Spinners, 1788–1886* (1960).

55 The following list is representative of the most notable contributions of this kind: T. W. Freeman, *The Conurbations of Great Britain* (1949); H. C. Darby (ed.), *Historical Geography of England before A.D. 1800* (1936); Rodwell Jones, 'Kingston-upon-Hull: a study in port development', *Scottish Geographical Magazine*, xxxv (1919), pp. 161–74; R. E. Dickinson, 'The regional functions and zones of influence of Leeds and Bradford', *Geography*, xv (1929–30), pp. 548–57; R. N. R. Brown, 'Sheffield: its rise and growth'. *Geography*, xxi (1936), pp. 175–84; E. W. Gilbert, 'The growth of inland and seaside health resorts in England', *Scottish Geographical Magazine*, lv (1939), pp. 16–35; G. de Boer, 'The evolution of Kingston-upon-Hull', *Geography*, xxxi (1946), pp. 139–46; H. A. Moisley, 'The industrial and urban development of the North Staffordshire conurbation', *Publications of the Institute of British Geographers*, xvii (1951), pp. 151–65; S. H. Beaver, 'The Potteries: a study in the evolution of a cultural landscape', *Transactions of the Institute of British Geographers*, xxxiv (1964), pp. 1–31. The British Association surveys contain some particularly good geographical writing, such as: M. J. Wise and P. O'N. Thorpe, 'The growth of Birmingham' in *Birmingham and Its Regional Setting*, ed. M. J. Wise (1950), pp.213–38; and W. Smith, 'The urban structure

It is not difficult to see that these various studies were in some sense responding to a tacit demand for historical research more closely related to contemporary economic and social conditions, just as the years of depression were beginning to evoke social surveys that wanted the facts about life in the half-idle industrial towns,[56] rather than speculations about the sociological meaning of urbanism *in vacuo*.[57] On the surface the urban past appeared to have little direct relevance to the urban present of the inter-war years, of which the most conspicuous features, apart from the depression of the basic industries, was the re-housing of the middle classes in the suburbs of the large towns on a totally unprecedented scale, and the more general shift of the centre of gravity of the whole population toward southern England. The town-planners were not unaware of all this, but as Clough Williams-Ellis showed, both in his little scorcher, *England and the Octopus* (1928), and in the impressively talented symposium he edited a decade later under the title *Britain and the Beast* (1938), the aesthetic penalities involved were inclined to be expressed more in rural than in urban terms.[58]

None of the studies undertaken to describe these processes would now be regarded as urban history, however much they belong to the history of urban society. The means of converting economic preoccupations to more specific urban history came originally from a much older industrial town, and was suggested most strongly by a scholar who was beginning to disengage himself from economic history to become the most formidable

of Liverpool' in *A Scientific Survey of Merseyside*, ed. W. Smith (1953), pp. 188–99. See also A. E. Smailes, 'The urban hierarchy of England and Wales', *Geography*, xxix (1944), pp. 41–51. His 'The Site, growth, and changing face of London' in *The Geography of Greater London*, ed. R. Clayton (1964), is a valuable synopsis of extensive research. H. M. Mayer and C. F. Kohn (eds.), *Readings in Urban Geography* (1959). For some valuable 'overviews' and further references, see: R. E. Dickinson, *City and Region. A Geographical Interpretation* (1964); A. E. Smailes, *The Geography of Towns*, 5th ed. (1966); P. George, *La Ville, Le Fait Urbain à travers le Monde* (1952). G. H. Dury, *The British Isles*, 3rd ed. (1965) is a useful textbook covering urbanism from the geographic view point.

[56] H. A. Mess, *Industrial Tyneside. A Social Survey* (1928); Sir Hubert Llewellyn Smith (ed.), *The New Survey of London Life and Labour*, 9 vols. (1930–5); D. C. Jones, *The Social Survey of Merseyside*, 3 vols. (1934); H. Jennings, *Brynmawr. A Study of a Distressed Area* (1934); University College of the South-West [Exeter University], *A Social Survey of Plymouth* (1935) and *A Social Survey of Plymouth: Second Report* (1938); Pilgrim Trust, *Men Without Work* (1938), which deals with Deptford, Leicester, Rhondda Urban District, Crook (Co. Durham), Liverpool, and Blackburn.

[57] David Glass, *The Town and a Changing Civilization* (1935) is an exception. Note also P. Cohen-Portheim, *England, The Unknown Isle* (1930), with its interpretation of English and Continental attitudes to urbanism.

[58] Compare the general approach of G. and E. G. McAllister, *Town and Country Planning. A Study of the Physical Environment: The Prelude to Post-War Reconstruction* (1941) and *Homes, Towns and Countryside. A Practical Plan for Britain* (1945).

pioneer of local history, W. G. Hoskins. His *Industry, Trade and People in Exeter, 1688–1800* (1935) was written with special reference to the serge industry, but it recognised in many ways the sense of community that prevailed in eighteenth-century Exeter. His work ultimately led others to develop a group of studies on industrial towns that are some of the most solid and revealing things to have been done in recent urban history: T. C. Barker's and J. R. Harris's *A Merseyside Town in the Industrial Revolution: St. Helen's, 1750–1900* (1954) is a particularly sanguine blend of the kind of economic, social, and broadly cultural factors that have played their part in the history of many such towns and, consciously or unconsciously, their work is being taken as a model by a number of other scholars.[59] Apart from C. R. Fay's *Round About Industrial Britain, 1830–1860* (1952),[60] it has not yet led to any comparative or general treatment of these basically economic themes. Another stimulus for urban history just after the war came from W. H. Chaloner's *The Social and Economic Development of Crewe, 1780–1923* (1950), which pioneered the study of a modern town from its very beginnings. It, too, has had a wide influence.

To realise how sharply one can differentiate between pre- and post-war interest in urban history it is necessary only to reflect how much out of fashion it had been to write on urban development—unless, like Ellen Wilkinson's *The Town that was Murdered* (1939) or George Orwell's *The Road to Wigan Pier* (1937), the words bit deeply on contemporary issues. One work palpably out of its time was G. M. Young's two-volume symposium *Early Victorian England, 1830–1865* (1934), in which R. H. Mottram and Sir John and Lady Clapham wrote two long, elegant essays on the social life in the towns of the period: they were almost the only general works of modern urban history to appear in the inter-war

[59] The best of the crop that has come from this tradition since Hoskins are: D. T. Williams, *The Economic Development of Swansea and of the Swansea District to 1921* (1940); E. R. R. Green, *The Lagan Valley, 1800–1850: a Local History of the Industrial Revolution* (1949); M. M. Schofield, *Outlines of an Economic History of Lancaster, 1680–1860*, 2 vols. (1946–51); T. C. Mendenhall, *The Shrewsbury Drapers and the Welsh Wool Trade in the Sixteenth and Seventeenth Centuries* (1953); W. E. Minchinton, 'Bristol: metropolis of the west in the eighteenth century', *Transactions of the Royal History Society*, 5th Series, iv (1954), pp. 69–89; J. W. Wardell, *History of Yarm: An Ancient North Riding Town* (1957); A. H. Dodd (ed.), *A History of Wrexham* (1957); W. B. Stephens, *Seventeenth-century Exeter: A Study of Industrial and Commercial Development, 1625–1688* (1958); John Prest, *The Industrial Revolution in Coventry* (1960); Roy A. Church, *Economic and Social Change in a Midland Town. Victorian Nottingham, 1815–1900* (1966).

[60] It included chapters on Birkenhead (J. E. Allison), Birmingham (Asa Briggs), Bradford (E. M. Sigsworth), Dundee and St. Andrews (J. W. Nisbet), Manchester (W. D. Henderson), and Sheffield (G. P. Jones).

period.[61] The most golden writing on urban history at the time was a monograph on London, a work which seems to have gone on adding to its stature ever since, Dorothy George's *London Life in the XVIIIth Century* (1925): it deserved to inspire many more writers than it has done,[62] though the study of Dublin by Constantia Maxwell, first published in 1936, should certainly not be overlooked.[63] Despite works like these, it is sad to think that the same factors which explain the unbridled spread of the built-up areas around Britain's major cities and towns at this very time probably go some way toward accounting for the failure to build up a more explicitly historical view of the process then at work; it seems equally true that too foreshortened a view of what was taking place allowed the worst to happen. It is interesting to notice that one of the sanest, but all too brief, glimpses of what was going on comes also from an historian.[64]

One historical perspective that could be discerned here and there was a commemorative one, for centenaries were beginning to turn up, and some of them were being celebrated happily enough in print. There was, for example, Laski's, Jennings', and Robson's *A Century of Municipal Progress* (1935), which marked the passing of the Municipal Corporations Act of 1835;[65] and Lady Shena Simon's modest salute to the chartering of Manchester in 1838[66] was followed by Arthur Redford's altogether more massive, officially commemorative volumes.[67] Not every such study

[61] See also H. A. Mess, 'The growth and decay of towns', *Political Quarterly*, ix (1938), pp. 389–407.

[62] R. J. Mitchell and M. D. R. Leys, *A History of London Life* (1958) is lighter in tone but provides a useful survey; C. Trent, *Greater London, Its Growth and Development through Two Thousand Years* (1965) is over-ambitious but better than any other recent study of this kind. The East End alone among the major divisions of London has had satisfactory general treatment: Sir H. Llewellyn Smith, *The History of East London from the Earliest Times to the End of the Eighteenth Century* (1939); M. Rose, *The East End of London* (1951).

[63] Constantia E. Maxwell, *Dublin under the Georges, 1714–1830*, 2nd ed. (1956). Her other major work, *Country and Town in Ireland under the Georges* (1940) is a valuable introduction to the whole urban history of the country in that period. T. W. Freeman, *Pre-Famine Ireland* (1957) supplements it well.

[64] See G. M. Young's introduction to the Penguin Special, *Country and Town* (1943). Another writer capable of taking long interesting views is John Betjeman, whose two brief writings on the subject have a distinct value: *English Cities and Small Towns* (1943); *The English Town in the Last Hundred Years* (1956).

[65] See G. B. A. Finlayson, 'The municipal corporation commission and report, 1833–1835', *Bulletin of the Institute of Historical Research*, xxxvi (1963), pp. 36–52, and 'The politics of municipal reform', *English Historical Review*, lxxxi (1966), pp. 236–55, in which he suggests that the administrative factors may have been exaggerated.

[66] Lady Simon, *A Century of City Government: Manchester, 1838–1938* (1938).

[67] A. Redford and I. S. Russell, *History of Local Government in Manchester*, 3 vols. (1939).

was laudatory.[68] R. W. Greaves' *The Corporation of Leicester, 1689–1836* (1939) also now appeared as an exemplary study of some of the antecedents to this phase.[69]

It is a pity that this commemorative inclination in English urban history should have strengthened its civic bias without notably adding to its stature. It would almost be true to say that not a single major British city has yet been made the subject of a major work of historical scholarship which covers all its principal phases. It is almost beginning to look as if none of them ever will. Nothing demonstrates the civic-centred tradition more clearly than the fact that the only substantial bibliography of the history of British towns should still be Charles Gross's *A Bibliography of British Municipal History* (1897), in which the lack of municipal institutions barred the inclusion of works on towns as self-evident as Bournemouth, Blackpool, and Tunbridge Wells.[70] (Aptly enough, it was the era of the long weekend which saw interest in the history of leisure

[68] See W. A. Robson, *The Government and Misgovernment of London* (1939); R. Sinclair, *Metropolitan Man. The Future of the English* (1938).

[69] Other work of this kind to have some value has been done by: G. P. Jones and J. E. Tyler, *A Century of Progress in Sheffield* (1935); H. Hamer, *Bolton, 1838–1938: A Centenary Record of Municipal Progress* (1938); F. Smith, *Coventry: Six Hundred Years of Municipal Life* (1945); Brian D. White, *A History of the Corporation of Liverpool, 1835–1914* (1951).

[70] The *Bibliography* was originally published in New York—trenchant fact—in 1897 but has now been reprinted with an introductory essay by G. H. Martin (1966). Dr. Martin is now preparing, in collaboration with Miss Sylvia McIntyre, a supplementary volume uniform in scope (and probably in size) containing an annotated bibliography of general works published on municipal history between 1897 and 1966; he intends adding other volumes later to cover works on individual towns. I am grateful to Dr. Martin and Miss McIntyre for giving me access to their very large collection of references. The contemporaneous work by K. C. Brooks, *A Bibliography of Municipal Administration and City Conditions* (New York, 1897) contains a vast amount of current material which is now of historical significance. A most instructive though patchy bibliography covering a very wide range, but especially good on architectural matters, is included in Lewis Mumford, *The City in History* (1961), pp. 579–634; still more catholic and better organised, but really a list of exemplary writing on the subject rather than a bibliography, is Philip Dawson and Sam B. Warner, Jr., 'A selection of works relating to the history of cities' in *The Historian and the City*, ed. Oscar Handlin and John Burchand (1963), pp. 270–90. Among more specialised bibliographies, the following are helpful: W. Bicker and others, *Comparative Urban Development: An Annotated Bibliography* (1965); Katharine McNamara, *Bibliography of Planning, 1928–1935* (1936). For the social history of British cities, including an excellent commentary on urbanism in Britain, see Ruth Glass, 'Urban sociology in Great Britain: a trend report', *Current Sociology*, iv, No. 4 (1955), pp. 5–76. A useful general list of works published in the last 30 years, with comments, is contained in W. H. Chaloner, 'Writings on British urban history, 1934–1957' in *Vierteljahrschrift für Sozial und Wirtschaftgeschichte*, xliv, Part I (1958), pp. 76–87; a review article of more interest for its comments on method than on the literature is Peter Hennock's 'Die neuere Stadtgeschichte in England', *Archiv für Kommunalwissenschaften*, 4th Year (1965), pp. 121–8. An increasing number of local librarians or individual enthusiasts is responsible for guides to the literature of particular towns, and most of these are printed, and are too numerous to mention here. Publications since 1960 are being covered as comprehensively as possible in each June issue of the *Urban History*

towns revive).[71] It seems ironic that Gross should have tackled his task, as Geoffrey Martin has explained,[72] because he felt municipal history to be neglected. The *Bibliography*'s scholarly premiss was Gross's own work on the merchant gilds of the middle ages,[73] and it may be acknowledged that a large part of the foundations of recent urban history were laid by historians of the medieval borough. The line of descent may not only be traced from Maitland,[74] through Gross to Carl Stephenson,[75] James Tait,[76] and others,[77] but, more faintly, to a wider circle of historians for whom municipal institutions are now of the greatest interest because of their bearing on the fabric of our own society.

The collectivisation of so much of our own daily round—as Sidney Webb once showed in a rare stroke of wit—has enormously strengthened that tendency, most evidently in the towns; and the centralisation tussle of mid-Victorian times,[78] the extension of the franchise,[79] boundary changes,[80] and the advance of the Welfare State,[81] have added to it even

Newsletter, which I edit. This also contains brief bibliographical introductions to the urban history of particular countries: Australia (Alan Birch, *UHN* 5); Ireland (R. A. Butlin, *UHN* 6); Scotland (William Forsyth, *UHN* 8); Poland (Geoffrey Martin *UHN* 8).

71 J. A. R. Pimlott, *The Englishman's Holiday* (1947) deals well with seaside resorts, but see also R. V. Lennard, *Englishmen at Rest and Play: Some Phases of English Leisure, 1558–1714* (1931). See also: A. Rowntree (ed.), *The History of Scarborough* (1931); F. A. Bailey, *A History of Southport* (1954); D. S. Young, *The Story of Bournemouth* (1957); W. J. Smith, 'Blackpool: a sketch of its growth, 1740–1851', *Transactions of the Lancashire and Cheshire Antiquarian Society*, lxix (1959), pp. 70–103.

72 Preface to Second Edition, p. [v].

73 *The Gild Merchant* (1890).

74 F. W. Maitland, *Township and Borough* (1898).

75 Carl Stephenson, *Borough and Town* (1933).

76 James Tait, *Medieval Manchester and the Beginnings of Lancashire* (1904).

77 See G. H. Martin, 'The English borough in the thirteenth century', *Transactions of the Royal Historical Society*, 5th Series, xiii (1963), pp. 123–44. A recent study of importance in this field is Gwyn A. Williams, *Medieval London. From Commune to Capital* (1963).

78 Royston Lambert, 'Central and local relations in mid-Victorian England', *Victorian Studies*, vi (1962–3), pp. 121–50. A more specific study is Henry Ferguson's 'The Birmingham Political Union and the government', *Victorian Studies*, iii (1959–60), pp. 261–76. For earlier views, see M. R. Maltbie, *English Local Government of Today: a Study of the Relations of Central and Local Government* (1897); Percy Ashley, *Local and Central Government: a Comparative Study of England, France, Prussia, and the United States* (1906); E. S. Griffith, *The Modern Development of City Government in the United Kingdom and the United States*, 2 vols. (1927).

79 T. R. Tholfsen, 'The transition to democracy in Victorian England', *International Review of Social History*, vi (1961), pp. 226–48, examines the rôle of the industrial towns in the mid-Victorian period in widening the franchise; Asa Briggs, 'The background of the parliamentary reform movement in three English cities, 1830–1832', *Cambridge Historical Journal*, x (1950–2), pp. 293–317 deals with Birmingham, Leeds, and Manchester.

80 V. D. Lipmann, *Local Government Areas, 1835–1945* (1949) sorts out much of the confusion, though anyone trying to construct a series of comparable census figures is likely to find it necessary to pay even more attention to the detail.

81 David Roberts, *Victorian Origins of the Welfare State* (1960), argues that the administrative

more. Private philanthropy both helped and hindered it.[82] Yet as one reads more and more histories of English towns and is taken steadily down the galleries of municipal progress, it is impossible not to speculate on the limitations that historians are working under here. How seriously have they been handicapped by looking longest at the Council Chamber and the official record? How important, and knowable, are the silent operations of powers behind the scenes, and the goings-on which one can but suspect in back parlours? The researches of both Dr. Hennock and Dr. Newton are certainly going to make a few of these shadowy happenings much less obscure.

The most skilled of the historians of civic affairs have done reasonably well with the centre—can it be the apex?—of urban life. Just the same, however well they recount the measurable achievement of municipal progress, they do not quite convey what it was like to be alive in these places and what people *thought* about what was going on in them. No one reading Briggs's deeply perceptive second volume of the *History of Birmingham*[83] could conceivably wish for a more sensitively drawn *total* view of a single urban episode as one community tackled the problem of organising its space and ordering its priorities. This is still easily the best general study of the social essence of any of our major cities—an exciting inter-play of thrusting non-conformity, small masters, a diverse economy, and the personality of one of the Victorian period's outstanding civic leaders, Joseph Chamberlain. The scale is heroic and the themes that are so skilfully plaited together produce a sort of *public* image of the place. Now one of the major tasks of second-generation research in this part of the field must be to discover Birmingham's private face. Diaries and personal reminiscences are probably too few and haphazard in any one place to do so unaided, though they cannot be overlooked.[84]

state did not come into being mechanistically in response to industrialism and urbanisation but depended very much on personalities and the conflict of attitudes and interests. We know too little about local aspects of social reform, but two studies that suggest what there is to be discovered are: T. S. Ashton, *Economic and Social Investigations in Manchester, 1833-1933* (1934) and J. F. C. Harrison, *Social Reform in Victorian Leeds. The Work of James Hole, 1820-1895* (1954).

[82] David Owen, *English Philanthropy, 1660-1960* (1965) contains some excellent information on its urban aspects (but see Brian Harrison, 'Philanthropy and the Victorians', *Victorian Studies*, ix (1966), pp. 353-74). Other valuable work on urban charity has been done by: W. K. Jordan, *Philanthropy in England, 1480-1660* (1959) and *The Charities of London, 1480-1660* (1960); Margaret Simey, *Charitable Effort in Liverpool in the Nineteenth Century* (1951); R. W. M. Strain, *Belfast and Its Charitable Society* (1961).

[83] C. Gill, *History of Birmingham*, Vol. I: *Manor and Borough to 1865* (1952) and A. Briggs, *History of Birmingham*, Vol. II: *Borough and City, 1865-1938* (1952). A third volume covering the years since 1939 is now in preparation.

[84] Nevertheless those printed are likely to number many more than W. Matthews, *British*

Agenda for Urban Historians

To distil any kind of social essence is difficult enough, whether in terms of a political or commercial ethos, or of a widely shared enthusiasm like league football or choral singing, or of the deep divisions and cohesions of religion or race.[85] To distinguish with any kind of certainty between rural and urban aspects of such phenomena, if such distinctions really exist, is more difficult still.[86] But most difficult of all is to unravel the common-or-garden domesticities of urban life, not merely to preserve a memory of its paraphernalia,[87] but in order to find historically the patterns of behaviour and attitude which we have learned to recognise almost instinctively in our own experience. Mr. Jones' thesis about the aesthetic of the industrial town will undoubtedly make us think more about this. One incisive exposure of the social anatomy of a city by a geographer is Emrys Jones' *A Social Geography of Belfast* (1960), and there are some sensitively probing examinations of particular towns, restricted though they are in time-scale, in which sociologists have made ordinary human lives more credible than many historians have done. Unique in its historical span and approach, for example, is a brief synopsis of some research conducted before the war into the history and social structure of the county town of Hertford since its foundation by the

---

Diaries 1442–1942 (1950) would suggest. The kind of work capable of yielding information not available anywhere else, for example, on London is A. R. Bennett, *London and Londoners in the Eighteen-Fifties and Sixties* (1924); William Margrie, *Roses and Kippers* (1930); M. Vivyan Hughes, *A London Family, 1870–1900* (1946); Frederick Willis, *101 Jubilee Road* (1948), *Peace and Dripping Toast* (1950).

85 The nature of these difficulties, for example, comes through works on religious worship like R. Mudie-Smith (ed.), *The Religious Life of London* (1904) or K. S. Inglis, *Churches and the Working Classes in Victorian England* (1963); see, too, V. D. Lipman, *Social History of the Jews in England, 1850–1950* (1954) and his unusual study 'Social topography of a London congregation: the Bayswater Synagogue, 1863–1963', *Jewish Journal of Sociology*, vi (1964), pp. 68–74. See also Ernest Krausz, *Leeds Jewry* (1964); Neville Laski, 'The Manchester and Salford Jewish community 1912–1962', *Manchester Review*, x (Spring 1964), pp. 97–108. Valuable studies of religious dissent include I. Sellers, 'Nonconformist attitudes in later nineteenth century Liverpool', *Transactions of the Historic Society of Lancashire and Cheshire* cxiv (1962), pp. 215–39; A. Brockett, *Nonconformity in Exeter, 1650–1875* (1962). On some other intangibles see: T. R. Tholfsen, 'The artisan and the culture of early Victorian Birmingham', *University of Birmingham Historical Journal*, iv (1956), pp. 146–66; S. G. Checkland, 'Economic attitudes in Liverpool, 1793–1807', *Economic History Review*, New Series, v (1952–3), pp. 58–75. There are too few local studies of small professional groups, trade union branches, clubs, and societies. One that is of exceptional value is R. E. Schofield, *The Lunar Society of Birmingham. A Social History of Provincial Science and Industry in Eighteenth Century England* (1963).

86 A valuable attempt to clarify some of the issues, including historical ones, has been made by Peter H. Mann, *An Approach to Urban Sociology* (1965).

87 Among the books which have done this the most revealing are: Marion Lockhead, *The Victorian Household* (1964); R. Dutton, *The Victorian Home* (1954); John Gloag, *The Englishman's Castle*, 2nd ed. (1949); John Pudney, *The Smallest Room*, 2nd ed. (1959). An unusually detailed study of domestic housing in one place is D. Portman, *Exeter Houses, 1400–1700* (1966).

Danes.[88] Among more contemporary studies Ruth Glass's *Middlesbrough: The Social Background of a Plan* (1948) continues to stand out, and in the last few years Margaret Stacey's study of Banbury,[89] Rosser's and Harris's of Swansea,[90] Peter Collison's of Oxford,[91] and Peter Willmott's of London's East End[92] have notably extended our whole perception of community life.

One historian who has been more successful than any other since the war in putting a whole community under the microscope and keeping it alive is Sidney Pollard, whose *History of Labour in Sheffield* (1959) brings into view the differences that were involved in being born into a working-class family bound up in one of Sheffield's light trades of cutlery, tool-making, or silversmithing, or in one of its heavy trades of steel-making, engineering, or armaments. This is a book which is the antithesis of municipal history. It deals with the urban masses whose reactions to decisions taken about them have normally tended to interest historians only when they were plotting or rampaging in a mob. George Rudé, Edward Thompson, and others are showing us that mobs and outrages themselves can be atomised and their structure and purposes better understood by a diametrical change of view.[93] What Pollard has tried to do in Sheffield, in his own phrase, is to make the ordinary people of that city over the last hundred years the subjects and not the accustomed objects of history—and, not surprisingly, he draws on the methods of the sociologists in order to do so. The prospects for the study of urban society from this standpoint are exciting.

Except for these extra-municipal glimpses we still know about even the core of community life, for the most part, in fairly general terms. The Webbs' great survey of local government is probably unrivalled anywhere, but they did not so much move the mountains of archives that confronted

88 E. Roper Power, 'The social structure of an English county town', *Sociological Review*, xxix (1937), pp. 391–413.

89 Margaret Stacey, *Tradition and Change: A Study of Banbury* (1960).

90 C. Rosser and C. Harris, *The Family and Social Change: A Study of Family and Kinships in a South Wales Town* (1965). See also T. Brennan, E. W. Cooney, and H. Pollins, *Study of Social Change in South West Wales* (1954).

91 P. Collison, *The Cutteslowe Walls: A Study in Social Class* (1963).

92 Peter Willmott, *The Evolution of a Community: A Study of Dagenham after Forty Years* (1963). See also T. Young, *Becontree and Dagenham. The Story of the Growth of a Housing Estate* (1934), which deals with an L.C.C. estate in the years 1922–32.

93 E. P. Thompson, *The Making of the English Working Class* (1963); George Rudé, *The Crowd in History: A Study of Popular Disturbances in France and England, 1730–1848* (1964); a more specific study is Rudé's '"Mother Gin" and the London riots of 1736', *Guildhall Miscellany*, No. 10, pp. 53–63. See also Charles Tilly, *The Vendée* (1964) for an analysis of outstanding importance for urban studies of this kind.

them as tunnel headlong into them.[94] Just how high these mountains are is only now beginning to be clear from the unwavering scrutiny of archivists,[95] and the more erratic readiness of local authorities to put some of their work into print.[96] Some of the unused spoil from the Webbs' excavations was sieved again by their research assistant, F. H. Spencer, for his study of private bill legislation in relation to local government in the formative period 1740–1835. His *Municipal Origins* (1911) has led the way for perhaps the largest number of researchers to have worked since then in any part of the field of urban history. The main emphasis in the work done on public health has been concentrated on the central institutions,[97] but several scholars have been trying to shift attention away from London and the period of parliamentary reform into the provinces and towards earlier phases of urban development.[98] Some headway has now been made in giving the growth of urban police forces,[99] the supply

[94] S. and B. Webb, *English Local Government*, in particular *The Parish and the County* (1924) and *The Manor and the Borough*, 2 vols. (1908).

[95] These comprise too large a class to be mentioned in detail, though it is one which contains some surprises. There is for example, no census even of medieval borough records, and there is no ready way of telling how widely held from recent times are such materials as rate books, street plans, or building licence records. For a selective list of materials see W. B. Faraday, *The English and Welsh Boroughs: an Historical Outline* (1951). Good examples of bibliographies for individual towns are W. Powell and H. M. Cashmore, *A Catalogue of the Birmingham Collection* (1918) and H. M. Cashmore *A Catalogue of the Birmingham Collection. Supplement, 1918–1931* (1931); E. R. Matthews, *Bristol Bibliography* (1916); Raymond Smith, *The City of London: A Select Book List* (1951). See, too, the critical selection in W. B. Munro, *A Selected Bibliography on Municipal Government in Great Britian* (1926).

[96] See Charles Gross, 'Town records of Great Britain', *American Historical Review*, ii (1896–7), pp. 191–200, and G. H. Martin, 'The publication of borough records', *Archives*, vii (1966), pp. 199–206, which deals with printed records since 1501. The records most commonly printed have been: lists of mayors, sheriffs, freemen, apprentices; descriptions of regalia; subsidy and assize rolls; calendars of fines; port books.

[97] W. M. Frazer, *A History of English Public Health, 1834–1939* (1950); S. E. Finer, *The Life and Times of Sir Edwin Chadwick* (1952); R. A. Lewis, *Edwin Chadwick and the Public Health Movement, 1832–1854* (1952); B. Keith-Lucas, 'Some influences affecting the development of sanitary legislation in England', *Economic History Review*, 2nd Series, vi (1953–4), pp. 290–6; E. P. Hennock, 'Urban sanitary reform a generation before Chadwick?', *ibid.*, x (1957–8), pp. 113–20. See too, A. Paley and B. Benjamin, 'London as a case study', *Population Studies*, xvii (1963–4), pp. 249–62; W. M. Frazer, *Duncan of Liverpool, being an Account of the Work of Dr. W. H. Duncan, Medical Officer of Health of Liverpool, 1847–1863* (1947).

[98] E. L. Sabine, 'Latrines and cesspools of medieval London', *Speculum*, ix (1934), pp. 303–321, and 'City cleaning in medieval London', *ibid.*, xii (1937), pp. 19–34.

[99] See C. Reith, *The Police Idea: Its History and Evolution in England in the Eighteenth Century and After* (1938); T. A. Critchley, *The History of Police in England and Wales, 900–1966* (1967); Jenifer M. Hart, 'Reform of the borough police, 1835–1856', *English Historical Review*, lxx (1955), pp. 411–27; D. G. Browne, *The Rise of Scotland Yard: A History of the Metropolitan Police* (1956); S. Walter, *Cuffs and Handcuffs. The Story of the Rochdale Police, 1257–1957* (1957). An important gap in the study of urban crime has just been filled by J. J. Tobias, *Crime and Industrial Society in the Nineteenth Century* (1967).

of water and main drainage,[100] the provision of fire services,[101] of public transport,[102] and a number of other facilities,[103] a local habitation and a name. We are beginning to learn more now about the municipal and commercial aspects of markets, the supply of food, the growth of shops, the rise of Chambers of Commerce.[104] Closer to the civic centre of things there has also been some useful work done on various aspects of local politics and local presses.[105]

100 For a general survey of the history of water supply, see F. W. Robins, *The Story of Water Supply* (1949); W. M. Stern, 'Water supply in Britain: the development of a public service', *Royal Sanitary Institute Journal*, lxxiv (1954), pp. 998–1004, which includes a valuable selective bibliography. Local studies include the Metropolitan Water Board's *London's Water Supply 1903–1953* (1953); H. W. Dickinson's *Water Supply of Greater London* (1954); T. F. Reddaway, 'London in the nineteenth century: the fight for a water supply', *Nineteenth Century*, cxlviii (1950), pp. 118–30; B. L. McMillan, *History of the Water Supply of Wolverhampton, 1847–1947* (1947); E. Hughes, 'The new river water supply for Newcastle upon Tyne, 1698–1723', *Archaeologia Aeliana*, xxv (1947), pp. 115–24. See also Nicholas Barton, *The Lost Rivers of London* (1962); slighter still is W. E. C. Chamberlain, *A History of Portsmouth Drainage, 1865–1956* (1957). Henry Jephson, *The Sanitary Evolution of London* (1907) is still a surprisingly rare, adequately researched example of its type.

101 G. V. Blackstone, *A History of the British Fire Service* (1957).

102 D. Ward, 'A comparative historical geography of street car suburbs in Boston, Massachusetts and Leeds, England: 1850–1920', *Annals of the Association of American Geographers*, liv (1964), pp. 477–89; G. C. Dickinson, 'The development of suburban road passenger transport in Leeds, 1840–1895', *Journal of Transport History*, iv (1959–60), pp. 214–23. W. B. Crump, *Huddersfield Highways down the Ages* (1949); Roy Brook, *The Tramways of Huddersfield* (1960); G. A. Sekon, *Locomotion in Victorian London* (1938); W. M. Stern, 'The first London dock boom and the growth of the West India Docks', *Economica*, New Series, xix (1952), pp. 59–77; S. Pollard and J. D. Marshall, 'The Furness Railway and the growth of Barrow', *Journal of Transport History*, i (1953), pp. 109–26. J. R. Kellett, 'Glasgow's railways, 1830–80: a study in "natural growth"', *Economic History Review*, New Series, xvii (1964), pp. 354–68; T. C. Barker and M. Robbins, *A History of London Transport*, Vol. I: *The Nineteenth Century* (1963); my two articles on 'Railways and housing in Victorian London', *Journal of Transport History*, ii (1955), pp. 11–21, 90–100, suggest one of the railways' vital contributions to urban ecology.

103 One special study of considerable value is: R. W. C. Richardson, *Thirty-two Years of Local Self-Government, 1855–87* (1888).

104 W. M. Stern, *The Porters of London* (1960) is a definitive work. Janet Blackman, 'The food supply of an industrial town: a study of Sheffield's public markets, 1780–1900', *Business History*, v (1963), pp. 83–97, deals with a somewhat neglected aspect of urban development. E. L. Sabine, 'Butchering in medieval London', *Speculum*, viii (1933), pp. 335–53, extends what is known of the cattle trade in a new direction. Local trade associations of all kinds remain very much in the dark, but see M. W. Beresford, *The Leeds Chamber of Commerce* (1951). On shops J. B. Jeffery's strongly economic study, *Retail Trading in Britain, 1850–1950* (1954), has now been supplemented in period and human interest by Alison Adburgham, *Shops and Shopping, 1800–1914* (1964), which is concerned with London drapers, dressmakers, and milliners; and by Dorothy Davis, *History of Shopping* (1966), which is the most extensive treatment of the whole subject yet available. Peter Mathias, *Retailing Revolution* (1967), covers mainly the development of the departmental and chain store.

105 Among the most interesting studies of the relations between economic interests and local politics are: Asa Briggs, 'Industry and politics in early nineteenth century Keighley', *The Bradford Antiquary*, xxxv (1958), pp. 1–13; T. R. Tholfsen, 'The origins of the Birmingham

34

The most coherent of these studies—the pick of them must be F. H. W. Sheppard's *Local Government in St. Marylebone, 1688–1835* (1958), A. Temple Patterson's *Radical Leicester, 1780–1850* (1953), E. W. Gilbert's *Brighton: Old Ocean's Bauble* (1954), and J. F. Ede's *History of Wednesbury* (1962)—have brought some understanding of wider issues to bear on local themes; and the best of those that have taken a narrower view—like W. Hooper's *Reigate: Its Story through the Ages* (1954) and Mrs. Gwen Hart's *History of Cheltenham* (1965)—have suffered from it.[106] Some towns and the neighbourhoods within them refuse to be wrenched from their setting without weakening their whole history; and it is the special merit of Ede's book that Wednesbury should have been placed with such care in relation to its Black Country neighbours and its physical terrain, as well as to the technical and economic manipulators of its changing fortunes which operated at longer range.[107] This is a difficult feat. More difficult still is the comparison, not merely of industries and types of employment, but of structures of society and prevailing attitudes. There are understandably very few such studies.[108]

There are some signs that the still more promising possibilities of discerning the larger movement in the microcosm are now being realised. I think they are becoming clearer, not so much by great vaulting com-

caucus', *Historical Journal*, ii (1959), pp. 161–89; E. Gwynne Jones, 'Borough politics and electioneering, 1826–1852', *Transactions of the Caernarvonshire Historical Society*, xvii (1956), pp. 75–85; David Cox, 'The Labour Party in Leicester: a study in branch development', *International Review of Social History*, vi (1961), pp. 197–211; J. R. Vincent, 'The electoral sociology of Rochdale', *Economic History Review*, 2nd Series, xvi (1963–4), pp. 76–90; Paul Thompson, 'Liberals, Radicals and Labour in London, 1880–1900', *Past and Present*, xxvii (1964), pp. 73–101 (the references are instructive). On the press, see D. Read, *Press and People, 1790–1850: Opinion in Three English Cities* (1961); Asa Briggs, 'Press and public opinion in early nineteenth century Birmingham', Dugdale Society, *Occasional Papers*, No. 8 (1949); Derek Fraser 'The Nottingham Press, 1800–50', *Transactions of the Thoroton Society*, lxvii (1963), pp. 46–66.

106 The following also deserve close attention: E. L. S. Horsburgh, *Bromley, Kent, from the Earliest Times to the Present Century* (1929); S. Middlebrook, *Newcastle upon Tyne: Its Growth and Achievement* (1950); Sir Frederick Rees, *The Story of Milford* (1954); R. Fasnacht, *History of the City of Oxford* (1954); J. M. Baines, *Historic Hastings* (1955); R. P. and E. Taylor, *Rochdale Retrospect* (1956); C. Stella Davies (ed.), *A History of Macclesfield* (1961); B. S. Smith, *A History of Malvern* (1964); W. R. Ward, *Victorian Oxford* (1965). Despite their pretentiousness, E. J. Warrilow, *A Sociological History of Stoke-on-Trent* (1960) and Winifred M. Bowmain, *England in Ashton-under-Lyne* (1960) contain some interesting material, insular though it is.

107 It may be compared with Professor Temple Patterson's more recent work, *A History of Southampton, 1700–1914*, Vol. I: *An Oligarchy in Decline, 1700–1835*, which has a tightly packed core of information on its central theme that is uncertainly related to outside events and tendencies. In this respect it also belongs to the *genre* represented earlier by Sir Francis Hill's *Georgian Lincoln*, and raises the same kind of doubt about its value.

108 Asa Briggs, 'Social structure and politics in Birmingham and Lyons, 1825–1848', *British Journal of Sociology*, i (1950), pp. 67–80.

parisons which erupt, *à la* Briggs, from a free-booting genius, but by the patient picking over of the masses of materials from which the mass portrait gallery of urban society must one day come. The paper offered to this symposium by Mr. Foster will, I think, be sure to move us more in this direction; and if Mr. Armstrong's pleas for equally disciplined inquiries as his are at all widely answered we shall advance even more rapidly that way.

It seems when viewed *en masse* that patterns of urban settlement expressed in statistical terms are sometimes so sophisticated, as they must be, that the imagination alone can supply the flesh and blood.[109] For the historian it is as dangerous as it is easy to be too clinical in handling such themes, though the problem of relating the quantitative and qualitative aspects of such studies can be exaggerated. Just the same, an historian who manages to move his readers without making them suspect his methods is rare, especially if he is working in some part of the field that has attracted few other researchers. We still know so little, for example, about the ways in which the millions of migrations that composed the cities were made. Ravenstein's,[110] Redford's,[111] and Cairncross's[112] cumulative efforts have been filled out to surprisingly little extent, both for the period before and during that covered by the census.[113] The researches of Buckatzsch and Lawton, despite their microscopic scale and quite different origins, vividly suggest how much we might learn of both these phases.[114] The paper which Mrs. Baker and I have contributed to this symposium also tries to make a tentative response to this gap in our knowledge. Our understanding of the ways in which migration to the cities has fitted in with movement into and out of the country is now being

[109] Professor Brian Berry and his team at Chicago are probably leading the way in the scientific analysis of patterns of urban settlement: see B. J. L. Berry, 'Urban population densities: structure and change', *Geographical Review*, liii (1963), pp. 389–405. An example of a brilliant generalisation without adequate historical support is Colin Clark, 'Urban population densities', *Journal of the Royal Statistical Society*, cxiv (1951), Ser. A, pp. 490–6.

[110] E. G. Ravenstein, 'The laws of migration', *Journal of the Royal Statistical Society*, xlviii (1885), pp. 167–235, and lii (1889), pp. 241–305.

[111] A. Redford, *Labour Migration in England, 1800–1850* (1926). See too, D. F. Macdonald, *Scotland's Shifting Population, 1770–1850* (1937). E. J. Buckatzsch, 'Places of origin of a group of immigrants into Sheffield, 1624–1799', *Economic History Review*, 2nd Series, xi (1958), pp. 303–6.

[112] A. K. Cairncross, *Home and Foreign Investment, 1870–1913* (1953), Chap IV.

[113] A recent statistical study of some importance is D. Friedlander and R. J. Roshier, 'A study of internal migration in England and Wales, 1851–1951—geographical patterns of internal migration', *Population Studies*, xix (1966), pp. 239–79.

[114] R. Lawton, 'The population of Liverpool in the mid-nineteenth century', *Transactions of the Historic Society of Lancashire and Cheshire*, cvii (1955), pp. 98–120. See also: H. A. Shannon, 'Migration and the growth of London, 1841–91', *Economic History Review*, v (1935),

amplified,[115] not only by genuinely moving works like Oliver MacDonagh's study of the traffic in Irish through Liverpool[116] or Lloyd Gartner's quest for the Jews arriving in the East End of London,[117] but by the sociological studies of immigration that are already passing rapidly into the literature of urban history.[118] But just how often, why, and under what constraints people ever moved house is far less clear than how far, or by what means, they journeyed to work.[119]

Housing itself is oddly neglected. Two or three scholars have written briefly on housing conditions in Leeds, Nottingham, London, and elsewhere,[120] and the subsidised phase of housing has been investigated from the Whitehall end,[121] but we have too few authentic tales of mean streets,

pp. 79–86; R. A. Pelham, 'The immigrant population of Birmingham, 1686–1726', *Transactions of the Birmingham Archaeological Society*, lxi (1940), pp. 45–80; H. A. Shannon and E. Grebenik, 'The population of Bristol', National Institute of Economic and Social Research, *Occasional Papers*, ii (1943); F. Beckwith, 'The population of Leeds during the Industrial Revolution', *Thoresby Society Publications: Miscellany*, xli (1945), pp. 118–96.

115 Brinley Thomas, *Migration and Economic Growth* (1954); A. K. Cairncross, *Home and Foreign Investment, 1870–1913* (1953). See also W. S. Shepperson, *British Industrial Emigration to North America* (1957).

116 O. MacDonagh, *A Pattern of Government Growth, 1800–60. The Passenger Acts and their Enforcement* (1961).

117 Lloyd P. Gartner, *The Jewish Immigrant in England, 1870–1914* (1960). It contains a valuable bibliography. Cf. W. Evans-Gordon, *The Alien Immigrant* (1903).

118 For example, K. L. Little, *Negroes in Britain: A Study of Racial Relations in English Society* (1948), which is based on Cardiff dockland.

119 The best general treatment is still K. K. Liepmann, *The Journey to Work: Its Significance for Industrial and Community Life* (1944). There are several travel surveys now available to supplement it in detail: J. Westergaard, 'Journeys to work in the London region', *Town Planning Review*, xxviii (1957–8), pp. 50–1; R. Lawton, 'The daily journey to work in England and Wales', *ibid.*, xxix (1959), pp. 241–57. See, too, the London Transport Executive, *London Travel Surveys* (1950, 1956).

120 On builders, see A. K. Cairncross, *Home and Foreign Investment, 1870–1913* (1953), Chap. II on the Glasgow building industry; J. R. Kellett, 'Property speculators and the building of Glasgow, 1780–1830', *Scottish Journal of Political Economy*, viii (1961), pp. 211–32; R. W. Postgate, *The Builders History* (1923); J. R. Jones, *The Welsh Builder on Merseyside: Annals and Lives* (1946); Marion Bowley, *The British Building Industry: Four Studies in Response and Resistance to Change* (1966) is mainly concerned with the twentieth century; both speculative builders and domestic housing in London get some attention in my *Victorian Suburb* (1961), Chap. V. J. Parry Lewis, *Building Cycles and Britain's Growth* (1965) brings together most of the material pertaining to building trends in different towns and regions and is a useful introduction to the growing literature on the subject; H. J. Habakkuk, 'Fluctuations in house-building in Britain and the United States in the nineteenth century', *Journal of Economic History*, xxii (1962), pp. 198–230, provides a valuable synopsis and interpretation. On housing itself there is very little: W. G. Rimmer, 'Working men's cottages in Leeds, 1770–1840', and 'Alfred Place Terminating Building Society, 1825–1843', *Thoresby Society Publications*, xlvi (1961), pp. 165–99, 303–30; S. D. Chapman, 'Working-class housing in Nottingham during the industrial revolution', *Transactions of the Thoroton Society*, lxvii (1963), pp. 67–92.

121 Marion Bowley, *Housing and the State, 1919–1944* (1945); M. J. Elsas, *Housing Before and After the War* (1942). There is a useful bibliography of such material in J. B. Cullingworth, *Housing Needs and Planning Policy* (1960), pp. 205–12.

The Study of Urban History

or of the making and unmaking of slums.[122] E. R. Dewsnup's *The Housing Problem in England* (1907) is still the most authoritative statement we have on the Victorian phase and H. Quigby and I. Goldie, *Housing and Slum Clearance in London* (1934) one of the very few accounts of a particular area. How, one cannot help wondering, has this slow-moving, complex machinery of urban renewal been set in motion, or brought to a halt?[123] Perhaps the most detailed historical knowledge we have refers still to the renewal of London from the ashes of 1666 and 1940-5.[124] It is the undramatic replacement of a city piece by piece and year by year that goes unnoticed. How great or small are the social costs and the benefits of an ageing environment, or of a new one? Can historians possibly say?

We know so little yet about a number of obvious things. Small towns that never grew big nor got stuck in amber as a neighbour did tend to remain unseen. There are too few studies of such towns.[125] Thanks to Maurice Beresford's unquenchable enthusiasm and scrupulous scholarship we are getting (just as this goes to press) a study of town plantation in the middle ages, something that we have known about so far only in scraps.[126] His inaugural lecture at Leeds, *Time and Place* (1961), contains

[122] See my paper 'The slums of Victorian London', *Victorian Studies*, xi (1967), pp. 5-40, which includes an extensive bibliography.

[123] Among recent work dealing with particular aspects of this topic, the following are of special interest: C. M. Allan, 'The genesis of British urban redevelopment with special reference to Glasgow', *Economic History Review*, New Series, xviii (1965), pp. 598-613; J. N. Tarn, 'The Peabody Donation Fund: the role of a housing society in the nineteenth century', *Victorian Studies*, x (1966), pp. 7-38; C. Vereker and J. B. Mays, *Urban Redevelopment and Social Change: A Study in Social Conditions in Central Liverpool, 1955-6* (1961), which deals with social structure and family life against the economic background of the Crown Street area.

[124] T. F. Reddaway's masterly account, *The Rebuilding of London after the Great Fire* (1940), could not have appeared at a more apt moment. It also seems fitting that the publication of the Improvements and Town Planning Committee of the Corporation of London, *The City of London. A Record of Destruction and Survival* (1951) should have been not only the best photographic document of the bomb damage but the most comprehensive coverage so far of the physical changes that have occurred since Roman times. There is a good deal of piquancy about the plans, given in full detail, for post-war reconstruction. For a more general and beautifully illustrated panorama of city growth and the possibilities for its design, see P. Johnson-Marshall, *Rebuilding Cities* (1966).

[125] See W. G. Hoskins, 'English provincial towns in the early sixteenth century', *Transactions of the Royal Historical Society*, 5th Series, vi (1956), pp. 1-19, reprinted in *Provincial England: Essays in Social and Economic History* (1963), pp. 68-85, which also contains a study of the town of Market Harborough. The following studies are all brief and have value: M. F. L. Pritchard, 'The decline of Norwich', *Economic History Review*, New Series, iii (1950-1), pp. 371-7; R. Mitchell, *Brighouse, Portrait of a Town* (1953); W. Haythornthwaite, *Harrogate Story: from Georgian Village to Victorian Town* (1954); W. Potts, *A History of Banbury* (1958); G. H. Martin, *The Story of Colchester from Roman Times to the Present Day* (1959); C. W. Chalklin, 'A seventeenth-century market town: Tonbridge', *Archaeologia Cantabriensis*, lxxvi (1961), pp. 152-62.

[126] M. W. Beresford, *New Towns of the Middle Ages. Town Plantation in England, Wales and Gascony* (1967).

a promise of more such studies of the seen and unseen, the lost and the
surviving, elements in the landscape, and he has now turned to contemplate the making of Victorian Leeds. It is a mistake to think that what is
most obvious is best understood, for the dark ages in urban history belong
still to the more recent past, in which our ignorance of the obvious things
may be less excusable. How much do we yet know about the actual
turning of cow pasture, say, into peopled streets; the convergence of
business interests upon building land and the creation of new titles to it;
the financial investment in building estates; the logistics, the risks, and
the rewards of speculative building. In the theatre, we know, the cherry
orchard comes down with a clean uncompromising stroke and the little
villas queue quietly for their entrance in the wings. But life itself is rarely
so well staged and we need to know about the history of the 'unplanning'
of towns to set alongside descriptions of the conscious artefacts.[127]
Professor Ashworth put us in his debt some years ago with his *The
Genesis of Modern British Town Planning* (1954) and he must be surprised
that so few people have wanted to supplement or modify his account in
detail.[128] G. F. Chadwick's *The Park and the Town: Public Landscape in the
19th and 20th Centuries* (1966) fills out one aspect of this magnificently.
Dr. Marshall shows from the scope of his paper, as from his writing,[129]
that he is thinking carefully about another of these themes.

Very recently, A. J. Youngson has delighted us by retelling the story of
Beauty and the Beast in *The Making of Classical Edinburgh, 1750–1840*

[127] On these, see F. Hiorns, *Town-Building in History: an Outline Review of Conditions, Influences, Ideas and Methods affecting 'Planned Towns' through Five Thousand Years* (1956); Helen Rosenau, *The Ideal City in its Architectural Evolution* (1959); L. Hilberseimer, *The Nature of Cities: Origins, Growth and Decline, Pattern and Form, Planning Problems* (1951).

[128] On one deliberately developed, if not consciously planned, town see the valuable series of articles: S. Pollard, 'Town planning in the nineteenth century: the beginnings of modern Barrow-in-Furness', *Transactions of the Lancashire & Cheshire Antiquarian Society*, lxiii (1952–3), pp. 87–116; S. Pollard, 'Barrow-in-Furness and the Seventh Duke of Devonshire', *Economic History Review*, New Series, viii (1955), pp. 213–21; S. Pollard and J. D. Marshall, 'The Furness Railway and the growth of Barrow', *Journal of Transport History*, i (1952–3), pp. 109–26. S. Pollard, *The Genesis of Modern Management: A Study of the Industrial Revolution* (1965) also includes some material on the industrial village. James Hole, *The Housing of the Working Classes* (1866) is still most valuable on the new industrial villages of Akroydon and Saltaire, but see also R. K. Dewhirst, 'Saltaire', *Town Planning Review*, xxxi (1960–1), pp. 135–44; A. Harris, 'Millom: a Victorian new town', *Transactions of the Cumberland & Westmoreland Antiquarian and Archaeological Society*, lxvi (1966), pp. 449–67. On later develop-ments there are P. H. White, 'Some aspects of urban development by colliery companies, 1919–1939', *Manchester School*, xxiii (1955), pp. 269–80; R. Trow-Smith, *The History of Stevenage* (1958). One earlier book is worth noting: Cecil Stewart, *A Prospect of Cities, being Studies towards a History of Town Planning* (1952); Leonardo Benevolo, *The Origins of Modern Town Planning* (1967) really adds nothing.

[129] Principally, *Furness and the Industrial Revolution* (1958).

(1966).[130] The political and speculative ins-and-outs of creating the New Town were touched in the end by a splendour which outlasted the city's subsequent decline, and this remains unsullied even by the parking meters which another onslaught on philistinism has brought on itself. The unthinking acts of a multitude of small men at work on the making of a city do not fall so quickly into a pattern. The *Survey of London*, which has for well over half-a-century been unpicking the tangle of London's architectural history, demonstrates vividly how much of this can be reconstructed, and how much has to be left in the dust. Dr. Sheppard's paper to this conference is likely to prove a sobering document.

If we are to understand how such places have grown we cannot concentrate on large coordinated developments or urban cores alone. It is excellent to have studies like Donald Olsen's sumptuous *Town Planning in London: the Eighteenth and Nineteenth Centuries* (1964), in which he looks searchingly at success and failure in the planned development and maintenance of two central London estates in the period; for he makes a gracious advance on what we knew of the beginnings of the West End from Sir John Summerson's classic, *Georgian London* (1945), and Gladys Scott Thomson's portrayal of the Russells.[131] Perhaps it is ironic that it is the account he gives of the unfashionable, foot-dragging estates north of the Euston Road—James and Muirhead Bone once caught their tone to a tee in half-a-dozen pages and a lot of charcoal[132]—which says most. It is indeed into the still more unmannerly suburbs beyond this that we should now be taken more inquisitively, into the kind of territory so gently satirised by the Grossmiths, so scathingly by Gissing and Wells.[133]

A. F. Weber, as in so many other directions, seems to have led for some of the way here. In looking beyond Mornington Crescent for that kindly light which might lure the working classes out of the slums and semi-slums into the suburbs, he was searching for a positive solution to some of the worst evils of the city. We see now that this was a fugitive solution to a problem which baffles us still. The unending story of London as a wen, growing blindly at the country's expense, begins under the Tudors and goes on in press, parliament and committee room throughout the nineteenth and twentieth centuries: the best places at which to listen

130 Cf. L. Wilkes and G. Dodds, *Tyneside Classical: The Newcastle of Grainger Dobson and Clayton* (1964).

131 Gladys Scott Thomson, *The Russells in Bloomsbury, 1669-1771* (1940). For information on two of the other large London estates, see Charles T. Gatty, *Mary Davis and the Manor of Ebury*, 2 vols. (1921) and B. H. Johnson, *Berkeley Square to Bond Street* (1952).

132 *The London Perambulator* (1925), Chap. IX.

133 George and Weedon Grossmith, *The Diary of a Nobody* (1892); George Gissing, *In the Year of Jubilee* (1894); H. G. Wells, *Anne Veronica* (1913).

in are Norman Brett-James' *The Growth of Stuart London* (1935), Stein Eiler Rasmussen's perenially suggestive *London: the Unique City* (1934), and Peter Hall's less-than-prophetic *London 2000* (1963).[134] The study of one set of minutiae in this process, the proliferating suburbs, is still in an early stage.[135] J. T. Coppock and Hugh Prince perform therefore a valuable service in acting, with their colleagues, as couriers along a frontier which was once so sharp that Regent's Park could be conceived as a garden suburb but is now so ragged that it has to be described in terms of an approach to an ex-urban zone. A great deal more work remains to be done, however, before the suburb becomes a clear historical entity. This cannot be so until we give more attention to its uncalendared annals, locked up even now in solicitors' black japanned boxes[136] or mouldering in heaps of auction particulars, and to the strangely moving apparatus of its scruffy little estates. One of the interesting possibilities contained in Dr. Reeder's paper in this regard is that we might begin to use the knowledge we do possess to recognise variety where once we saw only uniformity.[137]

It is here, too, that there are some inter-cultural comparisons worth making: room even for a new version of the 'frontier thesis', or a new kind of archaeology, or a new historical span for social psychology? Professor Leo Schnore's scrupulous study of the internal spatial structure of cities in the Western Hemisphere, in particular of the distribution of wealth and poverty at the centre and on the periphery, is highly relevant to this point and very suggestive for further research: his formal contribution to this symposium is an interim report on the progress of his work. Certainly, it is in towns large enough for suburbs, and especially the metropolitan centres, where the opportunities for studying the full spectrum of urban life may be at their greatest, as the Centre for Urban Studies' third report, *London: Aspects of Change* (1964), makes so clear. The Centre for Urban Studies at University College London, was established in 1958, with the object of contributing to the systematic knowledge of towns and linking

[134] Ministry of Housing and Local Government, *The South East Study, 1961–1981* (1964) provides one version of the present predicament. See, too, Paul Banks, *Metropolis or the Destruction of Cities* (1930).

[135] Two studies which concentrate in different ways on somewhat different suburban types are: H. J. Dyos, *Victorian Suburb. A Study of the Growth of Camberwell* (1961); R. E. Pahl, *Urbs in Rure: The Metropolitan Fringe in Hertfordshire* (1964).

[136] A rare glimpse is afforded by J. R. Kellett, 'Urban and transport history from legal records: an example from Glasgow solicitors' papers', *Journal of Transport History*, vi (1964), pp. 222–40.

[137] For a brilliant analytical typology of towns over 50,000 inhabitants in 1951, see C. A. Moser and W. Scott, *British Towns. A Statistical Study of their Social and Economic Differences* (1961).

this to social policy, in the tradition of Charles Booth. This report is its most ambitious co-operative publication so far and makes a distinctive contribution to the subject in both substance and method. Its theme is the cosmopolitan tangle of cultures, movement, and mobility to be found in contemporary London, and to understand them three of its contributors have examined related aspects of Victorian London: the localising tendencies at work in its labour markets; the effects of public transport on its social geography; the structure and unchanging typology of its eastern suburbs.

Physical and social distance are not unrelated here, but what does emerge with force is a new awareness of the relativity of urban life—networks of relationships rather than close-knit communities, overlapping and intermingling spheres of economic and administrative influence rather than discrete and monolithic zones. The present streaky look of metropolitan society has not occurred suddenly, though the juxtaposition of wealth and poverty in areas which are see-sawing between blight and fashion has not become marked until the last ten years. The rush into the suburbs represented one kind of development in urban life, and there are some strong implicit suggestions in *London: Aspects of Change* about what is relevant to an understanding of urban society in these and more general terms.

One practical implication of this is that London's present magnetic field cannot be depolarised by redrawing lines on maps nor its administrative problems solved merely by talking of regions. This conclusion fits well with one of the by-products of Jean Gottmann's commandingly over-stated thesis covering another urban zone, between Cape Cod and the Potomac, *Megalopolis* (1961). Such spheres of influence tend to be so nebulous that perhaps no country of the future can be so great as to keep them to their own corners. Indeed, it is possible that the present historical trend in highly industrialised countries is toward metropolitan explosion and the gradual extinction of the old extremes of population density.[138] That London's should still be the most blurred of all civic identities seems almost justifiable.

The closing of the gaps between historians, sociologists, and geographers which I hope this somewhat breathless review of the writing of urban history reveals, has had the healthy effect of making the historians more aware than they used to be of the visual evidence for the changes that interest them. Erwin Gutkind's *Our World from the Air* (1952) was one

[138] R. M. Haig, 'Toward an understanding of the metropolis', *Quarterly Journal of Economics*, xi (1926), pp. 179–208, 402–34 describes well the concentrative phase.

kind of eye-opener. Dr. Geoffrey Martin's *The Town* (1961)[139] is another, mostly at ground level. This is a lively guide to the human as well as the physical features of British towns since the middle ages, and in his paper here Dr. Martin will be sure to make anyone who has not used his eyes enough regret it. The urban scene is now changing really fast. Old, low-density building is making way almost everywhere for commercial boxes that are both cause and effect of rising land values, and the evidence that had been taken for granted is being wiped clean by the astonishing efficiency of demolition contractors.[140] We have nothing even remotely as ambitious in this country as *The Columbia Historical Portrait of New York* (1953) or Robert Auzelle's *Encyclopédie de l'Urbanisme* (1950), and there is a real need for a collection of photographs and plans illustrating the history of our towns with as much instruction and delight, and none of the wavering competence in disentangling the historical trends, as we are now getting in the best portrayals of our most photogenic cities.[141]

In what directions is the study of urban history in Britain moving now? That is not an easy question to answer, for it requires a review of the current commitments of at least four hundred active researchers in the field. This is the extent of the work listed in detail in the last issue of the *Urban History Newsletter* (June 1967), and by the time these words are read any detailed information based on that register of research will have become out-of-date. Just the same, there are some general indications of this that can be given quite briefly against the background of the work described in the last few pages, as well as the substantial number of university theses in this field that have never been published.

Most of the research now going on is, in fact, intended to be submitted in theses for higher degrees. The development of postgraduate research confirms the more general impression got from published work that the full force of the growth of interest in urban history has been felt only since about 1950. It is in the period since then that all but a fifth or so of the research for higher degrees to have been done on British towns since before the first world war (over 250 items) have been completed. Some of

---

[139] See, too, M. W. Barley, *The House and Home* (1963).

[140] Some slight impression of the scope of these erasures may be had from Harold Clunn, *London Rebuilt, 1897–1927* (1927).

[141] Ewart Johns, *British Townscapes* (1965) is a modest, competent study of the lie of urban land and the historical make-up of building texture; Quentin Hughes, *Seaport: Architecture and Townscape in Liverpool* (1964) is a dramatic kaleidoscope of surviving buildings, mostly Victorian; V. S. Pritchett's *Dublin* (1967) is a refreshingly beautiful, quasi-historical, portrait of a very human place.

this merely reflects the natural growth of the provincial universities, though the bulk of the work has in fact been done from, but not on, London; and the provincial universities have more often turned their students' attentions to other towns than their own.

The most obvious feature of this writing is its heavy concentration on the nineteenth century, which is now attracting about half the total number of scholars engaged on research of this kind; the proportion is probably greater even than this in practice because most of the general work excluded from this estimate is principally concerned with that period. It is interesting to notice that about a fifth of the research is given to the early modern period before 1800.

Much of this work is being devoted, as it has always been, to general studies of particular places and there is here a strong inflection of historical geography, and a preference for moderate sized towns like Exeter, Norwich, Peterborough, Stamford, Northampton, St. Albans. Less marked than it used to be is an interest in the economic and geographical aspects of ports and their hinterlands, industrial towns, and the location of industry within them, though this still comprises a substantial category. There also seems to be a growing preference for studying the urban aspects of a whole geographical region or a single conurbation. Closely related to this are researches on urban morphology, in a few cases very widely drawn indeed. A sprinkling of research students are investigating urban hierarchies and others specific changes in land-use, usually on some kind of comparative basis.

What is now more emphatic than it has ever been is an interest in both the detailed modulation of the urban landscape and various forms or phases of building. Some of this is concerned with changes in the central cores of towns, including shopping and business districts, and a little of this is related more broadly to civic design. Much more attention is being paid to housing and housing policy. The speculative and financial aspects of the housing industry are now being opened up for the eighteenth century and nineteenth century, and there are a few promising studies of housing activity in particular areas, including London, South Wales, and Ireland. More generally, there is a rapidly growing interest in working-class housing and its pathological aspects, both in London and provincial towns, some of it clearly related to present policy-making, some of it simply a reflex of the ageing condition of the industrial towns. Middle-class housing is getting at least as much attention, though this is much less specific and is to be included in the quite substantial number of projects concerned with suburban development.

The functioning and amenities of towns have never been very thoroughly investigated for their own sake and there appears to be comparatively little work going on in this sector now, except as an aspect of more general studies. One topic that is being looked at quite searchingly is the supply of food to the towns and its wholesale and retail distribution since the seventeenth century, though the specific rôle of road and rail in provisioning the towns and making them work, or fail to work properly, needs more attention. Dr. Kellett's forthcoming book should clarify several aspects of the impact of the railways on Victorian cities at least. One or two studies are being made of the development of local labour markets. Interest in public health and gas-and-water socialism has all but evaporated, it seems, and work on most other amenities is very scattered. One matter no longer so badly overlooked is the holiday industry and there are several pieces of work in hand on particular resorts, though there is more to be discovered, one suspects, about the geographical and social patterns of holiday-making, so much of which is still not done away from home. The urban underworld is being investigated to a very limited extent —largely owing to the lack, perhaps, of sufficiently reliable informers among the compilers of the judicial statistics and other records.

The characteristics of urban population movements are now being studied more closely than ever before, less for their strictly demographic meaning than for their ecological and sociological aspects. This kind of study is no longer being confined to the period covered by the censuses nor to the large towns, and it is to be hoped that Mr. Alan Armstrong may soon find a still stronger corps of researchers prepared to work comparatively in this field. Research into migration remains very largely a study of birthplaces, but it is being related particularly to the acculturation of various groups of alien immigrants since the middle ages and the local political issues to which they have given rise. Most of the research that is now being put into the practice of religion in the towns is also concentrating on the identifiable minorities, though one or two studies—inescapably comparative ones—are now afoot on broader aspects of the rôle of religion in urban society.

One of the largest historical spheres for urban research is now that of social structure and the politics which are most closely related to it. Apart from numerous less pointed projects levelled quite generally at the economic and social development of selected communities, there are studies aimed specifically at linking social and political with religious divisions or reformative zeal, others at identifying middle class élites, others at the sources of social and political conflict, or reasons for the lack of it. Apart from two or three inquiries into the roots of radicalism in particular localities, the whole of the study of urban politics is being concentrated on the period of parliamentary reform. There is considerable research going on into the politics of the major cities—London, Glasgow, Manchester, Liverpool, Birmingham, Bristol, Newcastle—over relatively short periods of time, but hardly any general study of small towns or suburbs; in relation to parliamentary elections the tendency seems to be to take smaller places as well. Apart from one study of Liberalism in Victorian Liverpool, all the research concerned with the formation of political attitudes and their implementation is concerned with working class movements, though one only with trade unionism. Comparatively little work seems to be in hand on the level of ward and local council politics, or the activities of local government. This is somewhat remarkable because local administration accounts for perhaps the largest single category of current research. A great deal of this is concerned with poor law or public health administration, though two or three projects do concern less hackneyed themes.

This very brief glimpse at the scope of the research now going on gives little idea of its content or of its methods. Yet its volume, taken with the published evidence of the current interest in urban history, almost tempts one to ask, Whatever happened to the anti-urban bias in English history? There is undoubtedly a great deal of research now taking place on most aspects of the history of towns, some of it purely incidental to that history, some of it bearing the signs of being derived a little mechanically from other lines of research, some of it highly original and, one hopes, rewarding. There can be no doubt that if volume were the test urban history is well on its way. But we all know that it is not. That list is itself a demonstration that the field is as yet a very ragged one and that those in it are a little confused as to what they are doing. What this paper may have done is to demonstrate how uncomfortably true that is.

The Growth of Urban History in France: Some Methodological Trends

François Bédarida

Owing to the vast and puzzling extent of the subject, I have deliberately chosen to limit this paper to three main themes. While trying to trace the general development of urban history in France, I shall consider its various trends from three points of view: the subjects selected as approaches to the study of town growth and city life; the methods used by investigators; the ideologies or theories underlying their researches, their hypotheses and their conclusions. Accordingly, the stress will be put upon a methodological reflection about the experience of French historians and social scientists. However defective and scattered this experience may be, some lessons emerge and some teaching comes out of it. In conclusion, therefore, I want to pay special attention to some highly promising lines of further research and to suggest some comparative views about British and French urban history. Such an investigation should demonstrate how far the general and impressive development of the social sciences during recent years must contribute to the promotion of urban history in particular.

Before coming to the core of my subject, let me make clear the limits which I have deliberately imposed on myself. These restrictions are of three kinds. First, I have omitted the period prior to the industrial revolution as well as that before modern urbanisation began. Apart from a few exceptional references here and there to earlier periods, this paper concentrates upon the nineteenth and twentieth centuries. Secondly, to avoid long and tedious lists of authors and books and to refrain from the style of a catalogue, I have selected a few typical works and ignored others, though often just as valuable. Such a choice leads to unavoidable and arbitrary gaps, of which I am fully aware. Thirdly, I have decided to leave out

47

sources. They will be mentioned only as far as their existence (or non-existence) impinges on the historian's choices and has some influence on his questions and methods.

If we consider the results achieved by urban history in France during the last half century, we must admit that the crop is meagre and rather disappointing. Even to-day this field of historical research is still in its infancy, and scholars at work in it are scattered among various departments and their teaching broken up in various lecture courses. Inevitably, therefore, it remains mostly unexplored.

Where is the origin of such a state of affairs? There is no doubt that for a long time historians—who reflect the cares and aspirations of their times—have shown but little concern for towns. They preferred to devote their energies to political, military or diplomatic developments, in which they saw the key factors of history. The towns were hardly considered as such: any study of them was generally for their government or their architecture. They did not rouse either the passions of groups or of private interests. They had no chance of developing a sense of solidarity drawn from history (as did for instance the Labour Movement, which took a great part in the development of labour history). Municipal patriotism or local pride was never strong enough to help and establish a link between the present and the past. We may hardly mention the rise of parliamentary democracy which wanted to trace back its ancestors in the communal movement of the middle ages: the liberty of the borough against the oppression by the manor. . . . All that this resulted in was the study of medieval cities.

In France, moreover, the countryside was still holding such an important position in the nation's activity that the urban phenomenon could not present itself as a major fact of modern civilisation. (We must remember that not until 1931 did the town population begin to exceed the rural population.) This explains why the urban past has long remained the province of the erudite, tenacious lovers of local history who patiently collected material. But these antiquarians were often not trained historians. They lacked method and critical accuracy: and even when they were historians their outlook remained too narrow. They did not really bother to connect their own town, studied with such loving attention, with the development of other towns, or the evolution of the country as a whole, and even less with the universal movements of history.

Indeed, even to-day while towns provoke a wave of curiosity, while urban development comes into fashion, one must mention a basic difficulty, very far from being overcome. History does not of itself provide a sufficient basis on which to rest a real understanding of the town. History must depend on the contributions of other social sciences. Everybody nowadays talks about the necessary co-operation of social sciences ('human sciences', as we prefer to say in France), about the need of multi-disciplinary studies. But unfortunately, it often remains a piece of mere wishful thinking.

So, for an historical approach towards towns, the first scholars came from disciplines other than history. After the pioneer work by Legoyt, a civil servant, and Meuriot, a teacher, who both devoted their labours to the statistical description of towns in the late nineteenth century[1] (anticipating by a few years the famous and more elaborate book of Weber in the States), the first scientific approach to the study of city growth, functions, and activitiy came from the geographers: they laid the foundations of the subject.

In 1912 the late Raoul Blanchard published his book, a classic now, on Grenoble.[2] From this model other geographers, belonging to the brilliant French school of human geography which flourished during the inter-war period, began to study French towns one after the other: Rouen, Clermont-Ferrand, Paris, and many other cities of smaller size.[3] In an article entitled 'The Method of Urban Geography' Blanchard himself had determined the rules which were to prevail in the geographical approach of towns. The problem, he said, was to 'analyse the mechanisms, to explain the birth, the growth, the ups and downs'. The merely geographical factors were unable to fulfil this task. They must be supported by the historical surroundings which are perpetually under change.[4]

After the second world war three scholars—all of them Professors of Geography at the Sorbonne—undertook to go beyond the local dimension, that is beyond studies of individual towns. They offered the first syntheses about cities: G. Chabot in 1948, P. George in 1952, and the late M. Sorre. With this new stage one changed from a monographic survey to a panoramic view.[5] At the same time urban geography was being

---

1 Alfred Legoyt [pseudonym of Hermann], *Du Progrès des Agglomérations Urbaines* (Marseilles, 1867); Paul Meuriot, *Des Agglomérations Urbaines dans l'Europe Contemporaine: Essai sur les Causes, les Conditions, les Conséquences de leur Développement* (Paris, 1897). See also the study by E. Levasseur entitled *Les Populations urbaines*.

2 Raoul Blanchard, *Grenoble: Etude de Géographie Urbaine* (Paris, 1912).

3 J. Levainville, *Rouen, Etude d'une Agglomération Urbaine* (Paris, 1913); P. Arbos, *Clermont-Ferrand* (Clermont, 1930); R. Lespès, *Alger, Etude de Géographie et d'Histoire Urbaine* (Paris, 1930); A. Demangeon, *Paris, la Ville et sa Banlieue* (Paris 1933).

4 R. Blanchard, 'Une méthode de géographie urbaine', *La Vie Urbaine* (1922), pp. 301-9.

5 Georges Chabot, *Les Villes* (Paris, 1948)—this research has been recently enlarged in collaboration with J. Beaujeu-Garnier: *Précis de Géographie Urbaine* (Paris, 1965); Pierre George, *La Ville, le Fait Urbain à travers le Monde* (Paris, 1952)—a new and more systematic approach gave birth to the *Précis de Géographie Urbaine* in 1961. Maximilien Sorre, a great geographer, tried to connect geography with other sciences, especially biology and sociology.

opened up in a big way as the subject of research for theses, not only on French towns, but of other continents and climatic regions.

One peculiarity of these geographical studies was to give to history a very large share of the explanation of the present characteristics and functioning of towns. Three of the most recently published and important theses may serve as examples.

J. Bastié, in a survey of the growth of the southern suburbs of Paris, underlined the part played by the various means of transport since the nineteenth century, and he described the successive stages in land-use, the old pre-1914 suburbs, the housing estates in the inter-war period, the new features of urbanisation (*les grands ensembles*) of the 1950s.[6]

In his book on the cities and their surrounding countryside in Langue-doc, R. Dugrand demonstated the link between the under-development of this Mediterranean region and the type of land ownership: while most of the land is owned by the *bourgeoisie* living in towns, the management of this real estate, capital and income, since the middle of the nineteenth century handicapped any modern development either of the towns or the country.[7]

In his thesis about the urban network in Alsace, M. Rochefort has attempted a more creative research. Going back to the eighteenth century, he has worked out the distribution of Alsatian towns prior to the French Revolution, and he has traced changes in rank and functions during successive periods. So he has thrown light upon the hierarchy of urban centres: from the regional metropolis—Strasbourg—at the top down to the small market towns. He has also demonstrated the zones of influence and the power of command exercised by leading centres. The result is a double analysis, geographical and historical, of an urban network. This is one of the seminal pieces of urban research to have been conducted in France.[8]

Two other features are characteristic of the geographers' approach: first, the stress put on the relation between the town and its region; secondly, the emphasis laid on transport. However, the sociological factors have too often been neglected in favour of the natural, historical, or economic elements.

Finally, a point which always appeared of utmost importance to the French School was to classify and define urban functions: administrative, commercial, industrial, military, etc. But this analytical concept, even if

---

[6] Jean Bastié, *La Croissance de la Banlieue Parisienne* (Paris, 1964).

[7] Raymond Dugrand, *Villes et Campagnes en Bas-Languedoc: le Réseau Urbain du Bas-Languedoc Méditerranéen* (Paris, 1963).

[8] Michel Rochefort, *L'Organisation Urbaine de l'Alsace* (Strasbourg, 1958).

it shows a clear description of the past or present state of things does not explain very satisfactorily the dynamic mechanisms of urban life nor its intricate and inter-related components.

On the other hand, although the geographers' contribution is so useful for history, one must admit that the historians' point of view is different. For a geographer the spatial factor comes first. His tools are maps and plans. His instrument of observation is his eye. His searches in the archives remain inevitably limited. An historian relies on the time-factor. He takes account of the duration and series of events rather than space and localisation. He aims at a causal chain in the process of time.

Another approach to urban history has been achieved by town-planners (*urbanistes*). A few were artists, creators, men of action, for instance architects having some scholarly interest in the past. But most of them considered town planning as a new department in the history of art. The most famous name to quote here is P. Lavedan (for many years Professor at the Sorbonne and Director of the 'Institut d'Urbanisme' at the University of Paris), the author of a monumental *Histoire de l'Urbanisme* from antiquity to the twentieth century.

The history of urban architecture, which studies the construction of towns, the layout and design, or in other words the development of streets, open spaces, monuments, etc., forms, as Lavedan claims in his thesis, 'a new chapter for the general history of art' (though not always escaping the danger of archaeology):[9] so urban history has found a province in the history of art. From this idea numerous monographs have been written dealing with town design, monuments, houses, squares, perspectives. Thanks to this work a new aspect of the urban past has been brought out of the dark.

During the same period between the wars, Marcel Poëte, Librarian of the Ville de Paris, entered upon a vast survey of the development of Paris, with a similar view, but with a different and greater ambition. From there he tried to define the notion of town-planning itself.[10] A creative mind, a contemporary and friend of Patrick Geddes, he agreed with the latter's views on the living and organic structure of towns, as well as the necessity

[9] Pierre Lavedan, *Introduction à l'Histoire de l'Architecture Urbaine; Définitions, Sources* (Paris, 1926), 3. Compare the same author's *Histoire de l'Urbanisme* (3 vols., Paris, 1926–52); *Géographie des Villes* (1936); *Les Villes Françaises* (1960). See also *Mélanges Lavedan: Urbanisme et Architecture, Etudes Ecrites et Publiées en l'Honneur de Pierre Lavedan* (Paris, 1954). For a more recent approach to *urbanisme*, see A. Chastel, F. Choay, the periodical *La Vie Urbaine*, etc.

[10] Marcel Poëte, *Une Vie de Cité: Paris de sa Naissance à nos Jours*, i–iv (Paris, 1924–31)—in fact, the survey stops with the seventeenth century; cf. also "Les sources de l'histoire de Paris et les historiens de Paris", *Revue Politique et Littéraire* (Nov. 1905), pp. 18–25.

of connecting the material and the spiritual side of town life. In spite of his limitations and debatable views, he helped to create a whole generation of *urbanistes*. He was particularly concerned to throw off too narrow a conception of the town. For him a town was not only a thing of walls, buildings, streets, and other pieces of physical superstructure; it was not even the sum of the houses plus their inhabitants; the town was nothing short of a whole human complex.

Unfortunately, in dealing with urban history town planners (or art historians) were hampered by two major restrictions. First, their approach was limited to a study of forms to the neglect of their inhabitants. While a town is a synthesis of structure and components (*le contenant* and *le contenu*), they selected the structure or the frame, and dropped the rest. The houses remained empty, or at best inhabited by abstract beings. From another point of view the artistic concern brought about a criterion of beauty or of functional quality. As P. Lavedan wrote, 'a town must be healthy, convenient and pleasant to live in.' In that sense it is beautiful, because beauty is 'the most precise adjustment to an aim'.[11] So a subjective judgement intervenes here, implying rules which vary according to taste. So it could be said 'science applies only to the universal, art to the particular.' Placed in front of such requirements so alien to his own ethic, the historian stands ill at ease.

A third line of research, initiated in the Faculties of Law, has avoided such difficulties. This legal approach to the history of towns has met with some success.[12] Here the stress is put upon institutions: local authorities and municipal bodies, their composition, election and legal powers, public services, finances and defence, privileges and liberties. Nothing else is taken into account. For a long time this approach, not unnaturally, led to a concentration on medieval cities, where all these features were more outstanding than during any other period.

It must be said to the credit of Pirenne that he was the first to suggest a new direction for studying medieval towns, in his famous book, first published in English.[13] He decided to show the part played by trade,

[11] P. Lavedan, *op. cit.*, p. 6.

[12] See, for example, Maxime Leroy, *La Ville Française, Institutions et Libertés Locales* (Paris, 1927) and *La Ville*, 3 vols. (Brussels, 1957). [*Recueils de le Société Jean Bodin*, Nos. VI, VII, VIII].

[13] Henri Pirenne, *Medieval Cities, their Origins, and the Revival of Trade* (Princeton, 1925), published later in French as *Les Villes du Moyen-Age: Essai d'Histoire Economique et Sociale* (Brussels, 1927). In *Les Villes et les Institutions Urbaines* (Paris and Brussels, 1939) are gathered all the studies written by Pirenne relating to towns (including the articles published between 1893 and 1898 in the *Revue Historique*, where Pirenne formulated for the first time his theory of town growth).

markets and fairs, merchants and capitalists, without neglecting the social life within the urban community. So he replaced abstract, cold and lifeless institutions with the excitement of human beings. And he introduced a new and fruitful era for urban history. One of the fruits of this was, for instance, the fine book by Ganshof about town development between the Loire and the Rhine.[14] Indeed, it is not merely by chance that so many of these investigations were undertaken in Belgium and northern France, regions endowed with an ancient tradition of town life and enriched by two waves of urbanisation: those of the thirteenth and fourteenth centuries and of the industrial revolution.

In contrast to the leading influence of the three disciplines just mentioned—geography, town planning, and legal history—three other branches of knowledge have had but a minor influence for a long time. But their recent, somewhat sudden entry into the field of urban history has proved both noisy and fruitful, not to say triumphant. Such is now the experience of sociology, economics, and demography.

In the case of sociology there were, it is true, some predecessors. For instance, there was M. Halbwachs, whose fine book on the inter-relations between land-ownership and the expropriations and lay-out of streets in Paris is even now more important as a pioneer in a new methodology than it is as a monograph on its chosen theme.[15] Halbwachs was also among the first to raise the question—hotly debated nowadays—of the connection between the structure of a town and the life of its inhabitants:[16] how and to what extent does its shape influence the behaviour of its inhabitants, and to what extent, if any, is the line of causation the other way round? However, for a long time the French school of sociology, led by scholars such as Marcel Mauss, was more concerned with social anthropology. It was less interested in ages past than it was in the present habits of savage tribes. Its links with sociological research pursued in other countries were few, irregular and unenterprising. For instance, the ecological method of the Chicago School has met with a very restricted audience up to a recent period.

It was the task of Chombart de Lauwe and his team of sociologists to

---

[14] F. L. Ganshof, *Etude sur le Développement des Villes entre Loire et Rhin au Moyen-Age* (Paris and Brussels, 1943).

[15] Maurice Halbwachs, *Les Expropriations et le Prix des Terrains à Paris* (Paris, 1907); the second edition, enlarged and revised, was entitled *La Population et les Tracés de Voies à Paris depuis un Siècle* (Paris, 1928).

[16] For instance, in *La Mémoire Collective*, pp. 134 *et seq.*, a posthumous work published in 1950. In the sociological field another pioneering author should be quoted: R. Maunier, *La Localisation des Industries Urbaines* (Paris, 1909) and *L'Origine et la Fonction Economique des Villes: Etude de Morphologie Sociale* (Paris, 1910).

undertake the leading and most attractive research on town life: the behaviour of townfolk, social integration in cities, environmental influences, aspirations and satisfactions, social values, relations between the citizens and public authorities—such were the main themes of their inquiries. But these sociological—or rather psycho-sociological—surveys, however rich in content, did not rely much on history. They restricted themselves to the present, or at best to the very recent years.[17]

This is even more the case with the economists' approach. Actually, in France urban economics started only a few years ago. The rare scholars in that field are kept very busy trying to ascertain the economic laws governing cities' growth, estimating the cost of urbanisation, of transport and of urban renewal, discovering the rôle of town centres, and applying economic theory and models to real towns (through cost-benefit analysis, input-output tables, etc.). Inevitably, they have no time to go back more than twenty or twenty-five years.

This is also partly the case with demography. Fortunately, however, the demographers have to work on a long-term basis, and a number of statisticians set to work long ago compiling the basic material. To use these data and to make new discoveries, the Institut National d'Etudes Démographiques and its periodical, *Population*, launched several projects and gave a strong impulse to historical demography which is just beginning to show its very promising possibilities. In a monumental piece of research Fr. Mols has demonstrated how deeply a rigorous method could be applied to European towns in early modern times.[18]

This whole development of the social sciences occurred at the same time as historians were showing a new interest in cities. The result was that, unlike the first wave of town studies originated by geographers or art historians, urban history, sociology, economics, and demography all marched abreast and closely related to each other.

It is now necessary to consider the achievements of the historians themselves, with its manifold trends and varieties of approach, and to suggest some of its shortcomings.

No doubt, we must begin by giving full credit to the *école des Annales* for the 'urban awakening' among historians. From 1929 onwards, under the leadership of Marc Bloch and Lucien Febvre—the two greatest French historians of this century—and with the help of their quarterly review, *Annales d'Histoire Economique et Sociale*, new horizons were

[17] P. H. Chombart de Lauwe and others, *Paris et l'Agglomération Parisienne*, 2 vols. (Paris, 1952); *Paris, Essais de Sociologie 1952–1964* (Paris, 1965); *Des Hommes et des Villes* (Paris, 1965).

[18] Roger Mols, S. J., *Introduction à la Démographie Historique des Villes d'Europe du XIVe au XVIIIe siècle*, 3 vols. (Louvain, 1954).

opened up for historians. L. Febvre and M. Bloch drew attention to the town as a major feature of civilisation. They indicated its huge conse-quences on economic life, society, culture, daily behaviour, and ways of thinking. Their journal, *Annales*, made a strong appeal to students of the subject, in insisting upon the necessary co-operation of various disciplines for such a task. They led the way by publishing many articles and reviews dedicated to urban studies.[19] Since the war F. Braudel has followed the same line, and in one of the major contributions to historical research, *La Méditerranée et le Monde Méditerranéen à l'Epoque de Philippe II*, he has drawn attention to the significance of the development rôle of towns all round the Mediterranean as centres of economic and social activity; his approach being to recognise cities somewhat as 'feedbacks' of civilisation. However, for the period we are considering, namely the nineteenth and twentieth centuries, one must admit that the editors of *Annales* were more concerned with the middle ages and the early modern period and directed less research towards contemporary towns.

Close to the *Annales* school, sometimes publishing articles in the latter's review, or taking advantage of the splendid facilities offered by the *Ecole Pratique des Hautes Etudes* (Section VI), yet activated by a different inspiration and methodology, another cluster of studies originated under the encouragement and direction of Professor Labrousse, whose influence has been of the first order among historians since the war. For the mem-bers of this school, the stress is placed on the quantitative aspects of historical research. Besides statistical series, new sources have been unearthed and largely used: not only prices and incomes or census data, but also fiscal archives, registers of voters, etc. Yet the psychological factors are not left out and the evolution of mental habits provides one of the fundamental points in Professor Labrousse's trilogy of economic basis, social structure, ideological frame.

This train of thought has already produced some valuable work. An important contribution to the social history of Paris has been provided by Miss Daumard, thanks to a systematic use of the *archives notariales* (solicitors' archives); through her study of marriage contracts and of successions has emerged an elaborate picture of the social hierarchy of

---

[19] G. Espinas, 'Histoire urbaine: directions de recherches et résultats', *Annales d'Histoire Economique et Sociale*, i (1929), pp. 104–25; iii (1931), pp. 394–422; vii (1935), pp. 353–90. Among other contributors, Halbwachs wrote articles on the urban sociology of Chicago and Berlin; A. E. Sayous wrote on Strasbourg. Close to the *Annales*, G. Roupnel studied Dijon and its relation with the surrounding districts of Burgundy, and more recently A. Chatelain has dealt with Lyons and the Rhone Valley. Cf. also L. Febvre himself, in G. Friedmann, *Villes et Campagnes* (1953).

the city,[20] its social mobility and class relationships. Other studies have dealt with provincial towns (e.g., Grenoble, Blois). But two high level researches, inspired by Professor Labrousse, should particularly be mentioned. P. Goubert has demonstrated with Beauvais how to make a splendid use of demography, especially of parish registers, in town and country history.[21] P. Vilar has endeavoured to link economic structure, social life, and national feelings in a peculiar Mediterranean setting.[22] Many other works of that type are still in progress; they relate to French towns (e.g., Caen, Lille) or to foreign cities (e.g., London, Cologne, Mainz). With regard to Paris, in the *Archives du Ministère de la Guerre*, are the files of the Communards, judged by special military courts after 1871, a first class source for studying the social structure of the population in Paris at that time. Some research of the same kind is being conducted on the *Journées de Juin 1848*.

Another centre of urban studies has spread around the *Institut National d'Etudes Démographiques* (I.N.E.D.) and the review *Population*. Yet it would be both unfair and erroneous to imagine each group as operating within a watertight compartment. There are in reality numerous interconnections between them, made the stronger by the fact that many scholars are at work simultaneously in several of them—a minor compensation for the prevailing disorder in urban history. Since 1946 the I.N.E.D., which boosted historical demography, has initiated many statistical investigations and given a stimulus to a large number of articles on towns, and urban patterns of life. It has moreover tended to assume responsibility for the publication in France of foreign works in this field.[23]

Professor Louis Chevalier's name reveals another tendency, an important and powerful one, in urban history. Holding a position by himself since the publication of his two theses about Paris and its region,[24] he became famous for his more widely circulated book, *Classes Laborieuses et Classes Dangereuses à Paris pendant la Première Moitié du XIXe Siècle* (1958). This brilliant and hotly debated work appears as a manifesto for a new methodology in urban history. According to Professor Chevalier's

---

20 Adeline Daumard, *La Bourgeoisie Parisienne de 1815 à 1848* (Paris, 1963); Adeline Daumard and François Furet, *Structures et Relations Sociales à Paris au milieu du XVIIIe Siècle* (Paris, 1961). About land ownership and property management in Paris, see A. Daumard *Maisons de Paris et Propriétaires Parisiens au XIXe Siècle 1809–1880* (Paris, 1965).

21 Pierre Goubert, *Beauvais et le Beauvaisis de 1600 à 1730* (Paris, 1958).

22 Pierre Vilar, *La Catalogne dans l'Espagne Moderne*, 3 vols. (Paris, 1962).

23 In turn the I.N.E.D. methodology influenced research conducted abroad, as acknowledged by E. A. Wrigley and P. Laslett for British historical demography.

24 Only *La Formation de la Population Parisienne au XIXe Siècle* (Paris, 1950) has been printed and published.

words, 'demography takes the lead'. In his view it illuminates the depths of city life as well as throwing important light on history in general. Its particular value lies in uncovering the biological, instinctive, unconscious world which other and more traditional approaches (including the economic approach) are unable to reach. Leaving aside such secondary elements as business cycles, class structure and class struggle, political doctrines and local organisation, L. Chevalier believes in placing emphasis on population movements, migration, birth and death rates, public health and epidemics, and so on. To him demographic influences are the most profound factors in history. Here lies the real explanation of a town's destiny, its physical and moral balance or its pathological disequilibrium, and it is here that one really plumbs the depths of history. Choosing Paris between 1815 and 1851 as an experimental ground, Professor Chevalier has insisted on pointing out every sign of urban pathology: criminality, vice, illness, and he draws a dark picture of the 'dangerous, unsound, frightening' city.

At this point demography itself is surpassed and the real roots of history are to be found in biological life. This explains why the last chapter of Professor Chevalier's book is entitled 'The Biological Foundations of Social History'. The material underpinning of urban life thus begins to appear as less of an economic structure—as it has been regarded for so long—and more of a biological one. This applies equally to the individual as it does to the community. All psychological behaviour is held to be governed by this primary factor: social habits, public morals, political attitudes, the barricades, revolution, concern for the public safety all reflect the deeper impulse of biological forces.[25]

Such are the main trends to-day in the study of urban history in France. Their most striking feature is their diversity. There is no one centre but a series of scattered initiatives, studies originating from various groups and at times encroaching on others, occasional gatherings of scholars, varieties of approaches. The concept of urban history itself remains confused: sometimes it is restricted to a narrow synonym of town planning, sometimes it is so enlarged as to mean social history at large, the city becoming the framework of the whole society.

Since any research implies a theoretical basis, at least in its hypotheses, urban history depends on various conceptions about town and social life. Doubtless this conceptualisation often remains hardly visible; it is most frequently hidden or underlying. But it is of first importance to bring out clearly the theoretical assumptions on which an historian's methodology

---

[25] In a recent article, L. Chevalier pleads in favour of a more qualitative approach: 'A reactionary view of urban history', *Times Literary Supplement*, 8 September 1966.

is based. Consciously or not, even the most empirical research is linked with ideology.

(1) The most common is the 'organic' or rather the 'organicist' theory. This view is to be found among town planners, geographers and not a few historians. Fundamentally the city is compared to a living organism. It goes through birth, growth, and decay, and its parts are organically linked together: hence the images of 'blood circulation', 'arteries', 'urban tissue'. Thus social history borrows its conceptions from natural history.[26] Although such a conception helps to evoke a certain total view of a town, it does seem in many respects irrational and confusing, and it fails to explain many of the economic and social factors affecting town life.

(2) Not far from this view, the 'biological' theory, brilliantly exposed by Professor Chevalier, encounters the same objections. It stresses an aspect of urban life which is admittedly too much neglected, but it does so in such an exclusive way that it either omits altogether or seriously under-rates other, at least equally important, features of urban life. Moreover, one cannot help regarding with some suspicion those mysterious and stranger forces of biology, the definition of which has not yet been made very clear.

(3) The 'functionalist' theory has been largely developed by geographers and economists. Both tried to define and classify urban 'functions'. But here again objections could be raised. First, the very idea of 'functions' is somewhat ambiguous: sometimes they are understood as living parts of a body—and then one falls back to the 'organicist theory'— sometimes as rational factors able to be translated into mathematical formulas and models. In both cases neither inter-relations nor correlations between various functions seems satisfactorily explained. Finally among some scholars it degenerates into a functional determinism—not very acceptable for historians.

(4) The positivist (or neo-positivist) school of thought places itself in a different direction. The aim here consists in avoiding any ideology. The positivists would limit themselves to an objective and scientific description of urban phenomena, relying as much as possible on quantitative data. Accordingly, the town is considered as a mixture of forces and mechanisms, ready for a strictly scientific analysis: the 'soul' or 'personality' of the town is ignored, as well as the citizens' own subjectivity. Such a view is supported by some demographers and mathematical

---

[26] This view, advocated by Patrick Geddes and Lewis Mumford, is widely diffused in France, but without such notable exponents.

economists, and it is shared also by many high-ranking civil servants, or civil engineers in charge of town planning. One can easily understand how such scholars or administrators indulge in the use of computers and mathematical models. But the most sophisticated among them are quite aware of the danger of restricting the urban complex to a mere cluster of statistics.

(5) Besides this mechanical conception we find the dialectical theory. Oddly enough, the Marxist method, which stimulated so much historical research over the last fifty years, has had very little to do with urban history as such. Marxist historians have given little attention to urban growth, to town life and even to the relation between town and country. This is in spite of Marx, who himself counted it as a major factor in the evolution of mankind.[27] From a socialist point of view, to overcome the existing opposition between town and country (which arose from the private property system and is a feature of the capitalist régime) constitutes a primary necessity before reaching the last stage of history, the communist stage. Actually, Marxist historians have neglected these ideas. They have preferred to devote their labours to mainstream economic history or to the study of class conflict.

(6) Another conception, which could be called 'socio-cultural', nowadays guides many historians. The city is looked upon as a decisive contribution to the history of civilisation: first as a network of economic services and human relations; secondly as a meeting place between the community and the individual. Therefore urban studies should bring to light the interaction between material conditions and psychological attitudes, environment and social values, town layout and town life.

As a conclusion I should like to present a very rapid survey of some problems, around which investigations are carried out today by social scientists. From these studies urban historians should have plenty to reap. Of course we must keep in mind that research in urban history, as in other fields of history, is largely dependent on the sources. According to the existence (or non-existence) of documents, their accessibility, and the possibility of computerising the data, historians could come nearer the questions raised by other social scientists and try to give them answers concerning the past. In any case, historians should be trying to respond to

---

[27] Cf. *The German Ideology*: 'the opposition between town and country begins when barbary turns to civilisation, when the tribal system gives place to the state, when local groups turn to nation. This opposition is to be found in all the history of civilisation up to now. . . . Here appears for the first time the division of population between two main classes, directly based upon the division of labour and means of production.' In fact, Marx partly gathered these ideas from Sir James Steuart. Cf. also the preface to the *Critique of Political Economy*. In his *Anti-Dühring* Engels amplified anew Marx's assertions.

as many of the questions thrown up by sociologists, demographers, geographers, town planners as they can. As brilliantly expressed by Lucien Febvre, 'the present offers us a lot of questions to be put to our beloved documents.'[28]

Research nowadays concentrates upon the following points, which should intensively attract the historian's attention:

(1) *Town growth.* What are its primary factors? Are they economic, demographic, social? What does the 'appeal' of the city mean? What are the rôle and consequences of decisions taken by public authorities in town planning? Is there a continuity or a breach in urban development from antiquity to contemporary urbanisation?

(2) *Urban network.* Instead of considering only one town or each town on its own, what type of relations have been established between the different towns in a country or in a region? Which hierarchy? Which distribution of forces, of political, economic, social, or spiritual power?

(3) *Migration.* From country to town and inside the city; social mobility and social integration; process of acculturation; national, regional, and ethnic groups. All these questions should also be answered by the historian.

(4) *Social structure.* As with the previous case, this study has to consider not only occupational stratification, but the whole pattern of social relations, household and family composition, relations between the town-dweller and the public bodies.

(5) *Environment and the image of the city.* Linking town-planning and social psychology, aesthetics and morals, such a research has to illustrate the relations between town and society, social values and town-dwellers' desires, urban myths and symbols.

To some people this huge programme could seem frightening. But at the same time it should be remarked how much, when raising these very questions, urban history could be helped by the most advanced branches of historical research and supported by the simultaneous progress of other social sciences. Therefore, the future should be faced with confidence. Even if urban history is still in its infancy, it can expect a promising youth and a fruitful mature age.

---

28 G. Friedmann (ed.), *Villes et Campagnes*, p. 31: this book gives the proceedings of an important and valuable conference in 1952 between historians and social scientists from every part of the field.

Discussion

The CHAIRMAN opened the discussion by asking Mr. Bédarida whether any evidence existed to show that the biological and 'organicist' schools of urban historians in France (by whom the town or city is likened to a living organism) were influenced at all by the Belgian poet, Emile Verhaeren, who wrote about the octopus cities in *Les Villes Tentaculaires* (1895)—as a sequel to his *Les Campagnes Hallucinées* (1893). Mr. BEDARIDA thought that on the whole this was not so, and gave it as his opinion that the biological and organicist schools of thought arose naturally out of current intellectual fashions, namely the theory of evolution and the prestige attaching to science in the nineteenth and early twentieth centuries. He considered, for example, that Bergson's evolutionary philosophy influenced Marcel Poëte, author of the *Introduction à l'Urbanisme: l'Evolution des Villes* (1904). He implied that Patrick Geddes' work was linked to the same ideas. Verhaeren, like his contemporaries, was merely a prisoner of this vision of the universe.

Mr. FREEMAN commented that the general evolutionary approach was highly characteristic of French geographical thought at that time and was the basis of Maximilien-Joseph Sorre's classic work *Les Fondements Biologiques de la Géographie Humaine* (1943); he also cited Raoul Blanchard's work on Grenoble, but felt that the idea had been stretched much too far. He noted the enormous advance made since that time by the modern American school of urban geography; and thought he detected a falling-off in mapping techniques among modern French geographers, with the exception of Chombart de Lauwe, which was unfortunate, since a great deal of urban history could be most satisfactorily expressed in map form: 'if the geographers don't do it how can you expect the historians to do it?' he asked. Mr. BEDARIDA commented that Sorre attempted to differentiate between physical environment, sociological factors and geography. He was one of the few Frenchmen of the time to be aware of the rising Chicago school of urban geographers, and towards the end of his life laid increasing stress on the importance of ecology (animal and human) and sociology in geographical studies.

Mr. BEDARIDA pointed out that first-class cartography depended on well-equipped and well-staffed map-drawing offices; Chombart de Lauwe employed the services of the cartographer M. Bertin, who enjoyed excellent facilities in the *Ecole Pratique des Hautes Etudes*. 'The quality of many geographers' laboratories explains the mean character of their maps,' he suggested. Professor CHECKLAND thought the trouble was not merely a question of money but of getting a sufficient understanding of the idiom so that a cartographer could be

briefed to produce the kind of results wanted. Mr. BEDARIDA agreed that collaboration between geographers and urban historians was important but thought
it could be fruitful only if the work of urban historians, geographers and car-
tographers were adequately 'programmed'. Learning the technique of this
programming took time and therefore historians were often tempted, in order
to save time, to leave out the maps or to rely on last-minute improvisation.

Most of the rest of the discussion turned on four topics that emerged from
Dr. Dyos's paper. These were: problems of definition, both of terms and
objectives; the proliferation of case-studies of individual towns and cities as
against comparative studies of two or more urban areas; individual research as
against collective research by teams; and the question of the 'personality'
of towns and cities.

On problems of definition, Professor CHECKLAND considered that the lack of
standard definitions of terms did not present a serious difficulty at the moment,
and he stressed the danger of adopting a rigid schedule of definitions prema-
turely. 'We have got to go a lot further in the development of method before we
start trying to resolve our differences of definition into a standard pattern,' he
thought. Dr. DYOS agreed up to a point. He thought we should 'very probably
never encounter the need to have standard terms' so long as we concerned ourselves exclusively with unique cases. All that was necessary was that historians,
geographers and sociologists, while using and expanding their terminologies,
explained their terms clearly at the outset. The question of standardisation of
terms would only arise, at any rate in Britain, if students of urbanisation
wished to weld these different contributions together into some more comprehensive view of the whole process of urbanisation, possibly with an underlying
unifying thesis: Professor SCHNORE had already mentioned to him the 'frontier
theory' in American history as a parallel in this connection.

Professor CHECKLAND was also not afraid of a proliferation of case-studies.
He thought that the dangers may have been exaggerated; research into the
history of major cities took time, and it seemed unlikely that an unmanageable
number of these studies would be completed within the next ten years. In his
opinion urban historians in Britain should simply concentrate on writing urban
history for the time being: he suggested that 'many people who are interested in
urban history are interested in a lot of other things as well, and they suffer from
this dichotomy.' He thought just the same that there did exist the danger that
mediocre studies of smaller towns might appear in very considerable numbers,
written by people 'who told the tale according to what turned up and according
to their own intuitive feelings about what was important.' If there were sufficient agreement on what were the agenda for urban historians and they were
sufficiently 'positive' in following them we could avoid standardising proce-
dures for a time. Dr. CHALONER observed that even at the moment it would be
possible to publish a guide to the writing of urban history on the lines of the
Rev. J. C. Cox's *How to Write the History of a Parish*, which would give adequate results, but perhaps of limited value. Dr. DYOS agreed that as far as
Britain was concerned the danger of an undue proliferation of case-studies was

less real in the short-run than in the United States, where Bayrd Still had drawn attention to the phenomenon 25 years ago, particularly in the case of the cities of the Mississippi Valley; but he held to his view that it was sensible to identify three or four sectors of the subject and to concentrate on these, particularly population movements and the shaping of the urban environment. 'In the short term,' he insisted, 'we have to be extremely modest and say that the most interesting and important parts of our present understanding of the history of cities can be classified under a few headings.'

Dr. J. R. HARRIS then raised the question of the difficulties which beset the urban historian in the choice of method of attack: is he to be a lone investigator (or at most one of a pair of like-minded people) writing the history of a town or city, and thus giving his account a certain literary unity, or is urban history better written by teams? He had the feeling that the team approach 'can produce a kind of synthetic town history but something which never achieves proper unification, and consequently doesn't give a living impression to the reader.' He also spoke of the need to live in the town in question 'to absorb its personality as well as its documentation' if one wanted to get a unified view of it. To Dr. KELLETT such 'really literary writing' of urban history made it more difficult to draw comparisons with other cities. He preferred to sacrifice the unified view for the fuller and more rounded view made possible by the collaboration of a team of researchers. Dr. HENNOCK agreed that there were no insuperable barriers to the co-operative method provided those involved had ample opportunities for discussion. But some disquiet was expressed less silence on vital matters in the finished work should be interpreted as agreement; clearly, the editor had a vital role to play in co-operative research and publication.

Dr. HARRIS, however, while regarding the approach of comparative urban history with some equanimity, expressed again his concern lest something of the 'personality' of individual towns might be lost if the emphasis shifted from the individual interpretations of specific historians to the collective study of a set of well-defined aspects of urban history imposed on future generations because they were fashionable now. Dr. MARTIN supported this point of view and hoped that too much emotional capital would not be spent worrying about the matter; those members of the various disciplines interested in the history of urbanism would best advance the cause by getting on with the job. Later on he returned to the point to make a strong protest against the general denigration of the literary method in historical writing that he thought he could detect. Mr. BEDARIDA put in a reminder that urban history was not merely the history of towns and cities but included the history of urban organisation, architecture, and so on, and that there were in these fields general concepts and notions that might be lost sight of in local detail and atmosphere. Dr. DYOS saw a difficulty in concentrating so much on a town as a whole. Towns were not homogeneous entities but extremely variegated ones, some elements of which were comparable with those in another place, which may be variegated in a different way. In his view it was important to proceed in such a way that one could compare

63

life in one part of a city not only with that in another but in another city altogether, and not to build up a 'total view of a city' all the time. He wound up this
part of the discussion by pointing out that the comparative method had to be
used for this kind of research and that it involved an understanding of the social
processes that were at work. If these were to be analysed some of the *terms* or
modes of expression used would have to be standardised, but emphatically not
the *types of approach* themselves.

These reflections led naturally to a long discussion of the concept of the
'personality' of towns and cities. Sir John SUMMERSON objected vehemently to
the use of the analogy between human personality and urban personality and to
the whole biological concept of urbanism. 'Did one have introvert and extro-
vert towns, and what neuroses did towns suffer from?' he asked; 'isn't the
personality of a town always a literary creation?' Dr. HARRIS, whose ideas on
urban personality were the target, was not to be toppled so easily. He pointed
out that to the outside observer the towns of northern England seemed very
much alike, and that although it was even more difficult to describe the personality of a town than it was of an individual, to those who knew them inti-
mately, Leeds was very different from Bradford, Wigan from Warrington.
(Later, Mr. BEDARIDA recalled that at another conference he had been charged
with confusing Sheffield with Leeds; but he had defended himself by saying
that both towns looked very much the same when viewed from Paris.) Dr.
HARRIS laid particular emphasis on the images projected by modern Liverpool
and St. Helens; these he attributed mainly to the high percentages of the two
populations who were of Irish origin. But there were other subjective impressions less easily explained: 'One's simply got to try to find out historically how
far this impression is justified.' Dr. DYOS, Dr. MANN, Dr. MARSHALL, and Mr.
TILLOTT all suggested that one's impression of these towns depended very much
on the observer's age, his social milieu, and his own personality. A Rochdale
millowner's son would have a different image of Rochdale's personality from
someone born in a Rochdale slum. Similarly, the protests by Manchester mill-
owners after the appearance of Mrs. Elizabeth Gaskell's *Mary Barton* suggested
that a town's personality was very much a literary creation and not an objective
concept. Sir John SUMMERSON and Dr. KELLETT mentioned the special case of
London, where the analogy of personality broke down completely, except
perhaps in the suburbs, e.g., Bayswater, which however were changing rapidly.
This suggested that personality was local rather than urban. In this context,
Dr. DYOS preferred to look, not for a sort of unified personality, but for conflicting attitudes and divided groups—a symbiosis rather. The trouble with the
concept of urban personality, as Dr. MANN pointed out, was that the same
evidence could sustain different judgements that were equally valid, and what
urban historians had to do was to state their evidence and give an operational
definition of the terms they used to evaluate it. This, he thought, was what Dr.
Dyos's paper meant by referring to the agenda for urban historians. Dr.
HENNOCK insisted that all would agree on certain differences between one town
and the next—which might be described as differences in personality or flavour

—but that in order to study such differences it was necessary to ask searching questions about class structure, demography, immigration, and so on. Mr. ARMSTRONG echoed this by saying that he saw no reason why historians should not write down their subjective impressions on the personality of towns, but that at the same time they ought to strive wherever possible to provide a solid core of objectively comparable statistical data.

The whole discussion reminded Professor SCHNORE of the attempts that had been made by some American anthropologists since the war to work over earlier research and 'impose a check-list on all these ideographic accounts' so as to generalise their analyses more objectively. The prospect that cities might be classified like tribes or their salient features recorded in a mechanical way now began to cause alarm, and Dr. MANN wondered if someone were trying to develop a theory of urban history. It was an uneasy note to finish on.

W. H. CHALONER

II

The Interpretation of the Census Enumerators' Books for Victorian Towns

W. A. Armstrong

This paper arises out of the experience of working with the census enumerators' books of 1841 and 1851 with the intention of producing a survey of the social structure of York in the mid-nineteenth century. It is essentially a sequel to the chapter which was contributed to a recent publication of the Cambridge Group for the History of Population and Social Structure, *An Introduction to English Historical Demography*, ed. E. A. Wrigley (London, 1966).[1]

The earlier chapter began with a discussion of the nature of the material in the enumerators' books. From 1841, the simple tally-sheet methods of earlier censuses were discarded, and working from the individual schedules distributed to each householder, enumerators had to copy down the details relating to each household into these books, which normally become available to historians when they are one hundred years old. Social historians have long made use of the printed census volumes to provide a basic framework for their researches (the printed volumes being simply abstracts from the enumerators' books), but in fact, only by going back to the original books can the historian *relate* the variables dealt with in the printed volumes (as well as others not mentioned there). For example, one can easily obtain birthplace, occupational, and age-sex distributions for a given Victorian town from the printed volumes: what one cannot generally do is to state what the age-structure (or birthplace distribution) of a particular occupational group was, or whether (generally),

---

[1] Hereinafter referred to in footnotes as *Introduction*.

indigenous inhabitants tended to be in more prestigious occupations: or what distinctions might be made in respect of family and household size, propensity to have servants, lodgers, etc., among such groups.

Apart from general observations of that kind, the chapter mentioned the minor problems involved in the delimitation of a population for study, which will often (though not exclusively) be an urban unit; and discussed in detail the methods used in preparing some York material for analysis. This involved descriptions of how to choose and test samples, and of recommended methods for notebook recording and the categorising and codifying of occupations, birthplaces, ages, etc., for use on punched card apparatus. A list of relationships and factors worth exploring was given, and the paper concluded with mention of the need for care in setting precise statistical confidence limits on estimates drawn from samples.

The chapter to which reference has been made was written during the summer of 1964. Like other sections of the book, it was published with the intention of being a useful guide, rather than a definitive and final treatment of the subject. Having observed the rapidly growing interest in exploiting the potentialities of social-structural and demographic sources, the authors shared the view that early publication would avoid 'more years . . . during which work without uniformity of method or benefit or acquantaince with recent advances in technique would have continued'. Since 1964 the number of persons interested in using the census enumerators' books has multiplied yet again, and now embraces a wide range of scholars from various disciplines. Local history tutors are especially concerned, for they feel that this is the kind of material which will interest their students, and at the same time produce results of more than parochial significance. There is similar diversity in the methods of data-processing currently being employed; the exercises mentioned in this chapter were handled by means of punched cards, but Dr. Dyos is now using a computer programme capable of handling very large samples, while local history tutors find that labour-intensive methods are altogether more suitable to their purpose.

Diversity in the actual mechanics of handling the data is unimportant and, strictly speaking, irrelevant. On the other hand, the presentation of results in forms that will allow for comparability is greatly to be encouraged.[2] It is also important that all those who use the enumerators'

---

[2] Common age groupings, etc., are an obvious case in point. Guidance on the definition of the 'household' and the 'family', etc. is given in Chap. VI of *Introduction*, and in this paper. Lists of occupations ascribed to various social classes in the York and Nottingham studies can be had from the author, while Mr. P. M. Tillott of the Department of Extra-Mural Studies at the University of Sheffield has available lists of the occupational groupings used in local

books should be aware of the potentialities and the limitations of the source. For this reason, the results about to be discussed should be of considerable interest to all working in the field.

This supplementary paper may be said to take up the matter where the earlier one left off, 'the point where the tasks of historical interpretation begin'. In the following pages, certain results from the York (and other) inquiries will be listed, together with brief comment on their possible historical significance. The rest of the paper will dwell upon some of the major difficulties that have been encountered in handling the raw data and interpreting the results. In short, what is offered is a sort of progress report.

We may begin by launching into a series of examples of the kind of results which the census enumerators' books can be made to yield with minimal complications. Mean household size in York in 1851 was 4·70 ($\pm$ 0·18), mean family size 3·45 ($\pm$ 0·14). For 1841, the figures were 4·56 ($\pm$ 0·19) and 3·41 ($\pm$ 0·15) respectively.[3] These average figures are of the same approximate order of magnitude as those arrived at by Laslett and others when studying the village household in pre-industrial society.[4] In ten selected English village communities of the seventeenth century, the mean average household size was 4·49 (ranging from 5·19 down to 4·03). Moreover, the distribution of household sizes was not dissimilar in the case of the York samples and eight of Laslett's villages (see Table 1).

Mr. Laslett contends that he has shown pre-industrial social structure to have been characterised by the nuclear family, and not, as has been falsely assumed by some sociologists and social scientists, by the extended family, or kinship system. The sceptical historian might grant the truth of this, but at the same time conclude that if the social structure has been

history classes in that area. It is hoped to deal more fully with this question in a forthcoming volume to be published by the Cambridge Group for the History of Population and Social Structure.

[3] The 1841 and 1851 mean family sizes ought not to be directly compared. Because details of 'relationship to head of family' were not demanded in 1841, a set of rules or conventions for allocating individuals to families had to be used. (See *Introduction*, pp. 229–30.) 1841 values for *different communities* could still be compared of course. Note also that both samples exclude a tiny minority of households with more than ten non-members of the head's family. It was thought that the inclusion of such quasi-institutional households might create undesirable biases. (See *Introduction*, p. 219.)

[4] All references to the size of seventeenth-century households, etc. in the following pages, are drawn from P. Laslett, *Remarks on the Multiplier: A Note on the Size of the Family and Household in England in relation to Family and Social Structure, especially in the late Seventeenth Century.* (Typescript paper prepared for the Third International Conference of Economic History, Munich, 1965, but not yet published.) Also from his 1965 volume, *The World We Have Lost*, Chap. III.

TABLE I

SIZE OF HOUSEHOLDS (*percentage distribution*)

	Persons per household												
	1	2	3	4	5	6	7	8	9	10	11	12	13 and over
Laslett— 8 English communities	7·29	15·79	18·35	16·06	14·06	10·38	7·29	4·43	2·35	1·43	0·95	0·39	1·2
York (1841)	4·94	14·49	19·43	17·68	14·97	10·19	7·17	3·98	2·55	1·91	1·27	0·96	0·4
York (1851)	5·12	14·98	16·01	17·67	13·57	13·32	6·66	4·48	2·94	2·30	1·15	0·64	1·1

virtually constant since the seventeenth century, its characteristics are so obvious that it scarcely merits serious study.

This would be quite wrong. Although average household size does not seem to differ greatly when the 1851 and seventeenth-century households are compared, important dissimilarities are concealed. Table 2 demonstrates the variations in household composition in a series of 1851 studies, in terms of social class.[5]

Laslett has written that 'the higher the rank of the head, the larger the household', which implies a gradation downward through the intermediate groupings (with household sizes of about the average), to the lowest (with the smallest households). A limited amount of statistical evidence has been put forward to sustain this view for the later seventeenth century, and the differences are held to arise largely (though not wholly) from the fact that the high ranking households were augmented by large numbers of servants, drawn in effect, from the children of the lower orders.[6]

In Table 2 below, household size comes out larger for the higher social classes in all three samples. We cannot be absolutely certain that this was so in Radford, but the conclusion will stand (in the statistical sense—at the 95 per cent confidence level) for York and Nottingham. This seems to be mainly on account of upper-class maintenance of more servants. It may be too, that there was actually a gradation downwards in household

---

[5] For brief reference to the nature of the scheme of social stratification which was used, see *Introduction*, Appendix D.

[6] Mr. Laslett has written to say that since his Munich paper was prepared, he has examined another 50 to 60 listings of inhabitants, and remains convinced that the same gradation of household size according to rank was very general.

TABLE 2

VARIATIONS IN HOUSEHOLD COMPOSITION, 1851

	Classes I–II	*Class III*	*Classes IV–V*
(a) *York, 1851*			
Number of cases	166	386	201
Mean: household heads	1·00	1·00	1·00
Mean: wives per family	0·58	0·78	0·71
Mean: children per family	1·54(±0·29)	1·93(±0·19)	1·73(±0·24)
Mean: family size	3·12(±0·32)	3·71(±0·20)	3·44(±0·26)
Mean: domestics	1·15	0·12	0·05
Mean: lodgers	0·42	0·46	0·63
Mean: relatives	0·41	0·29	0·29
Mean: visitors	0·21	0·08	0·07
Mean household size	5·31(±0·46)	4·66(±0·22)	4·48(±0·33)
(b) *Nottingham, 1851**			
Number of cases	181	757	285
Mean: household heads	1·00	1·00	1·00
Mean: wives	0·72	0·78	0·57
Mean: children	1·69(±0·28)	1·84(±0·14)	1·84(±0·21)
Mean: family size	3·41(±0·32)	3·62(±0·14)	3·41(±0·25)
Mean: domestics	0·72	0·09	0·02
Mean: lodgers	0·52	0·39	0·42
Mean: relatives	0·24	0·24	0·33
Mean: visitors	0·23	0·06	0·06
Mean household size	5·12(±0·40)	4·40(±0·11)	4·24(±0·25)
(c) *Radford, 1851*			
Number of cases	75	740	235
Mean: household heads	1·00	1·00	1·00
Mean: wives	0·68	0·87	0·66
Mean: children	1·96(±0·46)	2·42(±0·15)	2·08(±0·22)
Mean: family size	3·64(±0·57)	4·29(±0·16)	3·74(±0·25)
Mean: domestics	0·71	0·08	0·03
Mean: lodgers	0·32	0·25	0·26
Mean: relatives	0·47	0·20	0·24
Mean: visitors	0·03	0·08	0·07
Mean household size	5·17(±0·60)	4·90(±0·18)	4.34(±0·23)

* All Nottingham and Radford results quoted in this paper are owed to Mr. R. J. Smith, a research student in the Department of Economic History at Nottingham University.

size, in terms of social classes. Class III in all three samples has a higher mean than classes IV–V. Only in the case of Radford however, can such a difference be positively asserted. In all three cases, classes IV–V contained a fairly high proportion of incomplete families (see means for 'wives') which had important effects on family sizes, and hence on household sizes.

Lodgers were more commonly found in our nineteenth-century communities. Whereas outside London there were no lodgers to speak of in the seventeenth century (Laslett), the proportions of households with lodgers were 21·3 (±2·9) per cent for York, (1851), and 21·8 (±2·0) per cent and 13·7 (±2·1) per cent for Nottingham and Radford respectively. The gradual spread of lodging (insofar as it involved simply payment for accommodation in the house of another) may have been a function of the industrial and urban revolutions of the eighteenth and nineteenth centuries. On the other hand, there is a problem of different classification here: some proportion of those classified as lodgers in the York and Nottingham studies would have been classed as 'working servants' by Mr. Laslett, since the lodger category included apprentices and journeymen working for the household head and living in.[7] The case is less ambiguous with relatives. In York in 1851, 21·6 (±2·9) per cent of all households contained at least one relative, whereas there were very few relatives in the pre-industrial households. In Stoke-on-Trent in 1629, 'less than 10% of all households' had relatives of any kind.

The preceding paragraphs show quite conclusively that despite similarity of mean household size in the communities mentioned, there have existed a great many variations and mutations of the English household and family which will merit study for a long time to come. How would the parameters of nineteenth-century *rural society* compare with those of the seventeenth-century villages? How general, in mid-nineteenth-century towns, would be the patterns of variation found in York, Nottingham, and Radford? In particular, these investigations show an apparent tendency for the size of households to diminish as one moves down the class-structure, while on the other hand the *family* size of class III, the skilled artisan and small shop-keeper class, always seems to be the largest. Would this prove to be so in factory, residential spa, maritime, mining, or agricultural communities? Was the extended family structure, far from being destroyed by the industrial revolution, a creation of it in some sense? Etc. etc.

---

[7] Discussions on the problems of long-run comparability in studies of this sort have been commenced.

In addition to measuring household and family composition, one can shed new light on migration problems from the enumerators' books (see Table 3).

These percentage figures seemed to suggest above all that whereas York-born heads were especially likely to be found in class III, the immigrants tended more to be encountered at the extreme ends of the class-structure. So far as the latter were concerned, it seemed probable that

TABLE 3

BIRTHPLACES AND SOCIAL CLASSES OF HOUSEHOLD HEADS (YORK, 1851)

	Percentage of heads in:				
	Classes I–II	Class III	Classes IV–V	Class 'X' (not classifiable)	Number of heads
York (Parl. Borough)	20·8	54·3	21·6	3·3	269
North and East Ridings	17·6	45·2	33·0	4·2	221
West Riding	23·7	47·4	25·7	3·2	152
Contiguous Northern Counties*	26·8	55·4	16·1	1·7	56
Rest of England and Wales	35·9	48·7	12·8	2·6	39
Ireland	8·0	24·0	56·0	12·0	25
All household heads (including categories not listed above)	21·3	49·4	25·7	3·6	781

* Viz. Lancashire, Cheshire, Derbyshire, Nottinghamshire, Lincolnshire, Durham. Northumberland (though not contiguous) was also included on account of the large numbers born there. Westmorland (though contiguous), was not included, since few came from that county.

there was some relationship between social class position and distance of origin (excepting the special case of the Irish). However, since these findings were based on a sample, tests of significance of difference were required. While the ranges of error and working of the tests are not shown here, the findings were in fact:

(a) That the Irish were more likely to be found in classes IV–V than either the York-born, Northern Counties, Rest of England, or West Riding heads. There was also a significantly larger proportion of East and North Riding heads in this category than of York-born, Northern Counties, or Rest of England heads.

(b) So far as class III heads were concerned, one can positively state only that the Irish were below the general city proportion. No other differences can be substantiated.

(c) So far as classes I–II were concerned, longer distance migrants (Northern Counties and Rest of England heads combined), were significantly better represented than either the North and East Riding or Irish heads; but such tests just failed to show that a higher proportion of these groups were in classes I–II than York-born heads (although there was a significant difference between Rest of England heads *alone*, and York-born heads).

These positive findings do in fact, in the writer's judgement, make it possible to say that in this case, while the York-born heads were spread pretty generally through the class-structure, there was a definite relationship between social class and distance travelled—doubtless *in general*, the sort of man who would travel furthest had more education, skill, and capital at his disposal.

It has also been possible to show that while each of the three York urban sub-districts had a very high proportion of immigrant heads and wives, varying from 63·0 ($\pm$5·4) per cent to 72·5 ($\pm$4·9) per cent, the areas to the north of the river had a significantly higher proportion of East and North Riding born heads and wives (45·8 per cent) than those to the south (38·4 per cent). Significantly more West Riding born persons were to be found in the areas to the south of the river. Furthermore, using a 3-variable tabulation, it has been possible to show that of all York-born heads, those in the unsavoury Walmgate area were least likely to be in classes I–II: the same is true of the East and North Riding born heads. Clearly, the successful York-born, as well as the successful immigrants, preferred not to live in that area.

Results of that kind are drawn more or less exclusively from the internal evidence of the census enumerators' books. It is often possible to relate findings from this source to other background evidence in a highly meaningful way. For instance, Mr. Smith's studies suggest that both in Nottingham and the surrounding Radford district, the mean family size of the framework knitters was smaller than that of the more prosperous lacemakers. For both groups however, Radford provided higher averages. The differences in the sample figures arise principally from the fact that the framework knitters were generally older, and hence had fewer children. Radford was the more rapidly growing area (outlying industrial villages), and represented a more healthy environment (see Table 4).

As it happens, on the basis of the sample taken, some of these differences are not substantiable at the 95 per cent confidence level. They are

TABLE 4

NOTTINGHAMSHIRE FRAMEWORK KNITTERS AND LACE-MAKERS: SELECTED RESULTS

	Mean family size	Mean no. children	Percentage of heads aged below 45
(a) *Nottingham*			
(i) Framework Knitters (194 cases)	3·77(±0·34)	1·93(±0·27)	45·9(±7·0)
(ii) Lacemakers (88 cases)	4·11(±0·52)	2·41(±0·49)	56·8(±10·0)
(b) *Radford*			
(i) Framework Knitters (173 cases)	4·21(±0·29)	2·28(±0·30)	44·8(±7·4)
(ii) Lacemakers (208 cases)	4·87(±0·34)	2·96(±0·31)	71·2(±6·1)

highly suggestive figures however, when taken in conjunction with all the available information on the state of the two trades, and general living conditions inside the city and around it.[8] They will certainly be used to frame a range of hypotheses, which Mr. Smith will be able to investigate further, if necessary by means of larger samples drawn from these groups exclusively.

Let us move from a highly specific case to a more general description of how, in the York case, sample evidence has been related to background evidence. It can be shown, for example, that the York sub-district (Walmgate), most noted for its unsavoury public health conditions contained, both in 1841 and 1851, proportionately more class III–V residents and proportionately fewer class I–II residents than the healthier sub-districts (i.e., those sub-districts where not only were contemporary descriptions of health conditions somewhat less horrific, but also where the 'hard' evidence of lower death-rates supported the impression of their superiority). The same kind of result emerged when the social structure of other combinations of well, reasonably, and badly drained parishes were explored. The mean number of children aged 0–4 per 1,000 married women was, as far as could be seen, as high in the least savoury sub-district (852 as against 804 and 838—no assertion of difference was possible with these figures), implying that the known higher fertility of that sub-district made up for its higher infant mortality losses. Such a conclusion was strengthened by the census ratios of $\frac{\text{children aged 0–15}}{\text{total population}}$,

[8] See R. A. Church, *Economic and Social Change in a Midland Town: Victorian Nottingham, 1815–1900* (1966), especially Chaps. II, IV, and VII.

7

which worked out at 41·7, 41·2, and 42·5, respectively for the sub-districts. But Walmgate, as other reports can be made to show, was the least effectively schooled and churched area of the city.[9] And so one can go on, tying in one piece of background information with another, or with the social-structural information derived from the census, until a mosaic of clear patterns begins to emerge.

Having shown by specific examples and by general argument the sort of positive results that can be drawn from the census enumerators' books, it is now necessary to discuss certain of the major problems that have been encountered in statistical and historical evaluation of York and Nottingham census statistics. These include: problems inherent in the material; problems arising from the categories of analysis employed, etc.; problems of interpretation.

(a) *Problems inherent in the material*

The basic accuracy of some of the information is open to some degree of error, for example in the recording of ages.[10] No allowance can be made for this, although the critical student ought to be aware that the problem is there. One supposes that there could be a certain degree of error in birthplace statements, and perhaps in respect of recording the relationship to the head of the family. There may have been errors in the transcription of information from householders' schedules into the census enumerators' books, but it is likely that many more errors would be made at the next stage, i.e. the preparation of printed abstracts from the enumerators' books by the Registrar General's army of clerks (involving much counting). Generally there is little that can be done about suspected errors of this kind. Potentially much more serious are the complications connected with comparability.

The census of 1851 was a great improvement on its predecessor on several counts. More precise recording of birthplaces, exact ages, detailed occupations, and relationship of each individual to the family head were now called for.[11] Since the conventions used to analyse the inferior 1841 enumerators' books, and the limitations within which tabulations derived

9 See, *inter alia*, the Educational and Religious Reports of the 1851 Census: T. Laycock, *Report on the Sanitary State of York;* Royal Commission on the State of Large Towns and Populous Districts, 1844: Manchester Statistical Society, *Report on the State of Education in York* (1837), etc.

10 V. P. A. Derrick, 'Observations on errors of age in the population statistics of England & Wales', *J. Inst. Actuaries,* lviii (1927), pp. 117–59; J. C. Dunlop, 'Note as to error of statement of ages of young children in a census', *J. Roy. Stat. Soc.,* lxxix (1916), pp. 309–17.

11 The pamphlet entitled *Interdepartmental Committee on Social & Economic Research: Guide to Official Sources No. 2: The Census Reports of Great Britain, 1801–1931* (H.M.S.O., 1951) is remarkably useful for ready reference as to what is covered in successive censuses.

from the 1841 and 1851 censuses may be compared have already been discussed in the *Introduction to English Historical Demography*, we may concern ourselves here with the possibilities of post-1851 comparisons. It is important to notice that the form of the questionnaire remained *more or less unchanged* down to 1911.[12] This lessens our problem in one sense, for in the lengthy discussions of census comparability which have taken place, it is the comparability of the *printed abstracts* which is in question— i.e. the data after the census authorities had 'classified' and arranged it under varying categories, in districts of varying size, etc.

More difficulty may be experienced as a result of the looseness of definitions, principally over the question of what was meant by a household. Prior to 1851 census enumerators were given no specific instructions as to what constituted a house, but between 1851 and 1911 the definition employed was 'all the space within the external and party walls of a building'.[13] Enumerators were instructed to supply one schedule to each occupier (i.e. the resident owner or any person paying rent for the whole of a house), or (as a lodger) for any distinct floor or apartment. In filling up his enumeration book, the enumerator should, 'under the last name in any house (i.e. a separate and distinct building, and not a mere storey or flat) draw a line across the page as far as the fifth column. Where there is more than one occupier in the same house, he should draw a similar line under the last name of the family of each occupier, making the line . . . commence a little on the left hand side of the third column.'[14]

Of course, the vast majority of households in England and Wales constitute quite unambiguous cases. But (especially where towns are concerned) it will be found that the practice of enumerators in giving out schedules did vary. So too, did the extent to which they adhered to the 'ruling-off' regulations in their enumeration books, the most typical fault being a failure to rule off households at the foot of a page. In the York study, each fully ruled off enumeration schedule was regarded as a household and,

(a) where two schedules (or more) were used, and the household was seen to be divided properly by intermediate shorter lines between

[12] The questionnaire of 1891 demanded to know whether respondents were employers, employees, or own account workers, setting aside an additional column for this. Actually the authorities had always required this information, but had invariably obtained it imperfectly. Otherwise there were no major changes or additions until 1911, when a valuable range of questions on marriage and fecundity was introduced.

[13] *Guide to Official Sources, No. 2,* p. 66.

[14] 1851 Census: *Population Tables Vol. I (Report and Summary Tables),* cxlii. A facsimile of a completed page from a census enumerators' book is included in the *Introduction.*

each enumeration schedule, concluding with the longer line, all the inhabitants were regarded as members of one household.

(b) In cases where a household was not ruled off at the bottom of a page, the next unit starting at the top of a new page was regarded as a separate household, provided that it had a separate schedule number (except in one or two cases where the address was *precisely* the same as that of the preceding household, e.g., 3 North Road).

No confidence was felt in the separate schedule as the criterion of 'sharing'. Persons on the second or third schedule within a household were all treated as lodgers of the family on the first schedule. The household was regarded as sharing in cases where there was at least one identifiable family unit, either a married couple, or an adult with at least one child of his or her own, among the lodgers, regardless of whether they had been listed on a separate enumeration schedule from the head's family or not.

These rules should adequately cover all enumerators' books from 1851 onwards; for 1841 the marking off of families, households, etc., is distinctly more chaotic, and suggested rules for dealing with this census were described in the *Introduction to English Historical Demography*.

(b) Problems arising from the categories of analysis and method generally

Here we are referring to the categories of analysis employed by the modern user of the census enumerators' books, and our observations will refer principally to the schemes described in the *Introduction to English Historical Demography*.

It might have been useful for certain purposes to have had a finer breakdown of age groups over 50, and it is possible that a birthplace breakdown in terms of a series of concentric circles (0–9 miles from the city centre, 10–19, etc.) would have been more useful than the breakdown by counties, which was used in the York and Nottingham studies. This would also have allowed for standardised comparisons. In the early stages of data collection, however, this would have been very time-consuming.

Perhaps the greatest question mark hangs over the system of social stratification used—householders were classified according to the Registrar General's 1950 volume, *The Classification of Occupations*, with minor amendments.[15] That such a scheme is meaningful in relation to mid-

---

15 We lack knowledge of precise family and household income data which would allow for the sort of stratification used by B. S. Rowntree, for example, in *Poverty, a Study of Town Life* (1901). Stephan Thernstrom, in his *Poverty and Progress* (1964) writes that 'the terms "social

nineteenth-century society, seems to be confirmed by the following results for York in 1851.

TABLE 5

DISTRIBUTION OF DOMESTIC SERVANTS AND SHARING HOUSEHOLDS: YORK, 1851

	Class I (59 cases)	Class II (107 cases)	Class III (386 cases)	Class IV (103 cases)	Class V (98 cases)
rcentage of householders having at least 1 domestic servant	81·4(± 9·9)	57·9(± 9·4)	9·1(± 2·9)	5·8(± 4·5)	0·0
ean no. of domestic servants per household	1·88	0·75	0·12	0·10	0·0
rcentage of householders sharing with another identifiable family unit	1·7	1·9	4·7	6·8	10·2

On the other hand it is open to anyone to argue that the highest class (in the conditions of 1851) ought *all* to have had domestic servants. And on general grounds it could be said that to impose a pre-determined pattern from the outside at the outset, is undesirable. Given the range of data available for each household, and the extended possibilities inherent in computer analysis, it ought to be possible to allow the classes to select themselves, so to speak. One could examine which occupations were similarly placed in respect of variables a, b, c, etc., and construct classes on the basis of these, or some kind of weighted average of them.

Considerations of this kind apart however, it may be useful to include a few observations on problems which the scheme of social stratification for York did call forth. Table 2 showed the mean family size of class I–II households to have been 3·12 (and 1·54 children) while the results for class III were 3·71 (1·93 children) and for classes IV–V, 3·44 (1·73 children). But in terms of *individual* classes, the calculated values were shown in Table 6.

status" and "social class" raise perilously complex and disputed problems of definition. ... The historical study of social mobility requires the use of objective criteria of social status. The most convenient of these is occupation. Occupation may be only one variable in a comprehensive theory of class, but it is the variable which includes more, which sets more limits on the other variables than any other criterion of status' (p. 84).

TABLE 6

FAMILY SIZE AND DISTRIBUTION OF CHILDREN BY CLASS: YORK, 1851

	Class I	Class II	Class III	Class IV	Class V
Mean family size	3·39	2·98	3·70	3·22	3·65
Mean no. of children	1·85	1·37	1·93	1·52	1·94

This peculiar 'battlemented' series of results almost seemed to defy interpretation. Thus it was decided to combine classes I–II and IV–V with the results given in Table 2. We were then in the position of being able to assert there was a significant difference between classes I–II (combined) and III (in respect of family size), but not between III and IV–V, nor between classes I–II and IV–V. It is notable that the *pattern* of these results was repeated when the 1841 family sizes were analysed.

TABLE 7

FAMILY SIZE BY CLASS: YORK, 1841

Class I–II	Class III	Classes IV–V
2·88(±0·30)	3·76(±0·23)	3·65(±0·30)

How far was the procedure of combining results for the invididual classes justifiable? In the construction of the social classification system, a definite impression had been gained that the border-lines between the classes were on the whole, more strongly marked between classes II and III, and III and IV, than between I and II, and IV and V. (The domestic servant table, incidentally, strengthened that impression in some respects.) Statisticians warn that it would be unethical to combine disparate cases in such a way as to conceal part of the evidence—historians, too, have a similar sort of ethic. But we have a duty to interpret results as well as record them, and it is unlikely that harm will be done by combining categories in instances of this sort, provided that what has been done is clearly shown, and provided further that the necessary data for disaggregating results is duly given. Results which are initially difficult to explain may be suspected of having arisen merely from sampling error, or sheer chance, especially where the numbers of cases involved are small. But if they are seen to appear in successive studies of this type (e.g., if the 'battlemented' family size series were frequently repeated), then the historian who has combined categories may be guilty of providing wrong interpretations and concentrating on the wrong features: he could not, provided that the precautions listed above had been taken, be accused of misrepresentation.

On the broader question of general method, it may be appropriate to add a few comments on sampling, to the earlier remarks in the *Introduction to English Historical Demography*. Ten per cent samples (on a household basis) were used for the York and Nottingham studies, and this fraction has been quite adequate for general purposes. The gains have been those which one would expect, namely a saving in recording time and sheer tedium; on the other hand the need to acquire a working knowledge of this branch of statistics, and the volume of arithmetical exercises involved in calculating confidence limits, etc., have largely off-set this. (This disadvantage would cease to apply if those who had worked once using sample methods were to attempt successive surveys of the same kind.) Again, those who choose to sample may find that the absolute number of cases falls alarmingly (and the ranges of error rise dramatically), when it is necessary to relate not two, but three variables. For example, it was possible to show the distribution of York-born household heads, by class, in each of several areas of the city (see above p. 74). This could also be done with the East and North Riding born heads, who were also present in large numbers in the sample. But the absolute numbers of persons whose birthplaces were elsewhere did not run to making meaningful statements in respect of two other related variables at once.[16] Where important matters are at issue, however (e.g., the main characteristics of Irish households in York, this group being represented by only 25 households in the 1851 sample), there is nothing to debar the student from drawing appropriate sub-samples directed to answering specific questions.[17]

These observations apply to the possible drawbacks of a systematic general-purpose sample. There are many other possible types of sample that are equally legitimate, and may be appropriately used if the interest

[16] E.g. in the case of Contiguous Northern Counties heads, 55 heads were distributed by class and district as follows:

	Class I	Class II	Class III	Class IV	Class V
(a) Micklegate	3	4	11	1	2
(b) Bootham	3	2	7	2	0
(c) Walmgate	1	2	13	3	1

Obviously nothing meaningful can be said about the three comparative distributions.

[17] See *Introduction*, p. 220.

of the investigator is more partial, or specific. Dr. Dyos, with his interest in the life-cycles of urban property, is studying the social structure of given streets, from census to census. Dr. Thernstrom devised a scheme of analysis for the American enumerators' books which was designed to catch particular families and individuals in successive censuses, his interest being in social mobility.[18] Obviously a succession of general samples would not adequately serve such purposes as these.

(*c*) *Problems of interpretation: some general limitations of the census enumerators' books as a source for the social historian*

The information derived from the census enumerators' books is basically *social-structural*, a still glimpse of a moving picture. It is not at all easy to infer demographic trends from it.

David Eversley has succinctly summed up this kind of difficulty: 'We must also be aware of the general limitations of the static census analysis, at least as far as linking population and economic changes is concerned. Even if we know age and sex structure at a given point of time with some degree of accuracy, this does not in itself provide us with sufficient explanations of the process of change, though it may help us to include or exclude certain categories of explanation.'[19] In this field the use of original householders' schedules may enable us to determine the number of married couples, unmarried adults, widows and children per family, thus yielding further clues to change—but even then, needless to say, we do not know the size of *completed* families nor can we directly say what trends in fertility, mortality, etc. have produced the given social structure.

At the first level of analysis, results drawn from samples of this kind explain one another, e.g., the lower family size of upper-class households in York is largely to be accounted for by the fact that fewer heads were married males (i.e. a high proportion of households were headed by widows, widowers, or married women with husbands away). Again, the relatively low average number of children in the higher social classes also arises from this factor, as well as from the further fact that significantly fewer heads in the higher classes were aged below 45.

When we attempt to probe more deeply however, we are likely to move into areas where the evidence of the census enumerators' books is suggestive, but not conclusive. Let us take a case in point, with reference to the following tabulation.

---

[18] Thernstrom, *op. cit.* The American data gives more details than ours (in respect of property holdings, literacy, etc.), and is therefore much more amenable to social mobility studies.

[19] *Introduction*, p. 36.

TABLE 8

MEAN NO. OF CHILDREN AGED 0–4
PER 1,000 MARRIED WOMEN AGED
15–49, BY CLASS: YORK, 1851*

Classes I–II	Class III	Classes IV–V
783 (69 wives)	862 (232 wives)	814 (113 wives)

* The married women referred to in this table are
in fact wives of household heads *only*; no lodgers'
wives or married women among relatives, etc., are
included.

Fertility and the level of child mortality both have a bearing on these
results, and the enumerators' books will yield no more. As it happens,
since the calculated ranges of error overlap in all cases, no assertion of any
difference may be confidently made, but there remains a suspicion that
the upper classes in fact had lower fertility, and were perhaps limiting
their families to some extent. If there is one thing about which we can be
certain, it is that infant mortality bore more hardly on the lower classes
than the upper, and ratios pertaining to the upper classes ought (if
fertility was equal in all classes) to have been considerably higher than
those of the lower classes.[20] Possibilities of this kind, and the reasoning
behind them, ought to be included in historical surveys, even where
proof is impossible. They will be of value to others, and where there has
been uniformity of presentation, it may be possible at a later date to
agglomerate such findings, so reducing the ranges of error.

This section may be concluded by reference to areas of study where the
census enumerators' books are neither positive nor suggestive, but virtually useless. Much time was wasted in examining the *apparent* birth-
spaces of children in the 1851 samples, with a view to drawing some
conclusions on fertility, etc. This task was fraught with various difficulties, because (a) only families with at least two children could be included,
(b) unknown numbers of children would be away from home (at boarding-
school in the case of upper-class families, in service in the case of the

[20] The argument is crude, and it is true that *age-specific* ratios should ideally be examined.
The absolute number of cases in the upper classes did not allow for this however. It is of
interest to point out that in the case of 61 Nottingham wives (aged 15–49) of indubitably high-
class citizens (wives of surgeons, bankers, solicitors, fund-holders, landed proprietors, clergymen, physicians, attorneys, accountants, house proprietors, architects, army officers, lawyers,
and stock-brokers only: all with domestic servants) the comparable ratio worked out to 655
children aged 0–4, per 1,000 married women (1851).

lower-class), and (c) precise ages (in terms of months) could not be obtained for those aged over one year.

Various apparent birth intervals were calculated (ranging from 3·25 to 3·49 in the different social classes). But since the numbers of cases were relatively small, it did not prove to be possible to establish statistically significant differences between them. It was also noticed that the results were in effect a reflection of the ratios of children aged 0–4 per 1,000 married women aged 15–49, by class and by area. The latter ratios can be much more easily arrived at by using the punched cards, whereas the apparent birth-space intervals had to be laboriously extracted from the original notebooks.[21] Neither series, of course, is self-explanatory: both the ratio and the apparent mean birth interval are affected by both fertility and child mortality.

Another seemingly obvious line of investigation might be to trace fluctuations in immigration by reference to the ages and birthplaces of children. Such a scheme falls down on two points:

(a) A great deal of immigration was that of single people, whereas a scheme of this sort could only give the movement of married couples.

(b) When studying a given area, the earliest families to move in will stand a far greater chance of having move out again. Hence any curve of inward migration (say, over 10 years), will almost certainly be a rising one, since a greater proportion of more recent immigrants will still be there; i.e. the fluctuations in immigration, even of already married couples, may be grossly misrepresented.

Again there seems to be little point in attempting to use children's occupational data for the purpose of computing social mobility between class and class. In all likelihood the sons and daughters remaining at home will not be a representative cross-section of their generation and original class; on the whole, their social mobility would tend to be lower. This does not exclude the possibility of doing something with the census enumerators' books with an experiment expressly designed to look into the social mobility question, but meaningful data on this subject will not emerge from the general all-purpose samples so far attempted on York, Nottingham, etc.

There has been insufficient time and space to dwell on the more obvious uses of the census enumerators' books for urban historians. In general, examination of the contents of the work-house, gaol, hospital,

21 The original sample notebooks are described in *Introduction*, pp. 220-1.

almshouse, etc., present the investigator with no great problems, although it is right and proper that he should make use of such information.[22] Nor has it been possible to discuss the problems presented by the available background data. The Registrar General's Reports, for example, only give the numbers of vital events by sub-districts, which raises problems when one is discussing the demographic forces at work on populations other than those grouped within these geographical limits. Nowhere are there base populations for inter-censal years, so that estimates of birth, death, and marriage rates, and increments by immigration and natural increase are extremely difficult to make.[23] Always there is the problem of the shortage of wage and price data (in consistent series).

The census enumerators' books are not a remedy for the shortcomings of all other sources, yielding clear and unambiguous answers to all the questions one would like to ask in respect of the Victorian social structure. The reader may feel that even our more positive results are so hedged round with qualifications, 'ranges of error', etc., as to be of limited value. Some uncertainty is inevitable at this early stage, for, given the few results actually available, it is not altogether clear which are significant differences and which have simply arisen from chance error. In some important respects, nevertheless, a growing volume of careful analysis will enable us to measure the intensity of 'obvious' relationships as they varied between time and place—and sometimes we may be able to discover new ones. It should certainly be possible to delineate the field of Victorian social structure, urban history, and social history generally with growing sensitivity in the years to come.

[22] See M. W. Beresford, 'The unprinted census returns of 1841, 1851, and 1861 for England and Wales', *Amateur Historian*, v (1963), p. 266.
[23] In the York and Nottingham studies, inter-censal base populations have been calculated as follows: A. Total population increase (Population 1851 minus population 1841) was divided between natural increase (births minus deaths for the ten years, from Registrar General's Reports) and net immigration (Total population increase minus natural increase). B. One tenth of the net immigration was added in at each year. C. Thus, population for 1842 = Base population for 1841 (census) plus natural increase for 1841 (births minus deaths) plus one-tenth of calculated inter-censal net immigration, etc.

With the base populations having been calculated in the above manner, birth and death rates can be expressed in the usual way. Although the method is crude, it should be pointed out than an error of a few hundreds in the denominator would not affect (say) a death rate by more than a point or so in a sizeable town, i.e. important changes or demographic crisis years could still be detected.

The Possibilities of Computerising Census Data[1]

H. J. Dyos and A. B. M. Baker

We have been assured recently by a speaker at the annual meeting of the British Association that the human brain is still in many respects the most subtle and flexible computer that exists. Its enormous capacity, its speed of operation, and its ability to interpret many different kinds of data at the same time, are attributes of a mechanism which is also capable of discriminating between actions and results according to a set of values, and of reacting rationally to unfamiliar phenomena or to unexpected constellations of them. Fortunately or unfortunately, this intelligence is not mechanistic: the human brain can grow tired, make mistakes, become ambivalent, or merely get bored with the drudgery of repetition; and there is in fact all too little physiological evidence that it ordinarily works so well as communications theory would suggest. From all-too-personal knowledge we can say that its inherent capacity to handle certain kinds of quantitative data can sometimes be frustrated altogether.

To the historian confronted by problems which can only be solved satisfactorily through the analysis of a massive array of quantitative data there are two ways out. He can either rationalise his own limitations and

[1] This is a revised and up-dated version of the paper delivered to the conference. We are grateful to acknowledge the generous financial help which has been given to this whole project by the Leverhulme Trust and by the Research Board of the University of Leicester. We should also like to mention here the invaluable help we have had from several colleagues, notably Dr. J. R. Thompson and Miss Mary Simpson of the Leicester University Computer Laboratory, Miss Ann Russel of the London University Institute of Computer Science, and especially Mrs. Judy Lay of the Science Research Council's Atlas Computer Laboratory at Chilton, Berks. who has repeatedly gone out of her way to help us. We would also like to thank Miss Penny Wild for her careful coding of the data. Mr. W. A. Armstrong's generous advice and the 'demonstration effect' of his own work were in the earlier stages quite indispensable, and we are very grateful for his pioneering work.

insist that almost all the important questions are so precisely because they are not susceptible to quantitative assessment. He can conclude that problems involving quantification to this degree are therefore trivial ones.[2] Or he can use a machine to organise his data in such a way that he can discern their meaning more readily. One of the purposes of this paper is to describe the use we have been making of one such machine, the ICT Atlas electronic computer, in approaching the kind of problem outlined in the paper by Mr. W. A. Armstrong: though what we have to say in this respect is no more than a very brief report on research in progress. We begin, however, by saying something about the more general possibilities of using computers in a field of this kind.[3]

It is well to recognise at the outset what a computer can and cannot do in this respect. Whatever its more sophisticated mathematical possibilities are in other directions, a computer can only re-arrange those kinds of raw historical data that can be quantified, and treat them mathematically or statistically in order to get from them such quantities as means, standard deviations, and correlations. Despite some recent claims that machines can be made 'to think', we do not see how they can reason or develop spontaneously new hypotheses of their own: however elaborate or sustained their processes may be, they are for all practical purposes merely responding to sets of instructions prepared in languages of their own. Unless the instructions to a computer are meticulously precise, internally consistent, and ordered strictly logically, the machine will either throw out the case altogether or will simply utter numerical gibberish—sometimes with disconcerting flashes of entirely valid calculation. The true results that it will yield to faultless instructions will still lack significance unless their form has been imaginatively designed, and will in any case still be a *source* of information and not a considered conclusion. After even the most elaborate programming of data through a computer its output will simply be a re-arrangement of the raw data into a more intelligible pattern and cannot be regarded in any sense as the end of the line of research. It is indeed only the end of the beginning.

2 Arthur M. Schlesinger, Jr., 'The humanist looks at empirical social research', *American Sociological Review*, xxvii (1962), p. 770. For a contrasting view, see Thomas C. Cochran, 'The historical use of the social sciences', *Estratto da Relazioni del X Congresso Internationale di Scienze Storiche*, Rome 1955, Vol. I, reprinted in the same author's *The Inner Revolution* (1964), pp. 19–38.

3 Two very general introductions to the computer field at large are Brian Murphy, *The Computer in Society* (1966) and S. H. Hollingdale and G. C. Tootill, *Electronic Computers* (1965).

It would be absurd in the space we have here to pontificate about the tendency of many historians to behave as though quantitative data were, in fact, either trivial or at best misleading, and it would be even more ridiculous to pretend to be scandalised at their failure to use electronic computers. There are, we suggest, some serious technical pitfalls in the way of doing so—not to mention philosophical and psychological ones—and any tendency to make a new orthodoxy of historical statistics in place of conventional documentation would obviously be pernicious. Quantitative techniques can give precision to history but they do not seem capable of formulating new hypotheses, much less of bringing to it objectivity: our own historical standpoints shift about too much for us to be able to establish any timeless truths.[4]

Just the same, it is important to recognise the truth of the proposition expounded so well recently by Professor William O. Aydelotte, that much historical research is already implicitly quantitative in character:[5] the very terms 'typical', 'representative', 'widespread', 'most', 'on the average' are examples of the kind of generalised quantitative statements used by all historians, whether they are made precisely, casually, or even rhetorically. There are large areas of research for which a vocabulary of this kind, and the haphazard or even intuitive handling of quantitative data that lies behind it, are entirely adequate. Yet there are others in which the use of even very sophisticated quantitative reasoning is quite inadequate to explain how and why things occurred as they did. In economic history the scope as well as the need for quantification have always been very wide, and its problems and hypotheses have recently been assuming still more quantified forms in so-called econometric history. Political and legal history have, by contrast, required less of it. But in urban history, with its ton upon ton of deeds, directories, vestry minutes, rate books, school log-books, election data, surveyors' returns, medical officers' reports, census books and the like there seems to be a special need for more highly developed methods of classifying, counting, and cross-tabulating the more or less standardised entries which they contain. The electronic computer is a tool that might have been designed for this purpose.

The possibilities of using computers in the solution of historical problems are very new indeed. Indeed, it is really only within the last two years that computers have come at all effectively within the range of social

---

[4] One of the most interesting of recent discussions on this point is that of Peter Temin, 'In pursuit of the exact', *Times Literary Supplement*, 28 July 1966.

[5] William O. Aydelotte, 'Quantification in history', *American Historical Review*, lxxi, No. 3 (April 1966), pp. 803–25.

scientists at all.[6] The only papers known to us to have been written on the use of a computer as an historical tool were delivered in January 1965 to a Conference held at Yale University and to another the following November at Boston University.[7] The original pioneer in the actual application of computer methods to a particular historical problem is probably Merle Curti, whose study of the frontier period in Wisconsin's history, *The Making of an American Community*, was published only seven years ago. This involved the handling of manuscript census material covering the period 1850–80, though it could be said that the programme was not completely computerised; card sorters were also used. Apart from some well-known attempts to attribute authorship by the study of authors' vocabularies,[8] computers have been used recently in the analysing of Elizabethan trading companies, electoral, parliamentary, and bureaucratic behaviour, political disturbances, literacy, and urbanisation.[9] At the present time there are some very large-scale research projects in hand in the United States and Canada using some quite sophisticated computer techniques. These include study of demographic and electoral behaviour in Pittsburgh since the 1820s,[10] the social structure of Buffalo during the

[6] The release of the 1:1000 sample tape of the 1960 census in the United States led to an inter-disciplinary conference at the Joint Center for Urban Studies at M.I.T. and Harvard University in October 1964 on the possibilities of developing new computer techniques to handle it. See the mimeographed proceedings edited by James M. Beshers, *Computer Methods in the Analysis of Large-Scale Social Systems* (M.I.T.–Harvard, 1965).

[7] The proceedings of the first of these were published by Yale University Press under the title *Computers for the Humanities?* (1965); it contains a valuable 'beginners' introduction to the literature'. One of the three papers given to historical applications of computers came from Stephan Thernstrom [of the Joint Center for Urban Studies of M.I.T. and Harvard University] who also read a similar paper entitled 'The Historian and the Computer' to the Boston University Conference on computers in the humanities, though this has not been published. Thernstrom's second paper has been the principal source of our knowledge of the range of historical research with the aid of computers which has been published in the United States, though we have also benefited from correspondence and personal contact with a number of other scholars. A most useful symposium has also appeared just as we go to press: Edmund A. Bowles (ed.), *Computers in Humanistic Research* (New Jersey, 1967).

[8] See Jacob Leed (ed.), *The Computer and Literary Style* [Kent Studies in English, No. 27] (Kent, Ohio, 1966), which contains six specific studies of literary detection and two about computers in general.

[9] Theodore Robb's paper on the trading companies is being published presently. The other fields are: Lee Benson, *The Concept of Jacksonian Democracy: New York as a Test Case* (1961); William O. Aydelotte, 'Voting patterns in the British House of Commons in the 1840s', *Comparative Studies in Society and History*, v (1963); Charles Tilly and James Rule, *Measuring Political Upheaval* (1965). Tilly is now extending his work to cover the urbanisation and politics of France since 1830. Daniel C. Calhoun, Department of History, Harvard University, has been studying literacy in America in the nineteenth century with the help of a computer; so, too, has Edward Shorter, Department of History, Toronto University, in his work on social change in the Bavarian bureaucracy in the nineteenth century.

[10] Samuel P. Hays in the Department of History, University of Pittsburgh, is concentrating

nineteenth century,[11] social mobility in Boston since 1880,[12] the social geography of a segment of Chicago in the 1870s and 1880s[13] and of Toronto between 1850 and 1899,[14] the acculturation of the Irish in mid-Victorian London,[15] migration and occupational mobility in half-a-dozen Canadian prairie towns since the 1920s,[16] among others.[17] There is a clear lag between the development of computers in the social sciences in the United States and Britain but it appears to be even more marked in history, particularly urban history. So far as we know, the development

at the moment on a fairly comprehensive study of the recruitment of city councillors. He proposes later to sample the manuscript census returns in order to discover the socio-economic characteristics of the wards themselves. Professor Hays is also concerned with the development of an Inter-University Consortium for Political Research at the University of Michigan, which is just getting under way with the analysis of up to 100 variables defining the socio-political characteristics of elections for president, governor, congress, and senator since the 1820s. There is also a putative project at Pittsburgh on the relations, historically considered, between social class and mental illness in a working-class district of the city.

[11] Herbert Gutman and Laurance Glasco in the Department of History, State University of New York at Buffalo, have several joint projects in hand covering the family and household structure of two counties, including the city itself, as revealed in federal and state censuses, and by reference to deeds, mortgages, and so on; they are also studying occupational mobility in selected groups (professional, entrepreneurial, small shopkeeper, and skilled worker) between 1860 and 1900, using the 1860 census to derive names and to trace these subsequently by reference to directories; they are also looking closely at the whole negro population of Buffalo between 1855 and 1875 (about 700); and, lastly, making an intensive analysis of the state census of 1855 for the whole city (population: 85,000). This is probably the most ambitious project to have been started so far.

[12] Stephan Thernstrom is now extending the work he began for his book *Poverty and Progress* (1964), in which he presented the results of a punched-card analysis of several hundred un-skilled labourers in Newburyport, Mass., 1850–80, whose occupational mobility he was trying to assess. That study was based mainly on manuscript census data, supplemented by savings bank accounts, but he is now attempting to take his study down to the present by reference to marriage licence applications, birth certificates, tax records, etc. The census schedules after 1890 are still classified as confidential and not normally open to historical research; most of the 1890 schedules for Boston were in any case destroyed by fire.

[13] Richard Sennett of the Center for Urban Studies at Cambridge, Mass., is preparing a doctoral thesis on the ecological and socio-economic shaping of Westville (Chicago), 1872–90.

[14] Peter Goheen, of the Department of Geography, University of British Columbia, is making a factor analysis of the city assessments, 1834–99, along with the census schedules for 1842, 1861, and 1871.

[15] Mrs. Lynn Lees, now of the Joint Center for Urban Studies at M.I.T. and Harvard University, has been working on the census data for 1851 and 1861.

[16] Richard E. DuWors and Jay Beaman in the Department of Sociology, University of Saskatchewan. This study is dealing with the cities of Prince Albert, Sudbury, Toronto, Quebec, Moose Jaw, Regina, Winnipeg, Hamilton and Sault Ste. Marie between 1948 and 1964, and with Saskatoon, Edmonton, and St. Catherines at eight-year intervals between 1924 and 1956. The main source is city directories.

[17] We have heard that the following are also undertaking research of this kind but we have no harder information about any of it; Daniel P. Moynihan (Joint Center for Urban Studies, M.I.T. and Harvard), Seymour Mandelbaum (University of Pennysylvania), and Sam. B. Warner, Jr. (Washington University, St. Louis).

of computer methods in this country has been limited entirely to non-historical fields,[18] though the Centre for Urban Studies' *Third Survey of London* could probably be classified as contemporary history.[19]

The problem that is of interest to us is how to define and explain the social changes that occurred in the making of a suburb of Victorian London. The process of creating the physical superstructure of Camberwell upon a largely unsettled rural landscape has already been made the subject of a first volume in what is intended to be a much lengthier and more comprehensive study of the metamorphosis of a London suburb down to our own day.[20] What we now want to know is just how particular neighbourhoods came to be occupied, held, or vacated by different social classes, and just what kinds of communities these were in terms of the structure of families and households. Is the traditional picture of the suburbs, in which the middle classes, sensing the imminent loss of their own social exclusiveness by the outward movement of the working classes, decide themselves to move further out, a valid one? Did migration to the suburbs have any recognisable social patterns and, if so, what were their forms and chronology? What, in particular, were the relationships between phenomena of these kinds and the physical and economic circumstances already observed in some detail in the earlier work? In what ways did they bear on the structure and working of local and national politics in the area?

Quite obviously, the main source of information has to be the census books which, despite their well-known crudities,[21] do contain reasonably accurate information on the matters which concern us and do so in a standardised format capable of being treated in a uniform manner right through the second half of the nineteenth century.[22] Here it seems to us

18 For example, by Peter Willmott of the Institute of Community Studies, who is carrying out two town expansion studies for Ipswich and Northampton by means of ordinary random sample surveys. These involve no historical data at all.

19 This is to be a collation and analysis of existing sample surveys since 1931.

20 H. J. Dyos, *Victorian Suburb: A Study of the Growth of Camberwell* (1961). It is hoped to complete the study in three volumes, the second of which is to deal with the social structure and political organisation of the suburb down to 1901, and the third to treat the whole subsequent history of Camberwell during its period as a metropolitan borough (which ended in April 1966 with the reorganisation of the London boroughs in the Greater London Council).

21 See A. J. Taylor, 'The taking of the census 1801–1951', *British Medical Journ.*, 7 April 1951, and M. W. Beresford 'The unprinted census returns of 1841, 1851, 1861 for England and Wales', *Am. Hist.* Little is known in detail about the condition of the census books. We have been told by Mr. H. C. Binford (now of Harvard Graduate School of Arts and Science) that the census books for parts of Lambeth and Southwark for 1851 and 1861 are decidedly defective, partly due to missing pages, wrong classification, and misplacing and faulty numbering of pages. Fortunately we have no reason to mistrust the returns for Camberwell, but it is clear that the source material for this kind of research does need careful checking.

22 The census books do vary a good deal in their physical condition as well as their legibility

is a set of historical problems for which a computer appears to be the best means of re-arranging the very large body of repetitive data efficiently. A simple card-sorting machine could do most of the job, but it would be very slow and very expensive to use on a large project. As to the possibility of tabulating the data by hand and processing them with a desk calculating machine, this is defeated by the sheer size of the project, involving as it does more than 700 households per census. Our quest for a suitable basic computer programme began in December 1965 and it soon became clear that the programmes and languages most commonly used by the natural and applied sciences were not suited to a research project which belonged to what could be called a survey type.[23]

The reason for this is that computers so far have been used largely by the natural and applied sciences where the need is to subject variables to elaborate mathematical and statistical treatment. By contrast, in the social sciences most data can be handled by means of cross tabulations and fairly elementary statistical operations. The problems arise from the fact that data which are not primarily numerical have to be given a numerical value by coding and the programme has to allow for the association of variables by their code and, what is more complicated, for the graphing of variables where the size of the groups and the number of variables cannot be pre-determined. The programmes which have been developed for work in the natural and applied sciences are not well suited to the social sciences with their need for greater flexibility in data input and processing. So far as we know, there is still no basic survey-type programme available in this country of the kind which would be suitable for much of the research that could be done in urban history, and we are even inclined to think that one of the most urgently needed general aids to research in the

and a few of them are too badly damaged for particular pages to be read at all. However they do follow the same form and provide the same amount of detail throughout the century. The 1891 and 1901 schedules contain information about whether the person enumerated worked for someone else, was self-employed, or an employer; they also give the number of rooms occupied by the household. Unfortunately, these gains are at the expense of legibility, with many more lines being squeeezed on to each page. It must be remembered that under the ordinary 'hundred year rule' it is not possible to conduct *bona fide* research on the census books from 1871 onwards, but we are most grateful to the Registrar General for recognising the special needs of a research project of this kind and for making exceptional arrangement for supplying us with microfilm of the census books with all means of personal identification blocked out.

23 For some indication of the range of programmes available in the field of numerical taxonomy, for example, there is an occasional *Classification Programs Newsletter*, of which the first issue was made in March 1966: it originates with the Medical Research Council Microbial Systematics Research Unit at Leicester University. One other list that has come to our notice covers a biomedical series of programmes; this is used by the University of California and is the size of a telephone directory.

broad field of the social sciences would be a programme specifically designed for their use.[24]

For our purposes the best available programme appeared to be the Multiple Variate Counter Mark 5 (MVC) written by by Mr. Andrew Colin, formerly of the Institute of Computer Science at the University of London, which was designed to process surveys in which questionnaires were put to one person only in each case.[25] The Elliott 803 B in our own computer laboratory at Leicester could not handle the MVC

[24] Since writing this we have obtained more information about developments in the United States, and it is clear that a number of special languages have recently been developed there for a variety of purposes, among which are IPL and LISP for complex data manipulation, COMIT for language work, and SIMSCRIPT and SIMPAC for simulation. The basic computer language in use is I.B.M's FORTRAN, which is easily adaptable to a wide range of machines, and another array of computer languages based on it has now been invented, among them SLIP, IPL-V, DYSTAL, and DATA-TEXT. The primary aim of these new languages is to make it easy for social scientists to use computers with the minimum help from mathematicians, statisticians, and professional programmers; several of them enable the researcher to avoid using a completely numerical code and offer scope for verbal association (see James M. Sakoda, 'A general computer language for the social sciences' in Beshers, *op. cit.*, pp. 25–32).

Easily the most adaptable and potentially universal new language for the social sciences known to us is DATA-TEXT. This has been developed principally by Dr. A. N. Couch of the Laboratory of Social Relations, Harvard University, with the object of making FORTRAN more congruent with the needs of the social sciences and to do so in such a way that it is possible for the researcher himself to have direct and markedly simplified access to the computer, and to avoid depending so heavily on the many experts who at present stand between him and the machine: it is both a computer language for research in the social sciences—a very large one containing over 100,000 instruction words—and an actual programme for the implementation of that language. The special virtues of the system are that it performs a complete range of statistical operations of the kind already widely used in the social sciences; that it embodies a great deal of the processing which is usually necessary before, during or after the running of programmes, including the capacity to use the whole or part of the output of one stage as the input of the next; that additions may be made to the specification after it has been fed into the machine; and that by means of a novel system of group control cards the user may specify a complex series of statistical operations without the necessity of making technically difficult changes in the programme itself. The net result of these developments appears to be that the IBM 7090 or 7094, for which DATA-TEXT has been written, is the premier computer for work in this field. Unfortunately DATA-TEXT is written in a way which defeats any easy conversion to other computer systems, though there is the possibility that, in being re-written for the new IBM 360 series, it will become more convertible. In the meantime, the IBM 7090/7094 installation at Imperial College has the revised version of the system working and is available to users in associated institutions in the usual way. We are very grateful to Dr. Couch for information about his system and particularly for the opportunity of studying the preliminary manual, which was issued in November 1966; a revised version appeared in March 1967. From what we hear the system is already being widely used in the United States.

[25] Andrew J. T. Colin, *The Multiple Variate Counter*, University of London Institute of Computer Science [44 Gordon Square, W.C.1], Part I (June 1964), Part II (October 1964): the first part of this manual deals with the more elementary aspects of the system and is comprehensible without previous knowledge of computers; the second part is altogether more sophisticated.

compiler, so we turned to the Science Research Council's ICT Atlas Computer at Chilton.[26]

One formidable problem presented itself immediately. How is it possible to decide on the classification of the data without having examined them? To some extent this is a problem confronting any researcher faced with a really large array of data that he can afford to process once only, but using a computer—or any mechanical method of data-processing—presents the problem in an unusually acute form. The coding categories must be decided on before the coding can begin. In our programme all the data had to be assimilated by the computer in one of three forms: as a straight quantity (*numerical*); as true-false, in order to indicate whether any persons actually existed in a given category in a particular household (*binary*); as a range of multiple choice, in order to differentiate age, birthplace, occupation, and so on (*polylog*). Using *polylogs* forced us to adopt a more limited classification of jobs, and to be more arbitrary in using it, than would have been possible if we had been able to use the ingenious system worked out by Herbert Gutman in his study of the social structure of Buffalo in the nineteenth century. He has divided six columns into three pairs—the second pair providing sub-categories of the first and the third pair sub-categories of the second—so as to get potentially a million part taxonomy for occupations alone. This virtually allows the data to determine its own categories, but at the cost of preparing and implementing a very much more complex code.

We recognise that our own approach has a serious implication. Although it is true that computer data do not wear their significance on their sleeves, so to speak, any more than statistics commonly do when derived in other ways, it is also true that the form in which the results are cast is liable to suggest its own interpretation and that in this sense the author of a computer programme will tend to get the answers to the questions he asks. He will run the danger of prejudging the results of his work.

There are also serious practical difficulties involved here, particularly when the number of categories into which a given variable can be written has to be limited by the sheer volume of information that can be entered for an individual case, i.e. a single household. The practical limit to the number of variables permitted in a single case is more likely to be set by

26 Apart from MVC, an entirely new system is being developed at the Atlas Computer Laboratory which would allow great flexibility to the user and be more readily adaptable to certain other computers: see B. E. Cooper, 'ASCOP—A statistical computing procedure', *Applied Statistics*, xvi, No. 2 (1967), pp. 100–110.

the cost of coding than by the capacity of the computer itself, for even the most experienced coder is unlikely to exceed a rate of 50 cases (households) per day on systematic sampling using a standard 80-column system, and this means giving at least a month to code a 3 per cent sample of a population of 50,000 for a single census: using a coding system involving five times the number of columns does not reduce the number of cases that can be handled per day *pro rata*, but it does tend to cut it back by up to a third, and this factor needs weighing carefully when settling the amount of detail which is acceptable.

There is no disguising the fact that a process like this cannot be made empirical in any ordinary historical sense. Two things only can be done. One is to supplement the coded data by notes taken of unexpected or unclassified information during the coding process. These have been found to be most valuable in moderating the purely quantified data, provided the notes are not limited to the cases in the sample but cover incidental information on the location of factories, shops, pubs, and so on, and take some account of the general social characteristics of the neighbourhood, especially of the density of population. The other thing to be done is deliberately to avoid a selective approach and to devise a programme and table specifications making every conceivable combination of the basic data from the census books. This does help to avoid prejudgement to a considerable extent, though blanketing the ground like this does make interpretation of the results more difficult. However, we do not think that it is possible to get more than 80 or so tables of any consequence from the data in the census books and these, we hope, are within our limits of comprehension.

The second major difficulty was to write the programme itself: that is, the set of instructions to the computer as to what information to store and how to formulate this in tables; this part of the computer input is also known as the *specification* to distinguish it from the means that have to be used to translate the specification into the electronic impulses acceptable to the computer, and this is known as the translator or, more usually, the *compiler*. What we had to do was to adapt the M V C compiler programme to the specific task of accepting and storing coded census data pertaining to individual households, which were subsequently to be counted and cross-tabulated into some 80 tables per census. It should be remembered that once it had been accepted by the computer the first part of the specification could be changed only by completely re-writing it; the second part of the specification setting out the tables could be supplemented, if required, as the data was coded.

The real nub of our programming difficulties so far has been the necessity of repeating the same questions, not to each household as a whole, but to each member of the household. This point needs explaining. There are two basic approaches to the devising of programmes for analysing individuals and groups (families and households) in relation to each other as well as separately. One is to treat the individual as the standard case and the other the group (or household). In each instance it is necessary to give instructions to the computer as to how to aggregate or separate the different persons as required. The readiness with which this might be done depends very much on the type of compiler in use. Our own approach was to adopt the household as the standard case, partly because this appeared to be the central unit to be studied and fitted in with the Armstrong approach. We also thought that the alternative of allocating one 80-column card per individual would add enormously to the coding operation. In practice, we find that this would not have happened because the average number of persons per household is slightly less then five, which is the number of cards used per household in our programme.

We had expected to be able to aggregate or separate data easily enough because, although the MVC programme was not primarily designed for this purpose, the vector facility provided in the MVC compiler appeared from the *MVC Manual* to allow us to address the same question to a whole series of sub-cases (i.e. individual members of a household) but not necessarily to all of them. This part of the compiler had regrettably not been fully used before and had never been properly tested. The attempt to run our complete specification revealed that the compiler was, in effect, faulty and was incapable of handing what are described as 'unknowns.'[27] If, as in Gutman's study, each individual had occupied a complete card, and had been treated as a separate case, being put into a group later by reference to a household number, then no problems would have arisen as a result of the inability of the machine to ask the same questions of *different* people *within* a single case.

As vectors proved unusable, the specification had to be re-written so as to list the range of possible answers to each question for every possible member of the household. All known values have had to be distinguished from the unknown so that, for any household, only the people actually recorded there would be noted by the computer, and households with unknown values would *not* be thrown out. It has also been necessary to

[27] The vector facility was used satisfactorily by Peter Willmott on his town expansion studies (Note 18 on p. 92) but, being a straightforward survey project, it involved no 'unknowns'. 'Unknowns' occur because not all of the 38 possible members of a household actually live in any one household. The computer, using the vector system, rejected the whole case or household if there were any unknowns, i.e. in virtually every case.

use a combination of derived binary and derived numerical statements in the programme specification to permit the various groups of people which interested us to be counted. Thus, derived functions enabled us to get the number of male or female servants, the number of married males, bachelors and spinsters (unmarried men and women over 15), income earners, numbers of males and females, dependants of family head, mobility of family $\left(\text{defined as the } \dfrac{\text{number of children}}{\text{number of moves}}\right)$, and age groups (both of the total populations and a special further breakdown for children).

The final version of the programme, *sans* vectors, has come to be very much longer and more complex than we had bargained for because not only does each person have to be separately specified for each question but many of the tables have to be repeated for each person in a given category, e.g., lodgers, servants, relatives. This means that many raw tables have to be consolidated manually after the computer has finished its task. Writing and re-writing the programme took well over six months in an attempt to discover the capabilities of the compiler. The bulk of the effort required so far in getting the specification into a form which the computer would accept will not have to be done again, and the version that has now been made to work satisfactorily, with minor deficiencies, is available for processing census data for other places. If the project on which it is to be used requires exactly the same number of categories in the various classifications all that need be done in adopting it is to assign new names to them; otherwise it may be necessary to modify the specifications to a certain extent, or to leave some of its capacity unused, i.e. left as 'unknowns'.[28]

The rest of this paper is concerned with the unspectacular but crucial problems of classification and sampling of the census data.

As with the York study, we decided to take a systematic sample of the whole population by counting each nth household for each census from 1841 to 1901, a period during which the total population of Camberwell

[28] As we prepare this paper for the press, we hear that the vector facility has in the end been made to work satisfactorily and we shall be going over to a slightly revised version of our original programme for the rest of the project covering the topographical sampling of the area, the systematic sampling having virtually just been completed. Anyone contemplating using MVC for comparable work is welcome to get into touch with us and to have a copy of the full specification. It will save them much trouble. We are bound to say, however, that the specification which we hammered out last year and which is now producing valuable results is already becoming obsolete, its clumsy apparatus superseded by streamlined devices like DATA-TEXT, as described above. *Sic transit gloria mundi!*

increased from 40,000 to 260,000 approximately; the rate of intercensal increase declined slightly from the decade ending in 1841 to that ending in 1861, but then markedly accelerated, reaching its peak in 1871–81 (68 per cent), before falling sharply to the last decade of the century. With a very much larger and more homogeneous population to handle than in the York study, we felt we could safely reduce the size of the sample while keeping to a 95 per cent confidence level. Tests on an initial sample of 40 households and on published data for Camberwell indicated that a sample for 1871 of 631 households, or every thirtieth, which covered in fact just over 3 per cent of the total, would be large enough. We wanted to make the fullest use we could of the capacity of the computer to handle a much more detailed classification faster than was possible with a card-sorting machine and to carry out various statistical operations on the data. It must be recognised of course, that any classification of this kind involves some loss because it reduces the richness of detail in the census books to a limited number of categories; the Armstrong classification of industrial occupations was divided into five categories and birthplaces into six. By contrast Gutman's programme, using one 80-column card for each member of the household, makes it possible to use 34 major categories of industrial occupation and to divide each of these into sub-categories and sub-sub-categories; similarly there are 200 general birthplace categories divided into sub-areas. Needless to say, a project on this scale involves a large research staff and we had already limited our own scope more severely before we heard of it.

A second stage in the project is to select not more than a dozen small areas—single streets or groups of houses—in which to study the whole population in up to a hundred or more households. The object here is to study the way in which various types of districts were occupied by successive generations and classes. Apart from the intrinsic fascination of watching a succession of people take possession of premises in a neighbourhood which had not been developed for them, we thought that this topographical sampling of a large area offered two opportunities. One was to check the results of the systematic sampling, and the other to trace quite precisely the influence which various features of suburbia have had on the structure of suburban society: the proximity and convenience of transport to work; nearness to shops, schools and other family facilities; the moderating influences of open spaces, superior or inferior housing nearby, factories, public houses, churches and chapels; and so on. All suburbs are more or less volatile in their response to what sometimes seem to be quite trivial innovations, and we hope that in studying some streets over long periods, others for short ones, against a variety of circumstances, we shall learn more of the unrecorded history of otherwise unremarkable communities. Towns do have to be tackled on the microscopic as well as on the macroscopic scale.

It is not necessary in a paper of this kind to go very far into details of programming and coding but some general information about the manner in which we are handling the data does seem important. Our classification of each household extends to 400 columns (five standard cards), and this permits us to treat in sufficient detail the data relating to household head, wife, up to 12 children, 6 relatives, 10 lodgers, 6 servants, and 2 visitors; a maximum of 38 persons per household. These are not all treated identically. Every occupant has entries for age, occupation, and birthplace, though servants' occupations are classified in terms of household duties instead of the general categories. Heads, relatives, lodgers, and servants also have an entry describing their marital status. The relationship to the head of the household is given for relatives. Finally, an entry is made for the social group of the household head according to Armstrong's classification.[29] The programme allows for 21 occupational groups,[30] 36 birthplaces,[31] 12 industrial groups,[32] and 6 marital statuses;[33] there are also 12 possible relationships of relatives to the head of the household,[34] and 12 occupations for servants,[35] plus the column for Armstrong's 6 social classifications of family heads.

The divisions between households are usually clear enough from the enumerators' books.[36] In most households the head is marked as such, or the division may easily be deduced. For instance, the first person in the household might be listed as 'wife' and in the occupation column the entry might be 'supported by husband who is away' or simply 'husband away'. The convention adopted by enumerators of drawing double slanted lines (\\\\) at the end of each household continued throughout the period. Most households consisted of one family only, or perhaps one family plus relatives or lodgers. If there were servants or lodgers the convention was to divide them from the family by a single slanted line (\\). Although the enumerators' books are numbered by household some enumerators counted by addresses, some by number of household heads, and some by reference to both heads and lodgers.

There are two problems here. One is to overcome the varying practice of enumerators in discriminating between lodgers (belonging to the household of a family to which they were not related) and either tenants or independent households at the same address. There is, of course, no way of neutralising outright errors in the entries themselves but it is all too easy to increase them in the sampling process.

To ensure uniformity we decided that instead of simply taking, say,

29 A note on the sub-division in Class III is included under the discussion on p. 147. It is useful here to show the correspondence between the two classifications in the following sample drawn from the 1871 data:

Occupations of Household Heads in Camberwell 1871
(3 per cent sample)

Armstrong*		Dyos and Baker		
Class I				
Capitalists, manufacturers, professional classes, etc.	12	Managerial	8 ⎱	21
		Professional	13 ⎰	
Class II				
Small shopkeepers, lower professionals, etc.	83	Sub-managerial	40 ⎱	60
		Sub-professional	20 ⎰	
Class III				
Skilled labourers (including shop-keepers who do not employ others)	398	Petty entrepreneurial	106 ⎫	
		Clerical	61 ⎬ 332	
		Skilled labourers	165 ⎭	421
		† ⎰ Farm owners and workers	9 ⎫	
		Private and rentier income recipients	16 ⎬ 89	
		Retired and annuitants	28	
		Unemployed	3	
		⎱ Undeclared	33 ⎭	
Class IV				
Semi-skilled labourers	72	Semi-skilled workers	48	
Class V				
Unskilled labourers	44‡	Unskilled workers	54 ⎱	81
		Domestic servants	27 ⎰	
Class VI				
Housewives, spinsters, retired	19	Undeclared	33 ⎫	
		Retired or annuitants	28 ⎬	64
		Unemployed	3 ⎭	

* Based on the Registrar General's classification.

† Some part of each of these groups would fall into Group III; a retired person's former job or an undeclared widow's children's jobs may put them into Class III. Some part of each of these may belong to each of Armstrong's groups, especially Group III. There is no way of identifying exactly how many people in these categories fit into any particular Armstrong group.

‡ The discrepancy between a skilled and semi-skilled worker and Groups IV and V is probably due largely to the treatment of laundresses, charwomen, and other jobs poorer widows engaged in.

30 Managerial, professional, sub-professional, sub-managerial, petty entrepreneurial, clerical, agricultural self-employed, agricultural labourer, skilled labourer, semi-skilled labourer, unskilled labourer, private income recipient, rentier income recipient, retired, annuitant, unemployed, domestic, scholar, apprentice, undeclared, small child.

31 Camberwell, Peckham, Dulwich, St. George, Hampstead or Marylebone, St. Pancras or Paddington, Islington, Hackney, Poplar or Stepney, St. George in the East or Mile End Old Town, Bethnal Green or Whitechapel, Shoreditch, City, Holborn or St. Giles or Strand or Westminster, St. George Hanover Square, Chelsea or Kensington, Wandsworth, Lambeth, Southwark, Greenwich, Lewisham, Woolwich, Middlesex, Kent, Surrey, Sussex, Southwest, Southeast, Essex, Midlands or East Anglia, North Wales, Scotland, Ireland, Commonwealth, other countries.

each thirtieth entry we would distinguish households by reference to persons marked as head, or whatever term was used in its stead. This meant in practice counting each household separately wherever two or more of them were listed at the same address; lodgers or boarders were not treated as separate households of course. In a few cases pencilled notes in the census books gave supplementary information on this point, indicating that where several families were sharing a house each paid rent to an agent who collected it from the entire tenement. Even where no notes of this kind were made there is no reason to believe that the first household head listed at the address collected rent from the other heads living there, and households sharing the same address have therefore been treated as separate households.

The second problem to arise in classifying lodgers is more fundamental. When is a lodger not a lodger? Presumably, the acid test is whether the occupant in question takes meals with a given household and pays for the accommodation provided. Naturally this cannot be discovered from the enumerators' books, and there is the probability that some lodgers will have been entered as heads, and vice-versa. However, we have felt compelled to interpret the entries literally and in doing so have diverged from Armstrong's practice of taking the first person listed at a given address as the head of the household and treating all other occupants who are not relatives, servants, or visitors simply as lodgers. In our opinion Armstrong may be slightly inflating his count of lodgers and we slightly underestimating ours. Whatever may have been the extent to which addresses were shared in York in the 1840s, it is important to recognise that the practice tended to increase wherever the growth of suburbs was so rapid as to cause the middle classes to leave behind them relatively large houses which could be taken over and sub-divided by the working classes. This tendency helped, for example, to produce the situation in Camberwell in 1891—which makes a specially interesting case as containing the largest

[32] Agriculture, heavy manufacturing, light manufacturing, construction, transport and communication, distributive trades, gas and water, financial and professional, services, other services, government, armed forces, other or not specified.

[33] Married male, bachelor, widower, married female, spinster, widow.

[34] Mother, father, sister, brother, sister-in-law, brother-in-law, daughter-in-law, son-in-law, niece, nephew, grandchild, others.

[35] General servant, maid, nurse, governess, coachman or stableboy, gardener, cook, butler, others.

[36] It is unnecessary to describe their contents in detail as this has already been done very clearly by W. A. Armstrong in his paper, 'Social Structure from the Early Census Returns' in *An Introduction to English Historical Demography*, ed. E. A. Wrigley (1966), pp. 209–37. His thesis, *The Social Structure of York, 1841–51: An Essay in Quantitative History*, unpublished Ph.D. thesis, University of Birmingham, 1967, gives the complete picture.

proportion of Booth's 'central and comfortable working class' of any Registration District in London (72·5 per cent)[37]—in which about 70 per cent of all the addresses were shared.[38]

Three sources of ambiguity are step-children, shop assistants or apprentices living in the household, and servants' children. Step-children are being coded as children, partly because there probably were many more of them than are recorded as such and many parents appear to have listed them simply as 'children'. If an assistant in a shop owned or run by the household head or an apprentice to the head lived in the household he is treated as a lodger, whether the household schedule lists him as lodger or servant. Any servant's children living in the household are recorded as lodgers rather than servants unless there is some indication that they too were acting as servants in the house. In most cases children of servants were very young and are clearly to be regarded as lodgers, not as servants themselves.

It might have been possible for our occupational groups to follow those in the Registrar General's 1911 classified list of occupations or the list used for the 1851 and subsequent censuses.[39] The Registrar General's classification is, of course, by industry and all ranges of skill within an industry are included in any particular group, so it was necessary to make changes. We would have had to add some occupations which would have applied more specifically to children, but at the same time we could have eliminated some of the categories which would not apply to a suburb such as Camberwell. However, we thought we could make even finer distinctions in the data by including both an industrial and an occupational breakdown. Our industrial groups are rather similar to those of the Registrar General, though rather less precise because we could allow only twelve possible groups, or one column on a punched card. From these groups we hope to reconstruct the changing industrial structure of Camberwell and to show the inter-relations between changing industries and changing neighbourhoods.

The data in the census books cannot, of course, be used directly to determine social status. For example, one head of a household may describe himself as a carpenter and joiner, live in one of the better parts of Camberwell, and keep a servant or two; another, identically described,

[37] Charles Booth, 'Life and Labour of the People in London: First Results of an Inquiry based on the 1891 Census', *Journ. Roy. Stat. Soc.* lvi (1893), pp. 592–3.

[38] Based on our systematic sample for 1891. We have reason to think that this proportion of shared addresses may have risen quite sharply over the preceding decade or two.

[39] See Census of England and Wales, 1911, *Parl. Papers*, 1915 [Cd. 7660]; Charles Booth, 'Occupations of the people of the United Kingdom, 1801–81', *Journ. Roy. Stat. Soc.* xlix, (1886), pp. 314–435.

may live in the worst of slums with a large family in one or two rooms. It is clear that the two do not belong to the same social class, though in order to be consistent we must take the entries in the census books at their face value and must therefore enter both as 'skilled labourers'. It is quite possible that as the household schedules were originally filled in by someone living there some of them were embellished, but there is no way of checking this. Any real differences between similar entries—in terms perhaps of both degrees of skill and social status—cannot be shown from isolated entries taken from the census books alone. It is possible that the only valid way of judging social class from census returns is by looking at the whole neighbourhood and the kinds of jobs and households to be found all along the street. This is one reason for the hundred per cent 'topographical' sampling which we shall be doing. Even this procedure has to be followed very cautiously because some neighbourhoods appear to have been genuinely heterogeneous. It is also quite possible—especially in a rapidly growing suburb—for one or two families to be living among people of entirely different social status.

However, the census books do give invaluable data on the occupational structure of an area, and we hope that the occupational breakdown we are using will pick up as much information on the matter as can possibly be gathered from them. Booth was able to compare wage data from independent sources with the occupations listed in the 1891 census to determine social status for different groups in various parts of London.[40] In addition, he used information on the number of rooms per family collected in that and later censuses. Since this latter information was not available before 1891 and because we do not have any wage data for Camberwell for most of the period covered by this study it is impossible for us to learn much about social standing from these sources. The brief notes which now follow explain some of the salient features of the occupational and industrial groupings and of the birthplace classification.

Managerial and professional represent people 'at the top', merchants, large landowners, lawyers, doctors, and so on, but also including owners and/or managers of businesses employing at least five people. The occupation column sometimes gives sufficient evidence of managerial or professional status by including the figures of the numbers of workpeople employed (though we are inclined to distrust this information to some extent), and the household structure and address is also suggestive. Thus it was not uncommon for families quite far down the social scale in Camberwell to keep a general servant or two, at least before the 1880s; but

[40] Charles Booth, 'First results of an inquiry based on the 1891 census', *Journ. Roy. Stat. Soc.*. lvi (December 1893), pp. 557–93.

only a family of very high social rank would have had a large retinue of servants with clearly defined positions, from nurse or cook to coachman or stableboy. We take male servants and governesses as indications of high social class.

Sub-managerial comprises employees holding some responsible job, such as head clerk, police sergeant, or some kind of supervisor. In common with *sub-professional*—e.g., teachers, nonconformist ministers, auctioneers —these occupations normally involved some years of training or formal education or both, and their job description indicates that they were in some ways above the mass of employees. Although they may have been more apt to keep their children in school and to have had a servant or two, sub-managerial and sub-professional people may have differed little in their mode of living—to judge from the census books—from the next category.

Petty entrepreneurs, *clerks*, and *skilled labourers* seem to have comprised a fairly homogeneous class so far as their mode of living went. Some had a servant or two; others took lodgers; but most of these families had no-one else living with them, except perhaps for occasional relatives. Petty entrepreneurial includes anyone having a shop that gave employment to fewer than five persons; newsvendors, pedlars, rag collectors, and hawkers are not included since they had no establishment, however mean. People engaged in personal services, such as hairdressing or in shop industries like tailoring and millinery, are only classed as petty entrepreneurial if they appear to have run or owned the shop, a distinction seldom easy to make from the census books. Shop assistants make an extremely diverse group, which is very difficult to classify from the data given: for the most part they belong firmly enough to this general class, though there seem to have been some large differences in standing according to trade, and function in the shop. In classifying them with petty entrepreneurs we may have overrated them as a class to a slight extent. We have not attempted to sub-divide clerks, except to include any supervisory job under sub-managerial.

Agricultural self-employed and *agricultural labourers* were not always so sharply different in social status as might appear, though landowners operating on a very small scale were still superior socially to the men they employed. Market gardeners are assumed to have been labourers rather than self-employed persons unless there is evidence to the contrary: such people mostly lived in very poor neighbourhoods and apparently very meanly. 'Farmer' is a rare entry and is taken to mean self-employed.

Skilled, *semi-skilled*, and *unskilled labourer* correspond almost exactly to Armstrong's (viz. the Registrar General's) classification, but for the exclusion of clerks and petty entrepreneurs, and laundresses, ironers, grooms, maids, etc. who are included under our category of domestic servants.

Private income recipients may be distinguished theoretically from *rentier income recipients*. Many of the former were women or older people, often living alone, or in small households; the majority in both groups lived quite modestly. Some people listed themselves as drawing an income from property and we could have wished for the kind of detail available in the American census in order to distinguish from the altogether more substantial landlords those who had bought or built a few houses along a street and lived in one of them.

A distinction has been made between people listed as *retired* and as *annuitants* because the latter were receiving some pension, often associated with former, middle-class employment. Retired people sometimes listed their previous occupations; but not so the annuitants.

Unemployed is used only for those so declaring themselves but anyone who also gives an occupation is listed under it. Few persons did enter themselves in this way, and some that did so added that they were on parish relief.

Domestic servant applies to servants not living in their employer's household but living out and who give their occupation as servant. It also includes charwomen, and laundresses not working in a laundry.

Undeclared is a huge group, mostly of wives who are assumed to have stayed at home and acted as housewives. Anyone who gave no information or declared himself to have had no occupation is entered here. Children of school age stating no occupation are assumed to have been at home, receiving no education. Female heads of families with no occupation were often supported by husbands living elsewhere: we attributed social class according to husbands' occupations, if given, but wherever the wife was said to be supported by the absent husband she is coded as a private income recipient. A single or widowed woman who lists herself as a 'gentlewoman' is also put into the private income recipient group on the assumption that she must have some unstated income.

Children were 'undeclared', 'scholar', 'apprentice', or 'small child' unless they were old enough to have had one of the occupations listed above. They were listed as 'small child' if less than six years old, except for those recorded as 'scholar'.

The classification of industrial groups presents few problems. *Agriculture* in Camberwell consisted mostly of market gardening and employed few people during most of the period 1841–1901; there were also some cow-keepers. Apart from a few machine shops employing such trades as boiler-makers, or iron and steel workers, Camberwell had little *heavy manufacture*. *Light manufacturing* was the main source of industrial employment. Anyone making anything not classified under heavy manufacturing and not primarily engaged in selling it is listed under this heading rather than that of the distributive trades. Any employment involving the handling or sale of food is normally put under *distributive trades*, while anything related more directly to manufacture, from tailoring to wheelwrighting, goes under light manufacturing. *Construction* includes joinery and carpentry, painting, bricklaying, and all other builders' trades, which made a numerous class down to 1890 or so.

Little need be said about birthplaces. As one of the major objects of this study is to track intra-metropolitan migration, we are giving 22 of the birthplaces divisions to London alone. Boundaries are taken as those existing in 1871. Entries giving 'London' only—fortunately rare in Camberwell as a whole, but somewhat high among relatively unskilled people—go into the City of London; those giving 'London, Surrey'— again exceptional—go into Southwark.

How far our classification and treatment of the variables revealed in the census books will allow us to go in analysing the social structure of Victorian Camberwell we simply cannot yet say. What we certainly hope to have done when the computer has done its work is to clarify with reasonable precision the main outlines of that structure and the ways in which it changed as Camberwell received and discharged three or four generations of inhabitants, became, remained, and began to abandon the rôle of, a suburb of the greatest city the world had yet known. What we shall not have done is to explain how that happened or to comment upon its significance. The importance of such quantitative results as we can amass will depend entirely on what may be inferred from them, either directly or in answer to the questions they will undoubtedly raise. We shall simply have given this part of the evidence about the experience of living in Camberwell at any time during these 60 years a new shape, and it will then be necessary to bring to bear upon it every other kind of historical evidence that is relevant to the questions we are asking. Professor Aydelotte put this particularly well when he wrote 'Quantitative techniques . . . are nothing more than a means of deploying the evidence. . . . Once this subordinate and ancillary work has been done, however, the basic problems of historical interpretation still remain to be dealt with.'[41]

---

[41] *Loc. cit.*, p. 824.

On the more general point to which this paper has been addressed, we think there can be little doubt that computers are likely to prove extremely useful for historical research of the type we have been describing. We hope in any case that the specification we have now hammered out—or at any rate the approach through computers—may be used by others to establish a widespread basis for authentic census comparisons with other places. Yet it is already clear that the first steps in researching into these possibilities cannot be made without a good deal of frustration, and that the biggest computer in the world has not replaced the humble desk calculator, much less the card-sorter and the other well-tried facilities for statistical compution. There is a certain flexibility and simplicity in the more primitive methods which will cause them to be kept in use even in association with a project requiring a computer. Despite the incredible speed at which the computer itself does its work and every conceivable effort being made by its operators to give its users the last ounce of help, delays almost inevitably creep into the running of a project of this kind. The census-takers are themselves now using computers, of course, and a large proportion of the census data of the twentieth century is already in a form which fits it for ready computerising by historians when they get the chance. We think the possibilities now opening up are of the greatest value.

A NOTE ON STATISTICAL METHODS

Ideally, whenever a sample is used it should be possible to check the results against information known to be true for the subject of the inquiry as a whole. Thus, when samples are taken from enumerators' books for an entire Registration District, such as York, they may be checked against the published results in the census tabulations that pertain exclusively to all York households. The statistical testing of such samples—which is described in any introduction to statistics—is a means of indicating the range around the totals as published in the census volumes into which the sample proportions or answers must fall to be considered correct at a pre-determined level of accuracy.

Overall figures are not given individually in the census returns for every Registration District, as they are for the principal towns, and there are very few returns of any kind published for Camberwell separately and even fewer in sufficient detail or of the right kind to serve as a check on the sample. The practice varied to some extent in different censuses but the prevailing tendency was to lump the London figures in such a way that the figures for Camberwell cannot usually be abstracted. Down to 1911 there are separate Camberwell figures for total population, sex distribution, and some occupational data, though these are classified quite differently from ours; there are also birth and death rates in the decennial supplements to the Registrar General's reports. There has therefore been a limit to the application of the sort of tests used by Armstrong in our sampling of the data for Camberwell. For this reason the sample had to be made large enough for the results to approximate sufficiently closely to the distribution of occupations, birthplaces, etc. as to justify at least 95 per cent confidence in them. It was equally important for other reasons that the sample should be the minimum size that would give the desired level of confidence in the results.

Few statistical treatises give much help in determining sample size, though they do give numerous tests of accuracy of the samples once taken. Not knowing how large to make the sample before coding the data is a serious drawback in research of this type because months of coding could end in the discovery that the sample is not large enough. It is possible to determine the necessary sample size by deciding on the desired confidence level when the population size is known, as it is from the published census returns. For this purpose the formula to be used is

$$n = \frac{N}{1 + Ne^2}$$

where e is the level of error to be permitted and N is population size. We used a permissible level of error of 0·05 but rounded upwards in deciding how many households to include, so that our error is actually somewhat less (though more than 0·03). This test involves the use of the binomial distribution and should strictly speaking be used only in determining the sample size when one wants to know the proportion of the population having certain attributes; it should not be used for more general purposes as the *sole* indication of sample size![42]

To help determine the optimum sample size for the 1871 census we took an initial sample of 40 households. Tests were made on such relationships as mean ages in various occupations, the proportion of children of heads in different occupations in school, and the relationship between family size and the head's occupation. These showed that the sample should include slightly more than 2,000 people out of a total population of 111,000. In the event we took a sample of every thirtieth household, and included over 3,000 people. For 1851 and 1861 we took a 10 per cent sample, though a smaller one would probably have been all right for

[42] See Taro Yamane, *Statistics: An Introductory Analysis* (1964), pp. 547 *et seq.*

1861. For the 1881 to 1901 censuses we took a sample of one household in fifty. The following table summarises the various details:

	1851	1861	1871	1881	1891	1901
Households in sample	1,091	1,338	631	730	924	1,139
Persons in sample	5,097	6,357	3,052	3,653	4,482	4,693
Total population	54,667	71,488	111,306	186,560	235,344	259,339

Although it might have been possible to have had fewer households included in the later censuses, a less complete coverage might have introduced a bias toward the most common type of household. The count of each *n*th household might then have missed pockets of very well-to-do people and possibly even larger pockets of the very poor. Checks against the 1871 returns indicated that a sample of one in fifty over the larger population in the later censuses would have just as comprehensive a distribution as 1871, if not better. Checks like these do depend on the assumption that Camberwell did not change its social structure enough over any decade to invalidate such a procedure, and we felt there was sufficient independent evidence on this point to be satisfied that samples drawn in this way would not be biased.

After the sample data have been processed and tabulated by the computer, very extensive further work has to be done to evaluate the results. First, the tables need to be examined to see whether what they are saying has any meaning or relevance in the context of the current study, because it is possible that there can be a strong relationship statistically between variables where in fact any such relationship is meaningless. We have found that the tables coming raw from the computer do not always indicate very much of interest, but if they are combined, or if some of the variables are judiciously added together, more meaningful patterns and results appear. The most crucial operation in processing these results involves applying tests to see if the differences and similarities between the variables are statistically significant, and, even more important, whether these hold for intercensal comparisons.

There are several tests of significance of difference which are useful, depending upon the exact problem involved, and the form in which the data is returned from the computer. Moroney sets these out in some detail.[43] When the computer has given the mean and standard deviation of several variables it is possible to find that the difference between them is significant by looking at the ratios of the standard deviations to the number involved in each case (or, as it is called technically, the standard error of the difference: σ^2/n). For our purpose if the difference comes to more than two standard errors it is considered significant. In this case the variance is

$$(\bar{x}_1 - \bar{x}_2) = \frac{\sigma^2}{n_1} + \frac{\sigma^2}{n_2}$$

where x represents the mean, σ^2 the standard deviations, and n the number of people in each group.[44] This is the method we have used, for example, to discover whether the average age of those in a particular occupation is significantly higher or lower than in others. This test is valid only where large numbers are involved (i.e. over 30).

We have used a different test to discover whether or not the difference between two proportions is statistically significant. In the case, for instance, where there are figures for the numbers of clerks and skilled labourers having relatives living with them and we wanted to know whether the proportion of either clerks or skilled labourers having relatives in the household was significantly different from the other, we have proceeded as follows. We start with the null hypothesis that the difference is insignificant and test by the use of formulae:[45]

$$p = \frac{x_1 + x_2}{n_1 + n_2} \qquad q = 1 - p \qquad \sigma = \sqrt{\frac{pq}{n_1} + \frac{pq}{n_2}}$$

where x_1 = number of clerks with relatives in the household;

x_2 = number of skilled labourers with relatives in the household;

n_1 = number of clerks in the sample;

n_2 = number of skilled labourers.

The results obtained from plugging the actual figures into the above formulae are then compared with the difference of the proportions:

$$\frac{x_1}{n_1} - \frac{x_2}{n_2}.$$

The X^2 test provided for by the MVC programme can only be applied to entire tables, as compiled by the computer, so that when we are interested in the degree of difference between some of the variables only in a table, it is necessary to do separate X^2 tests by hand. For this we use

[44] *Ibid.*, p. 220.
[45] *Ibid.*, pp. 222 *et seq.*

the procedure described in Moroney, Chap. XV. Intercensal X^2 tests can be useful, but since the data from different censuses cannot be processed at the same time it is necessary for us to make such tests ourselves.

The computer does correlations where applicable and the significance of these must be decided upon, although in most cases where we have used them the strength of the relationship tested has been clearly significant without any further analysis.

The Use of Town Plans in the Study of Urban History

M. R. G. Conzen

The idea of using town plans in the study of urban history is not new and in western Europe goes back at least to the beginning of the seventeenth century, when some publications combined historical information with town plans in bird's eye view or elevational views of towns. More generally, the histories of individual towns were embellished by plans from the early eighteenth century onward, but the scholarly use of town plans for historical purposes began only in the late nineteenth century and has become more systematic in aim and method in the twentieth. In this later phase the historical interpretation of town plans has no longer been the concern solely of the historian but has also claimed the interest of the geographer, the archaeologist or antiquarian, the architect and the town planner.[1] The resulting exchange of ideas has been of general benefit and

[1] The following random references in no way give a complete list of European work: L. Gomme, 'The story of London maps', *Geog. Jour.*, xxx, Nos. 5 and 6 (1908), pp. 489–509, 616–40. F. Haverfield, *Ancient Town Planning* (1913). T. F. Tout, 'Medieval town planning', *Bull. John Rylands Lib.*, iv (1917) (repr. Manchester, 1934). W. H. St. J. Hope, 'The ancient topography of Ludlow', *Archaeologia*, lxi (1909), pp. 383–9. W. Page, 'The origin and forms of Hertfordshire towns and villages', *Archaeologia*, xlix (1920), pp. 47–60. H. J. Fleure, 'Some types of cities in temperate Europe', *Geog. Rev.*, x (1920), pp. 357–74. H. J. Fleure, 'City morphology of Europe', *Journ. Roy. Inst. of Gt. Brit.* (1932). H. J. Fleure, 'The historic city in western and central Europe', *Bull. John Rylands Lib.*, xx (1936). F. R. Hiorns, *Town Building in History* (1956). M. R. G. Conzen, 'Alnwick, Northumberland: a study in town-plan analysis', *Trans. and Pap., Inst. Brit. Geog.*, No. 27 (1960). M. R. G. Conzen, 'The plan analysis of an English city centre', *Proc. I.G.U. Symp. in Urban Geography, Lund 1960* (Lund Stud. in Geog., Ser. B. Human Geog. No. 24, Lund, 1962), pp. 383–414. P. Lavedan, *Histoire de l'Urbanisme*, Vol. I: *Antiquité—Moyen Age*; Vol. II: *Renaissance et Temps Modernes* (Paris, 1926 and 1941). M. Poëte, *Une Vie de Cité: Paris de sa naissance à nos jours*, 4 vols. (Paris, 1924–31). M. Poëte, *Paris, son évolution créatrice* (Paris, 1941). F. L. Ganshof, *Etude sur le Dévéloppement des Villes entre Loire et Rhin au Moyen Age* (Brussels, 1943). E. Oberhummer, 'Der Stadtplan, seine Entwicklung und geographische Bedeutung', *Verhand. 6. Deutsch. Geog.-tag Nürnberg* (1907),

has given greater direction to the historian's effort in this matter, notably in Central Europe. It has led to the current international project for the publication of a Historical Atlas of Town Plans for Western Europe.[2] However, after some 60 years of this development it can hardly be said that our work has got much beyond the pioneer stage. In spite of a large if scattered body of studies of individual town plans and some comprehensive works surveying the historical development of town plans as a whole it is only recently that plan study is developing more penetrating methods and, backed particularly by our increasing knowledge of the origin and development of medieval urban communities, is beginning to form a more effective body of general concepts. It is not surprising then that, with some notable exceptions, urban historians in the past have not made more use of town plans for the elucidation of the history of towns where documentary evidence is absent or inconclusive, and have rarely been prepared to consider the significance of any local case in relation to a broader pattern of urban development. Moreover, specialised work in

pp. 66–101. P. J. Meier, 'Der Grundriss der deutschen Stadt des Mittelalters in seiner Bedeutung als geschichtliche Quelle', *Korr.-Bl. Gesamtver. der Deutsch. Gesch.- und Altertumsver.* lvii (1909), pp. 105–21. P. J. Meier, *Niedersächsischer Städteatlas*, 2 vols., Veröff. Hist. Kommission für Niedersachsen, Braunschweig und Hamburg (1926 and 1933). E. J. Siedler, *Märkischer Städtebau im Mittelalter* (Berlin, 1914). W. Geisler, *Die Deutsche Stadt, ein Beitrag zur Morphologie der Kulturlandschaft*, Forsch. z. Deutsch. Landes- und Volkskde, 22, 5 (Breslau, 1924). O. Leixner, *Der Stadtgrundriss und seine Entwicklung* (Vienna 1925). J. Gantner, *Grundformen der europäischen Stadt: Versuch eines historischen Aufbaues in Genealogien* (Vienna, 1928). H. Dörries, *Die Entstehung und Formenbildung der niedersächsischen Stadt*, Forsch. z. Deutsch. Landes- und Volksk, xxvii (1929). H. Louis, 'Die geographische Gliederung von Gross-Berlin', *Länderkundl. Forschungen* (Stuttgart, 1936), pp. 146–71. F. Rörig, 'Der Markt von Lübeck' in the same author's *Hansische Beiträge zur Deutschen Wirtschaftsgeschichte* (Breslau, 1928), pp. 40–106, and his *Wirtschaftskräfte im Mittlalter* (Cologne-Graz, 1959), pp. 36–133. H. Planitz, *Die deutsche Stadt im Mittelalter* (Cologne-Graz, 1954). H. Strahm, 'Zur Verfassungstopographie der mittelalterlichen Stadt mit besonderer Berücksichtigung des Gründungsplanes der Stadt Bern', *Zeitschr. f. Schweiz. Gesch.*, xxx (1950), pp. 372–410. F. Gorissen, *Kleve*, Niederrhein. Städteatlas, Klevische Städte, H.1. Kleve 1952. F. Gorissen, *Kalkar*, Niederrhein. Städteatlas, Klevische Städte, H.2 Kleve 1953. F. Gorissen, *Nimwegen*, Niederrhein. Städteatlas, Geldrische Städte, H.1. Kleve 1956. O. F. Timmermann, 'Grundriss und Altersschichten der Hansestadt Soest', *Spieker*, v (Münster i. W. 1954), pp. 19–57. Th. Mayer (ed.), *Studien zu den Anfängen des Europäischen Städtewesens* (Lindau-Constance, 1958). E. Keyser, *Städtegründungen und Städtebau in Nordwestdeutschland im Mittelalter, der Stadtgrundriss als Geschichtsquelle*, 2 vols., Forsch. z. Deutsch. Landeskunde 111 (Remagen, 1958). *Westermanns Atlas zur Weltgeschichte* (Brunswick, 1956), plates 79 and 82.

2 This project was initiated by a sub-committee set up by the International Congress of Historians in 1955 to promote the study of medieval towns. The British Section covers the British Isles and has been allotted space for some forty towns. Mrs. M. D. Lobel, Oxford, was made responsible and has obtained the support of a large number of historians and geographers. A working committee for this section was formed in 1964 under the chairmanship of the late Sir Ian Richmond. Its present chairman is Dr. W. A. Pantin, Oxford, and the hon. secretary and general editor is Mrs. Lobel. The publication of the first batch of plans is in hand.

plan interpretation has suffered from excessive restriction to the consideration of street systems and a neglect of other significant plan detail, particularly the pattern of land parcels or plots and of the arrangement of buildings. This in turn has often resulted in failure to recognise the frequent compositeness of town plans which can give a clue to distinct stages in town growth of which a defective historical record may give no hint. Admittedly these aspects of plan interpretation are not without pitfalls for the unwary and have to be handled with care, but urban history would gain greatly if its practitioners would study town plans as a matter of course and might gain the same expertise here as in the use of written records. Existing and old town plans can shed much light on the history of urban communities, their size and structure at different periods, their phases of development, their institutions and the relation between them and the urban community which they serve.

This brings us to the question of what a town plan is and what it contains. The term 'town plan' is to be preferred to the more indefinite 'town map' in accordance with the widely accepted, though not always consistently observed, conventional usage of the Ordnance Survey. Thus 'plans' are any 'large-scale' maps showing essential detail of layout in recognisable and measurable form. In the case of town plans and particularly for our purpose the test is provided by the block-plan of the individual building. The map scale of 1 : 5,000 emerges as the smallest scale at which this requirement can still be reasonably satisfied. It is internationally recognised as such and accordingly has been chosen as the most economical scale for the Historical Atlas of Town Plans. It also follows that most 'plans' published in the more reputable types of guide-books are not 'town plans' in the strict sense but merely street-plans even if they show the block-plans of important buildings. Satisfactory as they are for their purpose, they cannot be used for historical or geographical research.

The Ordnance Survey does not publish plans on the scale of 1 : 5,000 but its so-called 25-inch plans (exact scale 1 : 2,500), and its plans on the scales of 1 : 1,250 and 1 : 500 are all of great use because of their accuracy and detail. Moreover there are earlier, now obsolete, Ordnance Survey large-scale plans of certain towns which are equally good and are of the greatest importance to the urban historian in Britain as they generally take us back to the middle of the nineteenth century, i.e. to the beginning of the climax phase of the industrial revolution, and frequently show detail of considerable interest to the industrial and social historian.[3]

In the few decades before that, town plans were privately produced and

3 [J. B. Harley & C. B. Phillips], *The Historian's Guide to Ordnance Survey Maps*, published for the Standing Conference for Local History by the National Council of Social Service (1964).

published, though often for town corporations in the case of larger cities or for big landowners in the case of smaller towns. They varied in accuracy and general cartographic quality, but the best closely approached the excellence of Ordnance plans and this applies also to those published or else produced only in MS during the eighteenth century. At this earlier period, however, it is rarely that one finds town plans on anything like the large scales of the Ordnance Survey, and paradoxically many of the larger cities with more independent corporations appear to have been less associated with the production of high-quality large-scale plans than some smaller market towns where big landowners occasionally had good surveys done for their own purposes. Similar considerations apply to the production of town plans in the seventeenth and late sixteenth centuries except that the volume decreases greatly as we go back in time and so does the cartographic quality in terms of accuracy and the detail of plots and buildings, save in the case of a dozen or so of the most renowned cities.[4] Erection of the buildings in elevation on the otherwise relatively undistorted plans of this early period is the rule, giving a 'bird's eye view' rather than a topographical plan proper.

This draws attention to the essential contents of a town plan and its relation to the townscape as a whole. In the strict sense the term 'town plan' means the cartographic representation of a town's physical layout reduced to a predetermined scale but in the literature it has gradually come to denote also the physical layout itself. The town plan in this last sense is part of the townscape and one of its fundamental form categories, the other two being the building fabric and the pattern of land and building utilisation. All of these, recordable respectively in the form of the town plan, the distribution plan of urban building types and the distribution plan of urban land utilisation, are interrelated genetically and functionally. In that general sense then the whole townscape is of interest as a historical document. But its record is not straight-forward or merely cumulative. Rather is the townscape a kind of palimpsest on which the features contributed by any particular period may have been partly or wholly obliterated by those of a later one through the process of site succession or in some other way. Some of this effacement can be extensive as in the case of building replacement during periods of economic prosperity or nowadays in central redevelopment and slum clearance. Some proceeds in piecemeal fashion and might affect only detail such as individual street lines and plot boundaries. In the last case the essential traits even of a medieval layout may remain quite well preserved. Where

---

[4] R. V. Tooley, *Maps and Map-Makers* (1949), p. 67, lists English examples.

this is not so, archaeological methods can sometimes help greatly in the reconstruction of early layouts within existing built-up areas and the second world war has provided many opportunities in this respect.[5]

For the historian the record of the townscape is complicated by the differential time response of the three form categories to the changing functional requirements of the urban community. Town plan, and, to a less extent, building fabric are more conservative in this respect as they tend to reflect the pattern of past landownership and capital investment more tenaciously. Therefore they present a greater range and quantity of traditional forms, i.e. those from the Roman period to c. 1850, thus contributing considerably to the historical stratification of the townscape. Land utilisation responds more easily to changing functional impulses and therefore the historicity of its distribution pattern is often weak. From the townscape as a whole, then, the town plan emerges as the form category of greatest value to the historian.

As implied earlier, the town plan is not merely a street plan but covers the rest of the built-up area as well. It consists of three distinct complexes of plan elements: the streets and their mutual association in a street-system, the individual land parcels or plots and their aggregation in street-blocks with distinct plot patterns, and the buildings or more precisely their block-plans and the arrangement of these in the town plan as a whole.

In the townscape these complexes do not exist in isolation but are interconnected in the sense that each element conditions the others' origins, physical relations, and functional significance, not just at present but in historical time. Thus the earlier forms and those of more general functional significance, like street spaces, tend to act as morphological frames conditioning the genesis and growth of subsequent forms and are often modified by them in turn. In this way streets, plots and buildings integrate in space and time to form individualized combinations of a dynamic rather than a static nature, recognizable in the town plan as distinct plan units. These again combine to form the major plan divisions of a town. Recognition and comprehension of the whole plan structure in these terms forms the subject of town-plan analysis.[6] All these plan components are of historical significance as they indicate phases of urban growth sometimes little known or quite unsuspected from the available

[5] K. Nahrgang, *Die Frankfurter Altstadt*, Rhein-Main. Forsch. 27, Frankfurt. a. M. 1949. F. Engel, 'Stadtgeschichtsforschung mit archäologischen Methoden', *Blätter z. Deutsch. Landesgesch.*, lxxxviii (1951).
[6] A demonstration of the method of town-plan analysis can be found in Conzen, *Alnwick* and Conzen, *Plan Analysis of an English City Centre*.

records. They also exhibit characteristic period traits and therefore suggest or at the very least corroborate or negate conclusions about various aspects of the socio-economic life of urban communities in different historical periods.

Thus the question arises as to the period styles in town plans, in Britain from the tenth century onward, if we disregard the direct site influence of Roman town planning in a few cases. The broad period styles in Britain as in Europe are well known, dividing town plans of the middle ages (c. 900–1500) from those of early modern times (c. 1500–1850), the climax phase of the industrial revolution (c. 1850–1900), the 'garden city' period and its aftermath in the inter-war period (c. 1900–1940), and the post-war period. Most of post-medieval town-planning is also fairly well understood because of its better documentation and large amount of relatively unchanged plan survivals, which has attracted a far greater volume of studies.[7] These have gone a good way towards plan analysis against the background of the increasing knowledge of our social and economic history in modern times in such aspects as technological innovations and changes in industrial production, the development of urban landownership particularly in relation to housing, developments in the social structure of modern society, and the rise of social services and associated technical aspects such as public health and housing. As this historical knowledge increases there is a continuing need of re-assessment in plan analysis. Conversely historians can use the town plan with increasing advantage for their own purposes, and recent local history has shown promising beginnings in this respect. But perhaps one might hazard the suggestion that because of their particular training historians as a whole have not been specially plan-conscious in their work and local historians have sometimes been preoccupied with the peculiarities of the place they studied without considering its significance for the broader theme of urban development. To illustrate the point, the building congestion of our old town centres during the industrial revolution is a well-known phenomenon and has been shown to be of a cyclic nature with recognisable phases.[8] This industrial 'building repletion' of medieval strip plots or burgages began at various times from the mid-eighteenth to the early nineteenth century according to local circumstances, though in a few cities like London or Edinburgh it is superimposed over much earlier building congestion of a traditional kind. It came to a climax be-

[7] For types of plan layout characteristic of various periods of post-medieval town growth in Britain see Conzen, *Alnwick*, pp. 71–3, 85–8, 97–104, and Figs. 15 and 19.

[8] Conzen, *Alnwick*, pp. 92–5 and Fig. 14. Conzen, *Plan Analysis of an English City Centre*, pp. 400–2, and Figs. 13, 14, 15.

tween the cholera years of the 1840s and the first world war and has been terminated by modern slum clearance or central redevelopment of various types. Though these broad facts are well-established we need to know much more about the regional and local variations of this 'burgage cycle' in order to recognise the specific historical character of internal urban growth in different parts of the country.

In contrast to the modern period, British town planning in the medieval epoch, spanning some 600 years and accounting for the great majority of our town nuclei, is very imperfectly known in spite of scattered studies of individual cases. Yet medieval forms still abound in our urban environment and condition urban life even now. It is therefore proposed to discuss further the use of town plans in research on medieval urban history and to indicate how plan analysis might assist in cases where the historical record is far from complete. In this country the gap in our knowledge of medieval plans is great and calls for a methodical approach in which the investigation of any individual example should aim at establishing clearly what is unique and peculiar to the place and explicable only from local conditions, and what is of generic significance originating in general historical causes or in the activity of important planning agencies and therefore represents recurrent phenomena inviting comparative study. This would lead to the recognition of significant sub-divisions in the medieval planning history of this country and its characteristic regional variations. As it is we have no clear conception even of such basic facts as the national distribution pattern of medieval market places of different shapes, or of different types of medieval street systems.

Part of the difficulty with medieval town plans lies in their greater age, which has rendered them more liable to later piecemeal alterations of detail. On occasion these can swamp the original picture and at all times they tend to impart an air of irregularity to medieval plans which is deceptive. A good deal of the post-medieval changes can be eliminated, however, if reliable plans are available for the 1830s, 1840s, or 1850s.

Careful study of individual cases and of groups of medieval towns in various parts of Europe has rather discredited the opposition of 'irregular' versus 'regular' plans and the unhistorical equation of these with spontaneously grown or 'unplanned' and 'planned' towns. What has emerged from this work is a genealogy of medieval town plans in Europe and of their components such as market places and street systems. It has drawn attention to the wide-spread compositeness of medieval town plans, characteristically reflecting the corporate organisation of medieval society, and to the influence on planning of the different level of technology, e.g. in transport and in the use of power sources. Thus the characteristically adaptive attitude of the medieval town planner to the natural site of the town and his equally free and flexible, but consistent notion of urban form have become apparent. In both respects he was different from the Roman and from the Renaissance and modern planner.

To appreciate the technical aspect of this fully, medieval town plans should be studied in relation to the relief of their site, most conveniently in terms of a contour plan. Unfortunately, town plans do not contain contours nor do the large-scale plans of the Ordnance Survey. Though it is not ordinarily part of the historian's personal equipment to be able to construct a contour plan for any particular town, a pattern of generalised contours can be produced in a relatively simple way without instruments other than an ordinary scale by 'interpolation' from the spot heights on Ordnance plans. Such contours should be corrected as far as possible by reference to the contours at 25-ft. vertical interval shown on the 1 : 25,000 Ordnance Survey maps, by field observation of slopes, and by allowing for post-medieval artificial and other changes in relief as indicated, e.g. by relevant sewer data, or, more rarely by archaeological evidence.[9] The correlation of such a contour pattern to the superimposed street pattern reveals the skill with which the medieval planner used the natural site to solve a frequently complex planning problem.

Sometimes the planner was faced not only with the natural site but with pre-existing man-made features on it which he might have to consider in the design of the new town plan and which would thus be incorporated as inherited outlines. Such features could be ancient route-ways, field boundaries, or a pre-urban nucleus in the shape of an ecclesiastical complex, a castle or occasionally a village.[10] In a few cases there might be several such pre-urban nuclei.

The contrast between uni- and multi-nuclear origins of towns introduces the subject of the compositeness of medieval town plans and the modes of their growth. Here the recognition of distinct plan units is of great importance and can often illuminate the growth stages of a medieval town, especially earlier ones, when available written records fail to give any information. Such recognition depends on the careful scrutiny of plan detail such as the behaviour of street spaces and their bounding street lines, and the shape, size, orientation, and grouping of plots, all such evidence leading to the identification of the 'seams' along which the genetically significant plan units are knit together. Keyser has dealt with this subject in north-western Germany in some detail,[11] and historians in

9 For a contour plan constructed in this way see Conzen, *Alnwick*, Fig. 4 on p. 26.
10 Conzen, *Alnwick*, Chaps. 4 and 5.
11 Keyser, *op. cit.*, see also Conzen, *Alnwick*, Chap. 5.

Britain, fortunate in being able to avail themselves of the very accurate Ordnance Survey plans reaching back to the mid-nineteenth century, are in a position to apply and refine the method on a really large scale.

The pre-urban nucleus, recorded in many parts of Europe as *urbs* if fortified or otherwise enclosed, is frequently though not inevitably the first plan unit in the composite medieval town plan. The open traders' and craftsmen's settlement developing below its gate as a subsequent plan unit is similarly recorded as the *suburbium*. Generally this takes the shape of a street-market often in spindle- or wedge-shaped form conditioned by the convergence of routeways and bounded on either side by a series of narrow strip plots that emerge in later town records as *burgages*. The early example of St. Albans, long ago described by Page,[12] comes to mind as one of the hundreds of cases dotting the map of Britain at an average lowland distance of twelve to fifteen miles or less. If because of favourable geographical position and support by the feudal lord such a place flourished subsequently it developed into, and was usually enlarged as, a commercially more important borough with corresponding privileges. This normally entailed physical growth manifesting itself in the addition of further plan units, more often in more or less eccentric block-wise or cellular expansion but sometimes concentrically after the fashion of annular rings. As the whole development might stretch over several centuries changes in the complexity of planning problems and in planning experience caused significant changes in planning style. These are well known from the great planning laboratories of medieval Europe like the territories of the Counts of Zähringen, those of the east German colonisation or those of Edward I. But the full implications for the historical interpretation of medieval town plans in Britain have hardly been worked out, particularly the progression from the more primitive and archaic to the more advanced and sophisticated solutions. Thus the generally earlier, simpler plans with but one type of street contrast with later plans characterised by varying but recurrent combinations of streets and by the functional differentiation of major traffic streets, subsidiary traffic and residential streets and auxiliary access or occupation lanes.

In late and post-medieval times this outward or additive growth was often supplemented by internal, more transformative growth of which 'market colonisation', i.e. the partial and piecemeal building over of market places with houses, was the most common early form,[13] while building repletion in the form of the burgage cycle, building replacement

12 Page, *op. cit.*
13 Conzen, *Alnwick*, pp. 34–38.

on the burgage heads, transformation of the burgage pattern and finally redevelopment are more recent forms.[14]

Another kind of urban growth associated with medieval plans concerns their peripheral areas or 'fringe belts', ultimately becoming 'inner fringe belts' in cases where modern expansion has gone beyond them.[15] These zones begin and subsequently develop further as distinct belts of peripheral land utilisation associated with the outer back fence, back lane or town wall of a medieval town as their 'fixation line' which divides the zone into an intramural and an extramural part. Urban friaries are common intramural fringe-belt features in medieval towns and town ditches, archery butts, bridges, certain hospitals, chapels, inns, and water courses are equally characteristic for the extramural parts. Often there are also triangular road widenings just inside or outside medieval town gates which may survive as testimonials of the former town margin long after its structural indices such as back fence, town wall or gates have disappeared, as Keyser has shown. In this and many other ways the medieval town margin may leave tenacious traces in the modern town plan.

As the reconstruction of the layout of a medieval town from modern plans, exemplified in some detail in the case of Alnwick, has already been referred to, it may be of interest to end this paper with a brief outline interpretation of two different examples, Ludlow and Conway. The interpretation is of a purely preliminary nature based mainly on scrutiny of the modern Ordnance Survey plans (Figs. 1, 2 and 3). The reader will bear in mind that the recognition of plan units depends, among other things, very much on seeing street spaces, plots and buildings in correlation.

Ludlow is a good example of a composite plan, and earlier views about its unitary origin require considerable modification. Hope's interpretation, now nearly sixty years old,[16] assumes an uncompounded 'symmetrical plan' with streets of more or less equal widths combining to form something like a 'chess-board pattern'.[17] This view is untenable in the light of what plan analysis of the 25-inch O.S. map produces and of what we now know about medieval plans in general. Its methodological weakness lies in the failure to recognize the genetic significance of the different 'styles' of street shapes, the functional differentiation between medieval streets of different widths and plan significance and the fact that functionally and

[14] Conzen, *Plan Analysis of an English City Centre*, pp. 400–4, 412, and Figs. 13, 14, 15, 16.
[15] Conzen, *Alnwick*, pp. 39–41, 56–63, 80–2, and Fig. 13. Conzen, *Plan Analysis of an English City Centre*, pp. 404–8, 412, and Fig. 17.
[16] W. H. St. J. Hope, *op. cit.*
[17] P. D. Wood, 'Frontier relics in the Welsh border towns', *Geography*, xlvii (1962), p. 61.

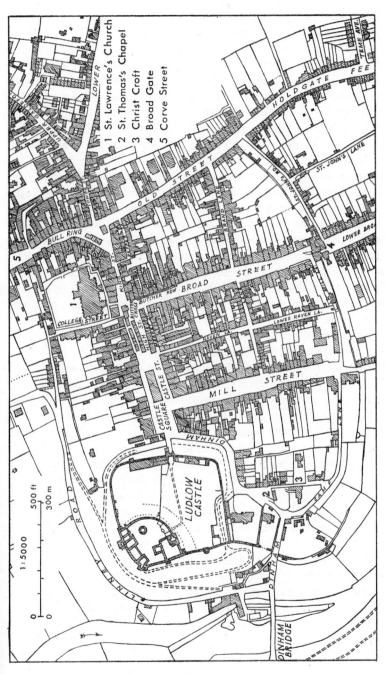

1 St. Lawrence's Church
2 St. Thomas's Chapel
3 Christ Croft
4 Broad Gate
5 Corve Street

FIG. 1. *Ludlow* (after 25″ Ordnance Survey 1926).

genetically street system and associated plot pattern belong together; they cannot be considered in isolation.

Within the line of the town wall Ludlow's medieval plan shows no less than five distinct plan units. The first two are the oldest and occupy the top of a WSW-ENE ridge conditioned by the asymmetrical and fault-accented structure of an underlying pitching anticline in Upper Ludlow and Downtonian rocks, and therefore having a short, steep northward slope and a long and more gentle southward slope to the River Teme. The plan units are: (1) the *castle* of 1086–95, enlarged by the 'outer bailey' in the later twelfth century on ground that may have formed part of the early village of Dinham and of the originally built-up urban area; (2) a northern plan unit occupying the top of the town ridge between the castle and the church and including the close grouping of small street spaces or the *street tract*, made up, *inter alia*, of Castle Square, Castle Street, *High Street*,[18] King Street and Pepper Street, together with the burgage series and church grounds between it and the wall and a few burgages fronting on to it on the south side; (3) an eastern plan unit merging into the last one and consisting of *Bull Ring* and *Old Street* and their burgage series; (4) a central and southern unit containing *Broad Street*, *Mill Street*, and their associated burgage series with internal back and cross lanes; and (5) a south-western plan unit consisting of *Dinham*, the western part of Camp Lane, Christ Croft and the plots associated with them.

Of these plan units the castle is the earliest, forming the pre-urban nucleus, the village of Dinham apparently having left no trace in the town plan. In terms of relation to the castle and favourable siting along the town ridge the High Street unit appears as the next oldest component in characteristic *suburbium* position as a generously dimensioned street market that may reflect a considerable livestock trade already in the twelfth century, i.e. in the first period of development of this border town. The unit included no doubt the church, at first a smaller building, probably facing the street market directly with its south side. The whole plan unit is likely to have had two equal burgage series originally, one on either side of the street market and uninterrupted by the subsequent cross streets. It suffered two alterations. An earlier one appears to be associated with the planned medieval southward extension of the town which, con-ceivably though somewhat unusually, defaced a considerable part of the southern burgage series in a re-orientation of plots towards the newly designed additional thoroughfares. A later change was more gradual and consisted of the *market colonisation* represented by eight narrow blocks on

18 Names in italics refer to those used in the key to Fig. 2.

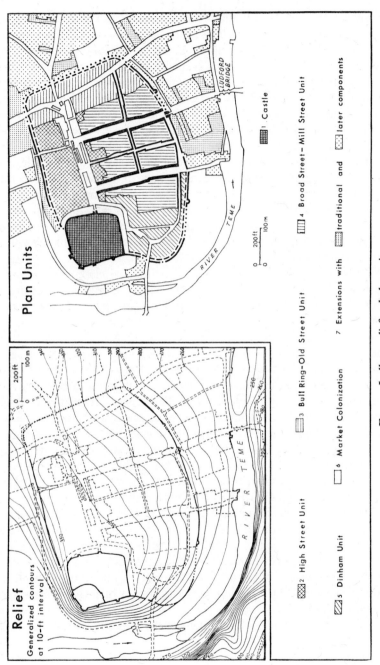

FIG. 2. *Ludlow: relief and plan units.*

the original street tract and a ninth block between Broad Street and Pepper Street that became attached to the eastern burgage series of Broad Street.

The Bull Ring-Old Street unit obtains its individuality from the marked convergence of informally shaped roads at the east end of King Street and from this appears to be contemporaneous with the High Street unit in its street system except that originally Upper and Lower Galdeford may have conceivably belonged to it and thus converged directly on the east end of King Street. Later their point of convergence would be displaced eastward when the town wall was built and Tower Street was constructed as the necessary intramural link. Corve Street outside the walls, Bull Ring, Old Street, Holdgate Fee, and an earlier ford across the Teme would represent the great regional routeway connecting the earlier suburbium of Ludlow with Shrewsbury and Hereford while Upper and Lower Galdeford gave access to Ludlow's fields and to the Austin Priory. The whole street system here would antedate the building up of the area and would therefore act as its morphological frame.

The Broad Street-Mill Street unit, though linked closely to the High Street unit, forms nevertheless a distinct plan unit with a very regular layout of functionally differentiated streets. It presents a *parallel-street system* in which Broad Street and Mill Street are major traffic and residential streets (*Verkehrsstrassen* or *carrières*, and *Wohnstrassen*) while Bell Lane, Silkmill Lane, Brand Lane, and Raven Lane provide subsidiary connections and back-fence or occupation lanes (*Wirtschaftsstrassen*) giving back access to the main-street burgages exactly as described for the French bastides of Edward I by Hudson Turner, the authority quoted by Hope.[19] This plan unit undoubtedly exhibits a more advanced style of planning catering for more developed functional needs. It is most unlikely to belong to the first period of Ludlow's growth but fits well into the thirteenth century with its general style and differentiated plan detail. In fact, it is more likely to be contemporaneous with or slightly earlier than the building of the town wall (late thirteenth century). It caused the main artery to the south to abandon its 'Old Street' and to be rerouted through Broad Street, Broad Gate and over the medieval Ludford Bridge. Hope suggests that peculiarities in the existing plot pattern in the interior of the street blocks east and west of this parallel-street system point to intended extensions of the unit on these sides. This seems plausible if we postulate occupation lanes in these places rather than the main streets visualised by him.

Finally, the Dinham unit abutting on the western one of the two

---

[19] Hope, *op. cit.*, pp. 387-8.

intended streets just discussed is the most difficult to interpret as the extension of the castle has evidently interfered with the original street layout and the present plot pattern is largely post-medieval. At all events this area, together with the outer bailey of the castle could have been the site of the early village of Dinham which preceded the castle and the town and was probably effaced by them unless the street layout immediately around the twelfth-century chapel of St. Thomas of Canterbury is original.

Ludlow's composite plan epitomizes much of medieval planning development and is instructive in its juxtaposition of pre-urban nucleus and early suburbium, its contrast of early street market and later regular street system with functional differentiation, its late and post-medieval market colonisation, and its incorporation of an earlier country road system as a set of inherited outlines acting as a morphological frame for the accommodation of additional burgages.

In contrast to Ludlow, Conway owes its medieval town plan to a single act of foundation in 1284 when it was constituted a free borough by Edward I in the manner of his other English *bastides* in Wales.[20] Yet, the plan is far from uniform. In its adaptation to an individual site and its structural differentiation in answer to a specific set of functional requirements it exhibits the distinctive quality of thirteenth-century town planning to perfection and is one of the finest examples in the country.

The site forms part of an eastward sloping plateau and occupies the acute angle between the lower Conway estuary and the flood plain of its tributary, the Afon Gyffin. At the tip of the angle a prominent and steep-sided rock knoll, consisting of the Conway Grits in the Bala division of Ordovician rocks and matched by a similar outcrop in the estuary nearby, presented the ideal site for the castle in terms of strategic requirements, defensive quality of site, and availability of reasonably flat land near it to allow for the attachment of a walled town as a kind of outer bailey to the castle. The only disadvantage was that the town site was already occupied by the Cistercian abbey of Aberconwy. However, Edward I caused the abbey to be removed to Maenan higher up the Conway valley and preserved its existing church to serve the new borough. As the new town was to be the regional focus for the Conway valley and the coast from Bangor to the mouth of the Clwyd, it had to be of sufficient size and contain at least a hundred burgages needing a total area of about 20 acres. The walled town actually contains approximately 21 acres and in 1311

[20] E. A. Lewis, *The Medieval Boroughs of Snowdonia* (1912). S. Toy, 'The town and castle of Conway', *Archaeologia*, lxxxvi (1936), pp. 163–93. W. G. Jones and Sir Cyril Fox, 'The castle and borough of Conway', *Arch. Camb.*, xcii (1937), pp. 365–7.

recorded 121¾ burgages. If the unrecorded size of these burgages was similar to that of the burgages at Caernarvon and Criccieth, i.e. 80 ft. × 60 ft., and the much altered plot pattern of Conway's plan vaguely suggests that, the burgages would have covered some 13½ acres leaving 7½ acres for streets, squares, public property, and non-burgage plots. Although such an area could have been entirely accommodated on the flat ground to the west of the castle with a more nearly north–south running west wall, this would have left part of the town dangerously overlooked by the high ground nearby and might have given a rather larger harbour area than was wanted. Instead, the siting of the town wall was determined by the location of the castle, the length of harbour front needed, the highest point to be included in the fortifications in the west, and the length of the flood plain along the Gyffin needed to use this defensive site feature to the best advantage. The result is the characteristic 'Welsh harp' shape of Conway's old town. The foundation of such a borough in recently conquered territory also required restriction of access to a minimum. The town had therefore only three gates, i.e. Porth Uchaf (Upper Gate) in the west receiving traffic from Gwynedd and the Conway valley, Porth Isaf (Lower Gate) admitting traffic from the port and the ferry and Porth y Felin (Mill Gate) giving access to the town mill on the Afon Gyffin. Only a postern, Porth Bâch (Little Gate) gave additional harbour access for the convenience of the castle.

Within the walls the chief requirements were rectangularity of burgages as far as possible, main-street or traffic location for the maximum number of burgages, provision of a market place in good site relation to main streets and gates, simplicity of street alignment for rapid surveying and laying out, proper connection of the castle with all parts of the town, and relative seclusion, yet accessibility, of the existing parish church. The present street system, containing modern additions in peripheral position only in the north-west of the borough and also near the castle, shows a masterly solution of this complex planning problem. Instead of connecting the two major traffic gates in an obvious but less satisfactory way by a single High Street in a straight line, a *staggered-parallel street system* was inserted between the two gates, thus more than doubling the amount of traffic-located frontage. It provided two main streets instead of one, each serving as a *feeder* from its own gate and connecting with the other by a number of traffic *distributaries*, the original market place, later extensively colonised by buildings, being one of these and extending towards the Mill Gate. Connection with the castle was effected by an additional *meridian street system* skilfully encompassing the pre-existing church in its central position. The parallel system no doubt accommodated commer-

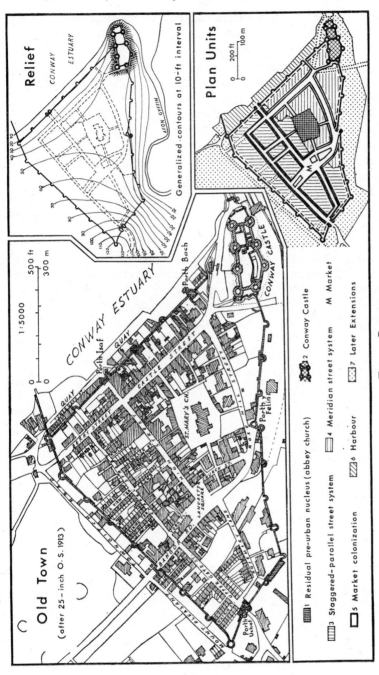

FIG. 3. *Conway.*

Relief

CONWAY ESTUARY

AFON GYFFIN

Generalized contours at 10-ft interval

Plan Units

0   100 m

0   200 ft

M

Old Town

(after 25 - inch O. S. 1913)

CONWAY ESTUARY

Porth Bach

Porth Isaf

QUAY

QUAY

CASTLE STREET

ST. MARY'S CH.

HIGH STREET

LANCASTER SQUARE

Porth Felin

Porth Uchaf

CONWAY CASTLE

1:5000

0   300 m

0   500 ft

1 Residual pre-urban nucleus (abbey church)

2 Conway Castle

3 Staggered-parallel street system

4 Meridian street system

M Market

5 Market colonization

6 Harbour

7 Later Extensions

cially valuable burgage land while some of the meridian system, even now characterised by relatively large plots, will have contained the holdings of royal retainers and of service population connected with the castle. The only other street spaces were minor occupation lanes and paths giving access to the church and including originally probably a continuous wall street.

The medieval method of solving complex planning problems by a combination of more than one plan idea in skilful adaptation to site conditions has had a history not only in the town planning of Edward I's French possessions but also elsewhere in medieval Europe. The colonisation of the East German lands provides perhaps the closest analogy to the Welsh *bastides*.[21] Sommerfeld in Lower Lusatia (founded 1210, now Lubsko in western Poland) provides indeed an almost exact analogy to Conway.

In modern times road improvements, though breaching the town wall in four places, and the coming of the railway, have not succeeded in destroying the unity of Conway Old Town as expressed by its magnificent fortifications and its medieval street system.

Perhaps the introduction of these two examples will stimulate the curiosity of local and urban historians and cause them to approach with more systematic interest the many hundreds of medieval town plans in Britain, to say nothing of the even greater volume of post-medieval plans.

[21] Cf. Siedler, *op. cit.*

Sources and Methods used for the Survey of London

F. H. W. Sheppard

HISTORY OF THE SURVEY OF LONDON

In 1894 C. R. Ashbee, a young architect prominent in the Arts and Crafts movement in the East End of London, was enraged at the demolition of the Old Palace of Bromley-by-Bow, a Jacobean country house which had been acquired by the London School Board. At that time London was expanding eastward very rapidly, and many fine old buildings were being destroyed. Ashbee decided to form a committee of volunteers for the purpose of listing and recording all such buildings within 20 miles of Aldgate.

Two years later the London County Council interested itself in the work of Ashbee's London Survey Committee. The area to be covered was extended to include the whole of the then County of London, and the LCC agreed to pay the cost of printing the Committee's lists or registers. The Committee soon found that it had embarked upon a much bigger task than Ashbee had originally envisaged, and the first volume described the monuments of only one parish—Bromley-by-Bow. It was published in 1900; the cost of printing was £100 and the selling price was 10s 6d.

Ashbee was not primarily a scholar. He was much more concerned with the Craft Guild which he had established in the East End, and he was not able to give the necessary time to the continuation of the Survey of London. The work was taken up by a group of enthusiastic members of his Committee, many of whom lived in Chelsea. They published half-a-dozen small monographs on individual buildings, but their main work was the compilation of a register of the monuments of Chelsea, and under the leadership of Mr. Walter H. Godfrey they published in 1909 a large volume describing the Cheyne Walk area. This was volume II of the main parish series of volumes of the *Survey of London*; it was much more elaborate in both form and content than volume I, and it set the pattern of the series for the next 45 years.

Its publication was quickly followed by the signature in 1910 of a written agreement between the LCC and the London Survey Committee. The LCC agreed to pay for the printing of all future volumes, and in order to expedite the work it also undertook to prepare the text of alternate volumes. The whole project was to be managed by a Joint Publishing Committee consisting of four LCC representatives and three representatives of the London Survey Committee.

This arrangement remained in force for 42 years, from 1910 to 1952, and during this period 23 parish volumes were published. Eleven of the volumes were prepared by the Committee, and 12 by the Council's own staff, and all 23 were printed at the cost of the LCC.

Thus there were virtually two separate series of parish volumes, united only by the Joint Publishing Committee. It is therefore not surprising to find considerable differences of emphasis between the volumes prepared by the Committee and those prepared by the Council. The Committee's parish volumes, and all the monographs on individual buildings (which they continued to produce independently of the LCC) were largely architectural in their approach; documentation was sometimes rather flimsy. The Council's volumes, on the other hand, while not neglecting the architectural aspects, were historical in approach, and more carefully documented. This development was due to the late Mr. W. W. Braines, who for many years prepared the Council's volumes of the *Survey*. The seven volumes which he wrote included three describing the Whitehall area, and the standard of historical scholarship which he set has been admired by all his successors.

After the publication of the fourth and last volume describing St. Pancras in 1952, the Survey Committee decided that it could undertake the preparation of no more of the parish volumes, and therefore asked the LCC to take over the whole of the remainder of the work. The Council accepted this request, and in 1954 a full-time General Editor was appointed. Shortly afterwards the printing and publication of the *Survey* was entrusted to the Athlone Press of the University of London—which is of course the publishing house of the University—and a number of changes were made in the layout of the volumes. The main part of the text is now printed in double columns, to save space, and each volume has a short single-column introduction which summarises the detailed findings of the main body of the text.

The London Survey Committee came to an end in 1964, shortly after the death of Mr. W. H. Godfrey, who had been its mainstay for over fifty years. In addition to its work on the main parish series of volumes it had published 16 monographs on individual buildings. Of these the most notable were those describing The Queen's House, Greenwich (by G. H. Chettle), St. Bride's, Fleet Street (by W. H. Godfrey), and the College of Arms (by W. H. Godfrey and Sir Anthony Wagner).

When the LCC came to an end in 1965 the Greater London Council assumed responsibility for the *Survey of London*. The staff at present engaged on the series consists of the General Editor, four history graduates, two draughtsmen, one architect and a secretary. The services of a photographer are available when required. Here I should like to pay grateful and affectionate tribute to the three senior members of this team, Mr. P. A. Bezodis, Mrs. M. P. G. Draper and Mr. W. Ison, who have all worked on the *Survey* for over 12 years, and from whom I have learned more than I care to admit.

SOURCES AND METHODS USED

C. R. Ashbee's original object was to produce a printed list or register of London's buildings of historic or architectural interest. This still remains the central purpose of the *Survey of London*, but the bare bones of listing have been covered with flesh and blood. The object, now, might be defined as to trace the topographical and architectural history of a given area, and to record the notable features of the building fabric by graphic and written means. This is a very general, even vague, definition, but the absence of strict terms of reference has the great advantage of flexibility. The danger is that the *Survey* may acquire a flabby, middle-aged spread—indeed, some people might think that it has already done so, and that a slimming course should now be prescribed. Slimming is always difficult, however, for physicians seldom agree about what should be excluded from the patient's diet.

In the preparation of a volume there are two phases of research—general and specific.

General research

First of all a provisional list is compiled of those buildings which it is intended to record. This involves sauntering round the area several times in order to acquire a working knowledge of it; dusk on winter afternoons is a particularly good time to stare through uncurtained windows into lighted rooms for traces of ceilings, shutters and other internal embellishments. [The Ministry of Housing lists of buildings of special architectural or historic interest are useful as a guide, but despite frequent revision of the London lists they are not entirely reliable, particularly where an old building has been refronted.] During these perambulations it is also provisionally decided how each selected building should be recorded—by photographs, and/or measured drawings and/or written description.

The *Survey* also aims to record notable buildings which have been demolished, however long ago—Carlton House is an obvious case in point. So, concurrently with the listing of existing buildings, a thorough general search is made for prints, watercolours, oil paintings, and architects' drawings, which are often the only graphic sources for demolished buildings. The collections at the British Museum (Map Room, Departments of Manuscripts and of Prints and Drawings), Victoria and Albert Museum, London Museum, Guildhall Library, RIBA Library, Sir John Soane's Museum, the Tate Gallery, the National Monuments Record (chiefly for old photographs), the Greater London Council's own collection, and the local public library are all searched. Relevant items are listed, and many of them are photographed at this stage. In the case of prints there is considerable duplication between these various collections. Facilities for topographical research are far better at the Victoria and Albert than at the Department of Prints and Drawings at the British Museum.

The draughtsmen, photographer, and architect can now get on with a large part of their work independently of the historical research workers, whose next task is to master and make notes on the vast amount of published material which already exists about all the central areas of London. This sounds obvious, but some historians do sometimes feel that they are not really doing research unless they are looking at manuscripts, and this has to be guarded against. At this stage, too, all relevant passages in the printed calendars of the Public Record Office, the volumes of the Historical Manuscripts Commission and the indexes of the Additional and other manuscripts at the British Museum are noted, as also H. M. Colvin's *Biographical Dictionary of English Architects* and Gunnis's *Dictionary of Sculptors*. Local Acts of Parliament are noted from a typescript list of London Acts in the GLC Members' Library.

During the last ten years a card index has been compiled of all London entries in *The Builder* from its commencement in 1843 down to 1892. All the entries which refer to the area under investigation are now copied out and filed.

Five out of the six most recently published volumes of the *Survey* have been concerned with areas where the original building development took place between about 1660 and 1750. Two very important sources have been used for the elucidation of this period—the Chancery Proceedings at the Public Record Office, and the Middlesex Land Registry at the

Greater London Record Office at County Hall. To exploit either of these sources systematically is exceedingly laborious, but very rewarding for the type of information contained in the *Survey*.

The indexes to Chancery Proceedings classes C 2 (Elizabeth I to Charles I), C 3 (Elizabeth I to Commonwealth), and C 3 to C 10 (which extend down to 1714), are arranged alphabetically under the name of the plaintiff, but the County and subject to which a dispute referred is also given, and the 'subject' column often gives the name of the parish. We have listed all cases referring to the parishes of St. Martin in the Fields, St. James and St. Anne, Soho, and as occasion has arisen during the last 10 years we have asked for and noted the contents of the documents themselves. This has proved to be a marathon task; in the mid-seventeenth century there were said to be over 30,000 cases depending in Chancery and only in a very few cases have we gone still further and looked up the Court Order Books (C 33), which should in theory provide the result of each case. Depositions (C 21, 22, 24) and Reports and Certificates (C 38) have also been used very occasionally.

After 1714 the indexes to the Chancery Proceedings contain no information about the whereabouts of the subject of dispute. In general it has therefore only been possible to use these later classes if we knew from some other source that there was a Chancery case of interest to our work, and if we knew the names of the parties to it. Very occasionally, when we have been investigating the career of some potentially litigious person, we have looked successfully in the post-1714 indexes of names and picked out cases which did prove relevant. The person in question must, however, have a very rare name, such as Burlington, or Turst or Cornelys, to make this search for a needle in a haystack successful. To use this procedure for a person with a name like Baker or White might mean looking at several hundred bills of complaint, and is therefore for practical purposes impossible.

The type of information contained in the Chancery Proceedings is infinitely various. Although Chancery was a court of equity the cases heard there were often concerned with matters of fact, and verbatim recitals of such things as title-deeds or building accounts are not uncommon. The bills of complaint and the answers were all written in English, in relatively informal language. They are, of course, written pleas, and are no doubt often tendentious or one-sided, but on the other hand this gives them a personal flavour which is never found in title-deeds, and is therefore very valuable. Some allowances do, nevertheless, have to be made; in order to bring a dispute within the jurisdiction of the court it was often necessary, for instance, to allege conspiracy, and statements on this subject cannot be taken at their face value. Prolonged study of the Chancery Proceedings is apt, too, to inculcate the erroneous idea that no building project was ever accomplished without litigious recrimination. When estate development proceeded smoothly, far fewer written records remain, and it would be wrong to suppose that all such operations ended, as did that in Soho in the 1670s and 1680s, in a field-day for the Chancery lawyers.

The Middlesex Land Registry was established by an Act of 1708 which provided that all sales, leases for more than 21 years, mortgages and wills affecting lands in the County of Middlesex (including Westminster) were to be registered before any subsequent transfer could be valid in law. Registration started in 1709 and continued until 1936, by which time some 12,000 large volumes of memorials and indexes had been accumulated.

The sheer bulk of the Middlesex Land Registry is the greatest obstacle to its use for historical research. Broadly speaking there is a separate index volume for each year, which is arranged alphabetically under the names of the vendors; a second column gives the name of the parish where each property was situated. In order to trace an individual entry it is therefore necessary to know the name of the vendor and the year of the transaction, but even if the searcher has this information he may not be successful, for deeds were often not registered until the property changed hands again, when registration of the first transaction became necessary in order to comply with the law.

In the preparation of the most recent volumes of the *Survey*, which have dealt with areas where the original building development was substantially complete by the middle of the eighteenth century, we have got round these difficulties by working through all the indexes up to about 1745 and noting on cards all entries relating to the parish in question. Then we abstract the essential information of each deed from the enrolments themselves, and arrange the cards by names of individual streets. In the case of an area such as the Burlington Estate (Cork Street and Savile Row, etc.), where development took place in the 1720s and 1730s, we then have a record of about 95 per cent of all the building leases. These give the date of the leases, the names of the lessor and lessee, the position and dimensions of the plot, and the ground rent.

The information contained in the Chancery Proceedings and the Middlesex Land Registry is supplemented by the parish ratebooks, which in the case of the Westminster parishes have survived with very few losses. Here again the material available is so vast that arbitrary selection has to be made. In this case it is not possible to abstract the names of inhabitants in all streets, so we have to confine ourselves to the principal streets, and doubtless some people of interest who lived in lesser streets are omitted in consequence. All names noted are checked against the *Dictionary of National Biography*, or if titled against *G E C*, or if of service rank, against the Army and Navy Lists. Even so, problems of identification often remain. Who, for instance, was the rate collector's 'Mr. Roosoe', living in Soho Square? Was he John Rushout, politician, or Jacques Rousseau, Huguenot artist? Or someone else?

The more we work on the ratebooks the more we become conscious of the difficulty of interpreting them correctly. Their obscurity is often greatest during the early years of the building of a new street, which is also the time when their evidence is most valuable. The rate collectors had not yet settled their perambulation into a regular route from house to house and street to street, gaps still existed between the different ranges of houses in an uncompleted street, and large numbers of the early occupants only remained for a year or two before removing elsewhere. The assessment figures can sometimes be used to help sort out these difficulties, but they often fluctuate too, and the problems of interpretation are occasionally insurmountable.

Taken together these three sources, the Chancery Proceedings, the Middlesex Land Registry, and the ratebooks, provide a very solid foundation on which to build. The only other registries comparable to the MLR are those for the Bedford Level (established 1663), and for the West (1703), East (1707) and North (1735) Ridings of Yorkshire.

Specific research

After two or three months of general research it becomes necessary to allocate specific tasks to each individual member of the team; so far as possible this is done according to personal choice. A task may consist of investigating the history of one building, such as the parish church, a theatre, or Burlington House, but more usually it means working out the history of an estate and of all the notable buildings there, both existing and demolished. Each investigator takes the notes already made which refer to his new subject and pursues his or her own line of research; ultimately he writes the account himself, which is then checked and edited by someone else.

The sources which may be consulted in this second stage of research are so infinitely varied that only a few can be mentioned. Two points— both very obvious—may be made at the outset. The work already done in the first stage will almost certainly contain clues for further research. Secondly, the *Survey* is concerned with buildings, and as all buildings stand on ground, the title-deeds, if available, will probably provide the most valuable evidence. Much time is spent in trying to find these deeds.

Most of seventeenth- and eighteenth-century London was built under long leases granted by the owners of the fee simple or their immediate under-tenants. Many of these estates still survive. The Crown Estate Commissioners, for instance, administer large areas of Crown property around Whitehall, Piccadilly, and Pall Mall; the Grosvenor Estate possesses much of Mayfair, the Bedford Settled Estates have much of Bloomsbury, and although they have sold Covent Garden they still hold the seventeenth- and eighteenth-century records. The Salisbury Settled Estates still own and administer part of the ground around Cranbourn Street which was bought as a speculation by Robert Cecil, first Earl of Salisbury, in 1609–10, and the counterparts of the building leases of the whole of the original estate are still at Hatfield. South of the Thames, the Duchy of Cornwall owns much of Kennington, and the Church Commissioners until very recently administered the extensive estates in Lambeth which formerly belonged to the Archbishops of Canterbury.

In the case of these great estates the chief problem is to obtain access to the owners' records. But we also often encounter areas where the original estate no longer exists and the records have been dispersed—often very long ago, as in the case of the Bakers' property around Piccadilly Circus, which was sold in the 1660s. These sales can sometimes be traced in the Close Rolls or elsewhere in the Public Record Office, and a visit to the National Register of Archives is almost always worthwhile. Through the NRA, for instance, we have found at the Buckinghamshire Record Office the deeds and papers of William Lowndes, who in 1693 bought the leasehold reversion under the Crown of ground to the east of Regent Street. More recently we have through the NRA found valuable material relating to Monmouth House, Soho Square, at the Northamptonshire Record Office, and this in turn gave a lead to an entry in *The London Gazette* which it would otherwise have been impossible to find.

The work of the British Records Association in salvaging old title-deeds from solicitors' offices and depositing them at local County Record Offices has proved invaluable to the *Survey*. An accumulation of deeds of the property of a family living in the country often contains London material, and there are few County Record Offices which we have not either visited or written to about such material. The Lincolnshire family of Nelthorpe, for instance, owned property in St. James's Street and Sackville Street, and the title-deeds are now in the Lincolnshire Record Office.

If all else fails in the search for title-deeds we enlist the help of the

Greater London Council's Valuer to discover who owns the freehold now. We then write to the owner and ask for permission to see his old deeds. Usually we receive no answer—County Hall is not the best address from which to make such requests—or a note saying that the early deeds have been destroyed or lost. But sometimes there is a favourable response, often from insurance companies or a very large firm such as J. Lyons and Co., which own much property, have well-organised legal departments and are often very helpful. It was, for instance, through the deeds held by the Prudential Assurance Company that the early history of the clubs managed by Almack, Brooks and Boodle on the north side of Pall Mall was unravelled.

This is an exceedingly laborious method of research which is gradually declining in value, for when a property changes hands the title is usually registered at the Central Land Registry. The old deeds then cease to have any legal validity and are often destroyed.

In any town there are, however, many properties which have been in the same ownership for very many years, and the deeds of these bodies can be exceedingly valuable not only for the history of their own properties but often for a large part of the surrounding area. First and foremost for the *Survey* comes the property owned by the Greater London Council itself. The history of the now defunct Newport Market was found, to take one example, through the deeds of the ground which the Council's predecessor, the Metropolitan Board of Works, bought in the 1880s for the formation of Shaftesbury Avenue and Charing Cross Road. All local authorities buy land for such purposes as parks, schools, housing, markets, cemeteries, or road widening; they tend to keep their old deeds, and access for any serious student can probably be arranged, perhaps after some initial reluctance. Other bodies which have allowed us to look at their old deeds include the Metropolitan Police, Newington Sessions, hospitals, British Railways, and a number of working-class housing charities such as the Peabody Donation Fund.

It is not at all unusual for any of these bodies to own land which they or their predecessors bought a century ago, or for the abstract of title on which the purchase was based to start in the early eighteenth century. The early parts of these abstracts often describe the descent of the whole estate of which the purchased property only formed a small part, and can therefore be of very great value. The deeds of Brixton Prison, held at Newington Sessions House, for instance, elucidated the eighteenth-century descent of the Manor of Stockwell, and the deeds of a small piece of land at Knight's Hill in Lambeth, now part of the railway line, contained similar information for the obscure Manor of Levehurst. British

Railways' collection of deeds is immense, for in building their lines the old companies had to buy up thousands of properties.

Enough has now been said to show that in the preparation of the *Survey* very great efforts are made to trace title-deeds. But unfortunately the information contained in even the most verbose of eighteenth-century deeds does not tell anything like the whole story of a building. Material relating to the embellishment and alteration is much more difficult to find, and, except in the case of churches, whose later history can usually be traced through the vestry minutes, is often completely lacking. Material relating to the building of the carcase of one of the finest mid-eighteenth-century houses in London, No. 1 Greek Street, Soho, can, for instance, be found in the title-deeds and supplemented from the Middlesex Land Registry, but the circumstances of its splendid interior embellishment by or for its first occupant, Richard Beckford, remain unknown. We have never found any detailed information about Georgian shop fronts. When investigating the history of the very fashionable Burlington Estate (Cork Street–Savile Row area) my colleague Mr. Bezodis traced and wrote to the descendants of a large number of the early inhabitants, but the results were extremely meagre. Peers living in Kenya or Kilburn have become parted from their family papers, and the depressing fact has to be faced that much of the information which we should most value does not exist. Building agreements, architects' and building tradesmen's correspondence and accounts, and all the written records for the planning and development of an estate are comparatively rarely found. In the 1670s and early 1680s a consortium of speculators—Richard Frith, a bricklayer, Cadogan Thomas, a timber merchant, Benjamin Hinton, a goldsmith, and William Pym, a 'gentleman'—were laying out and building a large estate of some 20 acres in Soho. They employed surveyors and scriveners as well as building tradesmen, but of course none of their 'office' records have survived, and so the story has to be pieced together from other sources, chiefly the Chancery Proceedings. The picture which emerges is really only a half-finished sketch.

In recent years the records of old-established banks have been used with some success by two of my colleagues, Mr. Bezodis and Mrs. Draper. These records consist firstly of title-deeds and family accounts of all kinds which were deposited at the bank for safe custody and never reclaimed; and secondly the ledgers of payments in and out to and from the accounts of individual customers. Banks to whose records we have been allowed access are Hoare's, Glyn Mills (who took over Child's), Drummond's (now a branch of the Royal Bank of Scotland), Coutts' and the Bank of Scotland.

This form of research presents difficulties. In the case of deeds and family papers the banks are sometimes reluctant to grant access for the good reason that these records are not their property, and however unlikely it may be that anyone will ever reclaim them, the banks feel that they have no right to allow inspection. Nevertheless, they do sometimes grant permission. In the case of the ledgers it is necessary either to know at which bank a particular individual had his account, or else to write to all the old banks asking whether the person in question was one of their customers. When the account has been located the ledgers will at best only give the payees' names and the amount of each individual transaction, and never, of course, the purpose of the payment. Despite these limitations bank ledgers have on occasion proved most valuable, when interpreted in the light of information obtained from other sources. The Duke of Kent's account at Hoare's Bank, for instance, showed that 10 days after the destruction of his house in St. James's Square by fire in 1725, the Duke opened a 'House account', from which payments to various building tradesmen were subsequently made. One of the entries was for £367 to the builder and architect Edward Shepherd. This suggested that Shepherd may have designed the Duke's new house, which still exists and is now the headquarters of the Arts Council. That Shepherd was indeed the architect was subsequently confirmed by a discovery made by Mr. H. M. Colvin amongst the Savile of Rufford papers at Nottinghamshire County Record Office.

In the course of our work it is often necessary to try to trace the careers of very obscure people—builders, perhaps, or craftsmen or tradesmen. The material used for this kind of research is, of course, infinitely varied, and includes many printed works, but it may be worthwhile to mention a few of the more out-of-the-way manuscript sources which we have found useful. Builders were often declared bankrupt, and particulars of their affairs may sometimes be found in the records of the Court of Bankruptcy at the PRO. Classes B 1 (Order Books, 1710–1877, 214 volumes), B 5 (Enrolment Books, 1710–1859, 111 volumes) and B 6 (Registers, 1733–1886, 219 volumes) are our favourites, and a search in *The London Gazette* is also useful. It may be noted, however, that there are no surviving records for the years prior to 1710; but conveyances of bankrupts' estates were, from 1571 onwards, sometimes enrolled on the Close Rolls. Information about people in the Royal service has been found in the records of the Lord Steward's Department (PRO, LS2 was used for the Fortnums of Fortnum and Mason) and in those of the Lord Chamberlain's Department (PRO, LC9 for the Soho tapestry weavers). The Guildhall Library has the records of many of the City Livery

Companies, whose apprenticeship registers can be valuable, and also the policy registers of some of the older insurance companies. There are also apprenticeship registers for both London and elsewhere at the PRO, class IR 1, 1710–1811, 79 volumes. Amongst printed sources for nineteenth-century biography I hope I may be forgiven for mentioning a work which until recently was not known to the *Survey*—Frederick Boase's *Modern English Biography*, in six volumes (reprinted 1965) which contains notices of many thousands of persons not in the *DNB* who died between 1851 and 1900.

Finally, a group of miscellaneous sources, beginning with the tithe maps made in the 1830s and 40s, of which there are copies at the offices of the Tithe Redemption Commission in Finsbury Square as well as the copies kept locally. (I only mention the tithe maps because I have the impression, perhaps quite wrongly, that they are not used as extensively as they might be for the history of urban areas.) If the parish ratebooks have not survived, or have only survived with gaps, the ratebooks of the commissioners of sewers are sometimes available; in Lambeth, where nearly all the early ratebooks had been destroyed, we also used the Land Tax books for the late eighteenth and early nineteenth centuries. The date of establishment of many public houses in Westminster has been traced through the licensed victuallers' recognisances at the Greater London Record Office (Middlesex Branch), sometimes with interesting results. The Shakespeare's Head in Great Marlborough Street, for instance, an outwardly uninteresting public house now fitted up in what the owners imagine to be a style appropriate to the Bard of Avon, was established in 1735 and evidently takes its name from its first licensees, Thomas and John Shakespear. The Scots Hoose in Romilly Street, Soho, an ugly nineteenth-century building decorated in the Caledonian manner, was formerly the George and Thirteen Cantons. This name was the result of a mid-eighteenth-century amalgamation of two taverns, the George in Moor Street and the Thirteen Cantons in King Street. This area around Cambridge Circus was in the early eighteenth century the centre of the Swiss colony in Soho, and the Thirteen Cantons was evidently the favourite resort of this particular foreign element.

In the foregoing account I have tried to describe the way in which the *Survey* is prepared, and to mention both the most important sources, such as the Middlesex Land Registry or the Chancery Proceedings, and some of the less well-known ones. There are, of course, very many others, as a glance at the references at the end of each volume will show. During the preparation of the *Survey* for the northern part of the Parish of St. James, Piccadilly, in 1961–3, we accumulated nearly three hundredweight of notes, exclusive of draft texts, etc. What C. R. Ashbee, the mercurial founder of the *Survey*, would have thought of this example of the ant-like industry of modern historical scholarship, it is (perhaps fortunately) impossible to tell.

GUIDE TO THE USE OF THE *SURVEY*

Parish volumes

There is very wide variation in the scope and quality of individual volumes. Roughly speaking, the more recent the volume the wider the coverage on all subjects, particularly since volume XXVI, where, for instance, Victorian buildings were first given serious consideration. In general there is more historical matter in the volumes whose texts were prepared by the LCC (marked with an asterisk in the list below) than in those prepared by the Survey Committee.

All volumes describe the history of individual buildings in detail and, in the case of domestic buildings, list their notable inhabitants down to about 1800 or sometimes later. All contain many illustrations, chiefly architectural, but also including topographical views, maps and plans. All are separately indexed. Sometimes there is a short general historical account at the beginning of a volume (or, where several volumes are devoted to a single parish, at the beginning of the first volume for that parish). Embedded in the main body of almost every volume is a vast mass of material relating to the manors, estates and building history of the area. Each volume or pair of volumes since volume XXVI has a short general introduction summarising the findings of the main text.

The series is designed to be used topographically, and it is much more difficult to use it to find information about a general subject, such as land values or railway history. For use in this way topography can often serve as a guide to find the appropriate volume, e.g., for railway development, see Southern Lambeth or St. Pancras; for tapestry making, see Soho.

Parishes described: an asterisk denotes volumes with text prepared by the LCC or GLC.

VI   Hammersmith. 1915.

VII   Chelsea. Part III (The Old Church). 1921.

*VIII   St. Leonard, Shoreditch. 1924.

IX   St. Helen, Bishopgate. Part I. 1926.

*X   St. Margaret, Westminster. Part I. 1926.

XI   Chelsea. Part IV (The Royal Hospital). 1927.

XII   All Hallows, Barking-by-the-Tower. Part I (The Parish Church). 1929.

*XIII   St. Margaret, Westminster. Part II (neighbourhood of Whitehall, Vol. I). 1930.

*XIV   St. Margaret, Westminster. Part III (neighbourhood of Whitehall, Vol. II). 1931.

XV   All Hallows, Barking-by-the-Tower. Part II. 1934.

*XVI   St. Martin-in-the-Fields. Part I (Charing Cross). 1935.

XVII   St. Pancras. Part I (Village of Highgate). (Out of print). 1936.

*XVIII   St. Martin-in-the-Fields. Part II (The Strand). 1937.

XIX   St. Pancras. Part II (Old St. Pancras and Kentish Town). (Out of print). 1938.

*XX   St. Martin-in-the-Fields. Part III (Trafalgar Square and neighbourhood). 1940.

XXI   St. Pancras. Part III (Tottenham Court Road and neighbourhood). 1949.

*XXII   St. Saviour and Christ Church, Southwark (Bankside). 1950.

*XXIII   St. Mary, Lambeth. Part I (South Bank and Vauxhall). 1951.

XXIV   St. Pancras. Part IV (King's Cross neighbourhood). 1957.

*XXV   St. George the Martyr and St. Mary Newington, Southwark (St. George's Fields). 1955.

*XXVI   St. Mary, Lambeth. Part II (Southern Area). 1956.

*XXVII   Christ Church and All Saints (Spitalfields and Mile End New Town). 1957.

*XXVIII   Hackney. Part I (Brooke House). 1960.

*XXIX, XXX   St. James, Westminster. Part I (South of Piccadilly). 1960.

Survey of London

*XXXI, XXXII   St. James, Westminster. Part II (North of
Piccadilly). 1963.
*XXXIII, XXXIV   St. Anne, Soho. 1966.

Monographs on individual buildings

All these 16 volumes were prepared and published by the Survey
Committee independently of the LCC. The later volumes, particularly
the last three, are greatly superior to the earlier ones. No. V, Brooke
House, Hackney, has been superseded by Volume XXVIII in the parish
series, and should not now be used.

I   Trinity Hospital, Mile End. 1896.
II   St. Mary, Stratford, Bow (Out of print). 1900.
III   The Old Palace, Bromley-by-Bow. 1902.
IV   The Great House, Leyton (Out of print). 1903.
V   Brooke House, Hackney (Out of print). 1904.
VI   St. Dunstan's, Stepney. 1905.
VII   Sandford Manor, Fulham. 1907.
VIII Crosby Hall, Bishopsgate. 1908.
IX   Morden College, Blackheath (Out of print). 1916.
X   Eastbury Manor, Barking (Out of print). 1917.
XI   East Acton Manor (Out of print). 1921.
XII   Cromwell House, Highgate (Out of print). 1926.
XIII Swakeleys, Middlesex. 1933.
XIV   The Queen's House, Greenwich. 1937.
XV   St. Bride's Church, Fleet Street. 1944.
XVI   The College of Arms. 1963.

Discussion

The papers by Mr. Armstrong and by Dr. Dyos and Mrs. Baker, both concerned with census book material and methods of processing it, were discussed together in the first part of the session. Those by Professor Conzen and Dr. Sheppard, each treating a quite different topic, were discussed separately in the second part. The session was a lively one which lasted for more than three hours.

In the first part of the session attention was devoted mainly to Mr. Armstrong's paper, for Dr. Dyos's and Mrs. Baker's did not lend itself so readily to discussion. Most members of the conference lacked the necessary technical knowledge of computers; and since the authors' research was still in a very early stage and they could not yet reveal any of their findings, any debate about the value of their methods was also ruled out. All in all, they had established themselves in an impregnable position. Nevertheless Dr. Dyos intervened repeatedly in the discussion and made a major contribution to it by his comments on Mr. Armstrong's work, many of which shed light on his own because of the comparisons involved.

Mr. Armstrong's findings, the product of a pioneer piece of research so far as Britain was concerned, proved highly controversial and provoked the fusillade of question and comment which he had expected, for—as he cheerfully confessed when the onslaught was over—he had gone out of his way to put his most contentious statistics into his paper. The very large numbers in Class III (skilled labour) in York, Nottingham, and Radford were discussed at some length. In all three places they far exceeded the combined total of Classes IV and V (semi-skilled and unskilled labour). In the York 1851 sample, the skilled were almost twice as numerous as the semi-skilled and unskilled, in Nottingham getting on for three times as many and at Radford more than three times. In his introduction to the session the chairman (Professor BARKER) asked: 'Did these Class III returns really all represent households at the head of which was someone earning, say, 25s a week or more? If so, then the social improvements resulting from industrialisation must have exceeded the optimists' most optimistic guesses.' Dr. CHALONER, recalling that Dr. Hobsbawm had estimated that the labour aristocracy constituted a mere 15 per cent of the working population, said that he had always believed that this figure was too low. 'Perhaps Mr. Armstrong's figures show ... that it's the urban proletariat [which] may be the aristocracy,' he added. Mr. ARMSTRONG explained that his Class III included not only skilled labour but also petty entrepreneurs—small shopkeepers and the like—who did not employ anyone. He admitted that it was unfortunate that they had all fallen together into one huge group, but it was 'rather difficult in respect of status to say what distinctions you would draw

146

between skilled workmen, shopkeepers and [other] petty entrepreneurs not employing anyone.' It was really necessary to have an industrial or occupational breakdown within Class III, for it was impossible to distinguish between skilled workers and petty entrepreneurs on the basis of status alone.[1] Dr. HENNOCK inquired whether it was, in fact, possible to distinguish between those who employed others and those who did not. His own work on the enumerators' books for Leeds had led him to believe that no such distinction could be made, in which case perhaps the reason that Group III was so large was that many allocated to that group would have been placed in Group II if more had been known about the numbers they employed. To this Mr. ARMSTRONG replied that the York enumerators 'seemed to be very good', either in noting '"emp. 2", "emp. 1" and so on' or in giving details of workpeople living in, but he conceded the possibility that some members of his Group III perhaps ought to belong to Group II. Mr. TILLOTT, siding with Dr. Hennock, said that in the rural areas which he had started to study, the evidence concerning numbers employed seemed very doubtful: 'If you analyse the farmers in order to check the numbers said to be employed against the numbers living in the household, it doesn't even add up at all.'

At this juncture the discussion took a more technical turn. Dr. DYOS pointed out that, by using a computer instead of punched cards he was not limited to 80 columns and therefore had room for further information about occupational or industrial groups—though not to go as far, in fact, as Herbert Gutman had gone in his study of Buffalo. (But even so, interjected Dr. HENNOCK, sticking to his point, it was still impossible to distinguish between the shoemaker who employed two assistants and one who did not if the returns did not give this information.) Dr. EVERSLEY raised his voice in favour of punched cards, pointing out that a computer was not essential for the processing of additional information about occupational or industrial groups; two or three cards could be used for each case. Dr. DYOS, however, drew attention to the cost of punching if outside contractors were employed and Mr. C. HARRIS pointed out that there were also difficulties about correlation if cards were used, and the process was slower. Mr. SPENCER noted that it was less convenient to store the information on punched cards.

After this brisk little exchange, to which most members listened with more awe than understanding, Mr. C. HARRIS brought the discussion back to the much-disputed Class III. Roundly condemning the Registrar General's occupational classification of 1950 as 'a lousy classification for any sociological purposes', he inquired why Mr. Armstrong had not chosen a classification

[1] According to some calculations made by Dr. Dyos and Mrs. Baker since the conference, for which they used the Armstrong classification, Class III contained 63 per cent of all heads of Camberwell households in 1871; Classes II and IV each contained about 12 per cent. Rather interestingly, they have been able to divide Class III reasonably accurately into petty entrepreneurs, clerks, and skilled labourers for this date, and they find that in Camberwell about half the total heads of households contained in Class III (and just over a quarter of all heads) were skilled labourers; a further 32 per cent of heads in Class III were petty entrepreneurs and 18 per cent were clerks.

nearer the period he was studying. To this Mr. ARMSTRONG confessed that, when he was preparing to start sampling, he did not have convenient access to the 1911 classification, the earliest he could have used; but a subsequent comparison showed that if he *had* used the 1911 breakdown, there would still have been an enormous Class III. In any case—and here he harked back to Dr. Hennock's point about the fullness and reliability of the original sources—it was not a good idea 'to use a highly refined system of stratification if your raw material isn't sufficiently well structured.' Mr. HARRIS, now fully roused and very fluent, returned to the charge. It was necessary to go back beyond 1911. Occupations could change over time—become less skilled for instance—even though the name might remain the same. 'If you wanted to compare the occupational distribution of two towns in 1851, I don't think it matters two hoots whether one uses either the 1950 or the 1911 classification. If one can show that they are different, this is perfectly valid. But if one wants to say that the occupational structure is somewhat different in 1951 from what it was in 1931 as compared with 1961' that was a different matter. In such fluid situations one had to pay the strictest attention to the choice of the base year and be scrupulously logical in making comparisons through time.

Interest then shifted from the Registrar General's changing categories to the actual enumerators' returns themselves. How reliable were the descriptions of occupation? Professor KÖLLMAN brought up this point by noting that in the Dortmund marriage registers most people, even though they were actually semi-skilled or even unskilled, wanted to be classed as skilled and gave appropriate occupations. This was particularly true in the nineteenth century when first-generation factory workers insisted upon giving an occupation, such as shoemaker or carpenter, which they may have followed in the countryside before moving townwards. Professor CHECKLAND drew attention to the difference in the size of Class III in York, Nottingham, and Radford and concluded from this that if a subjective self-estimate was involved, it obviously varied greatly from place to place. Mr. TILLOTT did not think that there was so much scope for a subjective self-estimate: 'The enumerators' instructions were, as they are now, to deliver the householders' schedule in the week before. The householder, of course, then filled it in. The enumerator then came along and copied the householder's schedule into his own books, clearly amending as he went along, because there is documentary evidence in the enumerators' returns showing this. On top of this, the District Registrar, where he was a good one—and I can show examples of this occurring—then went through the enumerators' books item by item and himself amended and checked—and, indeed often altered occupations where he clearly thought he had better knowledge than had been put down.' Mr. Tillott added, however, that he had only so far studied the enumeration of rural areas; market towns were the largest places he had investigated.

Mrs. BAKER intervened at this point to give her conclusions on this matter, gained from the Camberwell evidence which she had been recording. 'You have no way, from the census books,' she said, 'of telling the range or degree of skill within the stated occupation. . . . What you find is that a person gives an occupation which, on the face of it, looks skilled—let us say, a carpenter—and you can tell from the way [i.e., where] he is living that he is living at the same level as a man who is a bricklayer's labourer or someone like this. . . . You can't just look at the occupation and say from that occupation he is definitely within a particular social group.'

Mr. FOSTER thought that the only way out of this problem was to hold it to an incomes-earnings differential and define skilled in that sense, which he thought could be done with existing wage data. There was a big gap, in the three towns (Oldham, Northampton, and South Shields) which he had studied, between those earning 28s to 32s a week and others earning less than 22s. The former constituted Dr. Hobsbawm's 15 per cent. Mr. Foster agreed, however, that it was difficult to discover what were the earnings of shopkeepers, though 'one feels that many of them were probably a good deal more poverty-stricken than the 32s people'. Mr. BEDARIDA, who had been studying the 1851 census returns for London, emphasised the need to look at family, not individual, incomes. He, too, had discovered a huge Class III, but he thought that the main division came between Classes III and IV and not between Class II and III.

Dr. J. R. HARRIS changed the subject by turning to the size of households and particularly to the matter of lodgers. Professor Barker, in his introduction to the session, had raised this point by drawing attention to the large proportion of lodgers in Mr. Armstrong's returns. To what extent did nineteenth-century households contain more lodgers because of the large numbers of single people then moving townwards? Dr. Harris said that Mr. Oxley, a research student of his who had recently completed a thesis on the administration of the Old Poor Law in Lancashire, had shown that regulations concerning inmates of private houses were frequently enforced in the later sixteenth and seventeenth centuries. 'The very frequency with which you get these fines and amercements indicates that the movement of people to settle as lodgers in towns was far stronger than the administrative capacity to repel them.' It would seem, therefore, that the lodger may have been a more common figure in the towns of earlier times than Mr. Laslett had suggested.

Mr. C. HARRIS moved the discussion from household size to family size, another point which had been touched upon by Professor Barker in his introduction, when he had noted that some account ought, perhaps, to be taken of children of families in Classes I and II who were away at private boarding schools. Mr. C. Harris, commenting on Mr. Armstrong's 'array of figures' about family size, and having elicited from Mr. Armstrong that 'wives' in table I did not include married daughters, urged the need to build a demographic model on the basis of which one could then calculate what the distribution of household size should be if, in fact, it consisted of only husband, wife and unmarried children. Only in this way would it be possible, he believed, to discover whether an extended family household did or did not exist. Dr. EVERSLEY noted that the household tables in the 1961 census, broken down into about seventeen categories, could be used to explain the 'battlemented' effect observed by Mr. Armstrong. These tables showed which categories were out of series—the lower-paid white collar occupations, for instance. On the strength of this modern evidence Dr. Eversley thought that the 'battlemented' effect which Mr. Armstrong had found might 'not be just one out of line but all seventeen—all along the line.'

The first part of the session concluded with some conflicting evidence about the availability of nineteenth-century registers in local registry offices and with general agreement on the need to press for easier access by *bona fide* scholars to the later nineteenth-century records held by the Registrar General.

Professor Hoskins and Dr. Martin took the leading part in the discussion on Professor Conzen's paper, Professor HOSKINS setting the tone by boldly asserting that 'to publish a town history without maps is like publishing a book without an index; the book should be taken out of copyright straight away as a punishment'. He thought that urban parish boundaries were 'a marvellous source for getting back to the street and lane patterns of the twelfth century', for parish boundaries almost always followed streets, lanes and alleyways. There were difficulties, however, in places like Stamford, Lincoln, and York where small parishes had been amalgamated in the sixteenth century. Another snag in using modern maps for historical purposes was the need to make allowance for changed levels in the case of hill towns. At Exeter, for instance, 'two great steep-sided valleys, north and south, had been filled up in the nineteenth century and the streams had been turned into storm sewers.'

Dr. MARTIN supported Professor Hoskins in his censure of historians who failed to take advantage of maps. 'They've never seen them or have been frightened by them in infancy,' he complained, though maps were, he conceded, 'a damnably difficult and expensive business to construct.' It was characteristic that the British contribution to the International Atlas of Town Plans was being run on a shoe-string. At the same time, it was necessary to appreciate that there were many fewer maps of medieval English towns than of their continental counterparts. 'You don't find in the archives of English boroughs cartularies of the kind you find in the great cities of Flanders. They haven't the property; they haven't the interest in it. The only substantial property that they have is the waste land and they are not at all sure until the fifteenth century whether it really belongs to them at all because if the King gave it to them, he gave it to them in a fit of absence of mind. . . . Although Dr. [G. R. C.] Davis's handbook on medieval cartularies in this country refers to borough cartularies, there aren't any in the text, and this is not because he's missed them but because there weren't any. . . .'

Professor CONZEN agreed with Professor Hoskins's remarks about the value of modern maps as sources of information about medieval towns, but he was not sure how far he supported Dr. Martin's claims that the continental towns were better endowed with medieval maps than were the English. He had not been able, for instance, to find a really accurate and detailed plan of Hamburg or Hanover 'or any of the cities that were big commercial cities back in the mid-eighteenth century.' Yet it was true that an interest in cartography grew up

very early in towns situated on the main continental trade routes because of
their economic development. The detailed plans he had in mind contained not
only the street system but also information about the buildings contained within
the street system.

Dr. MARTIN drew attention to the fact that, from the fourteenth century
onwards, English towns in which the influence of the Crown was strong were
likely to be well documented. This led him on to extol the merits of the detailed
nineteenth-century ordnance survey maps of towns, and several other speakers
vied with one another to add their meed of praise and their own favourite
example. Professor HOSKINS recommended the early O.S. maps of Stoke-on-
Trent, one of the first places, he said, to be surveyed on the scale 1 : 500. It
showed not only every pottery but the use to which every building in that
pottery was put. Professor CONZEN recalled that the map of Alnwick contained
the most minute detail of the workhouse there, and Mr. TILLOTT noted that the
map of York identified the individual blocks within the prison. Dr. KELLETT and
Dr. MARSHALL recommended the maps drawn up by nineteenth-century
Medical Officers of Health and Improvement Commissions, which were often
based upon the Ordnance Survey. Mr. FORSYTH reported that Scottish towns
often possessed maps of the later eighteenth or earlier nineteenth century, 'all
superb and . . . all about 25″ to the mile.' Mr. FREEMAN believed that a map could
be an original source which was of as much value as any other original source
and urged a much more methodical search for privately produced maps which
were still in private hands. Maps could be particularly useful in helping the
researcher to discover when the decline in population of central areas of cities
had begun. Geographers would be very glad to help historians at an early stage
of their researches; but all too often the historian came along only when his
typescript was finished and said: 'Oh, I've got my manuscript all ready, and
I want to put a map in.'

This remark struck right home and was greeted with roars of good-humoured
laughter. But it was, nevertheless, realised that maps had their limitations as
original sources and this was brought out in the rest of the discussion on Professor Conzen's paper. The general drift changed when Professor CHECKLAND
raised the question of continuity. What was needed, he said, was not one
medieval map but a series so that the historian could get some idea 'at what
point the town became more than merely a servicing unit for the surrounding
countryside.' He was very sceptical whether, once economic growth had begun,
any of the old arrangements survived unless preservationists got to work. Why
was it, for instance, that medieval Glasgow became a slum while medieval
Lyon, encapsulated, became a tourist attraction? Professor CONZEN felt that
continuity emphasised the uniqueness of cities. Even the grid-iron pattern of
nineteenth-century towns differed from one another and gave each a distinctive
stamp—and 'when you get a town with a much longer history, that uniqueness
is even more pronounced.' Professor CHECKLAND doubted this, too. 'Is it not
true,' he asked, 'that really our cities have been built *once*, in the sense that
Bradford and Leeds, and I suppose a large part of Manchester and Glasgow,

were built in the course of the nineteenth century? They are not a *continuum* except in the sense that some of them may have a core which is continuous.' Here Dr. DYOS dissented from Professor Checkland, but not in a way that brought much consolation to the geographers. 'There is a constant process of renewal going on,' he argued, 'but most of it takes place in terms of changing two-storeyed houses, say, into three or four, rather than taking them over in ways which are normally represented on maps. . . .' Professor HOSKINS agreed that there had been 'constant changing in the most apparently immobile and fossilised city [and] . . . in many English towns . . . there was almost total reconstruction in the sixteenth and early seventeenth centuries when they wiped out much of the medieval plan and medieval buildings. . . .' It was left to Dr. MARTIN to sound a firm and final note of doubt. 'What we are *not* saying', he observed, 'is that there are a great many more points that historians can make readily and dramatically from maps than they can make in words. In the last resort there is no substitute for the word. What the historian has to say which is worth saying about the town is something which he can only convey in words to other people, because we deal in all kinds of imponderables which simply can't be written down in a pattern of black and white.'

The discussion was then switched to Dr. Sheppard's paper. In introducing it, the chairman, while praising the meticulous precision of the *Survey of London*, wondered whether some of the great effort and resources ought to be devoted to the consideration of the rôle of London in the economy as a whole rather than to such detailed studies of particular parts of it. To this Dr. SHEPPARD replied that the policy of the *Survey of London* was inevitably dictated by its architectural origins. 'It did start primarily as a record of London,' he explained, 'and unless one is really going to modify completely the whole purpose of the thing, or alternatively make it much bigger than it already is, I cannot see that it can contain social or demographic material to any appreciable extent.' The object of the *Survey*, he insisted, was to supply facts for other people to interpret and not to do the interpreting itself. The details of land ownership that the *Survey* contained were basic to the understanding of any town. Sir JOHN SUMMERSON warmly supported this view and pointed out that under Dr. Sheppard's General Editorship a much wider range of buildings had come within the *Survey*'s scope. 'The reason why one should most emphatically not try to get it to do more than it is doing', he added 'is that it is pinning down visual evidence of the history of towns which will not be with us for very much longer. . . . If one of our great national repositories of archives were gradually being eaten away by mice, we should all have terrible nightmares about it . . . But here is something of equal value, the visual evidence of towns.'

Having taken his stand on the value of the detailed information contained in the *Survey*, Dr. Sheppard found himself under criticism on its comprehensiveness. Dr. KELLETT complained that some of the detail about landownership in the *Survey* lacked vital information. He had found that it was not at all easy to discover, for instance, which estates were entailed. He also felt that it would be helpful if some of the rapid transfers of property which often occurred before

Second Discussion

improved ground rents were established could be set out in tabular form. Dr. SHEPPARD replied that the latter was already being done and that estate information of the kind that Dr. Kellett had asked for was also being given in the latest volumes. When Dr. KELLETT asked for the earlier volumes to be brought up to date as well, it was pointed out that after sixty years the *Survey* had still covered only one-third of the area of the LCC County of London. This caused Dr. DYOS to re-emerge as champion of the suburbs, though in a rather morbid frame of mind. 'With the desire, naturally, to record the buildings at the centre, which one wants to get down before the demolition squad gets at them', he gloomily reflected, 'it'll be ages—indeed, it might be your lifetime or that of your successor—before you get back into the suburbs.' Without confirming this depressing forecast, Dr. SHEPPARD agreed that unless there was a change of policy the likelihood of doing another suburb like Lambeth was very remote.

At this point Sir JOHN SUMMERSON changed the subject by bringing up the matter of building records which had also been raised by Professor Barker in his introduction to the session. 'It seems fantastic,' Sir John observed, 'that no economic historian has tackled the history of the construction industry.' Dr. DYOS reported that his attempts to find builders' records had not been rewarded with much success and Sir John recalled that he had also tried, 30 years before, to track down records of this kind for a series of articles; but all that the building firms had was 'a photograph or painting of the founder at birth and a few verbal traditions'. Cubbitt's did, however, possess some business records and these were being worked upon. Dr. REEDER thought that papers relating to other building concerns might be found among bankruptcy records.

Dr. NEWTON urged urban historians to study the records of estate agents. He had found these 'of great interest' for Exeter and there was also a good set of records for a family firm of estate agents and valuers in Trowbridge, though the useful bits of material had to be unearthed from huge masses of junk. The Exeter records would supply the researcher with information about capital values, rents and returns on capital. Dr. DYOS confirmed the view that estate agents' offices contained a few worthwhile records, especially auction particulars, hidden away amidst files of irrelevant paper. The real gold mine, however, was the solicitor's, not the estate agent's, office; but solicitors rarely welcomed historians. Dr. HARRIS drew attention to the fact that the British Records Association was conducting a survey of solicitors' historical records and Dr. KELLETT told the conference that at Glasgow University they had secured some valuable material from solicitors (who also fulfilled the function of estate agents in Scotland) about the high-class residential area of Western Glasgow. Dr. REEDER said that he had found insurance records helpful, for they contained information about loans to developers. Building society records, too, should be consulted. Indeed, they provided 'perhaps the most plentiful and abundant source of material', for so many of them had held on to their records.

The chairman thanked the authors for writing four papers which had kept the conference talking almost non-stop for the whole morning.

T. C. BARKER

Leicester, the Clock ower. The Clock Tower 868) is the hub, and so far its nature allows the heart, modern Leicester. The neteenth- and twentieth- ntury development of the y has moved the centre to nat was once an extra-mural ad junction. The tower nds just outside the site of e East Gates, where two untry roads, Belgrave Gate d Humberstone Gate, con-rged, crossed the line of a ad running once an extra-mural all, and entered the town to ake what is now called igh Street. Its origins have nferred a lasting restless-ss upon the scene.

(Ian Paterson)

eicester, the East Gates in 1867: the undistinguished clutter of Leicester's suburban development en the Clock Tower was begun. Photographs are among our most valuable sources of nineteenth-century an history, but like other pictorial material they need interpretation. There is a shabby inconse-entiality about the scene which no reconstruction could capture, but there is also some sense of occasion e, born partly of impending ceremony, and partly out of respect for the camera.

(National Monuments Record, Crown Copyright)

(H. W. Taunt, National Monuments Record, Crown C

3 (*above*) The St. Giles's Fair, September 1904. With the annual fair, local business and pleasure to precedence over traffic in St. Giles's, and they do so still to-day. This picture, one of a notable series by Oxford photographer, captures the whole feeling of a mechanised, but still more than half-rural, pub treat during the Victorian epilogue.

(*Sylvia N*

(*Keith Mirams, Essex County Standard*)   (*G. H. Martin*)

above, left) Colchester, East Bay, south side. Like Middleborough, Colchester (pl. 7) East Bay is a
marshalling-ground for traffic outside the town wall, formed not by a road junction, as at St. Giles's, but by
widening of the road outside the gates. Although its outline has been affected by road works and some
new buildings, East Bay has kept grass and trees, amenities which offered refreshment and shelter to horse-
drawn traffic rather as its present petrol stations serve the motor car.   6 (*above, right*) Colchester, Middleborough. The long loop of the river Colne at Colchester produced similar conditions outside both the North
and the East Gates. Incoming traffic crossed the bridge, and then found a resting ground on the level stretch
between the river bank and the hill leading up to the town's market.   Here it could wait before filing
through the gate to pay toll, or camp for the night after the gates were closed. Middleborough has suffered
more from rebuilding than East Bay, but in this photograph the broadening of the road can be seen between
the bridge—marked by railings on right—and the foot of the hill where the North Gate stood. The cross
road controlled by traffic lights is an extra-mural lane like the road outside Leicester's East Gate (pl. 2).

below, opposite) Oxford, St. Giles's in 1966, looking south toward the Martyrs' Memorial (1849),
St. Mary Magdalen, and the site of the North Gate (right). St. Giles's is now a boulevard, but was originally
a camping-ground made by the confluence of two highways: the road to Banbury and the Midlands on the
far side and the Woodstock road on the near side. There was at one time an island of suburban houses by
St. Mary Magdalen Church, where the Martyrs' Memorial now stands, and the street ended on the city
ditch (Broad Street) rather than at the North Gate.

below) Colchester, Middleborough. Seventeenth-century cottages on the east side, demolished in 1956.

(*National Monuments Record, Crown Copyright*)

8 (*above*) Conway, from the south. The walled town of Conway lies north of the castle, and even in t
twentieth century it is still confined on this side by its fortifications, powerfully reinforced by the railway

9 (*below*) Conway: a medieval gate which is still an entrance to the town, not masked by suburban buil
ings; although lamp-posts have sprouted here, there is also a shaggy growth of grass to emphasise t
frontier.

10 (*above, opposite*) Colchester, High Street, looking west. Colchester's broad High Street, the chief mark
of the town until 1961, owes its generous lines to the Roman street beneath it, but the development of t
market was probably helped by the blocking of the western section at the Balkerne Gate (pl. 11), whic
made the T-junction at the top of the town a less hectic market-stead than a cross-roads would be.

(National Monuments Record, Crown Copyright)

ɪ (*below*) Colchester, the Balkerne Gate. The Balkerne was the West Gate of Roman Colchester, a monu-
ʌental entrance which probably earned its name of the baulked or blocked gate in the fifth century.
ʌnly this south footway remained open, and the main streets of the town still show the effects of the
ʌange (pl. 10 High St. looking west). The western end of the walled town became an enclave, and the huge
ʌictorian water tower was raised on garden ground here in 1882.

(Keith Mirams, Essex County Standard)

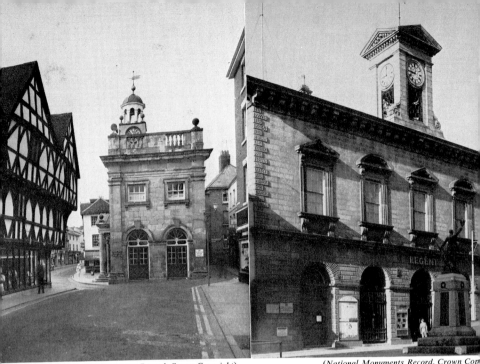

12 (*above, left*) Ludlow, the Butter Cross: a small town house of 1743–4, in a resolutely classical style, which has taken its name from the open ground-floor, a long-lived amenity in market buildings of that kind.

13 & 14 Truro, the façade (*above, right*) and penny-plain back (*below*) of the town hall (1845): a pleasant nineteenth-century essay in the tradition of the Ludlow and Shrewsbury town-houses.

15 (*above*) Shrewsbury: a nineteenth-century photograph of the council-house in the lower market; a large and handsome example, 1596, of the traditional town hall *cum* market-cross.

16 (*below*) King's Lynn, the Tuesday market: a broad twelfth-century market-place made regular and handsome by seventeenth- and eighteenth-century buildings, the most graceful being the Duke's Head, c. 1680, by Henry Bell, the Lynn architect. Bell also built a covered market-cross, but to-day the wide sweep of the square is interrupted only by motor cars.

17, 18 & 19 Kendal: 17 (*above*) the Market Place, looking east; 18 (*left*) the Market Place, looking west; 19 (*opposite*) Branthwaite Brow. Kendal's Market Place is only a fragment of the original wide market-stead at the top of Highgate. The first clue to its contraction is the presence of the old town hall (Brunskill's draper's shop) at the south-west corner (right in pl. 17, left in pl. 18). East of Brunskill's two narrow lanes lead to Finkle Street, which runs parallel to the market on the south. These lanes represent ways through the permanent stalls, on the site of which a whole block of buildings has grown up. Branthwaite Brow, which runs from the east end of the market into Finkle Street marks the eastern, as Finkle Street preserved the southern, boundary of the trading area. The effect of the change has been to reduce the market by more than half, and to place the old town hall at a corner instead of being, like Shrewsbury's council-house (pl. 14) in the centre of the square.

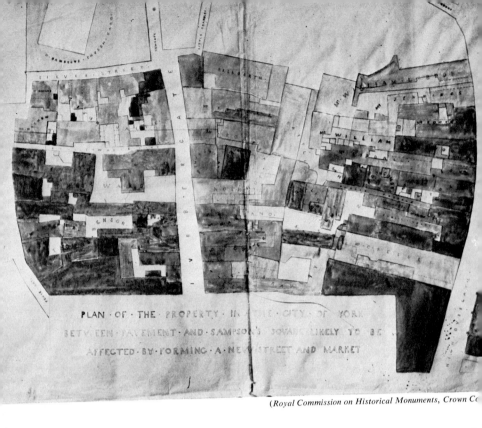

20 (*above*) York. A plan of the area cleared in 1836 to make Parliament Street. This scheme to improve th street markets marks an interesting stage in the cycle of accumulation, clearance, and renewal that charac terises the history of most towns.

21 (*above, opposite*) Colchester, High Street looking north-west, c. 1877. A photograph that can be date because it was evidently taken from the spire of St. Nicholas's church, built in 1876, and that show St. Runwald's, demolished in 1878. St. Runwald's was the survivor of a block of free-standing marke buildings called the Middle Row, which plugged the widest stretch of High Street. Notice the corrugatio of the road surface, sometimes called wash-boarding, which is a characteristic of unpaved roads su jected to hard-wheeled traffic, and can still be seen in small prairie towns.

22 (*below, opposite*) Colchester. An atmospheric picture of High Street decked for the election of 18 Photographs are a commonplace by this time, and the camera can record rapid movement; those that s vive are likely to record special occasions, but through them the century lives for us as no earlier one c

23 (*above, opposite*) Bath, the Royal Crescent (1763). The Crescent is a scenic design, a setting for the splendid play of Georgian Bath's high season. Its architect, John Wood II, took a segment of his father's imaginative Circus (1754) and made it a whole by his skilful use of the giant Ionic order and the addition of two pavilions. The design was a striking success, and one of the most influential devices in English architecture. This photograph records the Crescent's continuing beauty in an entirely different age: here in the second world war Bath has responded to the call to Dig for Victory by dividing the ground before the Crescent into allotments, and raised a thin web of bean-poles against the façade.

24 (*below, opposite*) Buxton, the Crescent (1779–88). Buxton struggled to keep pace with Bath, and it was appropriately the site of the first response to the Royal Crescent. John Carr's design is far enough removed from Wood's to have its own merits.

25 (*below*) Colchester, Vint Crescent (1939). The crescent's curves descended through the spas and watering-places of Regency England, and the quadrants of Nash's Regent Street, to the age of the close-packed, as opposed to the emparked, villa, and the semi-detached house, to which they have no relevance whatever. To call a loop of semi-detached houses a crescent is to make an emotional noise, not a statement; the historian's business is to discern its implications. There are many such crescents up and down the country on which to practise. The houses in Vint Crescent have green tiled roofs.

(*G. H. Martin*)

Tom Sharpe

27 (*above*) Cambridge, King's College chapel. To most visitors to Cambridge the quiet grace of the Backs is the very essence of the place, and the college's long ownership of the river bank seems a warranty that here if anywhere we have old Cambridge under our eyes. Yet the lawns and fine buildings overlie the quays, warehouses, and tenements of the merchant community whose consequence drew the scholars here in the first place. In this celebrated view of King's College we are looking over the site of the medieval salt-hithe, and of the busy lanes that connected the quays with the market, in the days before colleges were even a promising educational experiment.

26 (*opposite*) Shrewsbury, the Dingle and St. Chad's church. Shrewsbury has a pleasant park and promenade in the south-western bend of the Severn, where the ground falls from St. Chad's, a fine eighteenth-century church on the edge of the old town, to the river bank. The pond and rock gardens seen here are not a simple piece of municipal landscaping, however, but a remnant of the stone quarries worked for the town in the thirteenth-century, when the walls and gates were built on the proceeds of a special toll. Accounts survive in the borough archives describing the cutting and transport of the stone from here; the quarry itself survives as a gentle municipal amenity. (*Elaine Dennis*)

8 (*below*) Oxford, High Street from St. Mary's tower, looking south-east. In both Oxford and Cambridge the colleges were late-comers, and until the sixteenth century their privileged inmates, predominantly graduates, were greatly outnumbered by students living in halls, communal lodgings licensed by the University. Just as the lawns of King's overlie the staithes of commercial Cambridge, so Oxford's college quadrangles have spread over the halls and inns and houses of the medieval city. In this view the belfry of Magdalen is medieval—just—but the visible collegiate architecture is overwhelmingly seventeenth- and eighteenth-century, its Gothic forms at University (centre right) a tribute to Oxford's conservatism.

(*G. H. Martin*)

Welcome to Oxford – the home of

PRESSED STEEL

PRESSED STEEL COMPANY LIMITED

MAKERS OF:-
CAR BODIES. COMMERCIAL VEHICLE CABS. PRESSINGS OF ALL
TYPES. PRESTCOLD COMMERCIAL REFRIGERATION EQUIPMENT.
RAILWAY ROLLING STOCK. EXECUTIVE AND LIGHT AIRCRAFT.

PLANTS AT:-
COWLEY, OXFORD INDON, WILTSHIRE.
THEALE, BERKS. PAISLEY, SCOTLAND.
REARSBY, LE. RE, SHOREHAM, SUSSE

(G.

29 Oxford, the station approach, 1965. In the twelfth century scholars came to Oxford because it wa
lively centre of trade and traffic, but as the University developed it gradually subdued and dominated
city. The popular imagination having seized upon universities as places where truth is contemplated rath
than expounded, the modern industrial development of Oxford often comes as a surprise. There is more
say about Oxford than this hoarding said, but its self-consciously defiant message illustrated the cit
complex history very well. In its layers of meaning, it too was a palimpsest.

III

The Town as Palimpsest

G. H. Martin

Historians work with documents, and reach back through their written and printed text to people. On the way they use other material, adducing evidence from artifacts of all kinds, and calling as freely as they can upon common-sense, which is sharpened by experience. They ponder, in short, the marks that man leaves behind him. The historian's first and last concern may be, must be, with his text, but that text has a setting which is ultimately the whole sum of human activity, and to interpret the past we must be ready to come to terms with anything that has registered it. The historian of towns is concerned not only with people, but with communities, and with places. Communities, like individuals, have their own subtleties, but so do the places that they inhabit. In some sort a town is a document; it displays its history in its public face, as well as in its archives.

Towns are places where people live; that is the continuing secret of their strength and, to any tidy-minded person, their principal weakness. Successive generations leave their mark upon them, and some of the marks have proved surprisingly durable; they stay there to be read if anyone cares to read them. The visual evidence which is our concern here is the evidence that presents itself when we look at a town: the patterns of its streets and buildings, the blemishes upon the uniformity of the present that remind us of the past. If we think of what we see as a text, we recognise very soon that it is not a simple one: beneath the characters that we first trace, there are other words and phrases to be read: the town is a palimpsest.

Maitland found a happy phrase for our national habit of allowing institutions to grow by casual accumulation rather than by design. Speaking of the French revolutionary settlement he said, 'I doubt if we Englishmen, who never clean our slates, generally know how clean the French slate was to be.' To have called this paper 'the town as uncleaned slate' might have aroused unwholesome expectations about its subject matter and tone, but it is happily true that our urban slate has not as yet been scrubbed quite clean. It may be that the commercial pressures and the motor-traffic of the twentieth century will succeed where all previous generations have failed, and the places where we live will be ground to a monotonous and characterless smoothness. If that should happen, the historian who has a real curiosity about towns will be driven back to supplementing his texts with photographs, and drawings, and maps, and plans. Those materials are by no means overworked. Professor Conzen's paper has shown how much and how unjustifiably we have neglected one category of them.[1] Within this century the cinematic film too has added enormous wealth to our store of historical material.[2] Visual evidence of that kind is now abundant enough to be an embarrassment to us, and yet it is surpassed by the material that lies all around us: the scene in which we live. There are still many messages to be deciphered on the unclean slate; we might as well read some of them while we can.

Historically, towns have three functions, all inter-related: they are markets, fortresses, and seats of government. In this country the first two have done more to shape the towns than has the third, at least so far as we seek any formal manifestation of political power. Two of our kings, Charles I and George IV, can be credited with a desire to turn the suburbs of London into something like a capital city. Neither, as it happened, was a very energetic man, and though they were each served by an architect-manager of genius they were also each readily defeated by circumstances. The city of London itself has long, and perhaps always, been incorrigible. To the medieval Londoner government was apt to mean the Conqueror's Tower, and his successors were not much mollified to see it characterised instead by the urbane grace of the earl of Bedford's *piazza* at Covent Garden, or the Regent's street. London's interests are mercantile, as the glazed cliffs of the present City daily remind St. Paul's, and even its own civic tradition is deliberately casual: splendid, but very personal. The Lord Mayor's Show is a carnival mounted annually to celebrate the withdrawal of the monarch's hand from the city. In the middle ages the citizens' chosen magistrates presented themselves before

---

[1] See above, pp. 113–30. British historians seem to have paid little attention to the remarkable sixteenth-century plans and drawings of English and Irish towns in the Cottonian Collection: British Museum, Cotton. MS., Augustus I, 1 and 2. The bird's-eye view of Carlisle, *ibid.*, 1, 13, is of the first quality, and the Irish material in Vol. II is deeply interesting. See E. Croft-Murray and P. Hulton, *Catalogue of British Drawings* [in the British Museum] (1960), I, pp. xxiii–xxv.

[2] See British Film Institute, *Catalogue of the National Film Archive*, 3rd ed., 2 vols. (1951–60).

he judges in the exchequer, received the king's licence to manage their own affairs, and returned in triumph to their proper haunts. The carnival survives to-day, its origins forgotten. The mayors had no official residence until the Mansion House was built in 1739–53, and the corporation still uses its medieval Guildhall, a large but unassertive and unspecialised building around which the City once sprawled, and now looms.

London's attitudes summarise a national tradition, which we can assess with our own eyes. Until the nineteenth century our town halls were usually not impressive buildings; the early specimens that survive are prized rather for their antiquity than for their elegance, and the Victorians, who were more severe in these matters than we can afford to be, found them offensively undignified. Whether the many that were built or rebuilt after 1835 gained much in dignity is debatable; dignity is earned rather than bestowed, and efforts to introduce it into architecture are likely to be self-defeating. Yet both the unpretentious flint or timber walls of our few medieval guildhalls, and the gothic or baroque palaces of the nineteenth-century corporations and their successors, have something precise to say to us. Until 1835 the English borough was governed, managed, by something like a private club. A municipality might take a broad view of its duties, as the corporation of Liverpool often did, or a fairly self-regarding one, like the old corporation of Leicester, but it was nevertheless a club, with its own well-defined rules for admission, and a fair degree of freedom under the royal licence of its charters in managing its own property, the ancient royal lands and revenues of the town.[3] It consequently housed itself in a private, informal and domestic manner, buying an ordinary tenement like the Jew's house in St. Aldate's which the city guild of Oxford acquired in 1229, or the Tollhouse in Yarmouth which acquired its name when it was still a private tenement in the fourteenth century, with the council patching and altering it rather than rebuilding it.[4] London and York built themselves large guildhalls for civic business and civic pleasures, but they were halls and little more. A medieval patriciate wanted space, not hives of offices, and its

---

[3] Leicester became a by-word for unregenerate corruption because the corporation put up such a vigorous defence against the Whig reformers in 1833–6. Mr. G. A. Chinnery's *Leicester Borough Records: Hall Books and Papers, 1688–1835* (1965), Vol. V, shows that the old corporation's chief vice was secrecy, and that in its time it was an active and even a public-spirited custodian of the borough's patrimony. The fact remains that there was probably no municipal body in the kingdom to which the developed doctrine of public responsibility would have come as a more perverse and repugnant innovation.

[4] Ruth Fasnacht, *History of the City of Oxford* (1954), p. 44. The merchant guild seems to have rented another property, opposite St Martin's, in the twelfth century: H. E. Salter, *Medieval Oxford*, Oxford Historical Society, 100 (1936), p. 42. For Yarmouth see C. J. Palmer, ed.) *History of Great Yarmouth by Henry Manship* (1854), pp. 256–7.

quarters would often content its Tudor, and Stuart, and even it Georgian successors.

York's and Doncaster's elegant Mansion Houses (1725, 1745) migh seem exceptions to the pattern, but they were built as places in whicl the mayor could live and dine and entertain, not rule and administer. Exeter added a porticoed façade to its guildhall at the end of the sixteentl century, but councils were more often content to combine their chambe unobtrusively with a more generally-useful building, like the town hall o Ludlow, an essay of 1760 in a provincial classical taste, which for its pain was known locally as the Butter Cross, because its ground floor wa: thriftily contrived to shelter the dairy market. It had many fellows.

The traditional market house survived the reform of the municipa corporations—there is a pleasant specimen at Truro, built in 1845—bu the reformed corporations generally wanted and needed rather differen quarters. At first the new municipalities were not very active, because to a reforming temper the highest virtue was to spend no money at all, so much having been mis-spent, as it seemed, in the past. When they die build, however, and by the second half of the century most of them were forced to do so, it had to be in a manner appropriate to trustees of publi funds: not gaudily, but also not in a shame-faced manner. The inn parlour, club-room manner of the old civic life had to be dispelled. There were new rooms to be provided: a police station, a rates office with a public counter, rooms in which public business could be transacted openly and virtuously. The old corporators grazed their cattle on the common land, and occasionally, if there was a dividend to be disposed of had a modest treat. The new corporator pays rates. We have moved from the comfortable, exclusive ease of the dining-club into the chill, imper sonal world of the ruled-feint ledger: the buildings themselves say so.

It is a curious fact that as municipal government has grown more com plex and powerful, the buildings that house it have insensibly removed from the centre of local affairs. It is not only that the borough engineer's office or the school clinic will be found in some row of elderly houses between a car-park and a building site, but that the town hall itself has fallen victim to remoteness. No sooner did it allow itself a touch of grandeur to compel our attention and respect than it began to mark a dead stretch of pavement. The weakness was apparent in the nineteenth century, and it has grown. Albert Square may have many merits but it is

---

5 The town clerk of York hoped to secure a repository for the city archives when the Mansion House was built, but they seem to have remained in the Guildhall. The prime object of the building was 'to enhance the dignity of the lord mayors' by providing them with a house in which they could stand treat to the Commons. *Victoria History of Yorkshire: The City of York* (1961), pp. 536, 543.

not the heart of modern Manchester; Cathays Park at Cardiff is an enclave; the new guildhall at Norwich overlooks the civic church and the ancient tolbooth, but it stands back from the edge of the market. We can see in several earlier specimens a desire to make economical use of a valuable site, but in the twentieth century what one might suppose the natural place for the seat of local government—the centre of affairs, wherever that might be—has proved too valuable to waste on public buildings which, by serving all, bring profit to none.

What determines the centre of affairs, the place where, in the North American idiom, the action is, is a consensus, a sum of subjective judgements. It may offer its own satisfaction, like the angle of St. Mark's Square and the Piazzetta at Venice, but it is always worth considering. Leicester offers an instructive example. It is a city of some antiquity, older than the Rialto settlement at Venice, and very much older than most motorists or passengers on the Midland Region railway line might suppose from what they can see, yet it lacks, except in one or two secluded places, that repose which commonly marks antiquity. The centre of Leicester is not by the castle or the medieval guildhall; so far as there is a centre it is to be found at the clock tower, known locally as The Clock Tower, a case-hardened, stone, grandfather clock raised in 1868 at the east end of High Street. Undoubtedly the Clock Tower has some magnetic quality: it figures often in local conversation, and the policemen at its foot never lack company, but it stands at the junction of five roads, and it is no place for relaxed contemplation. That is not the fault of the motor traffic alone: it has always been dangerous to loiter at road junctions.

The principal street of medieval Leicester, and probably of its Roman predecessor, was not High Street but High Cross Street, which runs north and south across High Street about a quarter of a mile west of the Clock Tower. The Clock Tower in fact marks the site of the east gate of the walled town, and of the five roads that converge upon it, two, Churchgate and Gallowtree Gate, run along the line of the east wall, whilst Belgrave Gate and Humberstone Gate are country roads that meet here to enter the town. The nineteenth- and twentieth-century development of Leicester has moved its centre of gravity eastwards from the narrow streets and broad market place of the medieval town, and has given the city in the Clock Tower a hub rather than a heart. The motor car has added its own spice of anarchy to the scene.

Walls and gateways have had a powerful effect upon the streetplans of our medieval towns. They concentrate traffic outside the walls, a matter to which we shall return, and shape both the thoroughfares inside the town and the spreading suburbs. In some places, as at Caernarvon and

Conway, the walls substantially contain the modern town, and we can savour a thirteenth-century *bastide* there just as, on the seaward side of Berwick-on-Tweed, we can examine still the larger provision that the development of artillery in the sixteenth century made necessary. Elsewhere the fortifications have been swamped, but have left their mark in streets like those from which W. H. Stevenson traced the ramparts of pre-Conquest Nottingham.[6] Colchester to-day has the pattern of its main shopping streets determined by an alteration to the West Gate of the Roman town that was probably made in the fourth or fifth century. In the last days of the Roman town or early in the Saxon occupation a rough wall was built across the carriageways of the monumental West Gate which had been the main entrance to the *colonia*. The western arm of the cruciform main streets withered and vanished. The gate became a bastion, with only a narrow wicket for pedestrians, and medieval and modern Colchester have grown round a central T-junction instead of the cross-roads which was the universal pattern of Roman camps, towns, and their successors. This, and the substantial width of the main lateral street, High Street, governed the growth of the town's markets and, mischievously, the application of a one-way traffic system in 1963 which has brought a touch of pre-war Brooklands to the town centre.

Gates were not often blocked, and have usually been swept away by the pressure of traffic. Although over-exciting by our own standards, medieval England was a relatively peaceful and well-ordered country, and it was difficult even in the fourteenth century, when there was certainly still open ground inside, to stop towns spilling over their walls.[7] The gates were therefore often overlaid by suburban building, which spread along the roads for some distance in a way familiar enough to us before it began to expand sideways to enclose the old town in a new shell. If two roads converge on a gate they may draw the suburbs further out, although we must remember that tarmacadam surfacing and modern building can sometimes alter appearances. On the eastern side of the English Bridge at Shrewsbury there is an interesting confluence of roads on either side of the abbey church, St. Peter's, which plainly marks an important stage in the development of that frontier town. On the north side of the church are the Georgian and seventeenth-century houses of the street now known as

[6] See Carl Stephenson, *Borough and Town* (Cambridge, Mass., 1933), p. 197, and notes there. W. H. Stevenson's principal study of the ramparts appeared only in the *Nottingham Guardian*, July 1901.

[7] The bailiffs and commonalty of Ipswich leased a piece of land along the town rampart (*fossa*) in 1315–16, with the proviso that the earthwork should be maintained and that the town should have access to it in peace and war. Royal Commission on Historical MSS, *9th Report and Appendix*, Part I (1883), p. 233.

Abbey Foregate, but on the southern side the road is soon seen to divide
the church from the remains of its conventual buildings. What we see is
not an ancient junction at the bridge-head, but a piece of early nineteenth-
century engineering: the southern street is Telford's Holyhead road, and
the Abbey Foregate is the bypassed line of the earlier road. The present
arrangement is therefore quite modern, but the Benedictine abbey was
founded on the site of an earlier church, and if we looked back far enough
we might find the road displaced in 1083 to the line of Abbey Foregate,
and Telford's the accidental reinstatement of an older way, long buried
under the abbey cloisters.

There is a deceptive feature of a different kind outside the north gate of
Oxford, where St. Giles's Street runs from the church of St. Mary
Magdalen northward for more than a quarter of a mile to St. Giles's. This
wide boulevard with its avenues of trees, fringes of car-parks, and ample
carriageways looks at first sight like a recent and inspired contrivance in
a city which is not famed for the ease with which its traffic flows. The
clues to its origin lie in the division of the street at St. Giles's church,
which lies between the road to Woodstock and the Cotswolds on the west,
and a road of great historical importance which gives access through Banbury and Brackley to the whole Midlands and the North on the east side.
These roads merge, not into a single track aimed at the North Gate, but
into a broad plain like a parade-ground which ended on the city ditch
rather than at the gate. Outside the gate there was once a clutter of
houses on an island site now marked by St. Mary Magdalen's church and
the Martyrs' Memorial, but the wide expanse of the roadway has been kept
clear by traffic and also by the annual St. Giles's fair, held at the beginning
of September, and lingering on to-day, in an age when Oxford no longer
lacks excitement during the long vacation. St. Giles's is something of an
extra-mural seasonal market, and the rapid growth of the suburbs here
when post-Conquest Oxford developed as a cloth-making town, and above
all as a centre of trade and traffic, is indicated by the foundation of St.
Giles's church at the far end before 1133.[8]

There was always something to see at these entrances to towns because
they concentrated traffic, and often slowed it with tolls. They stopped it
altogether in the evening when the main gates were closed, even though
the wicket or postern might be open, that small needle's-eye which, a
well-read audience will remember, is a less stringent barrier to a loaded
beast than is the gate of Heaven to a rich man.[9] St. Giles's will have

---

[8] H. E. Salter, *Medieval Oxford*, pp. 114–16. St Giles's may also have been in regular use as
a cattle market; *ibid.*, p. 78.

[9] *Richard II*, V, 5, 17. 'It is as hard to come, as for a camel to thread the postern of a small
needle's eye': an ingenious gloss on Matthew, 19, 24. The Vulgate has *per foramen acus transire*.

served in its time as a marshalling ground for caravans, but there are two more-specialised examples of that forgotten amenity at Colchester, outside the northern and eastern gates. Both are now impaired by rebuilding, but they are each characterised by a wedge-shaped widening of the road, which opens gradually from the gate and then narrows sharply on the river to cross by a bridge or, in one case, by a bridge and a ford. That on the north side of the town, which is known for no obvious reason as Middleborough, exactly fills the space between the site of the gate and the North Bridge. It has kept some old houses on its margin, but has lost its cobble-paving since 1945. The other, called East Bay, extends from the foot of East Hill to the East Bridge. It is some 300 yards short of the site of the East Gate, which stood near the top of the hill. The slope was probably much steeper before the gate was demolished in 1674, and there could be no convenient resting place on the hill itself. East Bay is more cluttered with lights and signs and petrol pumps than Middleborough— the site is one appropriate enough for garages—but it has kept a strip of grass which would once have fulfilled the purpose of the present service stations.

Road-widening, paving, and rebuilding have destroyed many stamping-grounds of this kind and not only in this century. Colchester is lucky to have kept two, both engulfed by the modern town, but distinguishing the two gates in a striking way. It would be distressing for the preservationist to have to choose between them. If we turn now from the approaches to the town to the chief object of its traffic, the market place, we find a different process at work. 'Here's the town gate reached, the market-place gaping before us': the market places may be anywhere, but not often close to the gate. They are, despite the distinguished example of Shrewsbury, on top of hills rather than at the foot, and they are very often associated with the principal or civic church: St. Peter Mancroft at Norwich, St. Martin's at Carfax in Oxford, if we need to say more than St. Paul's at the end of Cheapside. Boston is an agreeable example of a single-parish town—always a sign of new riches in the middle ages, in contrast to the ancient multiplexity of Huntingdon, Bristol, or Ipswich— with the market place under one side of its splendid church, and the town quays on the other. At King's Lynn we still find the stalls of the Saturday Market under the walls of St. Margaret's, the mother church of the borough. Like many others, these are picturesque, fairly small market places, and we half expect our markets to crowd hugger-mugger in narrow streets even though we are gratified by such broad squares as Helmsley's when we come upon them. The Tuesday market at King's Lynn, at the north end of the town, is a market of that kind, a handsome, regular square like a French *place*. Although its principal buildings are seventeenth- and eighteenth-century it is a medieval square, laid out for the new land when the bishop of Norwich enlarged his investment in Lynn in the twelfth century.[10] It has not always been as open as we see it to-day, for in the seventeenth century it had a covered cross, a stone umbrella for market traders, like the medieval crosses at Chichester and Salisbury, designed by the Lynn architect Henry Bell, who built the Duke's Head hotel. Under its present crust of motor cars, however, it keeps its pristine shape, a clear space.

Markets are particularly likely to be built over; we are aware of the process, but we may not always give it its proper weight when we consider early town plans. The market cross and the market house are familiar buildings: Shrewsbury has a sixteenth-century hall with an arcaded ground floor that fills nearly a quarter of the present market place, but there are other and larger encroachments to look for. Professor Conzen calls the process market-colonisation, and Ludlow offers an excellent example of it, arrested at a point at which its nature is still clear: movable stalls become fixed stalls, covered stalls, lock-up shops, and finally private and public houses. If the block becomes large enough, the free space around it will look like a lane. The whole process can be seen in the derivation of the name Shambles, from the Old English *scamel*, Latin *scamellum*, a little bench, and so a butcher's counter, a place of carnage, as the dictionary picturesquely puts it, and at last a Tudor street in York that is constantly pressed into service to illustrate the medieval town, which it does not.[11]

Having identified the market block, we ought to consider it a little further. If it is large enough to be a nuisance without being impressive it is likely to be cleared again. Edinburgh had its Luckenbooths, another eloquent name, hard by St. Giles' church and the old Tolbooth, but even in that broad High Street they were an obstruction and were pulled down in 1817. Colchester had a line of shops called the Middle Row at

[10] E. M. Beloe, 'Freebridge Hundred and the making of Lynn', *Norfolk Archaeology*, xii (1895), pp. 311–34; an excellent topographical essay.

[11] There is a general account of this process in M. W. Beresford and J. K. S. St. Joseph, *Medieval England: An Aerial Survey* (1958), pp. 158–9, and further discussion and examples in M. W. Beresford, *History on the Ground* (1957), and W. G. Hoskins's *Local History in England* (1959), two highly-practised topographers and observers of the historic fabric of towns. For discussion of the markets of York, see *Medieval England*, pp. 159–60. The chief objection to the theory advanced there is that the in-filling would have had to begin very early, but it well could. We must also always keep in mind the abundant cattle of primitive trade, and their motor-car-like demands on space.

the widest point of its High Street market, and a church among them with an archaic dedication to St. Runwald. The houses were destroyed in the 1850s, but St. Runwald's lasted until 1878, when its demolition saved the twentieth century some heart-searching. Holy Trinity church in the market place at Richmond in the North Riding of Yorkshire, on the other hand, has survived with its attendant shops, and so have many larger blocks of buildings like those now on the north side of the church at Melton Mowbray.

The market place at Kendal opens east of Highgate, which is A.6, by what was the highest point in the town before the area called Fellside was built up above it in the late eighteenth century. Kendal has an intricate and ill-documented history, with two castles, a manorial *faubourg* called Kirkland at Nether Bridge at the southern end of the town, and a commercial centre to the north where the market is held on its hill. At its lower, eastern end, the market place narrows to a lane which runs into Finkle Street, a turning off Highgate which lies parallel to the market on the other shoulder of the hill. Between these two streets are narrow lanes, one called New Shambles. The Old Shambles lie across Highgate, to the west. It is clear enough in aerial photographs and then perhaps in maps, though not at all clear on the ground, that the present market square is only a fragment of the original market place, and that the whole space between it and Finkle Street has been built up by the process we have seen half-accomplished at Ludlow. The old town hall, now a shop on the corner of the Market Place and Highgate, therefore stood originally where one might expect it to stand, in the middle of the open market, on the main street of the town.

In their time there were further encroachments in Kendal. The present entrance to the market was plugged in 1754 by a chapel, St. George's, which afforded an extra shelter for stallholders at its east end, the mouth of Finkle Street was blocked by the Pump Inn, which had the fish market behind it, and Highgate was long encumbered below Finkle Street by a large free-standing block called Newbiggin, destroyed in 1803. If Newbiggin also had its origin in stalls then the original market covered a very large area, but the space above Finkle Street is generous enough. As the Old English dooms remind us, a large part of early trade was trade in cattle, and in the thinly-populated towns of the middle ages, which, beset as we are by people, we can only picture by the most strenuously imaginative efforts, there was plenty of room for trade of all kinds. Probably even the middle of Beverley, between the twin poles of the minster and the mercantile settlement by St. Mary's, was open in the same fashion. We can certainly posit two large markets there, reaching towards each other and now intricately built up; if we could see far enough back we might find only one.[12]

Like the history of urban parishes, an investigation of that kind reminds us that change is the normal condition of life: our historic towns are valuable because until recently their shifts of fortune have been written large in them. Even the most placid scenes have their restless moral. Oxford and Cambridge have lost some of their repose, but they stand to many people as the very pattern of old towns, and especially of medieval towns. Their belfries, gate-houses, mullioned windows, and angular passages keep the ages of faith and the medieval church's monopoly of learning fresh in the visitor's mind. In fact the colleges were not at all characteristic of the medieval university, where most students lived in halls and lodgings and would, *mutatis mutandis*, have found much more that was familiar in the life of a civic university of the 1930s than they would in post-Reformation Oxford or Cambridge. The view from the tower of St. Mary's in Oxford, which offers so many towers and spires and crenellations, is a record of the colleges' triumph in the sixteenth century and after, when they enlarged and beautified the miscellaneous properties that they had accumulated. The belfries of Merton and New College and Magdalen may cry out against hasty generalisation, but they would have stood higher above the tenements and gardens and waste lots of the medieval town.

However, the colleges have medieval roots, and some have fine medieval buildings. The chapel of King's College, planned in the middle of the fifteenth century, though not completed until the sixteenth, exemplifies all that its pious founder hoped for his great house of prayer and learning. King's chapel rising over the lawns and the riverside walk of the Backs is one of the most familiar images of ancient beauty and the learned life in the English-speaking world. As an Oxford man, and one particularly fond of Cambridge, I mind what I say: King's tells us something of the medieval university town.

Something, but not all; like Oxford, Cambridge was chosen by its scholars because it was a busy town, not a quiet one. Its famous bridge carried, as it still does, the great weight of traffic between the Midlands and East Anglia, and the castle above it was raised to guard the most important river-crossing in Eastern England. The later universities set their face against industry and Sunday trains and disagreeable innovations of all kinds, but originally learning would not have stayed in Cambridge

---

12 The demand for car-parking space and its attendant demolitions look like a modern twist to the story, but the city of York was compelled to carve out Parliament Street as a new market across the clutter of its old markets in 1834–6: *Victoria History, York*, pp. 488–9.

or Oxford if they had not been exciting towns to which people came and where things happened. The Backs, therefore, where to-day great, pampered ducks are fed and iron-tipped poles clink on the best punting-bottom in the country, were the site of the hithes or quays of medieval Cambridge, and the lawns of King's cover the site of the Salt Hithe, with the chapel imposed on a tangle of lanes and gardens and tenements and a forgotten parish church. By the time King's was endowed and built the site had already seen changes, as the demand for hostels for the growing university led to the rebuilding and regrouping of tenements, but the trade at the Salt Hithe would have been vital to the early borough. The delicate beauty of the chapel and its setting is the outcome of much hard bargaining and some sweeping demolitions. There is nothing entirely new under the sun.[13]

That said, King Henry spent his subjects' money well, and college lawns are more pleasing to the eye than the gravel waste of a car park, but the uncompleted scheme for King's would have made it a medieval college still, though on a splendid scale, built to a utilitarian rather than a monumental plan. We have to turn to Trinity College, where the Great Court was laid out on its present lines in the sixteenth century, and buildings demolished or moved and rebuilt to achieve regularity, to find the beginnings of that concern with appearances that lead on, with the revival of the classical styles, through Inigo Jones's Covent Garden to a world of symmetry and straight lines and neat edges. Since the Picturesque movement of the late eighteenth century we have been in fitful revolt against these values, although they have been strongly reinforced by the principles of the mechanical revolution. Indeed, we have now reached a point where we prize irregular buildings in a formal setting. Only by a prolonged and imaginative study of, say, the English water-colour school can we recreate the tumble-down, farmyard-like inconsequentiality of every scene of human occupation before the mid-nineteenth century, with mud and grass and loose timber everywhere, and animals as ubiquitous as motor cars to-day. As our kerbs and edges and walls have become irreproachably neat, so we have eased their unnatural constraint by cultivating other irregularities, and growing exotics indoors or on traffic islands. Like King's chapel, these things have their own story to tell, and despite its rapid transformations the urban scene is the more rewarding to study to-day because its elements are most diverse and richly mixed.

One robust feature of the modern town and its suburbs is the crescent. It has its origins in Bath, where the two John Woods, father and son,

[13] See the plan in R. Willis and J. W. Clark, *The Architectural History of the University of Cambridge* (1886), Vol. IV, p. 13.

created a setting for the eighteenth-century spa as sophisticated as the company that enjoyed it. The inventive progression of Queen's Square, the Circus, and the Royal Crescent, is a wonder of English architecture, and its influence has been very great. Queen's Square was the first square with a side planned as though it were a single large house; the Circus was the first circus in the country (and so an ancestor of the traffic roundabout, *inter multa alia*), and the Royal Crescent was the first crescent: half a circus, a terrace of houses curved for fun. Finely conceived itself, the Crescent represents a weakening inspiration, but it lent itself to imaginative treatment in other hands. John Carr's crescent at Buxton, a heavier but still impressive essay, was followed by crescents large and small in the seaside watering-places of Regency and Victorian England. The seaside, still one of the most neglected subjects in the whole neglected field of social history, is important architecturally because, as a scene of pleasure and originally of privilege, it has provided the most consistent inspiration for our own efforts to mitigate our great industrial cities and inland towns. The crescent moved inland again, although most of the experiments were made by the sea. Beaumaris, once a frontier fortress, but a respectable watering-place in the 1830s,[14] has a crescent with a convex front. Later in the century we find suburban crescents in southern Belfast, but the rapid social decline of the terraced house and the exigencies of building in developed areas probably checked their career.

In the twentieth century the fact that sweeping curves are better for motor traffic than sharp turns has increased the number of swelling or concave façades in our towns, but the crescent itself has fallen into a melancholy decline. It was used for the municipal offices at Bolton in 1939 to some effect, but it has also been used to lend what coherence a road can lend to semi-detached houses. The refined wiggle which gives such crescents their name does no great credit to the Woods, but if we observe and identify it correctly we can draw a small dividend even from the most dispiriting walks. Despite appearances there is little in our towns that happens by accident, though in this case the old text of the palimpsest is worn exceedingly faint.

Symbolism plays as large a part in our lives as ever it has done. The quirks of our builders' and planners' wilder fantasies are really efforts to state some principle and so reassure us all. A street is only a street, but it helps to call it Avenue, or Gardens—Chlorine Gardens in Belfast must give us all pause. To call it Crescent and to justify the name by the slightest of bends is to show that some real care has been taken. The

---

[14] See, for example, J. A. V. Chapple and A. Pollard, eds., *The Letters of Mrs. Gaskell* (1966), p. 16.

Victorians were past-masters of these delicate attentions. On the cliffs of New Hunstanton there is a brown stone public house like a sombre Cotswold farm, a town hall which is now dedicated to commercial Lotto, and in front of them a cross on a stepped pedestal. The inn is by Butterfield, as is a good deal of New Hunstanton. In a sense the cross is too, for it was brought here from Old Hunstanton to lend a touch of antiquity to the *caput* of the seaside resort. Abating the strangeness of its setting above the sea—and stranger things have happened, as Dunwich could have told us —the group is an effective one, a staid but ornamental appendage to the streets of boarding houses laid out to receive respectable Victorian families. It is also eloquent of a whole cycle of architectural taste, for, from the time when Beau Nash educated the patrons of Bath in the early eighteenth century, the health and pleasure resorts were aristocratic in their inspiration, and nascent resorts like Brighton lost no time in replacing cottages with terraces and crescents, and reckoning rents in guineas instead of shillings and pence. Now at the end of the nineteenth century the country inn and the cottage, or the simulated cottage, were in favour, and a village cross to which a gentleman might once have disdained to tether his horse could serve as the cynosure of a society which, if it was not urbane as the Augustans understood urbanity, had become the wealthiest and most powerful and demanding that the world had yet seen. The world was yet to see us.

From the seaside we might move again to the world of industry and endeavour. Shrewsbury is a town of the highest historical interest, with a fine collection of archives: its centre is a hill-top spread with handsome buildings, and circled by the Severn. It has been a frontier town, and a seat of military government, and the centre of a large textile industry. Its interest does not end with the old order of things, for Shropshire was a seat of the industrial revolution, and Shrewsbury saw the first iron-framed building raised anywhere. It has kept, from the same period, St. Chad's, an elegant round church built in 1792 on the western edge of the old town. Between St. Chad's and the river is a broad public park, falling to the riverside walk, and in this park is a hollow called the Dingle, with a small pond and a rock garden. It looks like any other municipal garden, but it is a much more ancient enterprise, for this is one of the quarries of medieval Shrewsbury where stone was cut for the town walls and gates in the thirteenth century, and where we can follow the weekly labour of the hewers and freemasons from the murage accounts which survive among the borough archives. The stone was shipped from the landing stages below to the bridge under the castle and the bridge towards the abbey, the English Bridge, and the work, sustained by tolls levied at the gates, filled more than a decade of Henry III's reign.[15] Then long after, the nineteenth century, solicitous of townsmen's welfare in ways that the middle ages had hardly guessed, laid out walks and a bandstand and brought in some rock plants to deck the raw stone above the pool. The vestiges of discarded industry are not often turned to such gentle and refreshing account.

To appreciate Shrewsbury's park we have to turn to the borough records. There are some features of our towns that speak for themselves, but it is the historian's business to turn to the records, records of all kinds, maps and pictures among them. At the same time it is always worth while, and usually very rewarding, to look at the scene itself. Sometimes it even offers its own texts. When the railway passenger to Oxford sees the city's towers in the gaps between its famous gasometers, it is time for him to take up his belongings. The view is not one that an innocent traveller might expect, but he can look for immediate reassurance. On the hoardings by the station approaches, Oxford's products are boldly advertised, and until this present year (the wording is a little different now) there was a large placard in bas-relief, which said 'Welcome to Oxford, the home of Pressed Steel.' It was an eloquent and thought-provoking text: a winning invitation to decipher the palimpsest.

[15] See G. H. Martin, 'The English borough in the thirteenth century', *Transactions of the Royal Historical Society*, 5th Series, xiii (1963), pp. 123-44.

(S. M. Haughton)

The Bank of England, Liverpool, undergoing cleaning. On each side we see buildings bearing the typical symbols of style and form that we associate with the formal values of architecture. The whole scene is closed by a façade of abstract forms and patterns which are nevertheless capable of evoking an emotional response. This equivalent of the modern art that is to be found in our 'advanced' galleries has been created by the scaffolding and fabric screens erected for the cleaning of Cockerell's Bank of England.

A Manchester street in the 1850s. This illustrates very well the boldness of incident and the surface texture. Note the spectacles, the telescope, and the variety of building forms.

(Manchester City Library)

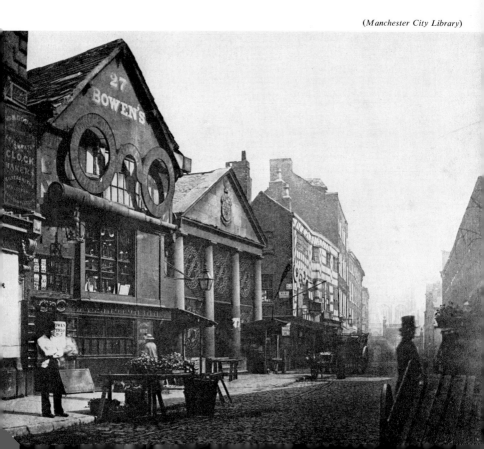

32 Market Street, Manchester, in the 1890s. This scene conveys very well the sources of traffic noise a the dirt of the street; the variety of signs, clocks and awnings gives a good idea of the mass of incident fro which the street scene was composed.

33 (*opposite*) Accrington, 1895. This map shows not only the small dimensions of a typical industrial tow but also the closeness of the active countryside to the centre. Notice the manner in which the developme of the town has created a variety of communities each readily identifiable to the inhabitants by the bou daries created by railways, roads and water and also by the siting of large buildings of one purpose another. It is still a pedestrian town.

(*Bolton Eveni*

34 35 In these two diametric views of Bolton even the very much enlarged town of to-day seems to have rural setting, especially when looked at from the moors above it.

(*J. E.*

(*J. E. Turner*)

6 Stoneclough, on the River Irwell. This is an almost classic example of a typical meeting place for members of a community in which gossiping and observation of the passing scene provide much of the attraction. Barges, fishing and cartage are brought together at a point surrounded by the industrial villages and towns of Lancashire.

(J. Allan

(J. Allan

(*above*) Colliers Arms, Orrell, near Wigan. The passage of time has not obscured the original elements
this scene: the patch of grass in the angle of the road, the split stone slabs of the fence, the lack of kerb.
ccretions like the new roof and reconstructed chimneys, more efficient plumbing, and new notice boards
not prevent us from seeing the original form. The old notice board remains, but the outside seat and the
tching posts have gone. This is a typical small isolated inn serving miners and farm workers in the week
d 'townees' who have walked out from Wigan at the weekend.

(*above*, *opposite*) Sowerby Bridge, Yorkshire, looking south across the densely-settled Calder Valley.
he dam pond in the foreground provides water for the woollen mill below it, dated 1862; the two build-
gs in the middle distance were erected as cotton mills, the larger one probably in the 1880s. More mills,
canal, railway lines, churches and chapels, rows of workers' cottages have gone on packing the valley floor
nce then (a multi-storey block of flats has recently sprung up on the extreme left) but have left the higher
ound relatively free.

(*below*, *opposite*) Mill at Brockholes, Yorkshire: a characteristic setting for rural industry. The large
uilding at the centre belongs to the late-eighteenth century, when the mill-stream provided the necessary
wer (the chimney came with steam-power later), but some of the low sheds around it did not appear
fore the 1860s, and the council houses on the left were added in the 1930s. The need for water for
dustrial purposes provided almost automatically an ambience which was either attractive in itself or one
which the inhabitants of successive generations found it easy to adjust.

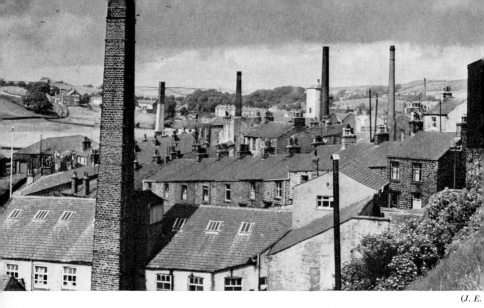

(J. E.

40 (*above*) Bury. Here is a sense of space that contrasts with closed streets, alleys and tunnels. The variety of forms generated by the different building types, their functions and topography has visual excitement. We must remember that these forms also had immediate and personal associations with the people of the town. Note the proximity of the countryside and its quality of belonging to the town.

41 (*below*) The rural ambience of the town edge mill. The bold simple statements of form in these towns are well shown in this view of a mill from the road. The close contact with the country and the variety of colour and texture provided by shrubs and plants in this kind of industrial setting, show up very well.

(J. E.

A Marshall Street Flax Mills, Leeds, built 1838–40.
B Denholme Mills, Yorkshire, built 1834.
C Manningham Mills, Bradford, built 1873.
D Joshua Hoyle's Mill, Summerseat, Lancashire, built 1876.

Mills were important human achievements so their very structure and detailing often deliberately pro-claimed this in symbolic terms: Classical, Egyptian, and Italianate influences are evident enough in this group of pictures. The mill in Leeds was the largest of its kind in Europe; that in Bradford originally had a frontage of about 2,000 feet.

43 Stubbins, Ramsbottom. Gradient can impose variety not only of forms but in a change from solid
void: the wall on the right stands on the edge of a steep slope. Just visible beyond the monumental chim
ney, which emphasises the bend in the road, can be seen a romantic tower. This is in fact part of a m
complex which lies behind the trees.

(J. I

(*J. E. Turner*)

The same street as in pl. 43 (*opposite*) looking downhill. The slope has forced these terraced houses into
[k]ind of private relationship but also opened a view over the slope to another part of the town. The per-
[sis]tence of the classic tradition is to be seen in the proportions of windows and doors; notice on the door
[ne]arest to the camera the double lintel which is a version of the entablature to be found in better houses.

Working class houses, Bury. Lightly textured surfaces of wood and wall, an enclosed scene, and yet a
[hi]nt of other spaces beyond the horizon. Notice again that although the housing is standard in form, the
[slo]pe creates not only special relationships of space and distortions of the normal design, but also creates
[sh]arp changes in form—as at the junction house of the two streets.

(*J. E. Turner*)

(J. E. Turner)   (J. E

46 (*above, left*) This typical example from a Northern industrial town of steps leading from one street
another illustrates the sense of enclosure in the angle of the high walls and the anticipation of space whi
can be seen as one approaches the steps. Notice once again the variety of form and texture in this sm
area.

47 (*above, right*) Stubbins, Ramsbottom. A pedestrian underpass giving a sense of contraction and releas
Notice the way in which the space is progressively restricted: the open iron railings defining the route b
allowing a view, next the brick walls shuttering off some of the sky, then the bridge closing it off altogeth
but not taking away the sense of direction and anticipation offered by the open view at the end of the tunn

48 (*opposite*) A Manchester alley-way in the 1890s. Passing through the arch at the end one emerges on
a busy street. The white-washed walls of the buildings form a decorative feature which contrasts sharp
with the grime-stained buildings of the public ways. Notice the lamps and the signs, which are as decor
tive in the alley as the ornaments inside the houses.

BULL'S HEAD HOTEL
BULL'S HEAD
HOTEL.
FREE FROM BREWER
OR WINE & SPIRIT MERCHANT.
SAMUEL ANDERSON, Proprietor
BULL'S HEAD
S. ANDERSON
HOTEL

(J. E.

49 (*above*) Bury. The changes in this row of houses and the paving are superficial. The whole scene is much as it has always been. Earlier taste would have demanded white steps, earlier still white windowsills, though it was acceptable later to wax them. Conformity in style was a product of social pressure. Note the gable of the chapel just glimpsed on the right.

51 (*opposite, above*) Wigan. Some typical polychrome brick and moulded brick detailing. The bye-law terrace seems a long way from Lombardy, but this detailing is the direct descendant of the architectural response to Ruskin's *Stones of Venice*. The dog tooth moulding is in red brick, the arch is in alternating pairs of blue and yellow bricks, the inner arch of moulded brick (obscured) is red, the quoins are in alternating light and dark yellow, the main wall is in reddish brown common brick. The door mouldings are original, but the letter box is not.

50 (*below*) Swan Meadow Road, Wigan. The buildings belong to the late nineteenth century although the earlier tradition of building in stone still prevailed to some extent. As the field lanes were developed the odd road shape formed accidental compositions and arrangements. As an abstract form the chimney equates to the church spire in a more orthodox architectural climax.

(J. E

(*J. E. Turner*)

(*below*) Caroline Street, Wigan. This section of a street commences with three houses faced in moulded
~ment stucco that is reminiscent of East Anglia; then comes a house rendered in vague reference to
~egency quality, with a carriage entry (coalman, builder or hackney); beyond that are five houses in a
~aper pattern of light header bricks and darker stretches; beyond that again comes painted render. This
~ one consequence of the small-scale builder developing in blocks.

(*J. E. Turner*)

(Manchester City L

53 This street scene of the latter half of the nineteenth century is of interest not only for the contrast between dirty hands and white aprons, but also for the contrast between the monumental railway arch and the restless pattern of colour and typography on the posters.

54 Warehouse packers taking their lunch hour in the sun, Liverpool. This narrow street hemmed in between the warehouses of wholesale food distributors is a good illustration of environmental factors in the use of space. The buildings angled so as to create shelter from the wind, an area where the sun warms the pavement, and where space for lounging permits gossip and observation of the passing scene.

(S. M. Ha

The Aesthetic of the Nineteenth-Century Industrial Town[1]

Francis M. Jones

The purpose of this paper is not to try to establish aesthetic standards by which the quality of an environment may be judged, but rather to describe some of the characteristics of an environment and the manner in which it would have been possible for human beings to adapt themselves to it, create compensatory situations, or find escapes, however temporary. Some accompanying plates provide a visual commentary on this theme (these are grouped between pp. 182–3).

It is necessary to begin, however, by defining the particular concept of aesthetic being used here. This is taken to include the physical responses of human beings to their environment and the actions based consciously or otherwise on such responses. It is patently not an aesthetic based solely on the visual quality of our environment although, since this sense is our most developed and widely used means of experiencing our world, it is inevitable that visual responses are to be looked for. Hearing, smell, and touch must also be considered. There are abstract qualities in architecture. While the intangible nature of our response to the quality of sound, heat or light and the tactile experience of surfaces will be appreciated readily enough, it may be more difficult to perceive that the visual organisation of planes and volumes and their sub-divisions may be achieved by individuals without conscious recognition of a regular formal ordering of the parts. The use of temporary plastic membranes to protect working areas, as may be seen on the temporary façade to the Liverpool Bank of

[1] This paper is based on research being conducted by the Housing Research Unit in the School of Architecture at the University of Liverpool, which is being financed by the Joseph Rowntree Memorial Trust.

England, suggests insights into the kinds of forms that are possible in our developing technology, and which, in time, will almost certainly extend to the permanent surfaces of buildings. Inherently 'abstract' forms will then become commonplace, however strange they may appear to-day.

It must be stressed that the aesthetic of architecture covers a much wider range of human experience than is expressed by the art critic; and that it involves more than the formal, spatial relationship of solids as definers of space, the modelling of the solids, or their surface decorative qualities. Architecture is the design of a controlled static environment for human use, and the interaction of physical and psychological realities of all kinds must be considered. Indeed, human behaviour in such realities may appear unreal, and decisions are taken whose origins are imponderable and whose consequences seem irrational. Modern research is moving into this field in an attempt to relate motives, however unmeasurable, to a functional base.

It will readily be appreciated that this view of architecture is of importance in considering the aesthetic quality of a town. Since buildings and their urban complexes are the hardware of a social organism, the form at varying levels of detail will reflect the responses of that organism to its environment—from the minutiae of clothing to the siting of a town hall. The persistence of vestigial forms as purely decorative features beyond their functional origin is a commonplace of experience. Yet we often fail to read back from the decoration to the conditions which brought it into being. Hence we do not appreciate the nature of the human responses at the point of origin of the decoration.

Let us consider, then, the aesthetic quality of the town in these terms, bearing in mind that for the majority of the population the creation of a personal aesthetic was more often than not a response to bad conditions in the general aesthetic. This discussion does not assume that aesthetic is to be equated with 'beautiful' or 'satisfactory' or that the general conditions of society permitted the enjoyment of a full life to those undergoing them. On the contrary, much of their activity was directed to salvaging some elements of human comfort and dignity from extremely disadvantageous conditions.

There were three special forms of difficulty to be overcome. First, there was the level and variety of noise. Transport was essential to the industrial town, so hard-wearing road surfaces to resist iron-shod hooves and iron-shod wheels were laid down. The best material was stone of granite hardness; for ease of laying this was in the form of blocks. Not only did it provide a fine surface, but the joints provided the rattle and clatter so frequently referred to in the prose of the era. Horse harnesses had chains to rattle; to control their charges the drivers shouted. Railways clanked, roared and whistled. Factories hummed, banged and shrieked.

Secondly, the dirt: the division of our roads into carriage-way and footpaths, with the latter raised above the gutter by a vertical step, reflect not only a desire for safe passage, but also a desire for a clean one. The carriage-way was a ribbon of horse droppings converted by rain into a morass which passing wheels threw on to the pavement; hence the polished marble, granite, glazed brick base to buildings lining a highway; hence, too, the crossing sweeper. The block or macadam carriageway slowly ground to dust; the manure dried up and powdered; grit and carbon poured from every chimney.

Thirdly, the smell: there were breweries, tanneries, dyeworks, gasworks. There was horse manure; there were defective or indifferent drains; there were unwashed people. The latter could hardly be avoided since a high density of building benefited society, not only in lowering land cost as a rent charge, but also in reducing walking distances to work —which was still a necessary feature of a town, even after the arrival of railways and tramways, since these were so inflexible.

The attack on smell that appears as Health Act provision came first because the desire to improve the health of the urban dweller involved good drains and piped pure water supply and both were associated in the mind with the unpleasant smells produced by their absence. As Humphrey House pointed out in *The Dickens World* (1941), 'In *Pickwick* a bad smell was a bad smell; in *Our Mutual Friend* it is a problem'. Equally, of all the disadvantages of the town the most difficult to escape from at an economic distance was the smell of the manufactures, so this had to be cured at source. Noise was not attacked in general terms but limits were imposed on the use of the factory hooters. The noise of traffic and manufacturing operations could be avoided by moving to the middle-class suburbs which had become a feature of the town towards the latter half of the nineteenth century. The noise was also held in check by religious sanctions in that Sunday, a day of rest, provided a period of quiet at regular intervals. Dirt depended, of course, less on its suppression at source than on its removal, and this depended in turn either on the employment of servants or on personal elbow grease.

All these disadvantages could be alleviated by physically removing oneself and family from the town, especially in an upwind direction, and those with the economic resources did this. The rest of the population reacted in a variety of ways, some of which were fortuitous in the sense that provision for one amenity tended to assist in providing others. Some of these reactions were apparently the result of applying rural traditions to urban conditions; some were direct counteractions to the effects of dirt and smell; some were direct, if temporary, escapes and varied from the gin palace to the open moorlands.

In examining these methods of coping with the prevailing aesthetic we must avoid the temptation to erect a model of what should have been done and dismiss as irrational any deviation from that pattern. This, unfortunately, tended in the past to be the approach of the reformers— whether social, artistic or technological. They were essentially persons educated to orthodox concepts of the formal aims of culture and tended to form models based on precedents which were essentially pre-industrial. Behaviour had not only to be middle class, but its cultural manifestations must belong to this rôle, or alternatively to derive from social rôles of a previous era. The visual organisation of space for architectural or 'civic design' purposes (the very idea of 'civic design' is revealing) had to conform to the canons of taste derived from the eighteenth century, and stylistic variations had little impact on this overall approach. There was therefore a specific 'Romantic' form with curving roads and carefully disposed objects at points equivalent to a happy surprise, and a specific 'Classic' form in which the relationship to specific axes of approach or view is established early and dominates the approach to climax objects.

The subjective response to the quality of space as manifested by light, sound, temperature, texture, and scope of movement were subordinated to the formal visual patterns conceived as appropriate to culturally respectable dogmas. These qualities had to be intellectually perceived and to be capable of description in words, so that literary quality became equated with the quality of subjective response expected from users of the space. It is not surprising therefore that the layman is taken aback at the sight of a back alley between rows of terrace homes and at being told that this is to be studied as an aesthetic experience. The orthodox views of the educated reformers, however, lie behind the solutions to town improvement produced by the bye-laws and planning regulations since the 'sixties of the last century.

The historian is at a disadvantage in that he cannot observe human behaviour in past time directly. He can however use documentary, especially literary evidence—and anecdotal evidence in the recollections of the living—and he can reasonably argue from observed behaviour of to-day that in the past similar action could be expected in terms of the environment. He must however be willing to accept behaviour as it manifests itself and not to assess it in terms of his own model or pattern. It is worth-while examining some such fixed ideas.

The first to be considered is the view that urban life meant complete

isolation from the countryside and condemnation to a prisoner-like existence in a jail of bricks. When it is borne in mind that in a quarter of an
hour an adult can walk a mile it will be found that even by 1914 there
were few towns in the United Kingdom that could not be walked out of
in this extremely moderate time. The walk in the country may have been
restricted to footpaths and roads in highly productive agricultural areas,
but this in itself was not necessarily defeating the purpose of the exercise.
Not only were there specific walks attractive and convenient to the town,
but the sense of purpose, even of climax, is to be detected in the aim of
such walks. The most common goal is a public house, and such places
might either be isolated—like 'The Eagle and Child' at Hale, the terminus
for a walk from Widnes—or found in villages, often associated with a
green space either common or private. Several walks of varying lengths
would be in the common itinerary of the townsfolk. Natural features
such as roads, streams and dells form another large group of goals for
such walks, and these are associated not only with public houses in the
vicinity but also with refreshments provided at a varying scale from
cottages and farmhouses. The well established custom of the picnic gave
additional value to the goal beauty spot. These areas surrounding a town
became part of the local experience and would form for differing classes
of society the focus of activities standardized to particular times of the year.

The fragmented and scattered suburbia of our own time tends to prevent
us from appreciating the sharp distinction that once existed between town
and country. The edge of the built-up area was the threshold of continuous
areas of countryside. This is seen very clearly when a view is taken across
the Lancashire plain from Warrington or Wigan, but is more forcibly
demonstrated by the view from the moorland tops, across the area in
whose valleys are the towns of Lancashire and Yorkshire. Hardcastle
Crags above Halifax provide a good example of this. This latter countryside gives greater scope to the walker since areas of land open to walking
tend to be more frequent—notwithstanding the problems of game-rearing
and preservation—but in addition to the goals of beauty spots or refreshment houses there are the kinds of possibilities opened up for Birmingham
people by the Lickey Hills—collecting wild fruits like whinberries and
blackberries. The experience of such places would extend beyond the
physical appearance and its facilities since many are associated with
historical or mythical events of general interest and inevitably of personal
and family value. Harrison Ainsworth's novel *The Lancashire Witches*
(1849), and other legends derived from Pendle Hill in Lancashire, give a
clue to what I have in mind here.

There were areas where the individual mills or workshops existed in isolation along some water course, whether natural for power or artificial for transport, and homes and the general buildings of community would be grouped at this point; these however did not amount to 'sprawl', since the dominance of the natural surroundings can be appreciated even in the present day when so many of these works villages can be still identified. Summerseat and Haigh provide characteristic examples of each type of settlement.

Within the town itself the same approach to the character of urban experience will provide insights into the quality of life during the nineteenth century. Again, it is necessary to query the exact character of the buildings, streets and open spaces of the town. For example, is it correct to picture the houses and other buildings as wholly black and colourless, with no relief? In housing especially we may be misled by present-day experience of dirty brick or stonework, rusting metalwork, and unpainted timber. We see this after a generation of rent restriction and rising costs when the income from housing could not cover outgoings. Prior to 1914 the renting of housing was an economically sound policy and maintenance, however it was organised, essential to the landlord. It follows that a general picture of neatness is to be anticipated; in addition, although the range of colour may have been limited to brown, green, black, or white, the woodwork and ironwork would have brightness.

In addition to the standard of landlord maintenance the tenants had common standards for the exterior of the house. This included sweeping the pavement and often even mopping it for the full width of the house. The window-sills were painted and polished, doorsteps were rubbed clean and colourwashed white or buff. Metal door furniture was either directly polished if brass or black-polished if cast-iron. The external woodwork, i.e., of door and lower windows, was washed regularly and polished. Through the windows clean curtains and shining metallic fittings would be visible. The general visual quality of the street was therefore bright, and even in streets consisting entirely of houses, uniformity did not necessarily mean a deadening monotony.

The image of terraced streets as a uniform series of dwellings only, withdrawn from the main roads which provided shops and public buildings, does not conform to the reality. The block pattern of such housing shows a variety of other uses, particularly shops and public-houses at the corners, and chapels often placed in the run of the terrace. These elements not only created a change of form but also provided colour and textual contrast, even where one landlord owned large units of housing and colour was standardized. The pattern of street blocks is in itself significant, since a system of short parallel blocks affords a greater choice of movement through the system than blocks of considerable length. The opportunity to create a variety of experiences of the environment was large because alternative routes provided alternatives of form.

The visual qualities so far applied to housing can, of course, be discussed in relation to other building types. It will however be necessary to mention other features created by buildings. Since they consist of vertical walls they provide not only screens from the wind but also reflectors and radiants of heat derived from the sun. It is reasonable to examine town layouts in detail to detect locations of natural congregation where such shelter was provided. Positions of this nature were associated with housing and places of work, but they could also be located for leisure hours, whether normal or enforced. They were normally associated with points of visual interest and the commonest of these was passing traffic. The group of people at the cross-roads in the centre of a small town persists to the present day, but it was a commonplace of road, rail and canal traffic in the past. Inevitably, such points of congregation are reflections not only of these reasons but also of a particular stage in the development of entertainment and social groupings.

Reference has been made to the formal concepts of town layout which appear to create these locations by the formation of squares and other geometrical open spaces bounded by public buildings. It is the failure to appreciate the function of such enclosures that leads to misconceptions in which the visual concept of enclosure is abstracted from its functional aspect and is then applied on a scale which makes the original function impossible.

The sense of shelter required could have been derived from the angle of a building, the angle of a building and an engineering structure, or the angle of a building and a natural feature. The visual quality of this space may have been nil in any orthodox assessment, but considered purely in terms of an organism reacting with all its senses to its immediate environment it has been 'right'. There is a possibility that the physical experience of shelter can be visually identified with specific shapes and hence such shapes whether for shelter or not are more acceptable or even more attractive than others. The idea of the 'nook', the 'peaceful square', or even a 'corner of old ──' are related to attitudes of this nature.

The arrangement of walls and spaces makes possible another kind of experience apart from the sense of enclosure. This comes with the relief of monotony, either by actual change of scene or the possibility of change. In this sense, anticipation, even if unrealized, appears to have value and many situations of little apparent interest have the ability to elicit an emotional response. This response will depend on the individual and may, of course, be one of fear or rejection, but the more usual reaction seems to be one of intrigue at the unknown qualities of the space hinted at. Arrangements that develop this response may be achieved by the juxtaposition of buildings, where the edges of planes indicate additional screened spaces, rather in the way stage sets are exploited. It may also be achieved by the shape of a road winding between walls, banks or vegetation unfolding new situations at every turn. Thomas Sharpe's description of the dynamic visual experience of the High at Oxford is a classic on this theme.[2]

In either case the discovery of new space may be heightened by the existence of objects in that space, which, whatever their quality in the formal art sense, will appeal simply because they exist in that particular location. As Patrick Geddes showed long ago, these objects may be trees, rocks, drinking fountains, gate-ways, memorials and other trivia of the roads. These changes of space need not happen purely on a horizontal plane, and it is obvious that even more dramatic situations are possible where flights of steps, ramps, and steep cuttings exist. Such positions occur in housing on steep slopes and where factories and water or rail transport are in association with hills. The impact of rising up a flight of stairs where the first climax is simply a view of the sky in isolation against the top step, and so on to the gradual development of a new environment as the head comes above the upper pavement level is a commonplace of civic design. Equally, the descent into a close confined stair or ramp and ultimate release at the lower level—usually through some form of gateway, whether actual or inferred is another frequent theme.

All gateways, whether as openings in boundary walls, small bridge tunnels under railways, or alley-ways through buildings, carry the same potential for new experience as one passes through them. They involve moving from a large open space through some constricted space and change of light and sound to a re-enlargement of the space into which they debouch. Although such routes would have been popular chiefly because they offered short cuts, the quality of change involved must have added something to their use.

The situations described up to now have been those in which individuals had to respond to situations outside their control, and it has had to be inferred that behaviour in these circumstances had some aesthetic significance to the individual. Within the home, however, the interior fittings, decorations, and modes of behaviour are largely under the control of the head of the family. It is reasonable therefore to conclude that we see here a more specific statement of choice, however constrained this may be. It

[2] See his article 'Oxford observed', *Country Life* (November 1952).

will perhaps be valuable to consider the nature of these constraints. Naturally the dominant one tends to be largely of money. This is not a reference to sheer poverty but to the difference between a range of choices related to equally pressing needs and another to the achievement of socially acceptable standards.

Standards in clothing as against standards in furnishings form perhaps the most obvious choice in the first of these cases; and funeral expenditure is perhaps the most obvious example of a social pressure. It is necessary to stress again that we should not be looking for standards in visual experience which are acceptable to some formal code of values, but rather to reflections and demonstrations of attempts to come to terms with the environment. Works like Dennis Chapman's *The Home and Social Status* (1955) and Richard Hoggart's *Uses of Literacy* (1957) have taught us that these standards are themselves a social issue since social acceptability depends for the housewife on achieving formal standards quite as rigid as those of the art critic in his special field.

The most obvious case of an environmental response having this kind of overtone is cleanliness. The aesthetic symbolism involved here however is too complicated for discussion in this paper.

Chadwick's advocacy of cleanliness as a major factor in health inevitably had an immense impact, but the comment of Treitschke that to the British soap was civilisation was perhaps truer than he had intended. It is important to appreciate one vital element in the statement of cleanliness, and this is *shine*. Not only has shine the value of light reflection or sparkle, but it is known to be associated with dust- and grease-free surfaces. The latter attracts social symbolism and is responsible for shiny lino, polished furniture, varnished woodwork and starched cloth. The effort required to keep a home clean in the period we are considering must have been immense: not only was there a simple relationship between the number of occupants and the size of dwelling in the problem of combating wear and tear and dirt, but there was the increasing dirt of the atmosphere as the towns expanded, thus creating heavier pollution underfoot and in the air. A major proportion of the working day for a servant or a housewife was spent in cleaning. This situation provided one of the principal drives to innovation at the simple level of providing surfaces with either permanent or easily developed shine. Linoleum is a very obvious example, but metal-plating, varnish, and glazed fabrics all show the same need. Ultimately, the diminishing ability of the middle class to keep servants started a series of mechanical innovations whose consequences are still reverberating around us.

The need for cleanliness stimulated a variety of actions and the use of a variety of materials having aesthetic value. For example, Sunday as a day for demonstrating particularly the value of leisure was also used to demonstrate higher social and personal values. At the weekend was developed a whole array of activities which were related to the ability to experience the cleanliness and leisure of the holy day. The dreadful memory of the day when one had to be clean, wear best clothes, be still, be quiet, have been embodied in innumerable recollections. Children could hardly see the reverse of the coin in that mother could, by means of such standards, gain some peace, and have a reasonable period for enjoying her efforts at cleanliness and order. The general tendency to dullness, offset as it may have been in the general colouring of the town, could be particularly relieved in the home where highly reflective surfaces like polished metal, mirrors and other reflecting or refracting objects could be used to make more light. The relatively feeble light of candles or oil lamps tended to cast an isolated pool of light in one section of the room and scattered reflections of this light will have enhanced its value in these conditions. The fireplace, of course, represented a principal source of light and was emphasised and exploited by being surrounded by a special array of polished metal, including the steel and brass fittings of the fireplace.

There are two further fields in which the sense of occasion manifested itself. One is the purely industrial. Here we have to ask ourselves whether we do not tend to forget, when considering the obvious economic struggles of the workers and employers in the period, that in fact there were many points at which a common sense of achievement manifested itself.

The design, siting and detailing of buildings and engineering structures show consistent attempts to achieve more than a purely utilitarian philosophy. The present-day appreciation of these efforts arises less from back-projection of our own conditioning by modern art, although we can now more easily detect the beginnings of our modern attitudes, but more from a less rigid set of formal rules than those imposed during the death throes of classicism in the first two decades of this century. There is the actual case of the Haigh foundry with its street party and celebrations at the successful completion of the Laxey Wheel, and many such occasions must have taken place during the various technical successes of the nineteenth century. The Black Country story of Enoch telling of the casting so big that they had to have a crane to lift the hole in the middle, could only have point in a culture in which workmen did boast of technical success. These occasions were marked by the processing of bands, the hanging out of bunting, the issue of medals or other tokens, or by works' meals with speeches.

This is an aspect of the matter in which we should, perhaps, be on our 1ard against our own pre-conceptions. The simple division of the conructional work of the period into industrial (hence ugly) buildings and ructures, and buildings of other kinds associated with the public weal)scures the fact that utilitarian aims could produce bridges, viaducts, 1d dams in which the scale of the construction, impressive enough in self, was emphasized by the judicious use of Classic or Egyptian details. he design of factory chimneys, entrance gates, workshops and engine)uses thus acquired significance, and the desire for achievement prevant in society produced work in which it is possible to argue that human :nsibilities were engaged. This may be seen, for example, in the Liverpool •ocks where buildings required for human shelter during dock operations 1ve received not only more detailed study in their design but even display ements of whimsy.

The fact that the composition of a scene depends less on the degree of :ill and taste brought to the design of the individual elements than their imensions and shapes relative to each other must lead us to ask whether 1e grouping of a church spire with trees is necessarily and intrinsically ifferent from the same composition embodying a factory chimney or ny other essentially industrial object of the period. We are willing to :cept the landscape in the vicinity of Rome with the Claudian and other queducts as legitimate elements of the rural scene; why, then, are we to 1dge the railway and canal viaducts of this later age in a different way?

It is a simple matter to discern the way in which detail of classical rigin was used to sharpen the quality of these objects, but details derived om Gothic stylistic pre-occupations, wherever used, achieved the same urpose. Polychromatic brick and stone-work and the use of terra-cotta re manifestations of this impulse. Although the principal demonstration f this development occurred in housing and public buildings it was)llowed, as the century progressed, by similar work in the construction f factories and mills. This response to the advance of technology is of 1terest since it depended on increased knowledge of the characteristics f different clays and their behaviour in firing and hence the colour range ossible with developments in the machine production of brick and :rra-cotta.

This made possible towards the latter half of the century a variety in esign which had been difficult to achieve economically in the earlier •eriod. It is legitimate to criticise the taste of the designers in this field, •ut before we do so we should ask ourselves whether the standards of ssessment of the educated art critic were really necessary for the actual njoyment of these objects by those quite unaware of these standards but who assessed them in the ways and the circumstances described in this paper. We must particularly ask whether we do not respond too readily to the set of symbols laid down by the members of the Arts and Crafts Movement under the impetus of their general attack on the industrial development of the nineteenth century and the support given to them by the more esoteric proponents of the aesthetic movement. Should we not perhaps pay more attention to the towns and buildings and the general evidence of objects of everyday use as attempts to come to terms with the environment? Although life was full of difficulty and anxiety we have here survivals indicating the will to live.

Discussion

The CHAIRMAN proposed that the contents of the two papers should be considered together as material for discussion on the whole subject of visual evidence. However, it at once became clear that Mr. Jones's paper had raised issues which required clarification. Professor ASHWORTH expressed two doubts. He asked how far people in the middle or late nineteenth century could be said to have looked at the visual scene with the eye of, say, Mr. Jones—i.e., the 'trained eye'. Could it, indeed, be proved—or disproved—that they were really much affected by their visual environment? Secondly, he wondered whether Mr. Jones had been consciously administering a corrective to the usually held view that all nineteenth-century working-class housing was contemptible.

Mr. JONES admitted willingly that the idea of a corrective had been in his mind and this led him to a consideration of the first of Professor Ashworth's doubts in a rather new light. He reminded the audience of the menacing noise, dirt and smells of the Victorian town. 'I can remember as a child, living in Liverpool, the horse-carts in the Dock Road and the noise of them, all the worse because they were in very constricted streets. This was true of London—otherwise why would they put straw outside sick people's houses?' As for dirt, Mr. JONES reminded the audience of the 'almost impassable barrier' of horse droppings; he had read a description of the Strand in which it was stated to be six inches deep. Hence crossing-sweepers, so often mentioned in Victorian novels. I could never understand what these crossing-sweepers were till I became aware of this particular by-product of horse-drawn transport!' Noise and dirt were accompanied by smells. 'I think, perhaps, that one of the values of Sunday in the nineteenth century must have been the unearthly peace and quiet that descended on the town.' There was 'sheer physical value in having Sunday as a day of rest and ensuring that everybody observed it'. Sunday suspended noise, but not, as the CHAIRMAN observed, smells.

Mr. JONES insisted that the brightness and cleanliness of many working-class homes was a keenly felt aesthetic defence against the general dirt and dullness. He emphasised the symbolic value of white. The standards laid down for hospitals from Florence Nightingale's time onwards placed emphasis on white not because it was hygienic but because of its symbolic quality (to-day white is replaced by green as causing less eye-strain). Mr. JONES claimed that although we could not say definitely that people reacted to their environment in this way or that, we could form a hypothesis and by studying behaviour on the one hand and environment on the other come to certain conclusions. One factor in behaviour was tradition, the results of a communal pressure, and this tended to be ignored by modern town planners. A serious error in twentieth-century planning could be shown to be the rejection of the life of the nineteenth.

The CHAIRMAN said that in the consideration of environment there seemed to be two quite separate factors. One was the traditional neatness and cleanliness *within the home*; this might be described as a kind of ritual. The other one was the *home itself*—i.e. the structure—and it was structures which Mr. Jones had mainly discussed and illustrated in his lecture. The two things need not necessarily be associated. The ritual, for instance, of whitened doorsteps might continue within a social group whether that group were in Manchester or Liverpool or set down in the Sahara or Peking. The fabric of the house, on the other hand, was something extraneous to this ritual. The original response to the actual shape of these houses was obscure. It was important not to assume that our present emotional reaction to them was anything like that of the people who first lived in them.

Then there was the question of the 'trained eye'. The CHAIRMAN suggested that the eye of a person having had experience of modern painting from cubism onwards might well be suspect as an instrument of historical investigation. Mr JONES replied that while he had been 'trained out of' the ability to react as an earlier generation would have done he had been trained to react consciously to things that others had reacted to unconsciously. We could see now in nineteenth century towns elements such as enclosures, colours and qualities of texture which would be conducive to some sort of emotional response, or, as he later expressed it, a psycho-physical response. He instanced the grouping of young people enjoying leisure in urban surroundings (Liverpool) where bright light or shelter from wind were factors in the choice of situation. He claimed that these and other factors being equal in a choice of various situations, the situation 'which had some kind of visual quality in the way of its form and texture' would unconsciously be chosen.

Dr. MANN said that he was aware of some confusion between the outline of the buildings under discussion and the things people did to express themselves within that outline. 'I wonder whether the inhabitants don't merely say: This is my dull house, I shall decorate this to brighten up my life.' Here, he thought, was a problem which concerned our attitude to housing where, as in recent blocks of flats in Sheffield, architects tended to express their own personalities while denying the inhabitants the possibility of expressing *their* personalities—everything was being done for them. Mr. JONES said that that was precisely the point he was trying to make. The Housing Research Unit, with which he was associated, was concerned with this matter and was opposed to housing being conceived in terms of homogeneous architectural blocks. Highly formalised situations were inevitable but the users should be allowed maximum freedom within them.

Dr. MARTIN interposed with a question on the use of ferns as an ingredient of popular taste, but to this there appeared to be no answer. Dr. HENNOCK asked about the bright colours he had noticed in some of Mr. Jones's slides and questioned whether a great variety of colours was cheaply available until recent imes: 'I would have assumed that whitewash and black-lead and brown chocolate was about the range.' Professor ASHWORTH agreed; he recalled that, in his own childhood in a northern industrial area, there was the tendency to keep the outside of a house spick and span, but this was not at all a question of brightness'. He was thinking of people living in the 'twenties whose tastes were formed back in the 'seventies; their taste in painted wood-work was for at least 95 per cent some shade of brown. There was not even much brass-work: iron rather than brass was the rule. It was true that there was colour sometimes on window ledges and door-steps, but the shops supplied only one tone for the purpose. There were two colours you could buy: one, bright yellow, the other a greyish stone colour. He thought that the impression of visual brightness was something which came with the 'fifties and 'sixties of the present century. Mr. JONES said that in this respect his slides, showing lively colours, could have been misleading and that when he talked about 'brightness' he was thinking of cleanliness rather than colour. Green was, in fact, the cheapest mass-produced paint for external surfaces until recently.

As a mitigation of nineteenth-century drabness, Dr. MARTIN instanced the exhibition of goods in the street under naphtha flares, to which Mr. JONES added the traditional processions with banners and brass bands, associated with some areas of town life. 'In Liverpool and Birkenhead we have the Orange Marches, with their different banners and the girls dressed up—very pretty and attractive, looked at in the abstract, not as a religious procession.' He instanced the Whit Walks in which all the children from the church and chapel walk in procession; also the processions of trade union branches. As for brass bands it appeared that in Wigan alone there was 'a fantastic number—the entire population must have belonged to one.' These processions were works of art in their way and it was interesting that they were necessarily 'linear'—the form dictated by the canyon-like streets of the city. The village equivalent had been the round dance in an open space.

At this point, discussion began to stray into various by-ways somewhat indirectly related to the main theme. It was felt, among other things, that town museums and the preservation of nineteenth-century interiors received less attention in this country than in some others. Mr. FREEMAN instanced a 'Victorian' museum at Bergen. The CHAIRMAN thought that authentic *ensembles* were probably most effectively captured by photography.

Professor COLLINS then introduced the subject of the urban environment as described in Victorian novels. He was reminded of the description in Mrs. Gaskell's *North and South* of Margaret Hale's first visits to the manufacturer's —Thornton's—house, when she was uncomfortably dazzled by its cleanliness: it seemed to her less for use than a display of triumph over the local atmosphere. He proposed an instructive comparison between two literary descriptions of Manchester—one ('Milton') in *North and South*, the other ('Coketown') in *Hard Times*. In the first, he recalled Margaret Hale's first move from the country when she talks of the factory smells and then, correcting herself, says It's not so much a smell as a lack of countryside'. Dickens' picture of Coketown, on the other hand, made a special point of its unchanging sameness—the same streets, the same hours, the same work, the same people, every day the same, every hour the same. Dickens' powerful impressions could not, of course, be taken as they stood. There was his famous use of fog in *Bleak House*. 'When I ask my students to write about *Bleak House* they say there's fog on every page. You point out that statistically there is fog on two-and-a-quarter pages out of eight hundred and it turns out that they have only read the first chapter.' The idea that Victorian London was always under fog was prevalent. Professor COLLINS recalled that when David Saule was feeling decadent and wanted a really delicious melancholia he decided to come to London 'because of all that *brouillard*.'

A threatening drift towards literature and sociology was sharply checked by Dr. DYOS with a reminder that the ordained theme for the day was 'Materials and Methods'. Had the conference been discussing materials or methods or both? Did the two speakers this afternoon conceive that they had been introducing an entirely new range of materials? If so, what disciplines were required to deal with them? What method was appropriate and could it be used on its own or only after a number of preliminary investigations?

Mr. JONES believed we were concerned now with materials and were looking for a new method of studying the relationship of human behaviour to environment. His own approach, he said, was not that of an art historian but of one handling a real problem of the present and future. The CHAIRMAN, on the other hand, replied to Dr. Dyos by instancing a problem in urban studies of a strictly art-historical kind. This concerned the degradation of style in suburban building. He gave an example of how it could be demonstrated by a methodical identification of stylistic sources and the use and re-use of motifs at different social levels. A more general answer came from Dr. MARTIN. The material, he said, was not something new. But 'visual evidence is, in a sense, the last part of our evidence . . . the historian's business is (is it not?) to say *what happened* and *what it was like*. In the last resort, as we are sentient creatures, we need to know what it was like visually.'

Dr. MARTIN then turned the discussion towards the need for conserving some parts of our towns as containers of history for people of the future to use with the new techniques they would doubtless bring to bear on it. It may be, he said, that the town is finished as an institution. It is desirable to preserve something to remind people of what it was like. It did, after all, 'seem to offer to humankind more than any other community which we have devised so far'.

Dr. DYOS took up the point of urban disintegration as being the logical consequence of the electrical grid system, the motor-car and the helicopter and producing, in principle, an even density of building over the whole country. This was in sharp contrast to the medieval conception of a town, whose logical consequence was a mile cube. This image prompted the CHAIRMAN to reflect upon the survival in modern times of ancient city ideals, of the new Jerusalem in *Revelation* and St. Augustine's 'City of God'. Were not images of this kind still operative in the way that people esteemed towns? Would we be here at all, discussing urban history, if it were not for the imaginative force of these images? There followed a brief dialogue between Dr. FISHER and Mr. TILLOTT on the subject of oral evidence and the urgency of recording statements by persons whose memories went back before 1914—the first world war being, in Mr. Tillott's view, the significant time barrier. Dr. DYOS joined in with a plea for the study of cinematograph evidence from the late 'nineties onwards, some of it preserved in the National Film Archive. On oral evidence, some cautionary observations came from Dr. MANN who described the extreme difficulty of persuading old people to recapture their attitudes to events at the actual time of their occurrence and not after a lapse of years during which a new attitude had formed which was the one recollected. It was vital for the research worker to know a great deal, beforehand, about the subject of his enquiries.

The discussion on oral evidence led Mr. WESTERGAARD to stress the importance of individual attitudes to the urban environment and the 'compartmentalisation' of people's lives. 'We can overview the whole city, so to speak, but for certain sections of the population the city consisted of small areas within which they spent practically the whole of their lives.' Evidence on this might be forthcoming through retrospective interview.

A few minutes before the discussion closed, Dr. MARSHALL threw in the neglected topic of late-Victorian paintings of towns, instancing a fine panorama of Bolton in 1880, in the library of that Borough. This reminded the CHAIRMAN of Crowe's painting of mill girls in the Manchester Art Gallery which Dr. HENNOCK at once characterised as 'historically extremely misleading'. Mr. JONES also entered a warning against the subjective character of paintings and their fallibility as evidence, but Dr. MARTIN turned the tables by declaring their fallibility an actual bonus, since a contemporary subjective statement was as useful as anything else. 'We do,' he said, in a phrase which made an effective tail-piece to the session, 'have to use our evidence in a sophisticated fashion!'

JOHN SUMMERSON

IV

Problems in the Quantitative Study of Urban History[1]

Leo F. Schnore

It has become fairly evident in recent years that the discipline of history itself is not about to generate historical data and interpretations on all of the many aspects of the city and its past that interest social scientists. This has inevitably led to the notion that each social science discipline will have to produce its own historians.[2] In other words, each field concerned with the city will have to devise its own studies of the time dimension in urban affairs. Such a development would lead to the recognition of new specialties. In addition to economic history, then, there would be 'urban economic history'.[3] Alongside the study of contemporary urban politics would develop 'urban political history'.[4] Another new specialty would be 'urban historical geography'.

But what of urban sociology? Here is a field that has been characterised —at least in the United States—by an utter lack of interest in historical questions and issues.[5] Moreover, it is a field without focus; it has no

[1] The author's current work, to which this paper refers, is supported by Grant Number GS-921 from the National Science Foundation for 'Ecological Patterns in American Cities: Quantitative Studies in Urban History'.

[2] This view is implied in Eric E. Lampard, 'American historians and the study of urbanization', *American Historical Review*, lxvii (October 1961), pp. 49–91.

[3] It has been argued that 'urban economics' is a very recent development. See Raymond Vernon and Edgar M. Hoover, 'Economic aspects of urban research' in Philip M. Hauser and Leo F. Schnore (eds.), *The Study of Urbanization* (New York, 1965), pp. 191–207. See also Wilbur R. Thompson, *A Preface to Urban Economics* (Baltimore, 1965).

[4] One can already think of examples—chiefly monographic case studies—in this field. Robert A. Dahl's historical analysis of New Haven is an outstanding instance. See Robert A. Dahl, *Who Governs? Democracy and Power in an American City* (New Haven and London, 1961).

[5] Gideon Sjoberg, 'Comparative urban sociology' in Robert K. Merton and others (eds.), *Sociology Today* (New York, 1959), pp. 334–59; Thomas O. Wilkinson, 'Urban structure and industrialization', *American Sociological Review*, xxv (June 1960), pp. 356–63.

overriding set of issues at the core of its interests. At times it would seem to be concerned with sociological aspects of anything that takes place in cities.[6] And in an increasingly urban world that means just about everything.

Perhaps it is unfair to characterise urban sociology as a field without focus. Without being too rigidly classificatory, it is possible to see most urban sociological effort as falling into one or another of four main categories: (1) demographic, (2) ecological, (3) structural, or (4) behavioural. These four categories correspond to the four sociological aspects of the urban community that one can discern at any one point in time, and it is to these four aspects of the urban community that I would like to turn at this point.[7]

Demographic aspects: population size, composition, and distribution

Perhaps the most fundamental aspect of the urban community involves human numbers. Community size is itself a key feature, in that it often seems to be associated with variations in other characteristics. But there is more than size at issue when we examine the *demographic* aspects of an urban community. To take Hauser and Duncan's widely-accepted definition as a point of departure, 'Demography is the study of the size, territorial distribution, and composition of population, changes therein, and the components of such changes, which may be identified as natality, mortality, territorial movement (migration), and social mobility (change of status).'[8]

In addition to size, then, population composition and distribution are at issue. It is important to notice that these three features—size, composition, and distribution—are *static* characteristics. They are subject to instantaneous measurement by means of a census, that is, an enumeration —whether complete or partial (via sampling)—of the number and characteristics of a given population at a given point in time. The cross-sectional character of a census is critical; it yields a 'snapshot', or an essentially static portrait of a population. Successive snapshots, of course, may produce an approximation of a 'moving picture', yielding a dynamic portrayal of change over time.

When an urban community is subjected to a census enumeration, all

6 Peter Mann, *An Approach to Urban Sociology* (New York, 1965).

7 The following section draws heavily upon Leo F. Schnore, 'Community' in Neil J. Smelser, *An Introduction to Sociology* (New York and London, 1967).

8 Philip M. Hauser and Otis Dudley Duncan (eds.), *The Study of Population* (Chicago, 1959), 2; see also Leo F. Schnore 'Social mobility in demographic perspective', *American Sociological Review*, xxvi (June 1961), pp. 407–23.

three of these features—size, composition, and distribution—are simultaneously ascertained. We learn the number of persons within the community, what their characteristics are, and how they are distributed in space. Thus, in addition to size, the 'make-up' or composition of the community is determined. We also learn the major facts concerning the distributional pattern of the city, for example, its population density in various subareas and sectors. A concern with the distribution of people and activities in space, however, leads quite naturally to another and more complex kind of inquiry. People are not randomly distributed, nor are their activities. People and activities tend to clump or cluster at certain points, and to be spread thinly at other points. The patterns assumed by these distributions are the key subject for 'ecological' investigation.

Ecological aspects: the spatial and temporal dimensions of community life

Human ecology has been traditionally concerned with the spatial and temporal aspects of the community.[9] As I have stated, human activities are dissimilarly distributed in space. The same is true of time; just as spatial patterns can be observed, there are distinct temporal patterns on view in the human community. In particular, there is a daily rhythm to community life that lends a high degree of predictability to community affairs. Like spatial patterns, these temporal patterns are not the same from one community to another. They vary, and often vary in an orderly fashion. For example, community size is a key factor in determining what the temporal pattern will look like. Like space, time serves as a dimension on which community structure can be observed and even measured.[10]

As in the case of time, space is employed differently in varying community contexts. In the small agricultural village, for example, there is a notable homogeneity of land uses. On the other hand, the giant metropolis is an intricate mosaic of highly differentiated land uses, in keeping with the rich variety of highly specialised activities that are carried on there. Every change in community size, then, might be expected to yield changes in the occupancy of space. Not only is the total occupied territory likely to be increased with each major increment in population size, but different pieces of that space are apt to be put to different uses. A dwindling amount of area is left to 'primary' (extractive) production, and more space devoted to 'secondary' (fabrication) and 'tertiary' (service) activities of many

[9] See James A. Quinn, *Human Ecology* (New York, 1950), and Amos H. Hawley, *Human Ecology: A Theory of Community Structure* (New York, 1950).
[10] See Amos H. Hawley, 'The approach of human ecology to urban areal research', *Scientific Monthly*, xxiii (July 1951), pp. 48–9.

varieties.[11] The residential uses of space grow and come to be differentiated, too, and there is initiated a 'sifting and sorting' process that yields a marked spatial segregation of activities and elements within the population at large.

Although I have veered into a kind of sequential description of spatial and temporal patterns, it is important to realise that these patterns can be observed at any one point in time, so that uses of space and time are also *static* aspects of the community. Even though the patterns are subject to change, they can be instantaneously observed. These ecological patterns in time and space are also evidence—along with certain demographic data —of another kind of order or structure.

Structural aspects: the organisation of communities and their parts

The spacing and timing of human activities reveal something about the organisation of communities, that is, about their *structural* features. It is the distinctive task of the sociologist, however, to investigate all facets of social organisation.[12] Not all of these facets are readily subjected to ecological mapping in space, nor are they amenable to strict ordering in time, but they are nonetheless crucial in determining the structural aspects of communities. A review of all the various 'institutional' arrangements on view within communities is well beyond the scope of this paper. Here I can provide nothing more than a general orientation toward the subject of social organisation.

A community is, in itself, a unit of social organisation. But it is more than that, since it *contains* numerous other organised units. To appraise this matter in its simplest form, consider the familiar roster of units that make up the typical contemporary community. First, such communities consist of a congeries of families and households. In addition, most of them contain a large number of business establishments engaged in the production of goods and the provision of services. Beyond that, a majority of them support a large complement of specialised units of a public or quasi-public character: governmental agencies, schools, churches, hospitals, and the like. Finally, besides these numerous operating units, there are substantial numbers of formal and informal associations. These associations draw upon the resident families and other units for their membership, and they may be loosely or tightly linked to each other in

[11] The terms 'primary', 'secondary', and 'tertiary' are taken from Colin Clark, *The Conditions of Economic Progress* (London, 1940).
[12] See Leo F. Schnore, 'Social morphology and human ecology', *American Journal of Sociology*, lxiii (May 1958), pp. 620–34, and Leo F. Schnore, 'The myth of human ecology', *Sociological Inquiry*, xxxi (Spring 1961), pp. 128–39.

still other and larger associations. Examples in the United States include the Red Cross, the Chamber of Commerce, and similar organisations; these associations undoubtedly have their counterparts elsewhere.

This bewildering array of units is what sociologists usually have in mind when they speak of the 'social organisation' of a contemporary urban community. But the complications in the analysis of urban community structure do not arise merely from the number and variety of units present. There is the additional complication of understanding the linkages between these units.

Some of these linkages are relatively simple and straightforward. The ties between the resident families and the local retail business establishments, for example, are not difficult to comprehend. The families of the community constitute the market for the goods and services offered by the businesses, and at least a few families provide the manpower required for staffing the community's business enterprises. Thus there are clearcut reciprocal relations between the two types of units. In other instances, however, the links between two or more organised units are not so easy to determine. The ties between families making up a 'social class', for instance, may be extremely tenuous, with limited interaction between one family and another. Indeed, some writers assert that 'social classes' are not groups but are statistical artifacts, created by the observer, with members lacking in self-conscious awareness of their common circumstances and rarely co-acting in any concerted fashion.[13]

Another complication in the analysis of urban community structure arises from the fact that such communities to-day are not perfectly insulated from the world beyond their borders. No community is an island, entire of itself. The links with the outside world are many and various. Kinship ties bind local conjugal families to other families, often over great distances. Local business establishments may be linked to dozens or even hundreds of similar units in other communities through the corporate ties of common ownership and operation. Labour unions are parts of non-local wholes. Churches are usually members of regional or national communions, if not world-wide faiths. And even the most ostensibly 'local' units—those of government—may be members of state leagues of municipalities and the like. Even if they are not, state and national governmental policy is likely to impinge at many points in their day-to-day operations. All of these manifold threads of interrelationships make the community a very complex system, indeed, and it is no wonder that the sociological understanding of urban community organisation is

[13] Werner S. Landecker, 'Class boundaries', *American Sociological Review*, xxv (December 1960), pp. 868–77.

at a fairly primitive level. Our understanding of the system as it now exists is limited, and we have even less grasp of the system as an evolving entity. That is, we have not even begun to grapple with the historical dimension.

Because of present ignorance, the analysis of urban community structure remains an important task for sociological effort. Viewed in its internal and external relations, the contemporary urban community is structurally complex; not only are the parts of the whole many and diverse, but the ties that bind these parts into a coherent whole internally —and that link the urban community externally—are equally numerous and varied.[14]

Behavioural aspects: social-psychological facets of the community

It may seem odd to speak of the 'parts' of the community as consisting of social groups—families, business establishments, institutions, organisations, associations, and the like. From another perspective, communities simply consist of individual persons. Indeed they do, and that fundamental fact has not been ignored by sociologists concerned with the community. In fact, the social-psychological aspect of the community has received considerable attention. Many sociologists actually stress the psychological dimension, and conclude that a community without self-consciousness is no community at all.

Perhaps the most fundamental assumption made by social psychologists is that an individual's group memberships are vital factors in influencing his behaviour. Attitudes and values are formed in a group context, and, according to this view, concrete individual behaviour is best understood in that context. The person and his actions, then, are to be studied with particular reference to the groups—past and present—with which he has been and is now affiliated.[15]

This assumption raises a number of questions. First, what are the most salient group memberships? Granting (for the sake of argument) that group membership makes a difference in a person's behaviour, which groups make the most difference? The answer, of course, may vary according to such things as the stage of the life cycle. The family may be most crucial to a person in the formative years of his childhood; the peer group may be more important to him in adolescence; and the occupational

---

[14] Perhaps the most thorough treatment of these matters is Roland L. Warren, *The Community in America* (Chicago, 1963).
[15] Theodore Newcomb, *Social Psychology* (New York, 1950).

group may be most salient to him in his adult life. The particular type of behaviour may be crucial, too, so that an individual's religious group affiliation may be vitally important in fertility behaviour, somewhat less relevant in political behaviour, and of virtually no consequence in economic affairs in general.

However, the question that is most vital for my present purpose may be phrased more generally: to what extent is membership in a local community significant in the understanding of an individual's behaviour? The answer depends on the particular area of behaviour that is being explored, but generally, the community of residence is fairly useful in many ways for the prediction of individual behaviour. One reason is that the community context will determine in a general way the number and variety of group experiences and opportunities for group member- ships.

Consider only the question of community homogeneity. If the area of residence should be a 'one-class' community (as many American small towns and suburbs are alleged to be), an individual's exposure to a variety of ways of life is likely to be sharply curtailed. The same is true with respect to racial and religious homogeneity; if all the other members of a community are of the same racial or ethnic group, or adhere to the same religious tenets, the behavioural consequences for the individual con- cerned are likely to be different from the behavioural consequences for one reared in a more heterogeneous setting.

Or consider the matter of the community size. A large community offers far more variety in personal opportunities and experiences than a small one. Differences of this kind are highly relevant, particularly in an individual's formative years. Consequently, social psychologists frequently ask for information concerning the kind of community in which the individual grew up. There are a number of interesting and important differences between people in outlook and in behaviour, according to whether their origin is rural or urban.[16]

The social-psychological aspect of the community clearly warrants attention in any full-scale examination of this social unit. The community is more than a population, arrayed in space, and organised into sub-units. It is also an assemblage of people, thinking, feeling, and behaving as individuals.

---

[16] See, for example, William H. Sewell, 'Community of residence and college plans', *American Sociological Review*, xxix (February 1964), pp. 24–38, and William H. Sewell and Alan M. Orenstein, 'Community of residence and occupational choice', *American Journal of Sociology*, lxx (March 1965), pp. 551–63.

The four facets in historical perspective

Now it should be fairly evident that these four facets of the urban community—the demographic, the ecological, the structural and the behavioural—do not offer the same possibilities from the standpoint of historical research. The data problems are substantially different. In fact, the order in which I took them up represents a rough grading from 'easiest' to 'hardest'.

In the Western world, urban demographic history is perhaps the easiest to contemplate. Blessed with long series of successive censuses, the historically-orientated scholar can hope to reconstruct the population composition of one or more cities with relative ease. In the United States, for example, we have decennial censuses stretching back to 1790. Now it is true that the items of information gathered have changed over the years; the list has become longer as items have been added. But the general comparability has remained substantial, so it is not too difficult to assemble a fairly long historical series.

Reconstruction of urban ecological history is somewhat more difficult. For effective work to be done, we must have demographic and other data for sub-parts of cities. Such materials are far more recent in origin. In the United States, for example, we have data for 'census tracts'—small and relatively homogeneous statistical sub-areas—for a small number of cities since 1920.[17] For the nineteenth century we have some data for political 'wards' (voting districts), but the amount of information for each ward is limited. Nevertheless, some historical work can be done on reconstructing ecological patterns of the past.

The reconstruction of a city's social organisation is quite another matter. The structural aspects of the urban community are most difficult to render for the present, let alone for the past. We simply do not have anything corresponding to a 'census' of social, economic, and political units. It takes a most imaginative and determined researcher indeed to present more than the most superficial account of structural changes. I am not saying that it cannot be done. An outstanding example, drawing heavily on old newspapers and other yellowing documents is Robert O. Schulze's historical study of the changing 'power structure' of Ypsilanti, Michigan during the nineteenth and twentieth centuries. Schulze was able to trace a distinct shift from a locally-orientated system to a 'metro-politanised' situation.

'The economic power structure [of Ypsilanti became] increasingly

[17] The list of tracted areas has lengthened considerably over the years, until we now have 1960 data for 178 cities.

dominated by large, absentee-owned firms, none of which were formally linked, neither with each other nor with locally-owned banks or industries. .... Our historical review has documented that, following the turn of the century, there occurred a marked withdrawal of the economic dominants [rich and powerful figures in Ypsilanti] from sustained, overt participation in its public life. We find, for example, that the 'average' economic dominant of the nineteenth century held over three times as many public offices and remained in them almost three times as long as did his twentieth century counterpart.'[18]

Unfortunately, Schulze's work is virtually unique, and we can find very few examples of historical investigations concerning truly structural matters.

Historical studies of the behavioural aspect of urban communities are clearly most difficult of all. I would guess that they are practically impossible. Some historian of the twenty-first century may be able to draw upon the great number of public-opinion surveys conducted in cities in this century for such a study, but the prospects for a contemporary are limited indeed. One cannot depend upon written accounts—diaries, journals, and the like—in order to assemble a portrait of the state of mind of residents of a nineteenth-century city, for there are severe problems of bias. Those who keep such records, setting down their most intimate thoughts, are hardly typical of those who do not. All in all, historical-behavioural studies appear to be virtually impossible, at least if rigorous standards of research are demanded. We shall have to continue depending upon impressionistic accounts concerning the attitudes and values of our urban forebears.

Historical studies of urban demography and ecology

If I were asked to make a recommendation, then, I would suggest a concentration of effort on historical studies of the demographic and ecological aspects of urban life. In other words, I would urge emphasis upon the two easier types of inquiry. I must admit that my advice is not an unbiased suggestion; my own work has focussed on precisely these aspects of the city—the demographic and the ecological.[19]

It appears that urban demographic history permits the investigator to grapple with the broadest set of problems. Eric E. Lampard has been particularly articulate in urging this kind of research:

18 Robert O. Schulze, 'The bifurcation of power in a satellite city' in Morris Janowitz, *Community Political Systems* (New York, 1961), p. 37.
19 Leo F. Schnore, *The Urban Scene: Human Ecology and Demography* (New York, 1965)

'[It] is a principal contention of this paper that social historians must begin to explore the underlying movements in community structure and organization that go much deeper than the epiphenomenal patterns of politics or the ferment of ideas. *An autonomous social history ought to begin with a study of population: its changing composition and distribution in time and space.*'[20]

This is no counsel of perfection, I am convinced, for much can be learned by careful inquiry into shifts over time in population size, composition, and distribution.

'The demographer, of course, is no magician; he cannot produce reliable results from unreliable sources. All census enumerations, for example, are subject to a variable degree of error: undercounts here, overcounts there, and occasional confusions of categories by the counters and counted everywhere. These shortcomings in the data are compounded for the historical demographer. Census categories are changed, items covered at one date are dropped at another and sometimes reappear later under a different title. Once the historian gets back before the first official census in any country, he must rely, for the most part, on fugitive sources, particular counts that have no claim to comprehension, such as directories, parish registers of births and deaths, 'books of souls', various lists of taxpayers, the wildest estimates of contemporaries, and so forth. If he lacks numerological powers, the historical demographer, nevertheless, has had to develop all the arts of the conjurer in manipulating even the official census data to make his results consistent and comparable over time. This fact alone accounts for the paucity of historical studies of urbanization.'[21]

Despite these difficulties, the field of urban demographic history appears to be quite promising, and I am fairly confident that the near future will yield some impressive results.[22]

As for urban ecological history, the picture is not quite as clear. I wish that I could be as optimistic about it as I am about urban demographic history. One difficulty, of course, is sheer data availability. Securing com-

---

[20] Eric E. Lampard, 'Urbanization and social change' in Oscar Handlin and John Burchard (eds.), *The Historian and the City* (Cambridge, 1963), p. 236; italics added.

[21] Eric E. Lampard and Leo F. Schnore, 'Urbanization problems' in *Research Needs for Development Assistance Programs* (Washington, D.C., 1961), p. 12.

[22] See D. V. Glass and D. E. C. Eversley (eds.), *Population in History* (Chicago, 1965), and D. E. C. Eversley, Peter Laslett, and E. A. Wrigley, *An Introduction to Historical Demography* (New York, 1966).

arable data for sub-parts of the city is just not as easy as compiling population statistics for the city as a whole. Moreover, there are fewer persons interested in this kind of inquiry. In the United States, for example, only 100 out of 4,200 members of the American Sociological Association selected 'human ecology' as one of their substantive interests.[23] And among these 100, a good guess is that only a handful are concerned with historically-orientated research. Nevertheless, there are exciting possibilities in this line of study, and I would like to spend the remaining time at my disposal in a broad over-view of my own current research.

Some current work on urban ecological history

My project is entitled 'Ecological Patterns in American Cities: Quantitative Studies in Urban History'. It is supported by the National Science Foundation, a federal agency of the United States government that underwrites research in the physical, biological, and social sciences. My own project began this past fall, and it will run at least three years. The focus of the research is the residential redistribution of 'social classes' in American cities. This is a topic that has interested me for many years. My first research dealing with the question was actually carried out over ten years ago, in connection with my doctoral dissertation, completed in 1955 at the University of Michigan.[24]

The main impetus, however, was provided by some more recent library research' done in connection with five years' service (1959–1964) on the Committee on Urbanization of the Social Science Research Council. This Committee was initially asked to review critically the extant assumptions and generalizations regarding the phenomenon of urbanisation, its determinants, concomitants, and consequences, including their applicability cross-culturally and historically.

'Surveying the sociological literature, in search of materials for such a critical review, one quickly gains the impression that a rather large amount of empirical effort has been devoted to *the internal spatial structure of cities.* This topic is not a sociological specialism by any means; geographers, economists, and others share an interest in the physical distribution of population and land uses within the urban agglomeration. For this reason alone, the subject of spatial structure

[23] Schnore, *The Urban Scene, op. cit.,* p. 33.
[24] Leo F. Schnore, *Patterns of Decentralization,* unpublished doctoral dissertation, Department of Sociology, University of Michigan, 1955.

seemed particularly appropriate for review by a group with multi-disciplinary representation.'[25]

I chose to work on the contrasts in spatial structure of cities north and south of the Rio Grande. There were two reasons for this: (1) it had been frequently asserted that Latin-American cities revealed a spatial configuration of social classes that was precisely the opposite of that on view in the United States; (2) at the same time, it had been repeatedly observed that Latin-American cities were tending over time to assume the 'Anglo'-American pattern. In other words, there were both cross-cultural and historical assertions interwoven in the literature dealing with the subject.

The literature held that the 'classical' Latin-American pattern showed the élite residing very near the centre of the city, with the disadvantaged located at the periphery. This is in sharp contrast to the pattern that so many observers—beginning with Ernest W. Burgess—have regarded as typical in cities in the United States. In that country, it was generally held, the lower strata are clustered near the urban core, with the élite located at the periphery, and especially in 'suburbia'.[26]

My 'library research' confirmed the fact that older Latin-American cities had indeed conformed to the classical pattern. It also showed that a shift in the Anglo-American direction was well under way. At the same time, this research suggested that older cities in the United States had—at one time in the past—resembled the classical Latin pattern. These facts raised the possibility of an 'evolutionary' sequence, wherein cities both north and south of the Rio Grande were sharing a common experience. I am confining attention to cities of the United States in my present research, but I am attempting to deal with historical developments

I am undertaking a series of intensive case studies in urban growth and development, complemented by a comparative research program that aims at quantifying the cross-sectional effects of historical trends in housing construction at the neighbourhood level. The focus of the

[25] Leo F. Schnore, 'On the spatial structure of cities in the two Americas' in Philip M. Hauser and Leo F. Schnore (eds.), *The Study of Urbanization* (New York and London, 1965), pp. 347–8; italics in original. The balance of this section draws heavily upon the earlier presentation.

[26] Ernest W. Burgess, 'The growth of the city: an introduction to a research project' *Publications of the American Sociological Society*, xviii (1924), pp. 85–97; reprinted in Robert E. Park, Ernest W. Burgess, and Roderick D. McKenzie, *The City* (Chicago, 1925), pp. 47–62 Insofar as it pertains to the residential distribution of the various social classes, the Burgess hypothesis was anticipated by writers dealing with London and Manchester in the nineteenth century. See Charles Booth, *Life and Labour of the People in London* (London, 1904), final volume, p. 205, and Friedrich Engels, *The Condition of the Working Class in England* (New York: Macmillan, 1958 edition), pp. 54–5.

esearch is the 'neighbourhood'. I plan to examine the population compo-
ition of urban sub-areas in terms of socio-economic status (education,
)ccupation and income), racial-ethnic make-up, and (occasionally) type
)f family.[27]

From an individual standpoint, these variables are linked in a familiar
way. A person acquires an education, which prepares him for an occupa-
ion that yields an income. All these factors presumably influence his
housing 'choices', perhaps exerting contradictory effects in some instances. Should he marry and have children, the size and composition of
his family will also exert an influence in determining his residential loca-
ion, and changes in family size will also influence his locational behaviour.
Then, within the limits of his housing 'needs', and within his 'capacities'
or buying or renting residential space, racial and ethnic considerations
impinge, barring him from certain areas or attracting him to others.

One difficulty in maintaining such a purely individualistic approach to
he locational problem—focussing on characteristics of the person and
his wishes—is the limited information available concerning all of the
many factors that limit his choices in the housing market. This particular
market is notoriously unstable over time and relatively unstructured at
any one point in time. Moreover, residential mobility is so frequent that
even the most sophisticated survey approach would be unable to construct
a long-term portrayal of urban growth and development by somehow
aggregating the residential biographies of thousands of individuals.

The approach taken in my research deals with these same variables in
quite a different way, and at a supra-individual level of analysis. In brief,
I regard the urban area as a kind of social organism that is subject to a
process that I call 'incremental growth and residues'.[28] Population change,
whether sustained or uneven, demands new housing construction; new
residential areas are developed, suited to a particular income range and
type of family, and the character of the neighbourhood tends to persist
for a time even in the face of considerable movement in and out on the
part of individual families. As the neighbourhood 'ages' it may undergo
the process which the geographers call 'sequent occupance' by different
groups. In any case, 'residues' of the past continue to exert an influence
on present structure. Housing is put in place, and families of a particular
ethnic and socio-economic status come to occupy it. I will be unable to
deal with all of the relevant factors in this process, of course, since many

[27] These are roughly synonymous with the three major variables involved in 'social area
analysis'. My research will not employ that particular technique, however, because I am
convinced that more direct approaches are sufficient.

[28] Leo F. Schnore, 'Urban form: the case of the metropolitan community' in Werner Z.
Hirsch (ed.), *Urban Life and Form* (New York, 1963), pp. 169-97.

of them elude measurement. The rôle of land speculators, real estate agents, local authorities in charge of zoning, and other strategically placed individuals and agencies can hardly be assessed in any but a narrative fashion. I do feel, however, that some salient aspects of this process of neighbourhood evolution—complex and changing as it may be—can be described in considerable detail and in a comparative fashion if a deliberate effort is aimed at quantifying the 'housing history' of urban areas.

Finally, I feel that the contemporary effects—the 'residues'—of past developments can be assessed in a meaningful way. Towards this end, I am undertaking two complementary lines of analysis:

(A) a limited number of detailed case histories, focussed on developments in residential construction in some 10 areas; and

(B) a series of comparative studies of some 200 areas, aimed at assessing the generality of the case-history findings.

The possibility that the 'traditional Latin-American pattern' might have been typical of North American cities of an earlier era raises a fascinating question—*does the residential structure of the city evolve in a predictable direction?* Casual observation leads one to believe that 'better' residential neighbourhoods are found near the very centre of small towns, even to-day, in every major region of the United States. Writing in the 'thirties, Homer Hoyt noted that, in small cities or cities of slow growth, the highest rental areas may occupy parts of sectors directly adjacent to the business centre.[29] Could not this have been the typical North American pattern of an earlier era, prior to modern transportation developments and rapid population growth?

Assuming that a real reversal has taken place, could one account for the shift in residential pattern from one in which the élite occupy the centre to one in which they abandon it for the periphery? At least three variables seem to be involved: (1) city growth, (2) local transportation technology, and (3) 'social power' to use Gideon Sjoberg's terminology. If growth is accompanied by commercial and industrial development there may well be new competitors for centrally located sites; in the face of this competition, residential areas may be abandoned to more intensive land uses. At the same time, the encroachment of business and factory uses, together with the traffic they generate, may render central areas undesirable for residence. For the élite to abandon the centre, however, technological conditions must allow them to maintain relatively easy access to the centre and its vital institutions. In the past, this was not the case, and still may

[29] Homer Hoyt, *The Structure and Growth of Residential Neighbourhoods in American Cities* (Washington D.C., 1939), p. 76.

not be the case. Speaking of Anápolis, Brazil, Carmin has observed that 'with no paved roads, and until recently almost no private automobiles, a residential site near the heart of town was and for the most part still is a prized location. Such a home site gives easy access to the shopping goods centre, the churches and the places of entertainment (coffee houses, bars, etc.) as well as to the business establishments owned and operated by many of those who dwell in Class A houses.'[30]

Sjoberg points to the technological factor as crucial, but introduces an additional consideration:

'How do we explain this [pre-industrial] distribution of classes as between the central sector and the periphery? Throughout feudal cities, values operate defining residence in the historic centre as most prestigeful, location on the periphery as least so. But reference to values alone cannot account for the ecological differences between the traditional and the modern community. Far more pertinent is technology. For one thing, the feudal society's technology permits relatively little spatial mobility, thereby setting limits to the kinds of ecological arrangements that can obtain. People travel mostly on foot, occasionally on animal-back; only the privileged ride in the human- or animal-drawn vehicles, slow and uncomfortable though these may be by industrial standards.

Assuming that upper-class persons strive to maintain their prerogatives in the community and society (here social power enters as a factor in ecology), they must isolate themselves from the non-élite and be centrally located to ensure ready access to the headquarters of the governmental, religious, and educational organizations. The highly valued residence, then, is where fullest advantage may be taken of the city's strategic facilities; in turn these latter have come to be tightly bunched for the convenience of the élite—patterns that are readily revised with the introduction of rapid transit, telephones, and so on.'[31]

In addition to easy access, however, the 'prerogatives' enjoyed by those with social (and economic) power include the ability to maintain a particular location in the face of competing alternatives, and the ability to capture the newest and most desirable residential facilities. The Burgess hypothesis tends to assume something about the occupancy patterns of the upper classes, i.e. that they will tend to occupy the newer areas. In

[30] Robert L. Carmin, *Anápolis, Brazil* (Chicago, 1953), p. 67.
[31] Gideon Sjoberg, *The Preindustrial City: Past and Present* (New York, 1960), pp. 98–9.

the United States, such areas have been peripheral in location, in Latin America, they are increasingly so.

Hence we come to a kind of 'common-sense' rationalization of the trends observable in both 'Anglo' and Latin America. Given growth and expansion of the centre, and given appropriate improvements in transportation and communication, the upper strata might be expected to shift from central to peripheral residence, and the lower classes might increasingly take up occupancy in the central area abandoned by the élite. Some of my earlier researches suggest that age of the city is a powerful factor in predicting the current residential distribution of socio-economic strata, but these were essentially cross-sectional studies and offer only indirect evidence.[32] It is now time to undertake direct longitudinal investigations of this 'evolutionary' hypothesis, at least in North America.

As I said earlier, my research involves two complementary phases: (1) detailed field studies and (2) quantitative comparative studies. I would like to examine some ten cities in some considerable detail. I would also like to develop a series of studies dealing with some 200 cities, representing a full range of relevant characteristics. Hopefully, the timing of this second phase will be such that the 1970 census permits 'up-dating' these materials by the use of new tract data.

(A) CASE STUDIES. I have drawn a preliminary 'sample' of 50 cities in the continental United States; from this list, about 10 will be chosen for intensive analysis over the next three to five years. The initial criteria used in developing the list of cities were as follows:

(1) the city should have had at least 100,000 inhabitants in 1960;
(2) 1960 census tracts should extend beyond the political limits of the city itself;
(3) the entire Urbanised Area (UA) and the entire Standard Metropolitan Statistical Area (SMSA) containing the city should each have had at least 200,000 inhabitants in 1960;[33]

---

[32] Leo F. Schnore, 'The socio-economic status of cities and suburbs', *American Sociologica Review* xxviii (February 1963), pp. 76–85, and Leo F. Schnore, 'Urban structure and suburban selectivity', *Demography*, i (1964), pp. 164–76.

[33] These two areal units are employed for reporting large amounts of statistical data. An Urbanised Area contains at least one city of 50,000 inhabitants or more in 1960, as well as the surrounding closely settled incorporated places and unincorporated areas. It is basically established by the use of a population-density criterion, and corresponds roughly to the 'conurbation' in Great Britain. The Standard Metropolitan Statistical Area consists of at least one city of 50,000 inhabitants, together with all counties (towns in New England) closely tied to the

(4) the entire UA and the entire SMSA should lie within a single state, in order that (a) legal and political factors will be 'constant' and that (b) single planning authorities will be present;

(5) insofar as possible, the city should be the *sole* 'central city' of a UA and of a SMSA, and it should be some distance from other cities of comparable size.

This last criterion has proved to be most difficult to handle. Obvious 'twin cities' (such as Minneapolis and St. Paul) and cities very close to each other (such as Dallas and Fort Worth) were excluded from consideration at the outset. But the criterion is especially difficult to apply, in any strict sense, within 'megalopolis', the heavily urbanised north-eastern seaboard. For example, the Boston UA connects with that of Brockton; the Bridgeport and New Haven UA's touch at the latter's south-western corner; the Hartford UA connects with that of a smaller UA (New Britain); Worcester's SMSA touches those of Boston (on the east) and Springfield-Chicopee-Holyoke (on the west). It would be very difficult to represent this region, in other words, without relaxing this last criterion to some extent.

In the actual selection of the 10 cities, certain additional criteria will be employed:

(1) I would like the 10 cities to represent a *substantial range in terms of* (a) *size*, (b) *age*, and (c) *regional location*.

(2) It will be desirable to have *tract data for census years prior to 1960*. Lack of perfect areal comparability will preclude strict comparisons over time in many instances, but the existence of tract data for earlier years should prove to be helpful; Lieberson has shown that reconstruction of comparable areas is feasible.[34] The use of this criterion would argue for the inclusion of such cities as Boston, Rochester, Atlanta, Cleveland, Milwaukee, Los Angeles and Seattle.

(3) Other things equal, I would like to work with a number of the *cities included in previous comparative studies* bearing on the main topics of this research, notably those of Lieberson, Wilkins, and Taeuber and Taeuber.[35] This would argue for the inclusion of Syracuse, Atlanta, Memphis, Cleveland, and Columbus.

central city (or cities) in social and economic terms. For a fuller discussion, see U.S. Bureau of the Census, *U.S. Census of Population: 1960*, Vol. I: *Characteristics of the Population*, Part A, 'Number of Inhabitants' (Washington, D.C., 1961), pp. xviii–xxvii.

[34] Stanley Lieberson, *Ethnic Patterns in American Cities* (New York, 1963).

[35] Lieberson, *ibid.*; Arthur H. Wilkins, *The Residential Distribution of Occupation Groups in Eight Middle-sized Cities of the United States in 1950*, unpublished doctoral dissertation, Department of Sociology, University of Chicago, 1956; Karl E. Taeuber and Alma F. Taeuber, *Negroes in Cities* (Chicago, 1965).

(4) I would like to include some *cities with different patterns of 'suburban selectivity'*.[36] This would argue for the inclusion of such cities as New Haven, Worcester, Birmingham, Charlotte, Memphis, Miami, Shreveport, Tulsa, Flint, Wichita, Albuquerque, Los Angeles, San Diego, Spokane, and Tucson—all of which depart from the 'expected' pattern, wherein suburban areas show higher socio-economic status as measured by school years completed.

(5) Finally, I will be guided by such *practical considerations* as (a) physical access, (b) the existence of active and research-oriented planning agencies, (c) the presence or absence of a major university or branch thereof, and (d) the availability of detailed 'city biographies' and other historical materials.

I have started the detailed case studies during the first year (1965–6) with Milwaukee, Wisconsin. It is close at hand; it has an active city planning department and it is also the focus of the research and action efforts of the Southeastern Wisconsin Regional Planning Commission. Detailed tract data cover the last three census dates, and 'community areas' have been modelled after the various local community fact books for Chicago.[37] The University of Wisconsin-Milwaukee has an inter-disciplinary Department of Urban Affairs. Finally the city has an excellent 'city biography' by Bayrd Still and a rich variety of other historical materials are available there and through the library of the State Historical Society of Wisconsin in Madison.[38]

Milwaukee, of course, is a relatively large and old urban area that exhibits the 'expected' pattern of city-suburban status differences. The second city chosen for intensive examination will be one that contrasts vividly with Milwaukee; my present inclination is to turn to Albuquerque as soon as my work on Milwaukee is completed. Other cities which appear to be likely candidates include Cleveland, Columbus, Flint, Detroit, and Wichita in the North Central region; Boston, Bridgeport, New Haven, and Rochester in the north-east; Atlanta, Baltimore, Birmingham, New Orleans, Memphis, and Miami in the south; and Denver, Los Angeles, Salt Lake City, and Tucson in the west. It goes without saying, however, that much more exploratory work will have to be done before final choices can be made, and that I am not committed to any one of these 20 cities at the moment.

---

[36] Schnore, 'Urban structure and suburban selectivity', *op. cit.*

[37] H. Yuan Tien (ed.), *Milwaukee Metropolitan Area Fact Book: 1940, 1950, and 1960* (Madison, 1962).

[38] Bayrd Still, *Milwaukee: The History of a City* (Madison, 1948).

(B) COMPARATIVE STUDIES. In order to complement the detailed case studies, and in order to permit the construction of generalizations with a wider basis, I am also initiating a series of comparative studies based on some 200 cities. I say 'some 200' because I do not know the exact number that will ultimately be involved. In some instances, all of the central cities of the (213) UA's and SMSA's recognized in the 1960 Census of Population will be examined, in other cases all of the cities for which 1960 tract and block statistics are available will be used.[39]

The first comparative study is an analysis of cities between 25,000 and 50,000 inhabitants in 1960. There were exactly 200 such places *outside Urbanised Areas* in 1960, but I have excluded some of these places, since they lie within the boundaries of SMSA's as officially defined by the Bureau of the Census. In any case, preliminary results for 1950–60 suggest that an examination of such 'quasi-metropolitan areas' (counties containing one or more cities between 25,000 and 50,000) throw further light on the 'evolutionary' hypothesis outlined above.[40] It is also proving feasible to extend some of the analysis back to 1940, in order to have a pre-war observation and a 20-year interval. While this is not much 'historical depth', it is at least longitudinal rather than cross-sectional in orientation.

Conclusions

Human ecology focuses upon certain spatial and temporal aspects of the structure and development of human communities. The studies I have outlined here are in the ecological tradition, emphasising patterns in urban spatial distribution, but I propose to deal with the historical or developmental dimension more explicitly than does most existing research on the American city.

As for *space*, I intend to retain a traditional emphasis of ecological attention: residential patterns in American cities. The spatial distributions of (a) socio-economic strata, (b) racial and ethnic groups, and (c) types of family are being examined within two 'samples' of cities, using a broadly comparative approach. The principal unit of analysis in the case studies is the residential neighbourhood rather than whole cities or other large urban units, as in most of my previous work.

With respect to *time*, I am examining processes of change in two ways:

[39] There are 1960 tract data for 178 SMSA's. For 136, the entire SMSA is tracted; for 17 only the central city is tracted; and for the remaining 25, the central city and part of the balance of the SMSA are tracted. City Block Statistics for 1960 have been published for 418 areas within the United States.

[40] Leo F. Schnore and James R. Pinkerton, 'The residential redistribution of socio-economic strata in metropolitan areas', *Demography*, iii (1966), pp. 491–9.

(1) by undertaking a series of intensive case studies examining the growth and development of some ten urban areas that have been selected to represent a wide range of existing situations; (2) by carrying out a much more extensive statistical investigation of some 200 urban areas, with a view toward assessing the present effects of variations in past growth and development. In both phases of this work, I emphasise the rôle of housing construction, and I plan to apply the demographic concept of the 'cohort' to neighbourhoods (rather than individuals, as in demographic inquiries) by identifying housing areas that have developed in different eras.[41]

In short, it may soon be my pleasure to join you—not merely as a guest at a conference on the study of urban history—but as an urban historian.[42]

[41] The most elaborate exposition of the 'cohort' concept in demography is Pascal K. Whelpton, *Cohort Fertility: Native White Women in the United States* (Princeton, New Jersey: Princeton University Press, 1954). For an application of the concept to urban neighbourhoods, see Beverly Duncan, Georges Sabagh, and Maurice D. Van Arsdol, Jr., 'Patterns of city growth', *American Journal of Sociology*, lxvii (January 1962), pp. 418–29.

[42] The most informed statement concerning the general range of problems considered here is William O. Aydelotte, 'Quantification in history', *American Historical Review*, lxxi (April 1966), pp. 803–25.

Discussion

The initial phase of the discussion on Professor Schnore's paper was illustrated, if not dominated, by a statistical table, written on the blackboard in answer to a question from Dr. MARTIN. A full version of the statistics used may be seen in Table 6 of Professor Schnore's article 'Urban structure and suburban selectivity' in *Demography* (1964), p. 172, but for the reader's convenience the relevant series referred to in discussion is reproduced below.

Size of urbanised area	'Tucson' type	'Los Angeles' type	'New York' type
1,000,000 or more	—	6·3%	93·8%
500,000–1,000,000	—	18·2%	68·2%
250,000–500,000	10·3%	27·6%	58·6%
150,000–250,000	16·3%	27·9%	41·9%
100,000–150,000	13·5%	46·0%	37·8%
50,000–100,000	17·0%	52·8%	20·8%

Census year in which central city first reached 50,000	'Tucson' type	'Los Angeles' type	'New York' type
1800–1860	—	7·1%	92·9%
1860–1800	—	11·8%	82·4%
1890–1900	2·8%	25·0%.	61·1%
1910–1920	8·3%	35·4%	50·0%
1930–1940	12·5%	53·1%	25·0%
1950–1960	28·5%	45·3%	17·0%

Dr. MARTIN's question sprang from mingled curiosity and scepticism concerning the recent course of urban development in the United States. Was it possible to maintain any strict division between suburb and central core in the case of cities like Los Angeles? Indeed, was Los Angeles an exception, or were there, as Professor Schnore had suggested in his classification, other urban areas demonstrating the same sociological trends, 'the spectre of 69 other Los Angeles'.

To answer this question Professor SCHNORE referred in more detail to his own findings, in which the measure of socio-economic status adopted had been the number of school years completed; though he later added that other studies undertaken as a cross-check, and based upon family income, had produced approximately the same results. Using his educational criterion of social status, three contrasted types of relationship between city and suburb could be distinguished. The 'Tucson' type, in which the highest educational grades were over-represented in the city, the 'New York' type, in which attendance at the higher school grades and college was over-represented in the suburbs, and an intermediate 'Los Angeles' type, in which both the highest and the lowest grades were over-represented in the central area.

The incidence of these characteristic types, Professor SCHNORE explained, seemed to be correlated to the size and the age of the cities under study. In other words the smaller or newer the city, the less it seemed to conform to the 'classical' Burgess pattern of a social élite inhabiting the suburbs, and the 'disadvantaged' living at, or near, the centre of the city. Judging purely by the criterion of educational privilege, therefore, Los Angeles was not a unique city. It shared with 69 others (out of the 200 cities chosen for study) the characteristic that both persons at the top of the educational ladder and those with no formal education or with very little schooling, were proportionately more numerous than usual in the central area.

From this point discussion led on to two main topics, both of them stemming from Dr. Martin's opening question and Professor Schnore's reply. The topics, which were treated in general methodological terms, and also in more detailed terms of historical techniques and sources, were as follows. First, was it possible, without gross distortion, to group together the many varied peripheral areas under the single homogeneous description 'suburbs'? And assuming that the simple two-part invention (to use Professor Schnore's phrase) was to be retained, what supplementary means could be found for studying and representing fairly the wide range in socio-economic status, population distribution, and functional rôle observable in different urban and suburban zones? Secondly, if the broad contrast between central area and suburbs were to be retained, as useful for the purposes of sociological comparison between large numbers of cities, the further problem arose of defining the frontier between central zone and outer area. 'There is a very large assumption,' Dr. DYOS objected, 'that one can draw a standardised line between the city and the suburbs, which tends to defy ordinary observation and other historical knowledge.' Was it not possible to be misled, suggested Drs. HENNOCK, KELLETT, and MANN, by the arbitrary nature of administrative boundaries upon which the statistical returns, and even the identification of the central zone depended? What provision could be made for the study of what Professor Schnore had called the 'annexation factor'?

In closer detail, the course of discussion upon these topics began with Professor SCHNORE's declaration, in response to questions put to him by Mr. FREEMAN, that his work so far had primarily been directed towards an overview. 'In these studies I have simply taken it as a mass . . . and I think that is all this sort of material provides; some kind of gross picture in which one can do most specific, careful jobs.' He was well aware that neither the city nor its suburbs could be taken as homogeneous areas. Although he had not conducted interviews and field work, he found it 'extremely helpful to actually go into the area for whatever personal observations can yield in the way of clues.' This was particularly valuable for some of the central neighbourhoods; 'they're not going to be around for direct observation for very long—urban renewal is proceeding at such a pace.' 'In other parts of my work,' he added, 'I have looked at specific suburbs in a detailed way, distinguishing for instance, residential suburbs versus employing suburbs'; and in the thesis and dissertation work which he had been directing he had tried 'wherever appropriate to have each student work on a couple of various specifics in the course of their more general statistical examination.' 'The amount of information one would really want to have,' he warned, 'is enormous . . . this kind of case-study is extremely time-consuming.'

Exactly what might be involved in studies aimed at doing justice to the internal variety of the central area or its suburban fringe, and what historical materials might be used for such an analysis, was illustrated by Mr. SPENCER, from his own current research in Liverpool. The method he was adopting was to take 10 per cent samples, at decennial intervals, from street and trade Directories for a small sub-area since 1841. It was necessary, of course, to guard against the partial nature of Directories' coverage. 'They are often criticised for not containing all of the population but only a certain proportion. . . . This proportion is always the middle and upper classes. The working classes were wiped out.' Since the area in question was a zone of middle class housing however, the range of error was reduced, and it was possible to trace changes in occupational structure, length of stay, and movement. Alternatively, an occupational group clearly associated with income and social class—such as solicitors —could be chosen, and their residential spread or concentration in various sub-areas traced over a period of time.

Professor SCHNORE, whilst lamenting the tedious nature of the exercise, accepted the fact that study of 'cohorts of neighbourhoods' might be possible upon the basis of similar material in U.S. city directories, giving the occupations of heads of households, 'and in southern border cities giving the colour of the person.' The alternative method, of tracing the residence of certain occupation-groups, was also being used for a study of Boston in the 1840s, with the difference that addresses were being drawn, not from Directories but from the registers of employees of 'certain centrally-located business establishments'. There was much to be said for these techniques. 'It's no worse than the census; perhaps in some instances it's better. The census was a one-shot affair throughout the nineteenth century. People were hired and not very well trained, and there are a lot of reasons for thinking the censuses are not particularly accurate.' Further questions on the U.S. census by Professor CHECKLAND and Sir John SUMMERSON elicited the information that, whatever its earlier limitations, the census now presented both individual and family income for the preceding year —a statement received with audible gasps and exclamations—and that the phenomenon of 'dual residence' was considered rare in the U.S. A few highly placed executives maintained a Connecticut home and a New York apartment; but the U.S. census 'asks for *usual* place of residence, which gets down almost to the individual's judgment as to where he spends most of his time.'

Discussion now shifted to the problems concerned with defining the central and suburban frontiers. 'The trouble as it strikes me,' Dr. DYOS observed, 'is that the graduation in any index you like to choose—whether it's density or social class—is likely to be so imperceptible that you can't tell for certain when you move out of one zone into another.' Such distinctions as might be drawn between zones would, moreover, vary with time and between cities, giving rise to 'a sort of moving frontier'. Dr. MANN pursued this point by questioning Professor Schnore about the fate of the transitional zone contained in Burgess's original hypothesis 40 years ago. 'What, in fact has happened to the transitional zone now? Is it still transitive or has it settled down?'

Professor SCHNORE's impression was that there still was, in Chicago, as in Burgess's day, 'a transitional kind of area, that is caught between residential and non-residential uses, where speculative holding involves not repairing, and maintaining slums, and so on.' Referring to Dr. MANN's further allusion to the Burgess hypothesis being 'based upon a *natural area* concept,' Professor SCHNORE discussed, at some length, the rôle of central governmental intervention, and civic or suburban initiatives in creating zones. 'In the large, zoning and indeed planning in the United States has been mainly adjustment to the existing situation—after the fact. Most zoning schemes take what is in place and try to rationalise it, try to patch up round the edges, and so on.' City planning in the United States had only started after the first world war, and 'any larger conception of an area of responsibility, is even more recent than that'. A most interesting control study which he hoped to undertake was of Houston, Texas, 'the only city that has no land-use control of any sort'.

This led Dr. KELLETT to refer to parallel difficulties encountered in the expansion of legal frontiers in British urban history. 'We have what are called "boundary questions" constantly cropping up in the history of every major city that we look at in the nineteenth century.' All were troubled with 'the problem of powerfully incorporated suburbs set up around them for quite often self-interested reasons'. The pattern, suggested during the discussion, by Professor Schnore—'cities that form a large fraction of the whole (i.e. 'whole' = city + suburbs) tend to be smaller, younger and show the 'Tucson' type social pattern'—was not apparent in British urban history; but it should be possible, Dr. KELLETT suggested, to undertake a study on a comparative basis here, and the private parliamentary bill procedure used meant that the records were central. Dr. MARTIN and Dr. DYOS also underlined the opportunities for work in this field. 'The spectacle of the filed minutes of evidence to any bill is a staggering one.' Some had been lost but the remainder of the unpublished select committee evidence was now 'well organised in the Victoria Tower', and only awaited a full bibliography.

At this relatively late stage of the discussion events took an unexpected turn. So far, although difficulties in method and definition had been stressed, no one had completely rejected the whole basis of Professor Schnore's paper. This Mr. BEDARIDA now proceeded to do. He questioned the 'law of urban development, at least in industrially-advanced countries, that the centre was deterioratng in social status, and the suburbs were growing with high-income people, better educated and so on'. This was not true in cities as different as Paris, Milan, Warsaw, Barcelona, Amsterdam, and Vienna, where the suburbs were left to the working class and seen as the worst part of the city without any facilities, with difficult transport and so on.' Professor Schnore's general argument was of great importance for the image of the city. 'What you are saying is an Anglo-Saxon pattern which, I entirely agree, exists in the United Kingdom, the United States, and Canada, but you have quite a different pattern in many other countries, not only Latin America.'

Professor SCHNORE was prepared to make concessions on this point. Upper East Side in New York, the so-called 'Gold Coast' close to the Loop in Chicago, Beacon Hill in Boston—'I'm sure there's one of these in every city. There's a tendency for one or two little enclaves of great wealth, despite the fact that on the average city inhabitants are much less well-educated, much poorer, and have much lower status occupations.' America, like France, could also show working class suburbs.' He would be quite satisfied to be able to make a generalisation about the Anglo-Saxon world, and looked for no universal law.

It was left to Mr. CARTER to intervene in support of the Burgess hypothesis. Even in a small, slowly-growing town like Caernarvon one could still trace morphological evidence of the movement from the old pre-industrial situation where the élite 'had concentrated near the centre of power within the walls'. I think the universality of the pattern is a thing worth stressing, in spite of the objections which can be made to it.'

At this point the CHAIRMAN wound up the discussion. Useful points had been made, both analytically and in discussion of possible source material. The sociologists, however, had remained disturbingly quiescent.

J. R. KELLETT

V

Colonisation as a Factor in the Planting of Towns in North-West England

J. D. Marshall

As is well known, water-powered manufacturing industries often demanded a compact, specialised labour force on or near the site of the manufacture concerned. The dispersal of such sites on streams or in river valleys sometimes forced the employer to build up a community away from any previously existing source of labour supply, especially in the early stages of the industrial revolution between, say, 1770 and 1820. Accordingly, one expects to find flourishing rural colonies in the field of cotton spinning and in the textile manufactures generally. A student who examines the earliest ordnance survey maps for Lancashire and the north-west will not be disappointed in this respect. He will find a variety of what were, undoubtedly, 'industrial villages'; he will also find that a number remain, either in relatively remote rural situations, or, as is more frequently the case, as constituents of the geological layers which are discernible in the great industrial towns of the post-1820 period. Most of these communities, or their names, do not appear in the now familiar litany relative to 'model' community-building; Cromford, Styal, Belper, Saltaire, New Lanark, and so on. In any case, the very concept of model communities raises some questions and begs others, and it may be that the circumstances of their creation justify Professor Pollard's thesis that the majority of such settlements, or colonies, were brought into being through the dictates of simple necessity rather than by virtue of the pursuit of social welfare *per se*.[1]

---

[1] S. Pollard, 'The factory village in the Industrial Revolution', *English Hist. Rev.*, lxxix 1964), pp. 513 *et seq.* and *passim*.

Historians may disagree profoundly over the motives of those who, by their business decisions, brought the colonies into being; but there will be less disagreement over the proposition that these colonies were distinct communities, with certain amenities—shops, schools, chapels, and so forth—provided by the main employer or employers. In the first instance the very nature of the industrial pursuits of the colony, and the social or demographic origins of its inhabitants, and the kinship patterns, ethnic characteristics of social customs of its immigrants, would tend to distinguish it sharply from the surrounding rural or semi-rural society. In other words, we can, profitably and with reason, regard the industrial colony as a sociological entity, and the question of whether its life and destiny were conditioned by a community of *interest* need not be allowed to dominate the discussion. It may well be that the operatives in some Lancashire mill colonies did in fact have a keen sense of such common interest, genuine or delusory, and it is important that urban social historians should bear this possibility in mind.

A colony did not necessarily lose its identity when engulfed by the spread of a wider urban environment, and there is an occasional indication that some colonies became the nuclei of whole suburbs or large suburban communities. The writer is very well aware that the evidence is, all too often, hardly of a very solid or conclusive kind, and the relevant data do not, in any case, always lend themselves to the types of quantification which seem to bestow a hallmark of respectability on central aspects of contemporary urban study. But the evidence is also susceptible to the probings of common sense. To give only one example, the inhabitant of such a colony was less likely to feel involved in the political and social activities of improvement commissioners, boards of health or borough councils than in the immediate exigencies of his job and the requirements of his workplace, or in the various overlapping groups within the industrial village itself, chapel, family, occupational, groups of similar rural or ethnic origin, and so on.

It remains to be discovered how far and how soon the growth of large towns and cities was instrumental in separating the worker and his workplace, the employer and his factory, the social or ethnic group and its main place of employment within the same neighbourhood. It may be that this process was a fairly rapid one in the generality of towns, and that the colours of the palette or paintbox were well and truly mixed, producing only the dirty grey of human anonymity which seems appropriate to the Bleak Age. It is well to remember, however, that colonisation did not cease in the early stages of the revolution in steam and textiles. It is a reasonably safe argument that the formation of colonies could play an important, if not a central part in the growth of some industrial towns, and that this process can be seen well after 1840, or whenever one chooses to terminate the first major phase of industrialisation in Britain.

When the spread of the railway network made the transportation of heavy raw materials both cheap and rapid, and when heavy engineering works, ironworks, and large colliery enterprises appeared in more or less dispersed situations, the industrial village, townlet or town of a single-industry or main-employer type received a new lease of life. Both Barrow-in-Furness and Crewe are obvious examples; but there are some of a less obvious character, and, indeed, a great many which were stillborn in the sense that their growing period and economic viability were alike limited, and in that they failed to give impetus to further urbanisation. One has only to look at the semi-derelict streets of, say, Askam-in-Furness,[2] to be sharply reminded of the latter possibility. But this was a consequence of attachment to too vulnerable a source of employment, or of too narrow an economic base in the surrounding neighbourhood or, even more simply, of isolation. This last word should not be left without qualification. Some industrial colonies grafted themselves on to already existing market or other villages, transforming their character in some measure while considerably extending their area of settlement or shifting their centre of gravity. In some salient instances, drawn again from the north-west, these have survived most successfully. Hence, despite vicissitudes, nearby Dalton-in-Furness, once an almost homogeneous community of iron ore miners grafted on to an ancient market town, has survived into the mid-twentieth century with some semblance of vitality—if only as a dormitory to its neighbour, Barrow. If the pre-existing community was, as often happened, on a main route, the prospects for survival of the industrial-based outgrowth would be that much better, no matter how apparently insecure the industry which created the latter, and no matter how isolated the industrial enterprise itself. Carnforth, the child of railway development and an ironworks, provides a good example.[3]

This last example will also remind us that town growth, even in comparatively small places, could take place through stages of colonisation based on different industries. Railway colonisation at both Carnforth and Barrow was far less spectacular in its effects than in the case of Crewe,[4] and did not result in striking town growth; rather, the centre of

---

[2] Cf. the account of Askam's development by Dr. Alan Harris in *Trans. Cumb. and West. Antiq. & Arch. Soc.*, New Series, lxv (1965), pp. 381 *et seq.*

[3] A. Harris, 'Carnforth, 1840–1900: the rise of a north Lancashire town', in *Trans. Hist. Soc. Lancs. & Ches.*, cxii (1960), pp. 105 *et seq.*

[4] Harris, *op. cit.*, p. 107; W. H. Chaloner, *The Social and Economic Development of Crewe* (1950); J. D. Marshall, *Furness and the Industrial Revolution* (1958), pp. 197–201.

gravity of settlement was pulled away from an already existing centre in each case. The real impetus in each of the Lancashire examples was provided by the establishment of ironworks, the effect of the latter on little Carnforth being so palpable that a contemporary commentator claimed that 'ere long, Carnforth may become a second Barrow'.[5] The social concomitants of industrial growth in these places included the settlement of more or less homogeneous occupational groups from a distance. Ironworkers from Staffordshire participated in the colonisation of both towns; Carnforth acquired a settlement called 'Dudley', and Barrow's Hindpool, made up originally of workers of similar origin, soon developed an attitude of aloofness as well as turbulence, the former sentiment finding apparent expression in the establishment of a separate co-operative society in what was still a comparatively small town.[6] Barrow's subsequent development involved the establishment of yet other social groups of common origin which, while becoming merged in the life of the town in various ways, yet established their identity, often through trade unions and church and chapel congregations as well as through common areas of settlement. The establishment of a shipyard in 1872 brought in men from the Clyde, who were given Glasgow-type tenements to live in; Irishmen, who had come as navvies, strengthened the Catholic contingent; and Cornishmen came as iron ore miners to form a distinct settlement at nearby Roose, with its chapel of St. Perran.

In the frontier conditions of the area and region, the services of the amenity-providing, town-ruling employer were at a premium, and a whole constellation of communities in north Lancashire and west Cumberland found the relationships of the workplace extended and transmuted in the pattern of social requirements beyond its confines. In the smaller communities the employers—as at Dalton-in-Furness or Cleator Moor—encouraged friendly societies and gave paternalistic approval to the formation of co-operative societies besides pursuing the more common paths of school, reading-room or church provision. It is by no means clear that the initiative came from one social level only, and the Cleator Moor and Dalton co-operative societies were markedly successful, much more, initially, than those in the more complex social organism of Barrow. In each case the industrial settlement concerned was a homogeneous one, largely of occupation in the Dalton example, but with the additional cement of common national origin in the case of Cleator Moor. Its large

---

[5] Harris, *op. cit.*, pp. 112 *et seq.*; P. Mannex, *Directory of North Lancashire District* (1866), p. 565.

[6] Marshall, *op. cit.*, pp. 310–11.

Irish contingent rapidly acquired some notoriety.[7] But there were also distinctive settlements of Cornishmen in the Millom district (drawn there by the great Hodbarrow mining enterprise), and near Egremont—at Moor Row, for example, there was a Cornish cricket club.[8] Messrs. Cammells, meanwhile, imported large numbers of Derbyshire men, known as 'Dronnies' by virtue of their Dronfield origins, into Workington. Generally speaking, however, the growth of Furness and Cumberland iron settlements and districts was sustained by local immigration, and the colonisation of the countryside by outsiders, often at the behest of individual enterprises but more often by a variety of firms, resulted in the growth of scattered urban districts rather than tight town communities. Barrow, concentrated as well as complex, stood out as somewhat unusual in its region, and there the rapid attainment of considerable size, the result of successive waves of immigration from a variety of localities, acted as a solvent comparatively early. Nevertheless, the interaction of the more or less distinctive social groups is worth study, even though the economic and class factor, expressed through trade union activity, was far more noticeable by the mid-'seventies.

The Furness and Cumberland examples provide what are undoubtedly classic instances of long-distance, railway-age immigration, falling within distinctive social, occupational and geographical groups and aiding the formation of industrial settlements of a clearly marked character. It still remains to be shown how far works-influenced ethnic or religious groups affected local politics, or how far they advanced or hindered the course of civic improvement, or even how far they kept their identity over more than a generation. It is obvious enough that the delineation of such influences promises to be no easy task, assuming that it is possible at all. Other more modest tasks, such as the estimate of the influence of such groups in trade unions, friendly and co-operative societies, mechanics' institutes, political clubs, local boards and town councils, clearly fall within the province of the urban and local historian. Equally plainly their importance should not be underestimated. It seems sensible, too, to make case-studies of the smaller colonies and work 'outwards' to the more complex examples.

As has been sufficiently indicated, sociological classifications may offer difficulty. This does not mean that they should be allowed to assume an unnecessary complexity, and the changing shape and visibly varying pattern of the colony—that is, its geomorphology—should always be the

---

[7] C. Caine, *Cleator and Cleator Moor Past and Present* (1916), p. 429.

[8] O. Wood, *Development of the Coal, Iron and Shipbuilding Industries of West Cumberland, 1750–1914* (unpub. Ph.D. thesis, University of London, 1952), p. 321.

dominant consideration. Moreover, colonies, like towns, exhibit characteristics of simplicity or complexity because they carry within themselves the most basic processes of urban growth in general, just as the development of cells may be seen to modify or direct the growth of a larger organism. But a colony is not always to be seen as a primal, basic or unicellular unit, although, as in the case of the classic factory village, built exclusively around a single mill, works or industry, it may be convenient to regard it as such. Factory villages, however, were not always single-firm or single-industry villages. Even when growing in a relatively isolated situation, they might still have their direction and form of growth determined by several factories or plants, a form of multicellular development taking place. This happened in a rapidly growing, complex colony and urban unit like Barrow-in-Furness. But it is also a characteristic of a colony that it comes into being through a major decision or a comparatively limited succession of major decisions. A fully developed town, on the other hand, takes steady shape by virtue of a multitude of decisions.

Symbiotic relationships obviously abounded, and an industrial outgrowth was often attached to an already existing, older community, as in the cases of Dalton-in-Furness and Carnforth already described. It could often happen, however, that the pre-existing hamlet or settlement was left isolated and separate from the new organism, or was so small as to have little effect on its growth. It is nevertheless useful to distinguish between two main types of colonising process: the *primary*, or clean-slate type, whereby an industrial town or village might be brought into being where there was no significant point of settlement before; and the *secondary* type, whereby there was development away from, or parallel to, that of a pre-existing town, perhaps before ultimate absorption in the latter. Secondary colonisation, as seen in these terms, was common in industrial Lancashire, and these broad distinctions will be found useful in the consideration of the examples that follow.

This brief study commenced, as was perhaps inevitable, by making reference to the early textile colonies of the water-power era. These last, as has been suggested, were fairly numerous during the period of relatively wide diffusion of mills and workshops. A single employer with the necessary capital, feeling the need for a stable labour force, would provide certain basic amenities and build houses. Such activities were common in the take-off phase of industrialism following about 1760, and advertisements of the sale of factories and their contents sometimes include references to factory-owned cottages. The creation of such small communities was not of course confined to cotton masters; the Duke of Bridgewater built houses at his Worsley headquarters,[9] canal companies generally aided settlement formation at transhipment points and other places, and mining companies, as at Alston Moor, engaged in this activity. All this is well known. What is less clear is the extent to which the formation of factory colonies actually aided or influenced town growth. Yet there is evidence that such colonisation was a recognisable part of urban development in the early history of some cotton towns. The term is here used in its wide, sociological sense, although the colonies concerned might have a distinct geographical and physical identity as well. Sometimes they sprang up in response to the requirements of a single factory owner, who might or might not have built, or caused to be built, the majority of the houses; in other cases, the building was speculative and the ownership of the dwellings diffused.

Such researches as the present writer has been able to pursue relative to a number of Lancashire towns suggest that mill-owners in an already developing urban area very rarely made themselves responsible for building activities and house provision, for the basic stimulus, that of sheer necessity, had disappeared, and the existing labour force would somehow find accommodation in the locality. But this was not always the case, even in the immediate vicinity of large and growing towns, before the third or fourth decades of the nineteenth century. By that time, large and self-contained colonies were sometimes established on the fringe of a built-up area, and were themselves incipient suburbs. The question which arises here concerns, once more, the speed with which the pre-existing settlement or colony lost its identity in the course of absorption into the wider urban mass. Here there was no sharp occupational distinction—iron-workers as against coal or ore miners, shipbuilders as against steelworkers, any of these as against farmworkers—for all were mill operatives as from one small locality to the next. Nor were clearly marked 'alien' ethnic groups likely to predominate, for, apart from a scattering of long-distance immigrants from a variety of places, the majority were Lancashire people[10] with Lancashire characteristics and attitudes. Surely, then, absorption into the greater, undifferentiated mass could proceed unhindered, and the creature of the village, with his narrow horizons, could become the urban animal with somewhat wider ones?

As urban historians may eventually confirm, the process of adaptation

9 F. Mullineux, *The Duke of Bridgewater's Canal* (1959), pp. 20–1. The general variety and pattern of colony promotion is described by Pollard, *op. cit.*, pp. 515 *et seq.*

10 These comments are based on some sample analyses of enumerators' sheets, for the 1851 Census, and on the published tables for the 1851 and 1861 census surveys relating to the birthplaces of inhabitants.

FIG. 4. *Freetown, Bury, 1845.* As can be seen, this detached colony housed a considerable proportion of the Bury population. The urban settlement of Freetown had, according to the Tithe Commutation map of 1837, taken this form by the latter date. The Hudcarr Mill (to the N.) was built c. 1822, and was later owned by Greg & Co. The Chesham Field Mill was Thomas Greenhalgh's property, and was on part of his estate.

or transmutation was by no means so simple. It has long been accepted that migration into the industrial areas proceeded in waves or short stages,[11] and census enumerators' entries, relative to the respective birthplaces of parents and to those of their children, show that a family might reside in a succession of places, both in towns and the countryside, before finally establishing itself in a main town or industrial district. Sometimes, on the other hand, the move from country to town was more direct, and the intermediate place of residence was an industrialised village or colony which had within the fabric of its life many of the patterns and attitudes

[11] The theory propounded by the late Arthur Redford in *Labour Migration in England* (1926), and a very fruitful one.

FIG. 5. *Freetown, 1894.* Although the colony had become absorbed into the more general urban mass, it retained a measure of self-conscious identity. The latter would be influenced by types of housing (the older streets were demolished about 1936), localised employment and family relationships, as well as by the social groups and recreations described.

of an earlier rural existence. On these the newer industrial régime was superimposed. Hence, the industrial colony of Belmont (on the moors to the north of Bolton, still little altered and a very fine specimen of its type), was subservient to two sets of overlords: the local squires, the Wrights, whose seat gave the colony its slightly exotic name, and who treated the local operatives as villagers of the traditional kind; and the owners of the local bleaching and weaving establishments, whose activities fostered the growth of a close-knit community packed in its stone-built cottage rows.[12] Of the immigrants (c. 1851) about one-third were already town workers by origin, but the majority were from the adjoining country areas.[13] Their industrial occupations notwithstanding, the latter still had deep roots in rural life. Observation shows that there were numerous country colonies of this kind in the mid-century, and it is a mistake to

[12] Cf. the revealing notes (MS) by the local historian of Belmont, Mr. C. M. Trevor, Bolton Reference Library, B914[B], based on the experience of a long lifetime in this colony.
[13] Census enumerators' sheets.

assume, whether in terms of urban boundaries or of social life, a sharp town-country antithesis in early Victorian Lancashire.[14] The centres of the textile towns outside Manchester were rarely more than 10 minutes' walk from the countryside, and that countryside was semi-industrialised already.

The foregoing example will help to make the point of the next one. As has been made sufficiently clear, not all colonies of cotton workers were 'remote'; and in some arresting instances, several grew up in what soon became the central areas of textile towns. One of the most striking of these appears in the growth-pattern of Bury between the early 1820s and 1840. The pioneering business history of the late Miss Frances Collier has been instrumental in drawing the attention of historians to the activities of the Peels in the Bury district, and, in about 1800, the Burrs Mill of that family had some 20 cottages there.[15] A generation later, however, the old township of Bury had acquired, not 10 minutes' walk from its centre, a large colony of cotton spinners known (significantly) as Freetown, its employment provided by two mills built to the north-east of the town on the Gypsy Brook. In 1846 it was stated at a parliamentary inquiry that between a quarter and a third of the population of Bury lived in Freetown.[16] The founders of the colony were Thomas Greenhalgh and William Rathbone Greg, a son of Samuel Greg of Styal—ironically in the latter case, because Freetown was described as 'a very filthy place' in the year mentioned. The dominant colony-builder, however, was Thomas Greenhalgh, who had developed a large freehold estate, on the unspoilt rural end of which was his private mansion, and on the other his 'very large factory and steam loom sheds' where he employed 'hundreds of people that live in his numerous cottages in Free Town'.[17] There is no evidence, meanwhile, that the employers in this colony were unusually welfare-minded;[18] but the suburban community which grew up had a vigorous life of its own, and it was a detached portion of Bury in a social

[14] The understandable obsession with large towns and populous districts has, perhaps, created a stereotype.

[15] Frances Collier, *The Family Economy of the Working Classes in the Cotton Industry, 1784–1833* (Chetham Society, 1965), p. 33.

[16] Published report of *Evidence before House of Commons Committee on the Bury Improvement Bill, 1846*, p. 29 (Bury Public Library).

[17] 'Veritas' [John Ainsworth], *Walks Round Bury for Sixty Years and Upwards* (c. 1842), p. 117.

[18] Infringements of the 1833 Factory Act were common in the area, the Bury employers being among the worst offenders in the country. Greenhalgh and the Gregs were high on the list: 'A return of the numbers and names of persons summoned for offences against the Factory Acts between 1 May 1836 and 1 January 1837', in *Brit. Parl. Papers, Accounts and Papers* (1837), 1. No folio number given.

as well as in a physical sense, with the atmosphere of a crowded, rather insanitary village. A number of local customs, still kept alive in the late nineteenth century, were of a character distinctly associated with pre-urban Lancashire society; pace-egging and 'morris dancing with May Day horse and turn-out processions'. Not only did the inhabitants organise sports meetings of a lively and ambitious nature, with traditional games; several of the public houses were very much more than drinking dens, their landlords organising concerts in the evening and providing hot coffee laced with rum for early morning visitors on their way to the mills.[19] Like other similar areas, Freetown was fairly well provided with beer-houses, and even a few chapels, and it is in any case obvious that the inhabitants had little incentive to wander beyond the confines of their own community into the centre of Bury, which can have had little to offer until comparatively late in the century. On the other side of Free-town were the countryside and the open moors.

It is not clear how many Freetowners lived in the colony and worked elsewhere; plainly, the tendency for a labour force to live at the factory gate would be strengthened where the main employers owned a large number of houses, though it is by no means certain that a cottage-owning firm would insist on the restriction of tenancies to its own workers. There is some evidence that the great Preston firm of Horrocks, Miller and Company did not impose such a restriction,[20] at least in 1831. But this eventuated in the conditions of a large and growing town, where the firm's labour supply was more or less assured. On the periphery of a town, or in the vicinity of a comparatively isolated mill or works, there was every incentive for the worker to live as near as possible to his place of employment, and, as the larger textile towns extended their boundaries and built-up areas to assimilate surrounding townships and colonies, transport problems would in any case become exacerbated, in so far as further mill-building led to demands for labour from a distance.

There are indications that colony-building could be prompted, and sometimes made imperative, in situations of this kind surprisingly late in the nineteenth century. Hence the firm of J. & J. Mellor, of Warthfold, between Bury and Radcliffe, had built works and cottages between 1863 and 1872, and had made roads, drains and laid gas mains in the vicinity of the settlement, acting as its 'own local board' under the nominal juris-diction of the board for Radcliffe. No fewer than 237 of its workers lived

---

19 'J.W.' in *Bury Times*, 30 October and 6 November 1948.
20 *Land Tax Book for Preston, 1831*, Lancs. Record Office, QDL 52/7. The firm did not own many cottages in any one area, but several non-textile workers appear, e.g. in one of their rows in Bolton Street.

in the firm's cottages by 1885, although 129 came from Radcliffe (a mile away) and 85 from Bury (the same distance removed).[21] Here again was a partially self-contained industrial village with its own school, provided by the firm, and a chapel. The firm's principal objected to the prospect of absorption into the town of Bury; he did not welcome the idea of beer-shops 'being about' and saw the danger of heads of households being 'dragged into excitement and demoralisation'.[22] Evidently the advantages of close moral surveillance were well understood. This employer's theme was taken up, in a different key, by another mill-owner from Walmersley, about a mile north of Bury; the outlying settlements were more healthy. But not only were they more healthy—they belonged to a different world. 'I could tell you a Walmersley man if I met him in Bury, as distinct from a Bury man. He speaks a different tongue, to begin with, and he has a far more robust and healthy complexion about him than the toilers in the slums of Bury.'[23] Perhaps the same could have been said of the inhabitants of Freetown in its earlier days, before parts of that colony, too, became merged into the 'slums of Bury'.

The owners or promoters of these tiny industrial empires could, then, prove difficult or obdurate in the face of tardily advancing local government[24] in the great Lancashire conurbations, all the more so because reason and justice appeared to be on their side; fresh air and clean brook water would tend to counterbalance the effects of foul and uncleaned ashpits.[25] And, as has been suggested, the inturned consciousness of the colony did not make for growing civic awareness at any level; the idiocy of village life might be rejuvenated and even strengthened in its new industrial context. Politically, too, the tight type of community, with its social relationships reinforced and hardened by those already existing within the mill, could present a problem. Foremen, whose houses occupied key positions at the ends of cottage rows,[26] and who themselves occupied key positions at chapel, might control a man's actions throughout the week. Could they, or the presiding deity, the employer, control a man's thoughts as politically expressed? The aftermath of the 1868 election in Blackburn showed that political divisions were not horizontal, or even

[21] *Minutes of Evidence, House of Commons Committee on the Bury Improvement Bill*, 1885, QQ. 2011–53 (at the Bury Public Library).

[22] *Ibid.*, Q. 2098.

[23] *Ibid.*, Q.1448.

[24] Cf. the important recent contribution by E. Midwinter, 'Local Boards of Health in Lancashire', in *Trans. Hist. Soc. Lancs. & Ches.* cxvii (1965), pp. 167 *et seq.*

[25] *Committee on the Bury Improvement Bill*, 1885, QQ. 1722, 1733–4; also B. H. Babbage, *Gen. Board of Health Report: Clitheroe* (1850), pp. 7–8.

[26] As at Dean Mills, Bolton; a fact revealed by the census enumerator's sheets for 1851.

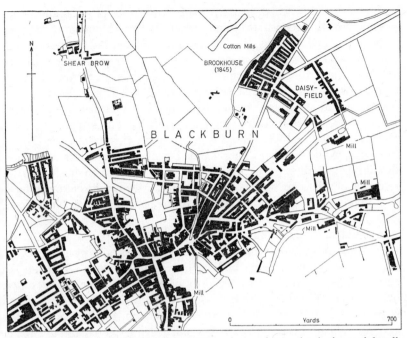

FIG. 6. *Brookhouse, Blackburn, 1845.* This was one of several colonies peripherally situated near Blackburn. The 1831 land tax lists for Blackburn suggest that there was little building in this locality at that date, and that the land was split up between a variety of owners. The mills on the N.W. side of the colony were constructed between 1828 and 1838. There was considerable development to the E. and S.E. of this area after 1850 (i.e. in Daisyfield), but the Brookhouse mill colony, dominated by W. H. Hornby, kept its political identity. The parallel terraces to the W. of the main road are still *in situ* (1967); the housing fronting the main road is of slightly superior quality, and bears the Hornby crest.

diagonal, but vertical in terms of mills; between 40 and 45 mills, out of 70 in Blackburn, were designated as Tory in allegiance. Blackburn was a town where the practice of intimidation, as between the operatives of politically opposed mills, and hence between their employers, was common and widespread. But, more significantly, a witness remarked that wholesale pressure of this character 'was first commenced at Brookhouse'.[27] The colony of Brookhouse[28] was virtually the creation of the Hornby family, and stood in much the same relationship to the town of Blackburn as did Freetown to the town of Bury.

[27] *Blackburn Standard*, 17 March 1869.
[28] G. C. Miller, *Blackburn, The Evolution of a Cotton Town* (1950), pp. 371–4; P. A. Whittle, *Blackburn As It Is* (1852), pp. 270–1. The area still has strongly marked characteristics.

The former town had, in fact, owed much of its physical and demo-graphic growth between 1820 and 1860 to the development of the three important colonised areas, Brookhouse, Nova Scotia, and Grimshaw Park Factory industry did not develop in earnest in the town proper until after 1819, at which time it was common for the established cotton masters to own a few houses. Hence, according to the Land Tax Returns of 1831 Messrs. Lund and Foster owned 84 cottages at Wensley Fold, Richard Lund, the proprietor, living near his operatives. The important firm of Banister, Eccles and Co. had 48 cottages in the vicinity of their Darwen St. Mills, while Fielden, Thorp and Townley owned over a hundred dwellings, including 72 back-to-backs which were distinguished in the returns from their 20 'stone-built' dwellings. Meanwhile, cotton factories had been established outside the limit of the built-up area at Nova Scotia (1822) and Brookhouse (1828). Neither of these at first developed a substantial mill community, but by 1847 W. H. Hornby and Co., the Brookhouse proprietors, employed 1,400 operatives, and by 1852, several hundred houses were being built in that locality. The 1831 Land Tax entries suggest that the great majority of houses in these colonies were owned by small landlords, although it is not likely that the major decisions regarding sale and use of land were taken by such. In 1837 the erstwhile solicitor William Eccles built another mill at Nova Scotia, and in 1852 he employed 1,900 workers there and at Wensley Fold. The development of Grimshaw Park was stimulated by the cotton mills of James Pilkington (a Liberal M.P. for Blackburn), who had a 'pretty residence' situated behind walls in the immediate vicinity. Schools, chapels, and public baths appeared fairly early; and the local historian Whittle (1852) re-marked, perhaps significantly, that 'Nova Scotia and Grimshaw Park bid fair to become an integral part of the borough'. In 1847 these areas, together with Brookhouse, contained the largest mills and about one-third of all the operatives in Blackburn.

Obviously it was much easier to control the politics of a tight, mill-centred community than a large amorphous one. ('Control' in this context does not of course mean the imposition of given views on an inert or passive mass of employees by some simple act of terrorism; it can also take the form of encouragement, persuasion, example-setting, and even that of turning a blind eye to joyful rowdyism.) But there was also deep loyalty to the mill, the village and often the employer.[29] Sometimes its manifestations were touching, and, in any case, the political orientation of mid-Victorian Lancashire mill operatives has never been adequately

[29] Cf. C. Townson, *The History of Farington* (1893), pp. 23 *et seq.* Farington was the site of a colony north of Leyland, and is now the nucleus of a suburb of that town.

accounted for, by labour historians or by others. The key may be in
some of the social, or sociological, ideas suggested here. The implications
for municipal history will also be apparent.

Colonies, and towns, embrace virtually the whole of human existence
at many levels. For this reason, the physical and geomorphological effects
of colonisation, or its architectural consequences, have not been unduly
stressed here. Needless to say, a great deal can be set out relative to this
topic. Colonisation as, again, in Lancashire towns, could influence the
pattern and direction of more general phases in house building, determining the layout and angling of streets. This was so in Preston, where,
despite comparatively little house ownership by mill firms, the factories
of the pre-1840 period, congregated along the Moor Brook in a striking
number of cases, tended to attract terrace rows in their direction. The
development of the main pattern of streets,[30] however, was conditioned
by the sale of a number of private estates, notably the Green Bank Estate.
The main house-owning colonists, Horrocks, Miller and Co., had early
developed a small settlement known as New Preston (c. 1800) on the east
side of the old London Highway, and, although their houses or cottages
were not numerous (about 130 in the whole of the town), the New
Preston street lay-out set the pattern for much of the New Hall Lane-
Ribbleton area, after remaining relatively isolated during the first half of
the nineteenth century. In other words, the sizeable firm of Horrocks had
it within their power to develop a considerable housing estate, for the
opportunity of acquiring more land must have come within their grasp
during such a long period. They did not do so; a pity, because their
housing and its sanitary arrangements were above the prevailing standard
of the time and place.[31] One can only conclude that managerial commitments and exigencies were such that estate speculation, even with the bait
of a 10 per cent return on occupied cottages, was scarcely feasible.

On this somewhat negative note this brief survey must end. There has
been insufficient space to mention the colonies with standards of housing
which can, albeit sentimentally, be designated 'model', which became
absorbed into urban districts but which signally failed to influence
architectural or building standards. There is a striking specimen, built
by John Horrocks Ainsworth, in the Halliwell district of Bolton about
the middle of the century, and consisting of a church, school, and heavily
Gothic cottages. Others remained isolated for too long to give effective
precept, and many single-employer, works-owned colonies were in any

30 I.e. to the north of the old town centre of Preston. Other observations here are based on
study of the early tithe commutation map (Lancs. R.O., 1840) and O.S. maps.
31 G. T. Clark, *Report of the General Board of Health: Preston* (1849), pp. 13–14.

case very small until the advent of the Bournville or Port Sunlight typ
of enterprise. The Halliwell colony mentioned was in fact established a
the onset of a time of rapid suburban development, but it hardly in
fluenced the style of a single subsequently built edifice, even in its ver
near vicinity.[32]

It is possible that preoccupation with the purely physical effects an
extent of 'model' colony-building has led historians to discount th
importance of more general types of colonising activity, especially in th
textile areas during the early and middle nineteenth century. But, as wil
have been made clear, the subject has much wider significance. It may on
day be shown that 'colony-mindedness' was part of an urban way of life

[32] These remarks, like numerous others in this paper, are based on that personal observatio
which is an indispensable part of urban study. Tawney's heirs in the sphere of heavily-sho
tramping now have to walk the town streets as well as the fields.

Phases of Town Growth in Wales

Harold Carter

This paper attempts to sketch in outline the major phases of town growth in Wales. No attempt is made to epitomise these in terms of an idealised example[1] for in many ways what is distinctive is the wide variety of urban features developed in a small country to which town life was completely alien. The paper is, however, accompanied by a table[2] which presents a synoptic view of the major growth phases, together with an outline of the prime controls of growth, which are the functions performed. In Table 9 these functions are recorded in relation to three aspects, the first is the general function as central place which *all* towns perform to some degree, whilst the third comprises those special functions which only *some* towns carry out. Between these, and related to both, is the second aspect of function, transport, for the effective working of towns depends essentially on accessibility. Town development in response to these functions is also recorded under three headings. The first is the design and layout of the plan, the second the general character of extension during each phase and the third the predominant buildings which distinguished the periods under review and which are still extant. Each town will have been differently influenced by the forces at work in each phase and in turn, the plan and fabric of each town will show individual responses, but it is argued that all the Welsh towns can be related to this tabulation and a consideration of phases of town growth is appropriately related to it.

When the structure of the table is considered, two particular sets of relations are immediately apparent:

1. The relation of the towns to external influences, that is to the stimuli impinging on the country from outside.

---

[1] See, for example, A. E. Smailes, 'Some reflections on the geographical description and analysis of townscapes', *Tr. Inst. Br. Geog.*, xxi (1955), pp. 99–115.
[2] This is in part derived from C. Tunnard and H. H. Reed, *American Skyline* (1955).

TABLE 9

PHASES OF TOWN GROWTH IN WALES

Phase of growth	MEDIEVAL First genetic phase	TRANSITIONAL	GEORGIAN
THE URBAN ROLE Central Place Functions	Anglo-Norman creation of embryonic towns Political, administrative and economic control through the borough Principle of separation ————————→	Market Towns: Sorting of created towns in relation to centrality Growth of 'native' settlements to town status Administrative centres by Acts of Union and Great Sessions ————————→Market Periodic Markets Fairs ————————→	Central place system stability in town/cou▮ relations Developed economic and social life Principle—————— Permanent market centres
TRANSPORT	Horse Coastal navigation	Horse Coach Coastal navigation	Regular stage coache▮ Market Carriers (Turnpike roads) Coastal navigation at 'Bristol Traders'
TECHNOLOGY Special Functions	Local crafts Military. See above	Local crafts. Woollens. Exploitation of minerals and early metallurgy	Water Power. Wool ▮ Flannel. Metallurgy ▮ beginning of Iron industry. Resorts. 1st P▮
TOWN PLAN and DESIGN	Crude agglomeration about castle nucleus Bastides or Villesneuves Axial and Grid Plans	Growth of 'native' settlements brings distinctive elements in urban layout No planned forms Internal reconstruction	Limited Renaissance ▮ Baroque influences New planned towns Internal infilling and construction
NATURE OF URBAN EXTENSION	Minor extra-mural extension Bridgeheads Market Places Religious Foundations	As across Linear extensions often from town gates	First major extra-mu▮ extensions Common land enclos▮ with rectangular deve▮ment
BUILDING TYPES	Castles. Defensive walls and towers Churches and Abbeys Local and imported stone	Market ⎫ Guild ⎬Halls Shire ⎭ Merchants Houses	Town Halls Assembly Rooms The Terrace. Stone a▮ Stucco Town Houses Boarding Houses and▮ Hotels

NDUSTRIAL I Second Genetic Phase	INDUSTRIAL II	MODERN	CONTEMPORARY
phase of sis. Growth of making towns k across old rated town/ try relations	Second part of second genetic phase Growth of coal mining settlements Crystallisation of service centres from amorphous industrial settlement	Integrated and stratified systems of central places: composite in character ↑ Growth of urban amenities	Country served and dominated by hierarchy of service centres Service, administration industry all urban directed 70% live in urban areas
———Industrial Principle———→ ————————————→		⟩	The urban region
e coach and ers stal navigation nroad al	Tramroad and canal Railways Port and dock development. Decline coastal trade in shop goods	Railway: system at maximum Omnibus Car	Railway: system shrinking Private Car Bus
m Power and Iron e	Coal and Iron. Steel Coastal migration of metallurgy Tinplate Resorts. 2nd Phase	Depression of heavy industry Introduction of light industry Trading Estates	Rationalization Strip mills and large mines Oil import and refining Further development of light industry and estates
e linear or grid rol or geometrical ning lel villages	Bylaw 'ribbing' over large areas Estate development in north-east Wales: planned resorts	Garden suburb Speculative development and villa 'studding'	New town(s) Redevelopment of town centres Renewal of residential areas
d unplanned vth ng control by and communi- n lines	Increased extension with only bylaw control Linear mining settlements Railhead areas	Extensive housing estates: private and municipal Ribbon development Conurbations	Housing estates: development continued Commuting and development of towns and villages
ages, wood and stone ling by Courts do Castles and nial halls Works	Degenerate terrace bylaw housing: stone to brick. Slate Growing embellishment Large family houses Chapels. Working Men's Clubs Commercial conversion of early terraces Banks Pit Heads. Iron and Steel Works Packmill	Villas: detached and semi-detached Brick, roughcast and tiles Municipal and National buildings Chain store façades Small factories—light industries	Prefab and Caravan. Villas: private and municipal. Terrace, reconstituted Point Block Flats Chain Stores and Office Blocks Larger light industrial establishments Integrated Steel Tinplate Works

2. Internal inter-relations, that is the evolving spatial distribution of towns and town growth consequent upon internal competition and relative dominance.

It is apparent, therefore, that growth is not solely due to internal generation, nor can it be ascribed to external pressures alone, but rather it is the alternation of external and internal forces which provides the key to the growth phases.

It has been customary to regard the Anglo-Norman introduction of towns into Wales as representing in real terms the beginning of urban living in the country. The contemporary situation is often referred to a well known extract from the 'Description of Wales' by Giraldus Cambrensis who had accompanied Archbishop Baldwin on his journey through the country in 1188. He wrote of the Welsh, 'They pay no attention to commerce, shipping or manufacture. . . . They neither inhabit towns, villages nor castles but lead a solitary life in the woods, on the borders of which they do not erect sumptuous palaces, nor lofty stone buildings, but content themselves with small huts.'[3] A modern economic historian has said the same thing in a more academic form, 'There are no towns of purely Welsh origin. This statement is true in so far as the privileged status of the important towns of medieval Wales was one of artificial creation or adoption rather than of natural growth. The making of boroughs in Wales originated with the Norman or English conquest about 1080. Up to this time the native economy scarcely required real urban centres, and the outside influences to which Wales had been subjected hitherto do not appear to have given much impetus to town life.'[4]

Before this view is accepted it is necessary briefly to consider the misgivings which have been expressed over the traditional view of the complete breakup of urban life in the immediate post-Roman period. Reservations have centred in particular about the identification of pre-urban nuclei which are claimed to represent an element of continuity. In Wales it is possible to suggest three types of such nuclei. The first would be the Roman forts which certainly appear to have influenced the later location of towns, probably through their tradition of central control, clearly an attraction to incoming town founders. The second type of pre-existing nucleus was the monastic cells founded by the Celtic Saints. Here too the evidence is tenuous and although the place-names of Wales indicate the

---

[3] W. Llewelyn Williams (ed.), *The Itinerary Through Wales. Description of Wales, Giraldus Cambrensis* (1908), p. 184.
[4] E. A. Lewis, *Medieval Boroughs of Snowdonia* (1912), p. 5.

importance of these churches, it was the conditions of much later times which transformed them into towns. E. G. Bowen writes, 'The Celtic Churches as such did not possess great nucleating power in the settlement pattern of Wales. . . . This general conclusion is understandable when we recall that the Celtic Church was in origin a hermit's cell specially sited away from the main lines of human movement. The church did not originate as a settlement or a centre of population however small, it only became such if later economic developments found it a pivot conveniently located.'[5] The third type of such nuclei was formed by the *Maerdrefi*, the centres of the native princes. Here, indeed, it is possible to perceive an emergent, indigenous urban character, for these settlements were places where dues were paid, where markets might develop and where trading centres might be established. The late Professor Jones-Pierce eloquently argued that this was so, particularly in the case of towns such as Pwllheli.[6] But the examples are limited and the functions nascent.

Although, therefore, tenuous examples of continuity can be identified in these three types of nucleus the main argument stands; it was with the Normans that the town was introduced into Wales and it is possible to isolate a clear genetic phase. The external links are clear and direct in that many of the Welsh town charters were based on that of Breteuil[7] and Edward's town at Flint had many general and one detailed point of similarity with Aigues Mortes.[8] The Welsh *bastides* are in the classic European tradition. Figure 7 shows Flint at the beginning of the present century. The rectangular characteristics of the blocks had been clearly preserved, together with parts of the defending banks. The detached tower of the castle is the part that compares in detail with the Tour de Constance at Aigues Mortes. This map also illustrates the point that growth phases might contribute a fairly static part to towns in terms of layout, but that land use and buildings are much less permanent; also, that not all growth phases are demonstrable in any one town. At Flint the outlines of the decayed *bastide* were followed by the cottages of the industrial period, which constitutes the second phase of genesis, while one element of this second phase, the railway, breaks across the chequer board plan. Two phases have been partially and unconformably super-imposed to produce the detail of this map.

This medieval plantation of urbanism places the country in a distinctive situation. Many attempts have been made to put cities into systems other

5 E. G. Bowen, *The Settlements of the Celtic Saints in Wales* (1954), p. 160.
6 T. Jones-Pierce, 'A Caernarvonshire manorial borough', *Tr. Caern. Hist. Soc.*, ii–v (1941–4).
7 M. Bateson, 'The laws of Breteuil', *Eng. Hist. Rev.*, xv (1900), p. 73.
8 W. D. Simpson, 'Flint Castle', *Arch. Camb.*, xcv (1940), p. 20.

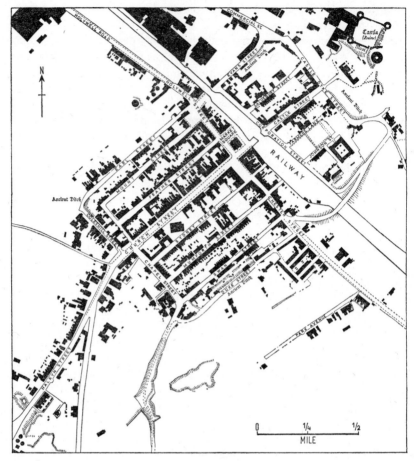

FIG. 7. *Flint in 1912* (based on the Ordnance Survey). The outline of the Edwardian *bastide* is clearly preserved but by a large number of industrial cottages which had been built in response to the growth of the chemical and textile industries which are to be seen in the large blocks to the north. The railway breaks the regularity of the medieval lay-out. Two growth phases have been superimposed with only partial conformity.

than those which are purely economic. It is argued that there are 'two processes of urban growth, primary and secondary, each with an associated type of city and a particular cultural rôle, in the former case orthogenetic cities and in the latter heterogenic cities.'[9] This is elaborated, 'Initiation

---

[9] B. J. L. Berry, 'Urban growth and the economic development of Ashanti' in R. F. Pitts (ed.), *Urban Systems and Economic Development* (1962), p. 53.

of primary processes of urbanisation is associated with the development of centralised social religious and political controls in previously non-urbanised societies. Such controls are organised from primate orthogenetic cities, which epitomise the traditions and sense of unity of the indigenous culture. . . . Secondary processes of urbanization assert themselves when an integrated system of cities develops, usually under the influence of forces external to local culture.'[10] This dichotomy is clearly not applicable to Wales, indeed in so far as it exists it is completely reversed. Certainly in a mountainous country lacking an obvious focal point, there was no form of centralised political control, even the boundary line of the Cymry, Offa's Dyke, was fixed externally. No town has ever epitomised 'the traditions and sense of unity of the indigenous culture' which has remained non-urban, a fact not without its significance in present controversy over new towns. But if this first genetic phase is not the consequence of internal forces it must be emphasised that only embryonic towns were created; in analogy one can use the parable of the sower, those founded towns were scattered seeds which could only become strong plants if the soil were fertile, competition limited and the site good. The translation of these scattered embryonic towns functioning in accord with Christaller's Principle of Separation into an integrated system of cities in accord with his Market Principle[11] is the consequence of internal forces coming into play and initiating a second 'Transitional Phase'. During this, accessibility was a controlling factor and the Transport Principle became dominant.

This seems in accord with the identification by Guttenberg[12] of three components in urban growth; Distributed Facilities, Undistributed Facilities, and Transport. Where transport is poor trade centres assume a distributed character but with the increase in the effectiveness of communication these facilities are concentrated in accessible points and become 'undistributed'. 'Thus Guttenberg maintains that urban spatial structure is ultimately tied up with the aggregate effort in the community to overcome distance.'[13]

This Transitional Phase cannot be given clear dates, but perhaps it can be looked upon as beginning with the relative pacification of Wales after the Act of Union. It is necessarily a complex period. The major purpose of the castle town carried the bases of its own decay, for the effective

[10] *Ibid.*, pp. 53–4.
[11] W. Christaller (trans. C. W. Baskin), *Central Places in Southern Germany* (1966), pp. 115 *et seq.*
[12] A. Z. Guttenberg, 'Urban structure and urban growth', *Journal of the American Institute of Planners*, xxv (1960), pp. 104–10.
[13] F. Stuart Chapin, 'Selected theories of urban growth and structure', *Journal of the American Institute of Planners*, xxx (1964), p. 54.

consummation of its task meant the subjugation and pacification of the countryside and the creation of those conditions in which the castle town as military strongpoint was no longer needed. Consequently unless the town was able to take on other functions it tended to decay and lose any distinctive urban character. These 'other functions' are in part those now regarded as the distinguishing features of towns, the carrying out of services for the surrounding countryside from a convenient or accessible locality. The town for survival had to become the *de facto*, not merely the *de jure* commercial focus of the countryside in which it was situated and also the centre of local administration and social life. This is in accord with the conclusions of Gideon Sjoberg who writes, 'Thus the political power variable explains urban growth and proliferation to the frontiers and beyond. It also accounts for some cities' decline. . . . Just as a city's capacity for growth is dependent in large part upon an elaborate political apparatus, so too, when this is withdrawn the city will shrink or disappear.'[14]

Within Wales the conditions of the early part of the post Norman period, a relatively disturbed countryside, lack of wheeled vehicles and poor communications, meant that neither the ability nor the opportunity existed to concentrate life in the towns. Again to this must be added the particular localisms of a poor, highly fractionated terrain and the traditional pattern of subsistence agriculture. The Welsh people must have had little use for towns, even in this period, and to some extent the countryside lapsed into its earlier condition where towns were not needed. The urban system which had been created in the process of conquest was in places too elaborate for the economic conditions of a succeeding age. When the military prop was taken away the economic was not yet strong enough to sustain a developed city system. Indeed the change over was largely made through the intervention of an administrative function as the created urban centres were used as the bases of the administrative pattern set up by the Act of Union and the Act of Great Sessions. All this meant a complex process of sorting which is still mirrored in the towns of Wales.

It is impossible in this brief statement to trace in full the physical implications of the functional developments outlined above. To some extent they are indicated in the table. But a number of features can be enumerated. The first is that there was no external stimulus in action so that no distinctive features of layout or design were introduced. The corollary of this is that as internal development of the town system

---

[14] G. Sjoberg, *The Pre-Industrial City* (1960), p. 73.

revealed gaps so rural settlements were given urban functions and a series of towns came into being outside the Anglo-Norman genesis. Tregaron is a good example and it has been demonstrated that analysis of its ground plan is dependent on the two features of the 'Llan', or church enclosure, and the 'Pentref', the medieval bond vill, and the generic name 'Treflan' has been proposed for such settlements.[15]

The second characteristic of this phase is the decline of Anglo-Norman towns either where they were poorly located or where there were too many. Examples of such decay are New Radnor, Montgomery and Harlech. The first in particular is an admirable example of a fossil town. In contrast the third feature of the phase is the minor extensions which took place in those towns which succeeded in growing. In nearly all cases these were ribbon like in form and usually directed towards a religious foundation outside the walls (Cardigan, Carmarthen, Brecon) or along a major line of communication (Cardiff). They were often transformed by later times but frequently play a determinant rôle in the character of the present inner parts of towns. At Cardigan the attraction towards the Priory and St. Mary's church dominated the earliest phase of extension, as Speed's plan (Fig 8a) emphasises, and the modern town displays a very distinctive closely built area of mixed uses which is the consequence of this initial line of development. At Cardiff (Fig. 8b) the earliest growth was beyond the East Gate attracted by the main through line of east–west movement and away from the marshy valley floor of the Taff. This was to become an area of fairly large town houses which in recent times have been more easily purchased to give large blocks of land. These in turn have provided good locations for the large chain and department stores which collected in this part of Cardiff in contrast with the market and the old 'family' stores which are to be found in High Street and St. Mary Street.[16]

The last characteristic bequeathed by this transitional phase is seen in the few buildings which remain in the present townscape. As against the castles of the genetic phase they are predominantly market or town halls together with merchant houses. The market or guild halls have mostly been destroyed, though in places the unusual wideness of streets within the old walled area (as at Cowbridge) or the small open area (as at Aberystwyth)[17] still shows in present plans. The most distinctive still standing

[15] Emrys Jones, 'Tregaron: A Welsh market town', *Geography*, xxxv (1950), p. 20.

[16] For a study, see H. Carter and G. Rowley, 'The morphology of the central business district of Cardiff', *Tr. Inst. Br. Geogr.*, xxxviii (1966), p. 119.

[17] H. Carter, 'Aberystwyth: the modern development of a medieval castle town in Wales' *Tr. Inst. Br. Geogr.*, xxv (1958), p. 239.

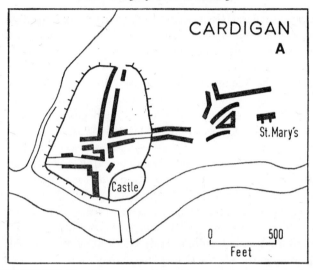

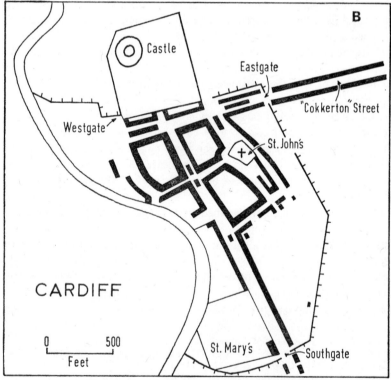

FIG. 8 A *Cardigan in 1610*, after J. Speed.
       B *Cardiff in 1610*, after J. Speed.

240

is at Llanidloes. The merchant houses too are more frequently met beyond the border and in the border towns, but a few fragments remain, as in the Tudor Merchant's House at Tenby.

The succeeding phase is designated 'Georgian'. In the accompanying table this implies dates which run from 1715 to 1840 though these are far too precise for the general way the name is used in the context. It may in some ways be regarded as a 'climax phase' before the next major genetic movement. By this period a hierarchy of commercial centres seems to have emerged . . . 'we can suggest some sort of progression associated with economic advancement: as one ascends the economic demographic scale the time space articulation of markets and fairs is replaced by a space articulation of permanent market centres; as specialization and interchange increase, the hierarchy of market centres becomes more highly differentiated into a greater number of levels performing the greater number of market functions now present.'[18] This hierarchy of centres can be demonstrated, though the stability of the period should not be overemphasised.

Although this was not a genetic phase three new towns were founded, Aberaeron, Milford and Tremadoc. These Lavedan called 'the last and distant echoes of forms which were born in Renaissance Italy'.[19] But now the influence of the continent was not immediate and military but remote and cultural and in consequence there is no distinctive layer of towns but only random examples. All were laid out on a rectangular basis and demonstrate the stretched and thin character of the cultural influence rather than central and classical aspects. Aberaeron was laid out at the beginning of the nineteenth century and is popularly associated with John Nash. It was given a central square, Alban Square which presumably is in direct line with Piazzas of Renaissance Italy and the Grandes Places of France (Fig. 9). But in this remote setting, in an area without the capital to sustain urban architecture at any level, and in a country where the true civic tradition of Europe never flourished, the square fails completely. The surrounding buildings are out of scale, for they are far too small for the large central area. This central area is not paved and embellished but is a hedged field more reminiscent of a village green. Nothing more sadly epitomises the fact that urban living was not really of Wales than this forlorn imitation of the great urban squares of Europe.

More important in a wider context is the fact that the emergence of the upper ranks of a hierarchy was accompanied by a marked phase of exten-

---

[18] B. J. L. Berry, 'Urbanisation and basic patterns of development' in F. R. Pitts, *op. cit.*, p. 14.
[19] P. Lavedan, *Histoire de l'Urbanisme: Renaissance et Temps Moderne* (1959), p. 276.

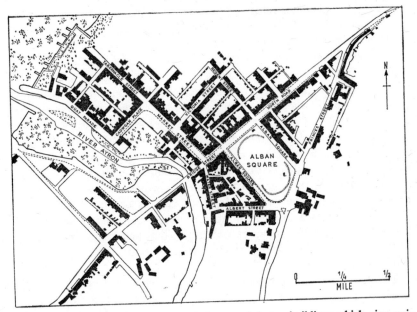

FIG. 9. *Aberaeron in 1965.* The regularly spaced, larger buildings which give uniformity to the surround of Alban Square can be identified by their slight protrusion. The Market Hall built for the town is at the junction of Market Street and Victoria Street.

sion which characterises so many of the regional capitals of Wales at this time. There were three interrelated aspects. In the first place this was a marked period of infilling of the open spaces particularly in the walled towns. This was usually in the form of short terraces which are very distinctive, even if they are severely limited. Second was a process of conversion of the existing buildings along the streets of the medieval plan. The earliest buildings of any consequence in Welsh towns are of this period, earlier survivals are very few indeed. The third aspect was a real extension, for in many towns this period saw the first extra-mural growth. This frequently took place on enclosed common land and a grid pattern is characteristic although in many instances only ribbons of development are found. This pattern in process of development can be seen in Figure 10 where the common land of the borough of Aberystwyth had by 1809 been laid out in plots ready for lease, an organisation which has determined the present street pattern of this part of extra-mural Aberystwyth. Later reconstruction has meant that much of the actual building has been obliterated and the present representation is in isolated terraces and sporadic town houses. These are sufficiently distinctive to produce an

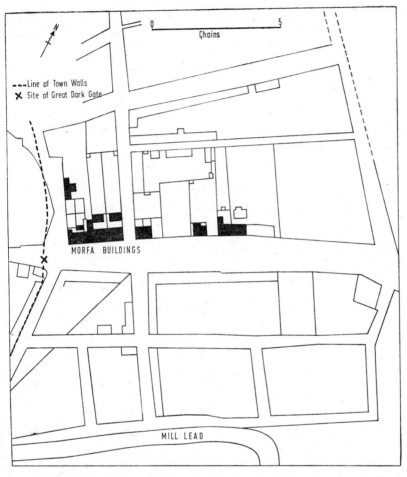

FIG. 10. *Extra-mural Aberystwyth in 1809* (after W. Cowling, *Map of the town and burgh of Aberystwyth in the County of Cardigan*, 1809). This shows the early layout of the former common lands of the borough on the former Morfa Swnd (Sand Marsh).

indeterminate fringe in most towns but never well defined areas. The best preserved sections are to be found in the resorts, such as Tenby, for the first phase of resort development took place during this period.

The main extant buildings are in keeping with the predominant functions. Town and Shire Halls were the expression of civic pride as the town became effectively the centre for the surrounding country, serving it through the hierarchy of subordinates. In reverse the countryside acknowledged the place of the town in the economic and social system by the building of town houses. The Assembly Rooms of the resorts are indicative of their early character, as indeed are some of the hotels and boarding houses.

The stability implicit in the above situation had barely been achieved before it was upset by a second major phase of urban genesis which accompanied the industrialisation of both south and north-east Wales. In terms of the actual genesis of towns there were two phases which are separated on the table. The first was the consequence of the development of iron working, particularly on the north-eastern outcrop of the South Wales Coalfield. Its beginnings can be dated to the Dowlais Lease of 1757 and it continued until the middle of the nineteenth century. After 1850 coal mining became predominant and the main creator of new settlements, such as those in the Rhondda valleys. This division does not correspond with the major influence on building itself, the Public Health Act of 1875, and hence to some extent the separation of these two phases is related to the economic circumstances of genesis rather than to real differences within the settlements themselves.

During the whole of the period under review a journey to work in its modern sense was never important, so that the houses of the working people were physically part of the producing machine; an element, and not the most important, in the mine or works equipment. Under these conditions South Wales displays all those extremes which arose from unfettered exploitation of natural resources in an era when the problems of urban planning were thrust aside by the vigour of economic growth.

The manner in which the new settlements were built is amply documented. Writing in a volume, rather inappropriately called *The Beauties of England and Wales*, one author recalls the Merthyr Tydfil of 1815 as follows: 'Nothing can be more offensive to the eye, probably nothing more injurious to the health of the inhabitants than the arrangement of streets and houses. Indeed it is scarcely correct to say that there is a place that can properly merit the name of a street. The houses were usually erected in the situation which best suited the proprietor of the ground without any regard to plan or even to the situation of similar buildings. As the increasing population called for new erections, the same method was successively followed, until the present collection of houses arose, spreading over an immense extent of ground in every possible direction.'[20] Again, the Committee of Enquiry into the State of Education in Wales gives a vivid picture of Aberamman at the time of their deliberations. 'This is a place that has risen entirely within the last

[20] T. Rees, *The Beauties of England and Wales*, xviii (1815), p. 646.

eighteen months. Its present population is about 1,200. . . . But Aberamman is not to be judged according to what it is now, but what it will be
in twelve months hence when the furnaces are at work. . . . There will be
here four furnaces. . . . Independent of this there are in this hamlet two
collieries, one just opened, the other beginning to work. . . . To judge of
the rapidity of the building here, there were in the hamlet today eighty
masons at work and fifty carpenters: there are also several rows of cottages
whose foundations have been commenced in the last few weeks.'[21]
These 'rows of cottages' became the main physical element of the new
settlements.

Occasionally, as in the houses constructed by the Harfords at Newtown
in Ebbw Vale, there were attempts to provide amenities in the form of
communal bakeries and wash houses, but generally these cottages were of
the meanest type. But the attempts by the ironmasters and the iron companies to accommodate labour produced a sequence that can be traced in
most of the industrial towns. The first stages consisted of the purchase
or leasing of farms for the location of furnaces, and particularly for the
disposal of the large quantity of waste material. The farmhouses themselves often became the earliest residences of the ironmasters, while a
disordered array of terraces of small cottages sprang up close to the
furnaces and were often surrounded by slagheaps. Further infilling of the
original farmland by these cottages produced the areas of poorest conditions to which the quotation above applies. The commissioners on the
State of Education in Wales recorded: 'In a sanitary point of view, the
state of Merthyr is disgraceful to those who are responsible for it. The vast
majority of the houses have no privies; where there is such a thing it is
a mere hole in the ground with no drainage. Indeed the town is to a very
small degree drained at all. This is the case nearly all over Wales, but in
a dense population the consequences of such neglect are more loathsomely
and degradingly apparent.'[22] These conditions resulted in the obvious
social consequences. In his report on the sanitary condition of Merthyr
Tydfil, Sir Henry de la Beche noted that, 'the most wretched part of the
town would appear to be that known as the 'Cellars', near Pont Store-
house, and supposed to contain 1,500 persons. Though so named they
are not cellars but a collection of small houses of two storeys situated in
a depression between a line of road and a cinder heap . . . an open, stinking
and nearly stagnant gutter, into which the house refuse is as usual flung,
flows slowly down before the doors. It is a labyrinth of miserable

---

[21] *Report of the Commissioners of Enquiry into the State of Education in Wales* (1847), p. 332.
[22] *Ibid.*, p. 304.

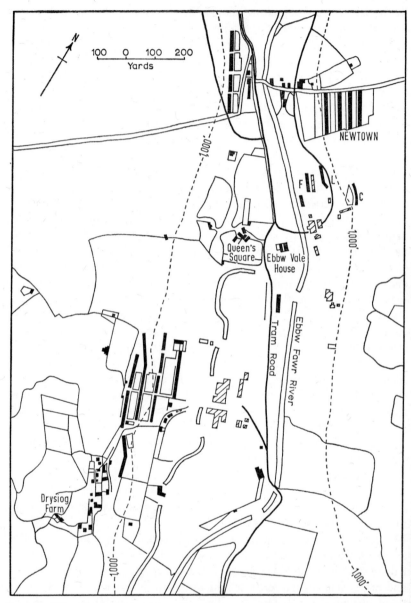

FIG. 11. *Ebbw Vale in 1842.* The earliest section is that to the north of Ebbw Vale House where Crooked Row (C), Limestone Row (L) and Furnace Row (F) are characteristic of the earlier cottages built in relation to the ironworks.

tenements, filled with people, many of whom bear the worst character.'[23] This area can be seen on Figure 12 to the south of Jackson's Bridge.

The next stage in the sequence was the attempt to remedy this haphazard process as settlements grew in size and conditions got out of hand, by building larger 'planned' residential areas or 'company towns'. Newtown at Ebbw Vale, already noted, was one example: at Merthyr Tydfil the three ironworks settlements of Georgetown, Dowlais and Penydarren were also of this type. At the same time the ironmasters built grander houses with their new wealth leaving the farmhouses for their under managers. Ebbw Vale house can be seen on Figure 11, while in Figure 12 Dowlais House, Penydarren House and the great mock medieval Cyfarthfa Castle appear. Figure 12, which depicts Merthyr in 1850, clearly shows the two stages traced so far. The early cottages are shown in black, except in the most complex area at Tydfil's Well—Caepantywyll—Jackson's Bridge. The company towns are left in outline. The older farmsteads, Gwaelod y Garth, Gwaunfarren, and Llwyncelyn have been superseded by the large houses, listed above, situated in their own parkland.

The third stage in the sequence occurred in the second half of the century which saw the local application, often in a tentative and *ad hoc* manner, of general measures aimed at the improvement of conditions. The main weapon in the control of physical building was, of course, the Public Health Act of 1875 by which local authorities could make bye-laws for the control of building standards and through this of physical layout also. 'In the past people have been allowed to erect houses without plans, without any formation of streets or roads, and without any system.' This was recorded at an early meeting of the Ystradyfodwg Urban Sanitary Authority and in 1879 a series of building bye-laws were adopted.[24] A few extracts from these will indicate the conventional measure of control introduced. Each new street was to be laid out 'so as to afford the easiest practicable gradients throughout its entire length'. These streets were to be of 36 feet width if intended for a carriage road and any new street constructed exceeding 100 feet was to be constructed as a carriage road. There was to be at least a 24-foot space in front of every building and at the back an open space exclusively belonging to the building of an aggregate of not less than 150 square feet. The distance of any neighbouring building had to be 15 feet and this was increased if the height of the building were over 25 feet. All these regulations were undoubtedly often

[23] Sir Henry de la Beche, *Report on the Sanitary Conditions of Merthyr Tydfil, Glamorgan* (1845).

[24] Ystradyfodwg Urban Sanitary Authority, Building Bye-Laws 1879. Min. of Housing and Local Govt. Welsh Office.

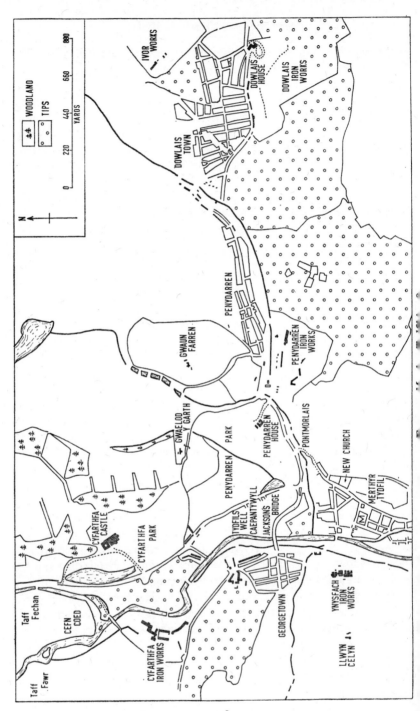

louted, but here were the beginnings not only of quality control but also control of layout in the enforcement of the construction of carriage ways and pavements.

Bye-laws such as these, which were adopted by nearly all local authorities, produced the long, monotonous, but structurally sound, terraces, which are such dominant features in South Wales towns. Where the site was open, the terraces cover large areas of the inner parts of the present built up area, as in Cardiff. Where site conditions were characterised by deeply incised valleys, there came into being the stereotyped long terraces on the valley sides. This pattern is the consequence of many factors combining. Development was rapid, speed essential, so that houses were built as quickly as possible without any organic planning. The divorce between workplace and residence was yet to come, and in a period where such employment was casual the need to be near the workplace was absolute. Moreover, there was competition for land, for space had to be found for canal, rail and road as well as the plant and spoil heaps of the mines. In this competition, housing was least able to win out. Add to this the physical characteristics of the valleys, and the controls of the resultant linear pattern are complete. As the terraces extended farther up the valley side the problem of slope became acute and this was met either by providing a long sloping front garden or by steps, if the house were above the road, and by adding a lower ground floor or basement if the house were downslope. In 1906, the following comments were recorded of Ystalyfera: 'The houses were built on the steep valley side, the ground being so steep that, on the lower side, the houses had basement rooms which unfortunately are frequently used as separate dwellings.'[25] Two years later in 1908, a survey revealed, 'In Ystalyfera practically all houses have underground dwellings with two entrances at different levels. They looked to be two storeys from the road, but were actually three or four.[26]

As the century progressed, so the terrace house became more embellished as fashion filtered down the social scale. Porches and bay windows, brick surrounds to the Pennant Stone and coloured glass made their appearance. In the larger towns, particularly Cardiff and Swansea, the houses of the entrepreneurs and merchants were larger, often detached and elaborately embellished. Cathedral Road at Cardiff is, perhaps, the best Welsh example of a large number of such houses forming a distinctive terrace in contrast to the massive bye-law areas.

The contrast between the earlier cottages and the later bye-law terraces can be seen in the accompanying map of Tonypandy (Fig. 13). The

25 Reports of Medical Officer of Health, 1904–8.
26 *Ibid.*

cottages bordered the old parish road and they were fronted by fairly large
gardens. The later blocks of terraces were built behind them on the only
land which was available and even so the slopes are inconveniently steep.
The front gardens of the cottages were built over as the old parish road
became the main street of the new town and shops were established.
Many buildings along the street line still preserve the old cottages at the
rear.

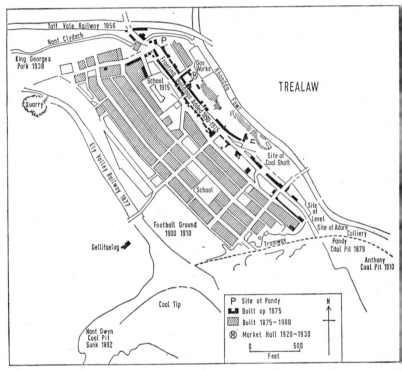

FIG. 13. *The growth of Tonypandy.*

Within this general pattern a number of buildings played dominant
roles, apart from the industrial establishments themselves. The largest,
as has been shown, were the homes of the entrepreneurs, but the most
widespread building was the nonconformist chapel. There is need for a
complete study of the rôle of the chapel in the formation of the Welsh
settlement pattern even as there has been one of the churches of the Celtic
Saints. Most of the settlements which collected about the isolated chapels
were small and in an urban context the chapel followed rather than
attracted settlement. But Bethesda in Caernarvonshire stands as an

example of a slate-quarrying town, the nucleus of which is a chapel of that name. Lastly the workingmen's clubs make another distinctive element in the townscapes of these industrial settlements, at times architecturally not greatly different from the chapels.

Although some detail of the two most recent phases, called 'Modern' and 'Contemporary', has been included in the table there is little point here in entering into any lengthy interpretation of the material. The major principle illustrated is that as after the first genetic phase so after the second there has been a period of transition, or 'sorting out', as the uncontrolled and haphazardly created products of industrial genesis are resolved into an integrated system of central places effectively serving the countryside. The parallelism can be shown to be quite marked. The extensive rebuilding which took place in the 'Georgian' phase can be also seen in the amount of urban renewal now in progress. Out of the early transitional phase, there emerged first the market hall and then the permanent shopping centre. Central area redevelopment schemes mirror this same pattern of adjustment at the present day. It could well be argued that the whole urban pattern of Wales could be interpreted in the context of two cycles which are made up of a major genesis followed by a transitional period of rapid change leading to one of relative stability.

TABLE 10

DEVELOPMENT OF EACH GENETIC PHASE

Stage of development	Dominant principle in distribution		
Genesis of unifunctional settlements	Separation of nodes	or	Distributed facilities
Transition: acquisition of new functions	Interaction: competition between nodes		Transport operative
Climax. Multifunctional settlements	Integration of nodes: system of central places	or	Undistributed facilities

In both cases the stimulus to genesis is in a sense derived from outside the country, certainly it is external to the cultural core, and the result has been a tension between things rural and Welsh and things urban and English. Many of the attitudes towards language and culture in Wales at present can best be understood through the consideration of urbanism and its development in the country. But that is another matter.

There are a number of points which are derived from this paper and which need to be considered in conclusion.

In the study of local detail it is essential not to lose sight of the fact that urbanism can be regarded as a cultural feature which has been diffused from sources in South-West Asia. From this point of view the interaction between urbanisation externally derived and the pre-existing traditions is basic to the broadest view of urban development; it is vital to the understanding of the social history as well as the social geography of many non-European areas.

It is important to see towns as forming part of systems and to direct attention to the general relations between cities on the broadest scale in both time and place. At the moment most suggested systems are economic but there are possibilities of developing other systems on cultural or social bases. In the post-war period the greatest stimulus to work on the location and growth of towns has been Central Place Theory as developed by Christaller and Lösch. Attempts have been made to apply this theory in an historical[27] setting but these have been sporadic and no historian has appeared interested in any of the techniques of modern urban analysis in this field and their application to the past.

Urbanism is a phenomenon which demands study as a whole. The urban fabric, layout, build, and function, is an epitome of the varied forces which have brought to bear on the town over a long period of growth. This demands, at some stage, a synoptic viewpoint which, if it leads on the one hand to generalisation and superficiality, on the other places in perspective the detailed investigation of more limited aspects.[28]

[27] H. Carter, 'The urban hierarchy and historical geography', *Geog. Studies*, iii (1956), pp. 85, 101; Lucy Caroe, *Urban Change in East Anglia in the Nineteenth Century* (unpub. Ph.D. thesis, University of Cambridge, 1965); also note R. L. Morrill, *Migration and the Spread and Growth of Urban Settlement* (1965).

[28] This concept was the principle of the author's work on the geography of Welsh towns: H. Carter, *The Towns of Wales: A Study in Urban Geography* (1965).

A Theatre of Suburbs:
Some Patterns of Development in
West London, 1801–1911

D. A. Reeder

'The vastness of suburban London distinguishes that city eminently from continental cities. A mile beyond Paris you are in a wilderness of bond hills, gypsum quarries, sterile rocks and windmills; beyond the walls of Rome there is literally an immense expanse of desert; whereas London... surrounds itself, suburb clinging to suburb, like onions fifty on a rope.'[1]

A substantial part of recent work in urban studies has been concerned with the structure and form of metropolitan cities, resulting in a much better understanding of the characteristics and functions of modern suburbs.[2] One example of this work is the classification of the London suburbs in terms of the social and economic characteristics which they display, and the degree to which they are dependent on the central area of the town.[3] William Ashworth has also shown how the character of some London suburbs can be traced back to the date and circumstances of their growth: he was able, for example, to identify and explain the persistence of four types of suburb that developed in Essex in the nineteenth and twentieth

[1] J. F. Murray, *The World of London*, 2 vols. (1843), i, p. 72.
[2] The point is made by Leo F. Schnore, *The Urban Scene, Human Ecology and Demography* (New York, 1965), p. 77.
[3] J. H. Westergaard, 'The growth and structure of Greater London' in *Royal Commission on Local Government in Greater London, Written Evidence* (H.M.S.O., 1962), v, pp. 668–99 and 'The structure of Greater London' in Centre for Urban Studies, Report No. 3, *London: Aspects of Change* (1964), pp. 91–144. Also relevant are the papers contributed by geographers to the volume, *Greater London*, ed., J. T. Coppock and Hugh C. Prince (1964), and Centre for Urban Studies, Report No. 2, C. A. Moser and Wolf Scott, *British Towns: A statistical study of their economic and social differences* (1961).

centuries.[4] There is, however, a wide gap between these ecological investigations undertaken mainly from the standpoint of the present century and the work of the historians of the London parishes, the majority of whom are 'local' in purpose and methods. There are still relatively few writers on London who have studied the history of particular places and estates to explain the nature of the process of suburban expansion or to exhibit some of the patterns of metropolitan growth and development.[5] One way in which the available material on the history of parishes can be used to examine the suburban development of London is by comparing the physical and social characteristics of different places as they changed from semi-rural communities into residential and industrial districts of London. This paper reports on a preliminary exploration of one theatre of operations to the west of London in the nineteenth century.

The rates of population growth in different registration districts provide a clue to some of the patterns of development. Maximum rates of growth were registered between 1831 and 1861 in places situated up to three miles from the City. Thus Paddington and Kensington reached peak rates of growth in this period when the means of transport were limited to the private carriage and the public omnibus. After 1861 the building of the metropolitan railways and their suburban extensions brought daily travel within the range of a much larger number of city employees.[6] This affected the development of places on the edges of London, such as Hammersmith and Fulham, and also places in Middlesex, such as Acton and Ealing; and these places registered maximum rates of population

4 'Types of social and economic development in suburban Essex' in *London: Aspects of Change*, pp. 62–87.

5 The first major contributions towards a history of London's growth since the eighteenth century were made by historians of architecture, notably S. E. Rasmussen, *London: the Unique City* (1937) and Sir John Summerson, *Georgian London* (1946) and his note on urban forms in 'The city as artifact' in *The Historian and the City*, ed., Oscar Handlin and John Burchard (M.I.T. and Harvard, 1963), pp. 165–76. This work on the physical history of the city has been extended recently by D. Olsen, *Town Planning in London* (Yale, 1964), a history of the Bedford estates and in a different way by an historical geographer, Hugh C. Prince, in 'North-west London, 1814–1863' in J. T. Coppock and H. C. Prince (eds), *Greater London*, (1964), pp. 80–141, who surveys the spread of building through the suburbs of north London. H. J. Dyos was the first economic and social historian to engage in a major study of one particular place in Victorian London in *Victorian Suburb: A Study of the Growth of Camberwell* (1961), the first volume of a longer term investigation into the nature of the process of suburban development. The most recent overall survey of London's growth and development over 2,000 years is Christopher Trent's one-volume essay, *Greater London* (1965).

6 Harold Pollins has attempted to relate transport and social class in London in the nineteenth and twentieth centuries in 'Transport lines and social divisions' in *London: Aspects of Change*, pp. 29–56.

growth between 1861 and 1891. On the other hand, the population of all these districts kept on growing by immigration as well as natural increase in the nineteenth century and it was not until 1911–21 that, with the exception of Ealing, the total of people moving out of these districts exceeded the total of people moving in. There were nearly three-quarters of a million people living in the registration districts mentioned so far in 1911, an increase of 26-fold on 1801.

The next step is to indicate some of the main features of metropolitan growth that affected the occupational structure of these registration districts and from this to start building up a picture of the phases in the development of these places. At the beginning of the nineteenth century some of the villages that lay to the west of the built-up area of London were already fashionable places of residence: the riverside villages in particular were situated in suburbs of great mansions and landscaped parks. Kensington was a suburb of this kind with the additional advantage of royal patronage: it was known as 'Imperial Kensington' or the Court suburb by the mid century.[7] The migration of the aristocracy into the western suburbs explains in part why those citizens of London interested in establishing a social position chose to live in the districts beyond the west end of town. By 1831 as many as 20 per cent of all occupied males over 20 living in Paddington and Kensington and 14 per cent of those living in Hammersmith were listed in the census returns as capitalists, merchants, and professional men.[8]

Paddington and Kensington were then affected by the building boom of 1837/8–1856 which was based, according to contemporary accounts, on the spending power of London's 'pursy' citizens who came out to populate these 'snug' suburbs.[9] The new housing districts were visible evidence of the formation of an upper middle class representing in the words of one directory of Kensington Town 'all those whom education and intelligence—tested by their professional and commercial pursuits—have rendered equally deserving of honourable and gratifying mention, forming as they do the bulk of what is termed good society.'[10] There can be little

---

[7] J. F. Murray, *A Picturesque Tour of the River Thames in its Western Course* (1845), pp. 65–78; Leigh Hunt, *The Old Court Suburb*, ed., A. Dobson (1952). The best modern account of the local history of Kensington is W. Gaunt, *Kensington* (1948).

[8] Calculated from the occupation tables of the census of 1831 in which these three parishes formed part of the Ossulstone Hundred, Holborn Division (Paddington) and Kensington Division (Kensington and Hammersmith): *Parl. Papers*, 1833 (149), i, p. 366.

[9] 'The building mania', *Builder* (1848), quoted in full in J. Parry Lewis, *Building Cycles and Britain's Growth* (1965), pp. 85–7. There were also regular reports on building progress in west London in the *Building News* (1854–60).

[10] Quoted from the introduction to a fashionable directory of south Kensington (a 'Blue Book'): *The Aristocracy of London, Titled, Untitled, Professional and Commercial* (1863). For

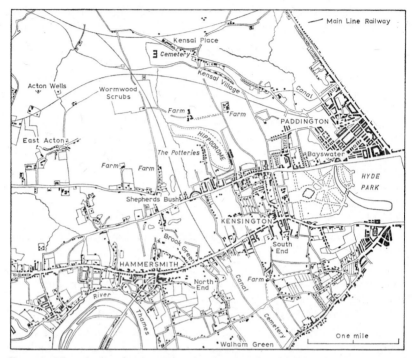

FIG. 14. *The suburban frontier*: West London in 1847, showing building development mainly along the roads that lay between the villages and fields. (Based on the Ordnance Survey.)

doubt that professional men and some members of the commercial classes could with conviction make a claim to gentility in the western suburbs of Victorian London. Yet there were several other districts in west London, including some in Kensington, that did not figure in the 'court' directories; they were more representative of what mid-Victorians liked to think of as the solid middle class. Charles Marriott observed in 1910 that one of these districts, the Ladbroke 'quarter' in north Kensington, gave him a stronger impression of social stability than any other part of London he knew: 'uncompromised and uncompromising, an airier Bloomsbury innocent of ducal associations, Ladbroke upholds the proper dignity of the English middle classes.'[11]

recent discussions of the social aspirations and rising scale of domestic expenditure of the urban middle classes in mid-Victorian England see W. L. Burn, *The Age of Equipoise: A study of the mid-Victorian generation* (1964), especially pp. 98–9, and W. J. Reader, *Professional Men, The Rise of the Professional Classes in Nineteenth Century England* (1966), especially Chap. IV.

[11] Charles Marriott, *Now* (1910), quoted with an account of the development of the estate in F. M. Gladstone, *Notting Hill in Bygone Days* (1936), pp. 111–31.

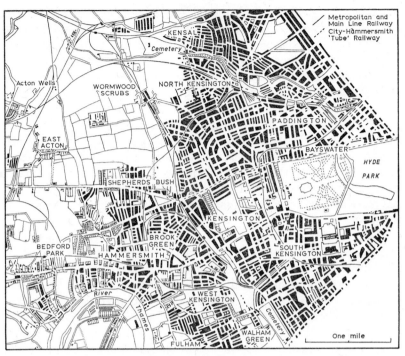

FIG. 15. *The development of the built-up area*: West London in 1904, showing the
physical absorption of most of the pre-urban settlements in the growth of London.
(Based on Stanford's London County Council map.)

After 1861 the development of west London continued to be influenced
by the movements of London's professional and merchant classes. Fewer
of them were moving into the inner suburbs: the 'best' district in Paddington (St. John, including Bayswater) actually lost more people than
it gained between 1861 and 1871; and the builders in Kensington had
difficulty in selling big houses in the 1870s and started to convert them
into flats.[12] Nevertheless, both districts still had a higher percentage of
professional people and merchants in their occupied male population
(over 10 years old) in 1901 than either Hammersmith or Fulham despite
the residential building in these latter places after the mid century.[13] An
increasing number of people were also going to live in Middlesex as main

[12] *Estates Gazette*, 15 May 1878.
[13] Calculated from the *Census of England and Wales*, 1901, *Parl. Papers*, 1902 [Cd. 1304],
L-R. The numbers in Class III and Class V-1, 3, 4, expressed as a percentage of the occupied
male population over 10 years old (the occupational ratio), were: Kensington (13), Paddington
(11), Hammersmith (10), and Fulham (9).

line railways provided suburban services. The development of Ealing as a middle-class residential suburb can be traced back to the 1850s when wealthy Londoners were installing themselves in country houses and Gothic villas: 16·8 per cent of the heads of the households in St. Mary, Ealing at the census of 1861 can be classified as professional and managerial, compared with only 4·5 per cent in the village of Acton.[14] Fifty years later, in 1911, Ealing had a larger occupational ratio of professional people and merchants than Acton, or for that matter, any other place in west London.[15] The impression which these ratios give that Ealing had a superior social standing to Acton was supported by the statistics of housing in the two urban districts in 1901 which showed that Ealing had more villa type and eight-roomed houses, and by the fact that Ealing also had more indoor domestic servants to every hundred families (68·6 compared with 24·5).[16]

The printed census returns cannot be used for any refined analysis of social class, but the increase in the number of clerks in the second half of the century can be regarded as indicative of the growth of a lower middle class. In fact, the occupational ratio of business and commercial clerks in Hammersmith, Acton, and Ealing in 1901 and 1911 was greater than the average for the Metropolitan County of Middlesex at these dates.[17] The lower middle class emerged in late-Victorian London from what Sweet Escott called the 'fusion of sub classes' brought about by the growing uniformity of educational and social disciplines.[18] Its origins

---

[14] W. H. Faulkner, *The History and Antiquities of Brentford, Ealing and Chiswick* (1845), p. 270. The calculations were made from the enumerator's returns, 1861, for St. Mary, Ealing (381 households) and Acton (310 households). The definition of professional and managerial is the same as that adopted by H. J. Dyos in an earlier paper, except that some private income recipients have been added. It is worth pointing out that the wealthiest residents in Acton in 1861 included members of an international capitalist class (the banker, Rothschild, Gunnersbury House), and of a local managerial élite (the London draper, J. Shoolbred). The rest of the heads of households in Acton and Ealing can be grouped in the following way: sub managerial, sub professional, petty entrepreneurs, clerks (with some annuitants and pension holders): 33 and 34 per cent respectively; skilled tradesmen and craftsmen: 30 and 25 per cent, respectively; semi-skilled and unskilled: 31 and 25 per cent, respectively.

[15] Calculated from *Census of England and Wales, 1911, Parl. Papers,* 1912 [Cd. 7018], x Part 1 (Tables of Grouped Occupations). The occupational ratios of Class III and Class V–1, 3, 4 were: Kensington (15), Paddington (12), Hammersmith (10), Acton (12), Ealing (18).

[16] *Census of England and Wales,* 1911; Middlesex County Council, *Report on the Vital and Sanitary Condition of the Administrative County of Middlesex* (1902), pp. 10–11.

[17] Calculated from *Census of England and Wales, 1901 and 1911.* The occupational ratios were: L.C.C. average (5·04 and 4·89), Kensington (4·9 and 4·3), Paddington (6·2 and 5·2). Hammersmith (6·7 and 5·9), Middlesex average (5·45 and 5·69), Acton (5·6 and 6·1), Ealing (6·2 and 7·7). Further information on occupational ratios for places in Middlesex, 1901–11, is contained in M. Rees, *The Social and Economic Development of Extra-Metropolitan Middlesex during the Nineteenth Century,* University of London, unpublished M.Sc. (Econ.) thesis, 1955.

were to be found in the growth of suburban commerce particularly in busy trading places like Hammersmith where more than half the male heads of households in the district of St. Peter were shopkeepers and petty entrepreneurs according to the enumerator's returns of 1851. By the 1870s the lower middle class contained not only those in commercial and most of the clerical occupations, but also those in relatively new occupations such as the elementary school teachers recruited mainly from the tradesmen and more ambitious artisan population to staff the new schools built in the suburbs from 1872.

The development of residential estates on the edges of London for occupation by tradesmen, clerks and better paid artisans can be quite closely related to the building of new transport lines. Thus the building of extensions to the Metropolitan District Railway in the 1870s really opened up the farther reaches of the south-west to the speculative builder of lower middle class housing and brought into being new suburbs in previously isolated places such as Fulham and the southern parts of Acton and Ealing.[19] Similarly the renewed activity in house building in Hammersmith, Paddington, and Acton in the late nineteenth century was connected with the building of tramways in the 1880s and 1890s and the belated interest of the Great Western Railway in increasing its suburban traffic. The major building boom in Acton and Ealing occurred at the turn of the century and by 1913 Acton was overstocked with low cost housing.[20]

Finally, account must be taken of the growth of an urban working class in west London as village settlements expanded into sub-centres of employment. The beginnings of this can be traced back to the colonies of pigkeepers, labourers, laundryworkers, and railway workers in the suburbs before 1861 which became the nuclei of working-class districts. Acton and north Kensington were particularly important as centres of the laundry industry in west London in the nineteenth century.[21] But at the census of 1901 workmen were mainly employed in building and construction, conveyancing, general labouring and metals (including machines

[18] T. H. Sweet Escott, *Social Transformations of the Victorian Age* (1897), pp. 193, 201. Changes in the composition of the middle classes in the nineteenth century are discussed by F. Musgrove, *The Migratory Elite* (1963), especially pp. 44–5. David Lockwood comments on different types of clerical work in *The Blackcoated Worker* (1958), Chap. I, and Asher Tropp looks at some of the ambiguities in the status of teaching in *The School Teachers* (1957).

[19] T. C. Barker and M. Robbins, *A History of London Transport*, i (1963), pp. 170–1, 209.

[20] *Ibid.*, and Edwin Course, *London Railways* (1962), pp. 176, 182; also S. B. Saul, 'House building in England 1890–1914', *Economic History Review*, xv, No. 1 (August 1962), pp. 124–5; W. King Baker, *Acton, Middlesex* (1913), p. 312.

[21] The first colony of laundry workers in Acton dates from about 1864 according to Percival Joliffe, *Acton and its History* (1910), p. 80.

and implements) in that order. The proportions of the occupied males (over 10) engaged in these industries ranged from as little as 27 per cent in Kensington, 38 per cent in Paddington and 34 per cent in Ealing to as much as 40–50 per cent in Hammersmith and Acton.[22] It is not possible to say much about the movements of these workmen as there are not many statistics on journeys to work, but the relatively smaller number of work-men's trains beyond Hammersmith (compared, for example, with the much better services provided in north-east London) suggests that fewer workmen lived in north-west London than in its eastern counterpart and that many of those living in the outer districts also worked there. It should also be said, of course, that the tramways in the west had no direct connec-tion with the central area; and, in any case, only one tramway offered workmen's fares. On the other hand there were complaints about the services for workmen from Acton to London.[23]

More workmen moved into the western suburbs between 1901 and 1911. One reason for this was that the London County Council provided new working class accommodation in Hammersmith, Acton, and Ealing except in so far as these new estates rehoused workmen already living there. Secondly, transport facilities were improved after 1901 with the electrification of lines and the building of the 'tuppeny tube' from the City to Shepherds Bush, Hammersmith. Thirdly, and partly as a con-sequence of these developments, opportunities for employment widened between 1900 and 1908 as north Kensington, Hammersmith, and Acton, with other places on the edges of west London, attracted manufacturing establishments, many of them concerned with producing electrical equip-ment and assembling motor cars. This was to develop into a new pattern of industrialisation in London between 1910 and 1920, 'when a limited range of industry provided a floating element that switched to a migration pattern weighted to the west.'[24] The effects of the growth of manufactur-ing establishments were reflected in the work-place data of the census of 1921 which showed that a number of places in west London, Hammer-smith and Acton amongst them, had become 'suburbs of production'

[22] Fulham was one place in which workmen represented 60–70 per cent of all householders, even in 1861. At that time Fulham contained mainly gardening labourers; but in 1901 it had more building workers than any other London borough: 53·1 per thousand in Fulham; 50·8 per thousand in Hammersmith (L.C.C. *Census of London, 1901* (1903); *Census of England and Wales*, 1910).

[23] London County Council, *London Statistics*, ii (1891–2), and 'Locomotive service', *Returns of Services and Routes* (1895), Part 1.

[24] J. E. Martin, *Greater London, An Industrial Geography* (1966), p. 80. Dr. Martin points out that Napiers took workmen with them to Acton in 1902, but that G.E.C. expected to be able to train local female labour when they moved into the buildings of the Osram Lamp Company in Hammersmith in 1893 (pp. 37, 41).

offering employment to some of their own workers and those of other suburbs as well. On the day of the census Acton even had a net inflow of workers. The places with the largest daily outflow of people in relation to their resident occupied population included late Victorian and Edwardian suburbs such as Ealing, but also some of the newer village suburbs in outlying parts of Middlesex.[25] Since the late nineteenth century the main line railways had brought residential building in detached and widely scattered communities to the clay plains of the north-west.[26] In these places the cycle of suburban development was starting all over again.

This brief account of the movements and changes taking place in some parts of this large area is intended, as it were, to set the scene for more particular descriptions of the developing characters of certain places. The upper middle classes were the first and the working classes the last to move into the suburbs, but they all kept on doing so while the available means of transport were changing. These patterns of migration affected the development of places in west London at different times and in different ways. Paddington became an early- and mid-Victorian residential suburb and a part of upper middle-class London, but along with parts of north Kensington, it subsequently developed symptoms of social and physical deterioration. The village of Hammersmith failed to maintain a reputation as a fashionable suburb of Georgian London and was turning into a lower middle-class place of residence from the 1850s. It also became a local centre of employment and entertainment. Acton and Ealing were hardly affected at all by suburban development in the first half of the nineteenth century, but after 1861 these villages became middle-class residential suburbs of outer London. The middle class appeal of Acton was epitomised in the open, pleasant, and freely planned neighbourhood of Springfield Park and the more famous 'garden suburb' of Bedford Park. Thereafter the migration of London's commercial and government employees and the impact of suburban industry dramatically altered its character. By 1911 it had a number of frankly working-class districts. On the other hand Ealing seems to have more successfully retained its late-Victorian character as a middle-class dormitory suburb, at least until 1921.

This paper does not deal with all these places and what follows now

---

25 *Census of England and Wales, Workplaces*, 1921. The figures of net daily inflow and outflow expressed as a ratio of the total population in each place were: Paddington (net outflow, 8·4), Kensington (net inflow, 5·1), Hammersmith (net outflow, 1·6), Acton (net inflow, 2·7), and Ealing (net outflow, 17·5).

26 James H. Johnson, 'The suburban expansion of housing in London 1918-1939' in Coppock and Prince, *Greater London*, pp. 144-5.

is mainly an account of some of the patterns of housing development in Paddington and Hammersmith to illustrate the salient features of these two places at different times. The two surveys are necessarily abridged and mainly descriptive, but they may serve to show the point of comparative studies of suburban development.

(1) *Paddington*

Paddington began to emerge from obscurity in the last decade of the eighteenth century with the completion of the Grand Junction canal. About the same time, in 1795, the approach of new house building encouraged the officials of the Bishop of London to apply to Parliament for approval to develop a building scheme on part of the church estates of 611 acres in the parish.[27] The ambitions of the officials and trustees of this church property to own a profitable but high class development was the main influence shaping the early Victorian character of a place that until then had been noted more as refuge for artists than for merchants. The Paddington estate was deliberately planned as an extension to the west end of the town, though it was some 30 years or so before it really began to compete with more established fashionable parts. The building scheme ran into difficulties from the start with drainage problems and building failures. Moreover, the managers of the estate found that substantial builders were reluctant to invest in notoriously risky undertakings on an undeveloped site still quite a long way out of town. Despite this, they persisted in leasing small plots to individual (mostly local) builders rather than hand the estate over to financial middlemen, in order to better control the development.[28] And this eventually paid off. During the 1830s the main thoroughfare (Sussex Gardens) was completed, lined with trees and provided with two carriage roads and a communal garden. The square and polygon had already been built. Thereafter building went forward rapidly, to such an extent in fact that the revenues from ground rents more than trebled between 1833 and 1843.[29] By then Paddington was beginning to acquire a new social status in the London directories as an 'elegant and *recherché*' part of the town, principally occupied by the aristocracy and opulent London merchants.[30]

[27] *Improved Plan of the Termination of the Grand Junction Canal at Paddington with the intended New Streets on the Estates of the Bishop of London and Mr. Crompton* (1799). Also *Paddington Estate Act*, 35 Geo., iii, c. 83 (Private, 1795).

[28] Minute Book, *Paddington Estate*, i (1805–23). The architect S. P. Cockerell was hired in 1805, but he had no actual dealings with the builders and on his death was replaced by George Gutch, the district surveyor of Paddington.

[29] Paddington Estate, *Building Contracts* (1 vol.) and Account Books.

[30] Such as Lucas, *Paddington Directory* (1843), p. viii, and Tallis, *Illustrated London* (1851), pp. 42–3.

The immediate impact of the rise of Tyburnia (as the place became known) on districts farther to the west was to encourage enterprising publicans and others to invest in providing tea gardens, bowling greens, archery grounds and even a suburban race course, the Hippodrome at Notting Hill. At the same time adventurous speculators began to lay out building estates, though few of them had the resources to see them through. The main phase of building on the clay lands to the west occurred after 1846 when substantial developers with the financial connections to sustain major schemes moved into the north-western suburbs.[31] Bayswater was the most prosperous of these new districts: it not only helped to establish Paddington's position as a place of genteel domesticity in mid- and late-Victorian London, but also provided locations for new commercial enterprise, leading to the emergence of an urban 'shopocracy'.

The rise of Bayswater began modestly enough in the 1840s, when villas and 'houses of a moderate class', embellished, to use the estate agent's phrase, 'in chaste decoration', were built along the curving roads of Westbourne Park.[32] Much larger town houses were erected in the 1850s in Lancaster Gate (fronting the royal park in Kensington) and in the long terraces that linked Westbourne Grove with the Uxbridge (or Bayswater) Road. The middle-aged and respectable heads of the Victorian households who moved into Bayswater paid £2,000 or more for some of these houses and also maintained a retinue of some six to ten servants per family. They also contributed quite lavishly to the social and educational institutions of the district: in fact the donations of new inhabitants were the main source of money for building the eight new churches of south Paddington at a cost of £10,000 to £15,000 each.[33] By the 1860s the social cachet of Bayswater had caught on to the extent of attracting the families of colonial administrators to whom the storied boarding houses on the banks of the Hugli were as familiar as those to be found in Paddington. Bayswater had become a symbol of Imperial London.[34] Finally, commerce followed after wealth and fashion as linen drapers, haberdashers, and silk mercers moved into Gloucester Road and Westbourne Grove where William Whiteley successfully attracted the 'carriage trade' to his new type of department store. Westbourne Grove was more of an organ than an artery of that part of the town, the centre of a largely self-contained

[31] A part of my unpublished Ph.D. thesis concerns the business operations involved in making these new pieces of London between 1801 and 1864: *Capital Investment in the Western Suburbs of Victorian London*, University of Leicester, 1965, pp. 230–65.

[32] Auction Particulars, *Westbourne Park Estate* (1853).

[33] Details of finance and seating are contained in the files of the Church Commissioners.

[34] *Bayswater Annual* (1885).

urban community with its own social apparatus of tea shops, circulating libraries, clubs, and colleges for 'young ladies'.[35]

In the last two decades of the century the social character of Bayswater became peculiarly complex. This was partly because some residential streets were taken over for shops, more boarding houses and private hotels. The district also contained a working population of milliners, shop assistants and others, for whom new commercial and social institutions were provided, mainly by the Westbourne Park Baptist Chapel founded in 1877.[36] Bayswater also became more cosmopolitan as Jewish and Greek families moved into the district.[37] But the fashionable Bayswater Road, still inhabited by men of property, kept up its air of social grandeur well into Edwardian times.

One feature of the development of Paddington was the proximity of suburban 'rookeries' and working-class districts to residential estates. This was the case in other parts of west London, too: even in south Kensington the High Street sheltered a slum for a time and the presence of a water works on Campden Hill was responsible for the formation of another.[38] Many of the scruffy cottages that were built in the inner suburbs were swept away as leases fell in, but some of these 'rookeries' survived to become densely populated urban districts. Notting Dale in the north-west of Kensington was one place with a continuous history of this kind, inhabited mainly by pig keepers in the early nineteenth century, but known as a West End 'avernus' by the end of the century when it housed a restless and migratory population without the skills or the social stability of artisan districts.[39]

The poorest—and most prolific—community in Paddington grew up round the canal basin at the very heart of the mid-Victorian suburb. It

[35] Details of these shops etc., are contained in Richard S. Lambert, *The Universal Provider: A study of William Whiteley and the Rise of the London Department Store* (1938) and Alison Adburgham, *Shops and Shopping 1800-1914* (1964), Chaps. 14, 15. Also the *Bayswater Chronicle* (1884).

[36] Until then, the intrusion of nonconformist chapels, other than Wesleyan, into Paddington had been successfully resisted by the owners and trustees of Church property. The history of the chapel and its social services is described by Sir James Marchent, *Dr. John Clifford, Life, Letters and Reminiscences* (1924).

[37] Bayswater had two synagogues and a Greek Church in Moscow Road: *Bayswater Annual* (1885), p. 13.

[38] The High Street 'rookery' known as Jennings Buildings was demolished to make way for Kensington House, the Victorian extravaganza of the financier Albert Grant. Places like these were investigated by the Metropolitan Commissioners of Sewers in 1849-50.

[39] Described at various times by Mrs. Mary Bayley, *Ragged Homes and How to Mend Them* (1853), London County Council, *Report on the Drainage of the Potteries* (1849), George R. Sims, 'Off the track in London', *Strand Magazine* (1904), and, more recently, Pearl Jephcott, *A Troubled Area, Notes on Notting Hill* (1964).

came into being in the early nineteenth century when the directors of the canal company formed what can only be described as a small trading estate.[40] Then the building of the Great Western Railway terminus, hotel and workshops from 1837 and the gas works at Kensal Green provided more work for artisans, particularly stokers, smiths and railway labourers, for whom houses were built at various points along the Harrow Road. By the late 1860s the pressure for cheap accommodation, intensified by the building of the Metropolitan Railway was beginning to affect the edges of residential districts. The medical officer claimed in 1869 that overcrowding in its worst forms did not exist, but he drew attention to cases where people had moved into back streets (mews) and had converted these outbuildings into workshops and stores.[41] From the 1870s workmen were being housed on what vacant pieces of land were left in south Paddington, but mainly in the open fields to the north-west of the Harrow Road on what became the wrong side of the railway tracks. Queens Park, built in the 1880s, was rationally planned as an experiment in suburban living for those workmen who could afford the rents of 6s to 13s a week charged by the Artisans', Labourers' and General Dwellings Company.[42] St. Peters Park, in contrast, was originally intended for occupation by the lower middle classes. This was a district that went wrong, partly because the houses were packed too closely together in the original ground plan, but also because the developer lost control over the project when he went bankrupt in 1872. By the 1890s some of the houses were in quite a dilapidated state, sub-let in tenements and converted into beer shops and bottle stores.[43] When Arthur Sherwell published a survey of west London in 1897 he was able to illustrate both the proximity of wealth and poverty in Paddington and the fluidity of social boundaries as streets filled up with an army of people who lived off the West End. As Booth pointed out a little later, the 'respectable' working class had already moved out of streets lying between the canal and railway, a classic site for the development of slums.[44]

[40] A monthly account of building progress was recorded in the minute books of the Grand Junction Canal Company until the 1850s.

[41] Annual Report, *Paddington Vestry* (1869), pp. 16, 21–3.

[42] *Select Committee on Town Holdings, Parl. Papers,* 1887 (260), xiii evidence Farrant; and *Artisans, Labourers and General Dwellings Company: A Short Account* (1883).

[43] Based mainly on the letters of complaint sent to the ground landlords who could do little about them as they were unable to trace the head lessees of property fallen into disrepair: Church Commissioners, File no. 41784, Part 1, and 58206, Part 2.

[44] *Life in West London* (1897) and C. Booth, *Life and Labour in London,* 3rd Series, 'The inner west', pp. 123–4. Also H. Lazarus, *Landlordism: An Illustration of the Rise and Spread of Slumland* (1892).

(2) *Hammersmith*

The population of Paddington rose by increases of 370 per cent, 420 per cent, and 54 per cent in the census periods ending in 1831, 1861, and 1891, but the rate of growth of Hammersmith's population was much less dramatic with increases of 82 per cent, 140 per cent, and 296 per cent in the same periods. Moreover, residential building was a less important cause of these increases in Hammersmith before 1861 than in Padddington, and the expansion of the suburban economy more important. Hammersmith was chiefly known for its prosperous farming gardeners whose capital-intensive methods had established it as the great 'fruit and kitchen' garden, north of the Thames. It was also a trading place with a number of suburban industries. In fact, the village had a local life and character of its own where people rising in the middle classes—traders and nonconformist ministers, for example—looked after the parish council and gave the place a somewhat dubious reputation for independent thinking on national issues.[45] This might be compared with the situation in Paddington where property interests converted the parish council into a select vestry and the instrument of financing residential amenities on new estates.[46]

On the other hand, Hammersmith was known to writers such as Thomas Faulkner as a fashionable place of residence in Georgian London because of its situation along the river side and its connection with the Great Western Road, the main avenue of ribbon building in the south-west.[47] According to them it housed one of a number of exclusive communities to be found between Chelsea and Hounslow, and it had, in common with these other places, the distinction of possessing reputable boarding schools. Information on the sources of income of the heads of households living in the Georgian houses in St. Peters Square, George Street, and Hammersmith Terrace taken from the enumerator's returns of 1851 may help to give some idea of the sort of people who had gone to live there. Thirty of these had private incomes (two of them were baronets) and thirteen were professional people. The others were a really mixed lot of people, including four merchants (three retired), a cement manufacturer, a tavern keeper, clerk, an artist, two master craftsmen, and a lady 'dependent on friends'. Few of these households employed more than two servants.

✳

[45] P. D. Whitting quoting the researches of C. G. Thorne in 'Backcloth to Hammersmith' in *A History of Hammersmith* (ed., P. D. Whitting for the Hammersmith Local History Group, 1965). Also Eleanor J. Willson, 'Farming, nursery and market gardening' in the same volume (pp. 88–100).
[46] W. Robins, *Paddington Past and Present* (1853), p. 211.
[47] *The History and Antiquities of the Parish of Hammersmith* (1839).

The most obvious difference between mid-Victorian Paddington and Hammersmith was that the greater part of the latter place was still on the suburban frontier in 1851, with the real concentration of people living near the riverside village. But there were also important and widening social differences as the reputation of Paddington as a fashionable place to live improved and that of Hammersmith's declined. Whereas Paddington became associated with the prosperous district of Bayswater, the image of Hammersmith changed for the worse in the eyes of old inhabitants with the development of new places away from the river. By 1861 the clerk who lived at Brook Green and Shepherds Bush in Hammersmith had through Leech's *Punch* cartoons become a recognised type.[48] Hazlitt's verdict a bit later on was that the place had been taken over by the 'vulgarer forms of modern suburban life'.[49]

The differences in the rate and character of suburban migration into Hammersmith compared with other places in west London became marked soon after the development of omnibus travel when Hammersmith was, for a time, the terminal of the main routes from the City and in direct competition with established but still relatively undeveloped suburbs —such as Brompton—further in. Local pessimists complained that Hammersmith in the 1850s was a *terra incognita*, unable to hold its old families who were 'departing for more favoured locales'; but this sort of talk may just have been a way of raising support for a local railway promotion. The first business trains ran from Hammersmith to the City in 1858, but only two of these were provided and they took 53 minutes on the up journey.[50] A more important social change was the increase in cottage building, especially on the swampy lands of the parish. Builders ran up cheap and insanitary cottages near to Brook Green, for example, in order to house the Irish labourers and their families who settled there.[51] No doubt the construction of main line railways (including the notoriously unsuccessful West London Railway) and the increase in brickmaking brought them in. Hammersmith was not the only place in west London to become a reception area for the labouring poor, as we have seen, but they seem to have created more problems in this parish than elsewhere. One problem was the sharp increase in the poor rate during the 1850s to a level higher than in neighbouring places; and another was the threat

[48] Quoted in Whitting, *A History of Hammersmith*, p. 15.
[49] W. C. Hazlitt, *The Hazlitts*, ii (1912), pp. 65, 165.
[50] P. Roos, 'Public transport in Hammersmith', in Whitting, *A History of Hammersmith*, pp. 226–38.
[51] Brook Green became a Catholic 'colony' in the west with some wealthy residents such as Countess Tasker, whose philanthropic activities for the Irish labourers in the district are described in A. White, *A History of Holy Trinity Church, Hammersmith* (1903), pp. 38–9.

which poor drainage and insanitary cottages contained for a suburb with a reputation as a healthy place. One survey of 1856 showed that only 2,000 houses or so had piped water laid on: for the most part Hammersmith was still in the era of open wells and cesspools.[52] The effects of all this must not be exaggerated however: Hammersmith was still a respectable place in 1861. Yet it had relatively fewer landowners than in other places able or willing to invest in parish 'improvements' and attracted less ambitious speculators. The character of middle-class housing development can be illustrated from the kind of building at Shepherds Bush, a place that was no more than a mile up the road from the scenes of substantial housing projects for at least the moderately well-to-do in Kensington. At Shepherds Bush the small freeholders sold land to the highest bidders and the district to the west of the Green was covered between 1841 and 1861 with two- and three-storey villa houses and small shops bought up by traders, lesser manufacturers, warehousemen, and commercial clerks, with the aid of loans provided by the small building and freehold land societies that had interests in the development of the district.[53]

It cannot be said that the social divisions of west London were created by the railways as they were already established before the Metropolitan Railway penetrated Hammersmith in 1864. But they did accelerate the pace of development and in particular they opened up parts that were previously inaccessible from the main roads. The building of stations in the open fields encouraged speculators to buy up small holdings and to form larger estates of houses of a similar type and design. The progress of the metropolitan drainage scheme was also another factor influencing the development of places on the outer edges of London, and the extensive operation carried out with the assistance of the Fulham District Board of Works in Hammersmith from 1856 helped to make the physical condition of this place more attractive to the builders of middle class housing. Even so, builders still managed to run up cheap houses in the 'mud and water' districts of Fulham (Sands End, Moor Fields) before the engineers

[52] Annual Reports, *Fulham Board of Works*, 1856 and 1857; also P. D. Whitting, 'The beginnings of Public Health in Hammersmith', *Historical Record* (a publication of the Local History Group, 1963).

[53] Information from the building leases of the district. The rôle of building societies in the development of lower middle class housing in west London is described in my thesis. The West London Building Society founded in Chelsea in 1856 was an example of the type. The depositors appear to have been mainly domestic servants, single professional women, and shopkeepers, and the shareholders and borrowers mainly tradesmen and builders. This society financed new building as well as the purchase of houses.

arrived on the scene.[54] One rather crude index of what were quite subtle differences in the character of particular districts built in Hammersmith was the price of houses, which ranged from £250 to £300 each on the Oaklands estate, developed by Peter Broad a city auctioneer, to £20 to £30 towards Starch Green and Leyfield Road. These prices varied according to the number of rooms and kind of fittings.[55] For the most part the Hammersmith developers built houses to sell quickly by meeting the demands of the 'respectable' lower middle class for solid but moderately priced homes. A contemporary description of the building of west Kensington after the extension of the District Railway to North End, Fulham in 1873 illustrates this. Building was 'rapidly carried on', this reporter claimed, 'where speculative builders had money or credit; the tall houses, detached or semi-detached, or in closed lines improperly called "terraces" which ultimately became the sides of streets, rose up in a few months, roofed and windowed and calling for tenants.'[56] Finally, the old-fashioned, plebeian name of North End was dropped, much to the disgust of Burne Jones who was living at Grange House nearby.[57]

West Kensington was literally a builder's invention: in fact, one of the progeny of the firm of Gibbs and Flew Ltd., the largest building firm in terms of housing output to be operating in west London during the long upsurge of building, 1876–1881. This large-scale operator made the biggest profits from selling 'improved' building land, so the firm built roads to give convenient access and economised on the use of land. On the other hand, the houses which the firm also built sold well because they contained all the latest fittings: according to one report they were provided with 'hot and cold water, and bathrooms with electric bells; while the encaustic tiles, stained glass and marble fenders gave them an attractive appearance not often to be found in houses of this class.' The builders were able to provide these relatively cheaply partly because of the economies of scale which they obtained from buying materials in bulk, but also because they made some of the fittings in their own workshops. The result was that west Kensington, unlike some parts of the contemporary development of St. Peters Park in Paddington, secured the kind of inhabitants for whom the district was intended.[58]

54 The medical officer of health frequently reported on this kind of building to the Fulham Board of Works in the 1860s. It seems, for example, that cesspools overflowed into the basements of houses built in Fulham 'New Town'.
55 W. S. Clarke, *The Suburban Homes of London* (1881), p. 401.
56 *Illustrated London News*, 23 August 1884.
57 W. Lockhead, *The Victorian Household* (1964), pp. 174–81; and 'North End, Fulham' [a publication of the Fulham Local History Society] (1963).
58 Details of this firm's operations from the *Builder*, xlvi (1884, Part 1), and *West London Observer* (1886–7).

The rise of these suburbs also affected the character of Hammersmith by stimulating the growth of religious and social institutions. The Baptists, Presbyterians and Congregationalists made, for example, a major advance into suburban territory from the 1860s.[59] Another social change which can only be referred to here was the impact of new residents on the educational facilities in Hammersmith, particularly the provision of commercial schools and colleges. But the chief social feature of the new suburbs was the pursuit of outdoor recreations reflecting the youthfulness of the residents and the new image of the suburbs as a place for bringing up children. C. F. G. Masterman complained that in places like Hammersmith people were drifting away from the realities of life, but he admitted that the infinite boredom of mid-Victorian villadom was being replaced by a 'scene of busy activity with interest in cricket and football results, "book talk", love making, croquet, and tennis parties for young men and women'.[60] He should have added visits to places of public entertainment to this list. Hammersmith not only acquired a number of out-of-town theatres and suburban music halls but also quite new forms of entertainment such as the spectacular performances provided in the Olympia—built in 1888—which drew audiences from all over London.[61]

By the 1890s, when the main period of residential building was over, Hammersmith gave the appearance of being more socially homogeneous than Paddington, with less obvious physical contrasts between its different parts. The impression given by local writers is that despite industrial growth and some poverty and overcrowding, Hammersmith was a trim and quiet residential suburb. The influx of workmen was most marked in some of the older parts of Brook Green and Shepherds Bush where 'West End' type industry and new catering establishments (including the business of Joseph Lyons and Co.) had taken over converted houses and other buildings. Workmen also lived in the south near to the riverside industries and in the far north where new industries had been started on pieces of open land between the canal and the railway, adjoining the open common of Wormwood Scrubbs.[62] The main pockets of poverty and overcrowding were located in these two extremities of the parish: the cramped streets of the old village were a natural breeding ground; whilst the Latimer Road in the north was really an extension of the over-

59 J. Stoughton, *Congregationalism in the Old Court Suburb* (1956).
60 *The Condition of England* (1918), pp. 74–7, 83.
61 Eleanor J. Willson, 'Theatres and entertainment' in Whitting, *A History of Hammersmith*, pp. 190–6. Paddington also had a music hall (The Metropolitan, Edgware Road), but the only place for outdoor recreation was a piece of waste land that was eventually bought for a recreation ground.
62 John S. Usher, 'Industry and employment', *ibid.*, pp. 185–9.

crowded district of Notting Dale in Kensington. The number of missions founded in Hammersmith since the 1860s was one indication of the condition of the people living there.[63] Yet many parts of Hammersmith were not socially depressed, and the parish had less poverty and over-crowding than Paddington. When Charles Booth arranged localities in order of social condition Hammersmith was well up the list at the top of which was Brompton (south-west London) and Hampstead (north London).[64]

*

These accounts of the main features of the development of Paddington and Hammersmith, though far from complete, may have served to indicate the kind of developmental and comparative approach that I am adopting in studying the history of London. The work done so far needs to be extended and strengthened by taking in more places and by attempting to define more precisely the movements of London's élites and their imitators, as well as the social and physical changes consequent upon these. There is plenty of statistical information embedded in the census returns, the rate books and the suburban directories which might be used to provide a sophisticated analysis of the spatial and social mobility of Londoners.

The conclusion that can be reached, even on the basis of this limited study, is that suburbia had many complexities. Different places passed through a number of phases of development as the growth of central London and the building of the inner suburbs triggered off and influenced the character of those further out. Certainly, the development of Padding-ton and Hammersmith did not correspond to one pattern or type, but produced two quite distinctive historical styles. The same can probably be said for other places in this heterogeneous complex of suburbs, and it seems likely that more detailed comparisons will reveal still greater diversity between their development. There are clearly many more facets of this whole experience awaiting research.

---

63 Jean De H. Simons, 'The development of nonconformity', *ibid.*, pp. 77–87.
64 Quoted in 'Backcloth to Hammersmith' *ibid.*, p. 16.

Discussion

One might have expected that by the fifth session of the Conference, participants had made up their minds on the meaning of the main words used by the historians of towns, and on the nature of their task. That this was not in fact so is shown by the discussion—which went on for three hours—of these three papers. Very little was said which could be used for a direct comparison between urban growth patterns, the resulting social structures, or the political characteristics of different towns. Instead, the meeting was devoted largely to the attempt to evolve a general typology of towns, and a division of labour between different disciplines which might all study urban phenomena comparatively, in order at least to achieve a common language for those engaged in research.

Although the theme led to a concentration of interest on British towns, the meeting benefited from the contributions of Professor SCHNORE from the American standpoint, and of Professor KÖLLMANN on the German experience of the nineteenth century. Even with these broadening influences, however, it did not seem possible to produce a system of general validity capable of spanning differences of time and place. If comparative study means a uniform description of scattered phenomena and the production of a set of explanations satisfactorily accounting for the heterogeneity of observed events, then urban historians are still a long way from achieving their goal. This session really contented itself with exploring the kinds of explanation which might be used in this comparative study.

Perhaps the most interesting positive outcome of the discussion was the identification of a few distinct patterns of settlement with their attendant social, economic and political characteristics—additions to the historians' vocabulary which, without claiming to cover a significantly large portion of all urban history, at least prove the advantages of an inter-disciplinary typology. Thus, the word 'colony' in a western European and industrial sense entered into the contributions of both Dr. MARSHALL and Professor KÖLLMANN. Mr. C. HARRIS's account of the settlement of the Swansea Valley found an echo in Mr. FREEMAN's Huddersfield. This was not the case of finding facile comparisons: we were warned by Dr. WESTERGAARD that the relationships between the economic typology of industrial patterns, the physical typology of the land forms and the social and political typology dependent on the other two, were all capable of being linked in many different ways, and at different levels of intensity and causality. The implication of this was that we should abandon any search for a single definition of the city or urbanisation. 'The worst definitions of the city', he said, 'are influenced by the stereotyped conception of the metropolitan city as

Fifth Discussion

the true city towards which all urbanisation proceeded—a top point in what I think is probably a non-existent continent.' This proved to be one of the main themes of the discussion.

The CHAIRMAN began by reviewing the different kinds of historical scholarship represented by the papers and discussants. All historical writing had to begin with description—few of us thought that one ought to begin with a model and then try to fit the facts into this framework. He was himself convinced that 'it is better to start with a sound documented historical narrative which will throw up its own hypotheses which you can then test quantitatively afterwards'. There was little argument about this, though there were warnings, which presage the sociological and systematic approach, that the historian must from the beginning learn to state not only what was there and explain this, but also observe and account for what was not there, or did not happen. This was exemplified by Mr. Carter's paper on Wales. Many of his old urban settlements like Tregaron, Montgomery, and Harlech, are remarkable just because they did *not* grow. The reasons were different in each case and it is possibly as illuminating to examine them as to try to show why Cardiff or Swansea *did* become large cities. Why did Milford Haven *not* become one of the country's great ports, and why, in Dr. Reeder's study, did Ealing flourish when Brentford languished? Any causal study dependent only on successes deals with only half the phenomena to be explained. The 'city square' of Aberaeron in Mr. Carter's contribution which remained a village green (symbolising for him the failure of the urban tradition in Wales) is as illuminating as that Greenwich Village which remains a small community in the heart of New York.

Fact-finding, then, makes a start, but systematisation to bring order into the chaos of data comes from hypotheses. Of such there was no lack. The real test came when theories had to be tested. There was underlying agreement that such testing had to be of a quantitative (numerical) kind, though this did not necessarily mean with quasi-censal material, and there was also the possibility of topographical (archaeological) verification, which is a substitute measurement in some cases where historical statistics are not available. It was clear that the effort to quantify was wasted if one did not ask the right questions, and if the category to be measured was not adequately defined. This came out in several ways. Dr. REEDER insisted on the need for *specific* quantitative inquiries rather than general ones: for example, 'the patterns of internal migration into and between the suburbs, and to look down even into the detail of the changeover of inhabitants in particular streets.' Professor KÖLLMANN picked up the same point in discussing German miners' fertility when transplanted into an urban environment and the subsequent 'social and professional sorting out into groups'. In a similar vein, Mr. FREEMAN warned against accepting urban boundaries at their face value and showed how complex the journey to work was in the Manchester conurbation. In other words, we must not blindly try to quantify everything, but carefully select the important indices which really throw light on structural differences.

By this time the conference was anxious to define its working terms more accurately, but soon ran into difficulties. In the United States a corporate city may be a tiny rural settlement, in England any cathedral town is a city, and in Germany the right to be called a *Stadt* was a privilege acquired with some difficulty, so that the juridical definition serves to identify the category. The complexity of London, as described by Mr. WESTERGAARD, was such that it formed a category of its own, but that apart, how do we in Britain know when a town emerges? (Leaving aside the question whether for much of the time covered by our discussions, all Britain was not already urban, with statistically insignificant exceptions.) Most people seemed to know what a village was, and as Mr. FREEMAN and Dr. MARSHALL both showed, some of the settlements which were part of the urban production process retained the character of a village in size, isolation and internal social relationships, so that any similarity to a townscape was, as it were, accidental. This is also true of mining villages in Durham, as shown by Dr. MARTIN, though they might be larger than many towns so described. Somewhere, the village makes the transition to 'town-hood' but this threshold was hard to define. For Dr. PAHL, there was some doubt whether the adoption of urban living forms itself constituted urbanisation, and he shot off a quiver of quotations. 'Is "urbanisation" the way that one suburb or one village coalesces with another? Is it a change in the "way of life"? Do people's fertility patterns change when somehow the density of their houses increases? Does "place" have a fundamental sociological significance?' Professor KÖLL-MANN's remarks about some of the Ruhr settlements bore this out: urban habits, urban industrial occupations, even urban architecture—but not necessarily towns. As Mr. C. HARRIS, in a long and spirited *exposé* of the Swansea valley insisted, that 'although being industrial, these settlements were unquestionably villages rather than towns'. In other words, a static analysis did not yield satisfactory results. Dr. HENNOCK suggested that it was partly a matter of concentration, partly of scale: both density and size entered into the matter; and Professor SCHNORE, quoting from American authors, added 'heterogeneity'. But however many examples of precedent were added, we did not succeed in producing a test by which any settlement could be identified as 'urban' simply from a still photograph, so to speak. One speaker after another said, in essence: a town is a way of life, and we know when we feel we are in an urban environment. (There was a strong warning, from Dr. HENNOCK, though, not to take middle-class criteria of environment and amenity as the yardstick of urbanity— a mistake usually made by architectural critics when looking, for instance, at new towns.)

The same difficulties were encountered in static attempts to define a 'suburb' —as opposed to the edge of the core settlement—as shown in Dr. REEDER's, Professor SCHNORE's and Mr. WESTERGAARD's discussion of the suburb in terms of the journey to work. If we say that a 'suburb is an area from which people travel to work by public or private transport to central city areas', we are in difficulties: some people work in suburbs in which they live, some commute in the reverse direction, some *walk* to work in the city, some retire there. There were many different labour markets in a large city like London. Some suburbs have a separate existence although physically indistinguishable (as in Mr. FREEMAN's description of some parts of the Manchester conurbation) and others are individuated only by courtesy of the boundary-drawers. The suburb, Dr. DYOS pointed out, had to be defined in dynamic terms: 'there is', he said, 'a constant shift in the spectrum, and you want really to find terms which you are ready to give up when the place changes its character.'

The consensus of this part of the discussion was that two ways had emerged in which urban areas may be classified more meaningfully than by tying labels to them which are soon shown to be inadequate. The first way is to differentiate places by building a kind of continuous hierarchy with respect to some important characteristic, and to identify them by their positions in different rank orders. This may be done in relation to size, to industrial significance, to their importance as a labour market, the distances people travel to or from the settlement, or any other variable. If Bolton has a distinct place, as Mr. FREEMAN insisted, in the hierarchy of 'separateness', Münster in Westphalia, in Professor KÖLL-MANN's description, is the only large town in his area without a significant industrial base. (At the other end of the scale would be a town which has nothing but industry.) From such evaluations, it seemed, there emerge multiple labels, which enable us to produce a topographical, occupational, or social differentiation making each place at once unique in its combination of descriptions, and 'typical' of a number of others which have similar characteristics in respect of a single chosen variable.

The second useful approach is through the dynamics of town growth (and decline). Instead of labelling a place only by its eventual function, or its topographical characteristic at the time of its foundation, we learn to draw composite (but nevertheless comparative) pictures by taking the process of town building over time. One could begin with the problem of the nucleus, as in Dr. MARTIN's classification—mining centres tied to a geological peculiarity, rural mixed economy outposts of urban trading centres, deliberate plantations started by employers drawn by considerations irrelevant to town makers into building their mills in a particular place, and so on. This is in most cases reasonably easy, though once again one has to beware of successes. Everybody seemed to be able to explain, as the CHAIRMAN said, why Birmingham is where it stands to-day; except that when one really begins to examine the supposed topographical advantages, they are seen to have been possessed, when Birmingham was only a village, by other places in the vicinity, and in much greater measure.

From the nuclear definition, one comes to growth-rates, directions, agencies. Inertia is a recognised growth factor, and 'inertia towns' can be identified. That is to say, no special advantages were added to those which dictated the original foundation, and may even in time have become irrelevant, but growth continues for lack of any obviously suitable and cheap alternative. Speculators played their part here, and where they were successful, like the colonies of the manufacturers, we applaud their foresight, but need not believe that their initiative was a 'sufficient cause'. We were reminded that growth is not automatic, and may in some cases be deliberately hindered, even before the days of planning. Swansea wished to remain non-industrial, and grew mainly for commercial reasons, and Professor KÖLLMANN demonstrated what can happen to a town like Iserlohn which refused to have the railway when it was offered, and thus became a backwater. Without commenting on their general significance for town growth in the nineteenth century, Dr. KELLETT suggested that the railways could also blur our view of what was really taking place. He challenged the idea that because a city can be shown in a series of maps as 'spreading outwards like an inkblot, it *is* growing outwards', and suggested instead that suburban railway stations were opened in what he called 'a nucleus of people who are already there'. Growth, then, is partly a matter of factors over which developers have control, and partly those which are given by situation and natural resources.

It became clear that if one looks at urban growth over time, it also becomes easier to come to terms with the demands of the sociologists that we should define the urban peculiarity in terms of human reaction to environment. By following the evolution of a settlement, we can perhaps more clearly say that at a given point in history it was still a village-type community (leaving aside the question of what is characteristic of the village) and that at some specified later date it had become a town. This is what we call urbanisation—and though Dr. PAHL thought that this word was redundant, he clearly meant to convey by this only that we need not use it if all it means is that there is recognisable social change in an agglomeration. It remains a useful term if we mean by this that a certain place has accomplished the transition from the village-type community to an urban-type community.

Although the earlier part of the discussion had necessarily touched on this point, it was only a little later that the meeting finally faced the question whether there were not important differences precisely on this matter between the various sorts of social scientists: how they would recognise urban forms if they saw them evolving. This is a subtly different problem from that of what constitutes a city legally or in a hierarchy of places: it means identifying a set of urban characteristics (like community, cohesion, heterogeneity, density) in relation to a particular place, when all the accidents of industrial form, topography, and administrative law conspire to make it difficult to recognise the common phenomena. The way the question is put is clearly sociological: but geographers and historians were able to demonstrate that they were familiar with the necessity to clarify the issue. Mr. WESTERGAARD thought it was confusing to try to distinguish between historians' and sociologists' definitions of urbanism; he pointed instead to a distinction applying to both, namely that between definitions for 'operational purposes' and those which ultimately result from a study of this 'multi-dimensional phenomenon . . . which there is not much sense in trying to reduce to a single thing' any more than there was in 'trying to arrive at a single definition of class' because one had set out to analyse class structure.

Recognition of a set of categories in a given situation does not preclude some differences in method. To Dr. PAHL, the 'actual physical form of a settlement is a confusing issue', a remark prompted by the spectacle of Yoruba settling in urban agglomerations in Nigeria, and peasants in southern Italy living together in nucleated settlements far from their fields. To a geographer like Mr. FREEMAN, however, physical form is not at all confusing; it determines relationships. It is really a matter of a starting point. It was clear that the social geographer examining the Yorkshire valleys would expect, given apparently similar forms of production, that social relationships would vary according to the lines of physical communication. If, on the other hand, one begins by looking at a community and one measures the degree and type of social cohesion encountered (e.g. by discovering, as Dr. THOMPSON reminded us, whether there was a *Gemeinschaft* or a *Gesellschaft*), then one inevitably regards physical characteristics only as one element in a whole series of determinants which are all interlinked and none of which can claim primacy. The Marxists present did not insist that forms of production were the only or even principal determinants of urban community structures. And political scientists would certainly find (as Dr. MARSHALL reminded us in relation to Lancashire) that the combination of topography, economic system, and accompanying social structure would determine political attitudes and, ultimately, the form of political organisation, from trade unions to county councils. Equally, the sociologist could retort that these political institutions in their turn are a significant determinant of later social structures. However, none of these processes are ever 'one-way'. Professor KÖLLMANN showed how important centres of political power can become industrial concentrations, and thus achieve even greater significance (Berlin, Düsseldorf) when people in England might have thought that, after 1832, it was economic importance which led to a redistribution of political power.

It seemed that this discussion left the historian, *qua* historian, un-moved: he would not expect any single growth factor to be paramount in the chain of causality, or identifiably deserve the accolade of chronological primacy. Their attitude was that whilst it is trite to say that all causes inter-act, it is only good sense to show that the communal life of a highly-developed country like Great Britain is far too complex to allow itself to be resolved into a few simple sets of pressures and responses.

It emerged from these discussions between the makers of many different types of systems that there was no conflict between the desire of some to establish recognisable categories and that of others to prove the uniqueness of each place and event. There was room for both. Almost every mention of a town produced the response that there was another just like this—or if not absolutely alike then similar in some important respect—whilst clearly unique with some other criterion in mind. The 'place' itself was often no town from the Municipal Calendar, but a hamlet, a suburb, a central area, or some other part of a whole. As Mr. WESTERGAARD pointed out, in a town a metropolitan structure may co-exist with surviving villages round the core, all within the same boundary. In his own words, 'There is a co-existence of different patterns, not only in the city or the town as a whole, but differently for different sections of the population, so that the working-class experience of urbanisation and of different segments of the working-class at different stages of that process, would be quite different, say, from that of the middle or the upper classes.' Equally, if Greenwich

Village is unique, Jane Jacobs has shown that there are many places with all the separate identity of a Greenwich in other American cities, even though these have nothing else in common other than that they are palpably different from their host communities. Mr. Carter's chapel-based Welsh villages are clearly something nobody would ever mistake for anything else, topographically, sociologically, ethnically. But as economic units, in their poverty, their lack of attraction for anyone except those tied to them by birth or occupation, of their suffering in adversity, they are like thousands of other such villages elsewhere and therefore the social responses to outsiders, for instance, are likely to be parts of larger categories.

Even the familiar stereotype of John Bull as a countryman looks different in a larger comparative framework. The chairman drew attention to the Englishman's moral and intellectual objections to the town and the rural imagery and tangible forms it had generated. 'The example of the Eisteddfod is to me a very mild example of our pretentious rurality; we bring up our children on a diet of the Bible, Shakespeare and the pastoral poets; we never have conceded the fact that we have industrialised. What is the semi-detached house except the desperate nineteenth-century attempt to try and maintain an outlook on your own plot of ground?' However, the flight, from the town into the suburb, then beyond the rim into the country and eventually back into the sham rurality is not peculiar to England. Nor is anti-urbanisation as such. What Dr. PAHL called 'the declining commitment to the City' was evident in Professor KÖLLMANN's account of recent German movements: in search of a better environment, people leave towns. This is not a question of 'back to the land' but rather 'forward to a happier life'. The same may be observed in the emergence of the *pavillonaires* in an area which is as highly committed to urbanity as the Paris region. The peculiar price-support structure which derives from a high value being placed on the survival of agriculture, and therefore rural life forms, is common to Britain, Germany, the United States, and other countries.

The discussion had not tried to settle in any final way the logical complexities of urban historiography, though the questions raised in considering comparative methods had exposed a number of them, and thus anticipated the final session of the conference. The subject was turning out to be rather similar to urban sociology, and in the end the most important areas left for future research and discussion were precisely those which have recently become the main preoccupations of many different kinds of social scientists. The term 'structural differentiation' was not apparently used in discussion, but the concept was present. The mobility of social groups, their segregation by physical area, the formation of new social and political organisms to meet the needs of these separated populations—these are the structural differentiations which underlie the process of urban change and give scope for the comparative approach.

To describe this process, to measure it, to draw categorical conclusions from it—this is no small research task. The conference produced, at least, some useful bricks for the total structure, and perhaps sharpened some tools. No single approach was dismissed as being useless. Narrative or statistical analysis, urban archaeology or migration model-building—all these will be used. City, West End, Suburb, Nucleus, Industrial Village—the words have no unique meaning, but this does not deny us the right to make use of them. At the end, one came away with the feeling that what was needed was more of the same kind of work, more exchanges between students of different disciplines, more challenges to others to explain their meaning, or to support their hunches derived from literary sources by references to hard figures. Urban science in the United States is probably more highly developed than in Britain, but the total knowledge of our urban past accumulated by our historians is not negligible in volume, and the authors of some of the most detailed urban historical studies who were present made it clear, in this session, that they are not incapable of hypothesising or of sorting complex phenomena into neat categories. What they stoutly refused to do, and this seems entirely to their credit, is to be forced into a common mould by accepting certain concepts as possessing universal application. This would not have been justified, on the evidence of our diverse experiences. The final impression which remains is that there is probably no one system, however intricate, which will meet all cases, but this is no excuse for failing to put the comparative study of urban history on a much more systematic footing. Towards this goal the fifth session made some contribution.

D. E. C. EVERSLEY

VI

Nineteenth-Century Towns—
A Class Dimension

John Foster

'It must always be kept in mind that the social war is avowedly raging in England; and that whereas it is in the interest of the bourgeoisie to conduct this war hypocritically under the disguise of peace and philanthropy, the only help for the workingmen consists in laying bare the true state of things.' ENGELS 1845[1]

'It is however to be considered ... whether the state of Oldham is likely ... to be at any future time better able to do without a military force than at present; and also whether, it being deemed advisable that such a force should be kept there, it is not highly expedient that that force should be such a one as under any possible circumstance would be able to act in an efficient manner and act at all events to protect itself against such a body of people as might in the event of serious excitement be poured upon it. ... The force now in Oldham I look upon as totally inadequate. ... Two companies of infantry never exceeding 120 men would be placed in a very trying and dangerous predicament in such a town.'
   MAJ. GEN. BOUVERIE, 'The defence of Oldham', report to Home Secretary, 21 July 1834[2]

A WAY OF COMPARING TOWNS AS A WHOLE

This paper puts forward a method of comparing nineteenth-century English towns; comparing them in terms of the class consciousness of their inhabitants. This, it will be argued, provides a way of comparing them as a whole—not just bits of them (birthrate, street-plan, council composition). *As a whole* (or nearly so) because the degree to which labour was politically and socially united very largely determined a

---

[1] *Marx & Engels on Britain* (Moscow, 1962), p. 248.
[2] Bouverie—Home Office, 21 July 1834 (HO 40/32/214–225).

community's mass social structure—housing and marriage, language and politics. *As a whole* because class consciousness or labour fragmentation refers to a community reaction to the essential nature of contemporary English society; a reaction to it as a structured, politically-endorsed system of economic inequalities.

A comparison on these lines must involve working out the local implications of the country's total social make-up; and coming to grips with the incompleteness of the town as a social community. To start with, then, it is worth restating the basic characteristics of nineteenth-century England. English society was organised along class lines: in other words, there was a gross 'unfairness' in the way opportunities of social success were distributed—with the country's underlying economic organisation placing the real interests of the privileged and the non-privileged in long-term opposition. More particularly, the underlying organisation was capitalist: so the structural unfairness involved the inheritance of accumulated capital (or the means of production). In addition, English capitalism was imperialist: the continuation of an industrial economy depended one way or another on the subordination of other economies (thus introducing a critical inhibition into any mass movement produced by the class situation).

Wherever a man lived, and whatever the particular economic make-up of his community, this was the over-riding political reality he had to face. And, equally, though social reactions differed, they were all designed to solve in some way the problem of having to live in a capitalist society. Anyone without capital had to come to terms with the knowledge that socially he counted for nothing; and, even more difficult, that there was nothing he could do—at least within the law—that would make the slightest difference. Success meant capital: to the worker obviously because it meant physical well-being; to the men with capital (and the power that went with it) because they had to justify their authority *socially*. But the essence of the system—the inheritance of accumulated capital—meant that socially (in the rewards it held out) capitalism contradicted itself. Society, to use R. K. Merton's term, was 'anomic'—there was a 'disjunction between culturally defined goals and means'.[3] Or, as people said more forcefully at the time, capitalism turned men into 'things'; in terms of capitalist society labour could have no meaningful social (or human) existence.

This was the basic social organisation—all too fixed and solid. In contrast, the ways people reacted differed a great deal. And attempts to accommodate and live with social 'unfairness' (and the variants of

[3] R. K. Merton, *Social Theory and Social Structure* (New York, 1965 ed.), pp. 131 *et seq.*

behaviour this entailed) were, of course, quite as much the product of a class society as labour solidarity and class consciousness. The grouping of such reactions into some sort of typology has been a major preoccupation of social scientists (both non-Marxist and Marxist) for the past generation; developing a dimension of community reactions from total accommodation to total rejection—isolating the variables that disposed a community to a particular place along the dimension. The results provide the historian with what is potentially a very powerful comparative tool.

The way people reacted (labour fragmentation or solidarity—in effect, the community's social structure) depended on their social consciousness; and it is important to stress its straight political content. When and where there seemed a strong chance of overthrowing the whole system (which could only be very infrequently), labour had good reason to become conscious of itself as a class, and act politically as such. More usually, when capitalism seemed immovably permanent, class consciousness became irrelevant, and labour was socially fragmented.

Before going on to look at class formation in particular towns, it would be useful to examine the reaction to capitalist permanence (as the typical capitalist social structure) in slightly more detail. It was described by Engels as 'the social division of society into innumerable gradations, each recognised without question, each with its own pride but also its inborn respect for its 'betters' and 'superiors''.[4] This type of reaction (sometimes called a 'status system' to distinguish it from the 'caste system' developed by the unfree labour of feudal-serf societies) protected people from irrelevance within society at large by allowing them to build up smaller sub-cultures with their own small-scale versions of success. Consequently, to avoid disruptive comparisons, the members of each sub-group had to have roughly the same life-chance, and, thus, the same type of job, income and pattern of expenditure. Place in society (or social function) fixed each group's identity—an identity in terms of the existing order. Each group had its 'pride' but also its 'respect'. The church-and-king labourers carried their branches of oak; the sailors their 'loyal standard'; the clerks their paper collar 'gentility'. Each group also defined itself *against* other sub-groups—particularly groups with lower incomes or those prevented by race from properly identifying themselves in terms of the existing order.

The immediate task of this paper is to suggest reasons for the diversity of community reactions within mid-nineteenth-century England; and methods of measurement. The following section will sketch the back-

---

[4] Engels-Sorge, 7 December 1889 (*On Britain*, p. 568).

grounds to labour politics in three very different towns; and the last section will discuss variables and their measurement.

LABOUR IN THREE MID-NINETEENTH-CENTURY TOWNS

1. *Oldham*

Oldham parliamentary borough was formed in 1832 out of four industrialised Pennine townships six miles east of Manchester: Oldham, Chadderton, Crompton, and Royton. The area's population ran: 4,000 (1714), 13,000 (1789), 21,000 (1801), 50,000 (1831), 72,000 (1851). Industrialisation went back to the mid-eighteenth century when weak apprenticeship and rapid population growth made it profitable for merchants to promote outwork production successively in wool, hatting, and cotton. The area also had coal.

By 1851 two thirds of the borough's 40,000 labour force was employed in cotton, coal, and engineering. All three industries had been fairly fully capitalised, and control was concentrated in the hands of a small number of families—most of whom combined interests in more than one industry. Over three quarters of the cotton workers were employed by 60 firms with over a hundred hands (mean labour force 240); 80 per cent of the engineering workers by three big firms; and almost all coalminers by one combine or the subsidiaries of cotton firms. This structure ruled out any chance of a man working his way into the employer group; and there was certainly no chance of marrying in. Nor was there much mobility during the period of factory-building: a survey of early firms shows only one manual worker coming up—the rest, predictably, were small landowners switching over from outwork manufacturing. In fact, land and (critically) coalownership restricted large-scale operations to the tight group of families who, as yeomen manufacturers, had been in at the mid-eighteenth century beginning.

Thus at mid-century there were 12,000 worker families selling their labour to 70 capitalist families. The capitalist families were very rich—annual incomes ranged between £3,000 and £10,000—and most owned estates in other parts of the country. Incomes of worker *families* ranged from £50 to £100—insufficient to keep any but the top 15 per cent of high-paid craft workers *permanently* out of primary poverty.[5] One worker child in five died before its first birthday. One female mill worker in seven died while in the age group 25–34 (mostly of TB). One miner in every five

[5] Poverty survey: earning potential and consumption minima (1851 census schedules) with variable wages, prices, and employment simulated for 'normal' times (Summer 1849) and 'bad' times (Spring 1847)—using the Rowntree poverty line as modified by Bowley (A. L. Bowley, *Livelihood and Poverty* (1915)). No account is taken of secondary poverty.

could expect to be killed during a normal working life. Up to 1850 mill hours were never much below 12 a day, six days a week. Nor could the system guarantee even this minimal existence. There were regular periods of mass unemployment—sending the proportion of families in primary poverty at *any one time* well over 40 per cent. This was the class situation with which people had to come to terms.[6] For the first 50 years of the century their reaction was to fight it.

It is not easy to give a satisfactory assessment of class formation in the small space available. Probably the best thing is to document the success of working-class leaders in getting hold of local government—an operation that manifestly demanded mass organisation, and, in terms of union control of poor relief and police (especially during strikes), was of critical importance for working-class living standards; and also brought headlong conflict with the state.

The working-class leaders ought first to be defined—they were something more than plain trade-unionists or friends of the poor. Right through from the 1790s to the 1840s Oldham possessed a coherent and stable group of social revolutionaries, linked to a succession of national organisations, frequently in prison, and working for the overthrow of the existing pattern of ownership and production. These were the people who directed the 'social war' in the Oldham area and whose activities in 1834 ultimately forced Bouverie to evacuate. In the early 1790s these revolutionaries were a minority and could be persecuted.[7] The military and economic disasters from 1795 on reversed the position and by 1801 gave them a mass following.[8] By 1812 they had captured control of Oldham vestry, and at least by 1816 of the subsidiary northern township of Royton; and thus got their hands on police and poor relief (which, with expenditure running at around £5,000 a year, was a useful source of political influence).[9] Similar trends in the country at large provoked the 1818 Vestry Act imposing cumulative voting by ratable value and the 1819 Act requiring

---

[6] It is obviously not possible to list in detail the sources used in this and following analyses—the most important are discussed in the last section of the paper. Any doubts about the social consequences of Victorian capitalism can be quickly set at rest by a glance at contemporary estimates of national income distribution; at actuarial tables giving workers half the life expectation of a 'gentleman'; or just at the annual reports of the Registrar General—which (looked at in human terms) have something of the enormity of mass graves.

[7] Rowbottom Diary (Oldham Public Library) especially 4 January 1793 and 21 April 1794. Samuel Bamford, *Early Days* (1849), pp. 45–8.

[8] Rowbottom, 29 May 1797, 20 May 1800, 3 May 1801. Hay-Pelham, 7 June 1801 (HO 42/62): captured papers show Oldham United Englishmen with a paid-up membership (including Lees) of 426—also enclosed is a fragment of the Crompton subscription list.

[9] Chippendale-Fletcher, 23 April 1812 (HO 40/1/1). Fletcher-Becket, 14 September 1816 (HO 42/153). Chippendale-Fletcher, 23 March 1818 (HO 42/175).

poor relief to be managed either directly by magistrates or by select vestry.[10] Neither act shook working-class control in Oldham.[11] In 1821 the crown revived its right to dispense with vestry elections and appoint constables direct through the hundred court leet.[12] This gave the authorities nominal control over the police, but left them unable to prevent the vestry blocking funds. In 1825–6 a local act was put through parliament enabling commissioners to levy a police rate—and fixing the minimum commissioner qualification of £60 ratable value.[13] This 'police commission' functioned as intended for five years, and then the working-class (using large-scale intimidation) again got control, and cut the town police down to size.[14] In 1832 the caucus was able to put Fielden and Cobbett in parliament without much trouble.[15]

The 1830's saw the crest of the wave. The police were neutered, and the experience of the military (especially in 1820, 1826, and 1834) made commanders reluctant to commit any but impossibly large detachments to garrison duty. As a result, there was no help nearer than Manchester or Rochdale, and the unions could safely act as 'schools of war'; wage rates from the 1820s were significantly higher in Oldham than Manchester.[16] In 1838 the caucus felt confident enough to appoint the secretary of the spinners' union as secretary of the poor relief fund (a man who had been an organiser of the 1812 fighting and was held on treason charges in 1817 and 1819).[17]

From then on, however, working-class power declined—the whig 'reforms' were beginning to take effect. In March 1841 police recruited under the 1839 County Constabulary Act (and controlled by the Lord

10 58 Geo III c. 69 (3 June 1818). 59 Geo III c. 12 (31 March 1819). At a mass meeting in Ashton-under-Lyne on 15 May 1818 the proposed 1818 bill was attacked as 'a death-blow to their rights and privileges—that now what was called a gentleman would gain no less than six votes'. Thackeray-Fletcher, 16 May 1818 (HO 42/177).

11 To avoid magistrate control of relief a select vestry was formed in April 1820. The unionists still controlled the annual elections. *Manchester Guardian*, 20 October 1821. First Report, Royal Commission on the Poor Laws, 1834, *Parl. Papers*, 1834, xxviii, Appendix A, Part I [*Reports from assistant commissioners*], pp. 909a–19a.

12 *Manchester Guardian*, 20 October 1821. The inhabitants appealed to King's Bench without success. *MG* 24 November and 1 December 1821.

13 7 Geo IV c. 117 (26 May 1826). Hobhouse-Collinge & Lancashire (cotton manufacturers), 26 February 1827 (HO 41/7): 'Mr. Peel is glad to find that the workmen have again returned to their labours and particularly that the provisions of the New Police Act have had so good an effect in accelerating that desirable event.'

14 *Voice of the People*, 19 February 1831.

15 The caucus maintained a fairly close supervision over its MPs. See especially Knight (secretary to both the Oldham spinners and the Oldham Political Union)—John Fielden, 21 January 1835 (I am indebted to the late Professor David Owen, Harvard, for transcripts of this and other letters).

16 Eckersley-Hobhouse, 19 September 1826 (HO 40/21/523).

17 *Manchester Advertiser*, 31 March 1838.

Lieutenant) were brought in to break a colliers' strike.[18] The Act of 1842 transferred all police to the control of the magistrates, and the same year a permanent military garrison was established.[19] 1842 also saw 33 local leaders arrested on sedition charges.[20] In 1847 the new Poor Law was finally introduced with its cumulative voting, secret ballot and *ex officio* magistrate guardians (the new secretary to the board was also, neatly, secretary to the cotton employers' association).[21] That year for the first time the working-class failed to carry the parliamentary elections. In 1849 the supersession of the 'corrupt' police commission by a corporation did away with the last stronghold of popular government.[22]

To make sense, the sketch needs to be filled out a bit. First, how did the working-class get hold of local government? Right through voting was restricted to property-owners; which in Oldham largely meant shop-keepers. These shopkeepers were dependent on working-class custom, and 'exclusive dealing' or blacklisting was the method used to bring them to heel. Three quotations will show this worked. The first comes from the preface to the 1832 poll book. 'When this trust was conferred upon them [our electors] it was unjustly withheld from you who possess superior claims to it—who are they who do not earn their bread by the sweat of their brow? . . . We are well aware it is in the interest of the shopkeepers to uphold the cause of the working-classes—but the question is, are they resolved to do this? . . . The great majority of this portion of society ranked themselves on the side of tyranny. What guarantee have we for their future better behaviour? I'll tell you . . .' And the writer goes on to list shops to be blacked.[23] The second quotation comes from an 1834 military report. When the vestry disallowed barrack expenses, Bouverie inquired whether the 'delegates of the class of shopkeeper voted this way out of hostility to the presence of the military, the answer was "they darst not vote otherwise." '[24] And the third dates from 20 years after the breaking of Oldham's working-class when Platt (the MP owner of the largest machine works) still felt frightened enough to speak out for the secret ballot. 'For many years the small shopkeepers, for fear of violence,

[18] 2 & 3 Vict c. 93. Butterworth Diary (Oldham Public Library), 5 March 1841.

[19] Arbuthnot-HO, 12 December 1842 (HO 45/268). Barker-Graham, 29 June 1843 (HO 45/350). Parish Constables Act, 5 & 6 Vict c. 109.

[20] The arrests continued spasmodically all Autumn. *Manchester Advertiser*, from 27 August to 19 November 1842.

[21] R versus Overseers of Oldham (10 QB 700), 29 May 1847. Oldham Poor Law Union Minute Book 1847–50, 22 September 1847 (Lancs. Record Office).

[22] PRO PC 1/851, 852, 853, 855.

[23] *William Spier, Member of Oldham Political Association, A List of the Voters in the Borough* (n.d.) (OPL).

[24] Bouverie-Phillips, 11 August 1834 (HO 40/32/234).

had had to place in the windows of their houses the names of the candidates for whom they intended to vote, and sometimes pickets were actually stationed to stop customers. . . . This was what was done by those turbulent and unscrupulous men who formed the minority of operatives . . . and who were at the bottom of all strikes. . . . He believed the Ballot would have a conservative influence because it would . . . take away the power possessed by small sections of the working classes.'[25] All this nicely reveals both the strength and weakness of the Oldham working-class. The method used to influence elections provides a foolproof demonstration of careful direction and organised *mass* allegiance. But the power had to be gained by proxy and used within the legal forms. In the same way that local trade-unionists had to keep their demands within 'competitive reason', so the politicians had to operate inside the system. And their efforts to break the system (intensified during the ruling-class counter-attack of the late 1830s and 1840s) were hamstrung by the contradictions of national leadership and policy that could not, in the broader circumstances, be avoided.[26]

So Oldham's working-class cannot be seen as a properly mature class movement. But it came very near. Certainly it was a great deal more than 'boss politics' or short-term political trade-unionism. The feeling of class is unmistakable. A frightened coalowner of 1817 describes a mass meeting of colliers and cotton workers—making their point with a timeless menace that could come as much from twelfth-century France or 1925 China. A journeyman mechanic had got hold of a loyalty declaration by the 'principal inhabitants'. 'The signatures he read over one by one with a considerable pause betwixt each of them. This pause was filled up by some sort of indecent remark accompanied by a characteristic gesticulation . . . all the most respectable people in the town for character and property were made the subject of public derision.'[27] When people laugh off a lifetime of caste and subjection, they risk a great deal, and will only do so when the old sanctions seem to have failed altogether. The essential pre-condition of class consciousness is that people *think* it possible to change things. Though all the national movements failed, and had to fail, they can only be understood while it is remembered that for fifty years people believed themselves on the brink of a new age. 'The people are in a most insubordinate state, and set the law at defiance. Out of 92 summons issued

[25] *Hansard*, ccvii, c. 612 (26 June 1871).

[26] Fielden was especially aware of these contradictions—the difficulty of reconciling his own demand for the state regulation of industry (wages and investment as well as hours) with the country's dependence on foreign markets and commodities. See his important speech *Hansard*, xlvi, c. 805 (18 March 1839).

[27] Chippendale—Sidmouth, 10 February 1817 (HO 40/10).

for 17th July [1819] only three of the parties appeared—they damned the constables and told them that in three weeks their day would be over.'[28] An old Oldham cotton worker remembered 1848. 'The near prospect was that of the monarch dethroned and all her dependents and followers ... in headlong flight to escape the vengeance of an oppressed and vindictive people. This is no fancy sketch; it is a fair picture of the wandering day-dreams of the whole body of what were called the working classes forty years ago.'[29]

In this sense, even though national revolution had repeatedly to be cried off, it remained a reality. And locally the explosion of popular con-sciousness that this sustained produced a critique of capitalism that cut pretty near the bone. Here is the Oldham's spinners' secretary in 1834. 'Your employers seem to know no way of meeting a declining market but that of getting more work out of you and paying you less wages. . . . It is high time for all English workmen to awake ... and no longer be driven along the road to ruin by their blind employers. . . . We must learn to look beyond the improvement of our own particular branch of business. . . . and improve the whole body of English labourers. . . . With this view we ought to ascertain the *intrinsic* value of labour; for until we have learned that it is impossible to ascertain to what extent we are robbed of the fruit of our labour.'[30] And four years later the following resolutions were passed at a mass meeting of Oldham workers. 'That labour is the source of all property; without a surplus of labour has been performed and property produced no accumulation of capital can take place. . . . That it is an indisputable fact that the various classes of capitalists have the whole power of making and administering the laws, which is almost uniformly done for their own benefit. . . . That the time has now arrived when Englishmen must learn to act instead of talk.'[31] It would be easy to go on—'the working classes should form a nation apart and govern them-selves'[32] and so forth. But the point to be made is obvious. The analysis of the Oldham workers was in terms of class; they were asking what was wrong with the community, and not how an interest group could better itself. Looking at Oldham, they saw the basic contradiction as capital and its inheritance. And they defined themselves as Labour—in an analysis that could only make sense in terms of conflict and change.

This leads to the last and, from the historian's angle, the most important

---

[28] Chetwode (Ashton-under-Lyne recorder)—Sidmouth, 17 July 1819 (HO 42/189). The 'three weeks' doomsday was headed off by Peterloo.
[29] Benjamin Grime, *Memory Sketches* (Oldham, 1887), pp. 1, 81.
[30] John Knight reported in *Herald of the Rights of Industry*, 1 April 1834.
[31] *Northern Star*, 17 March 1838.
[32] Benjamin Harrop at Tolpuddle protest meeting. Butterworth, 27 March 1834.

aspect of Oldham's class consciousness. Working-class power depended on a solidarity that stretched to all sections of the labour force. The power, and the terrorism and blacklisting that went with it, was real enough. But it needed organising. Keeping hold of local government and fighting off the employers meant something near semi-permanent mobilisation. The network of control had to penetrate every corner of working class life—union, factory, shop, and beerhouse; and, to maintain it, the solidarity slogan had to be banged out incessantly. The great, traditional divisions of an English working population were, for the moment, suspended. In 1834 a mass meeting demanded the elimination of wage differentials and the levelling up of labourers' pay.[33] The year before there had been a call for an end to coercion in Ireland.[34] And throughout the period a predominantly English population was willing to accept Irishmen among its leaders. The very fact of class formation meant that the controlling spell of the ruling-class had been broken, and, with it, the sub-group system by which people accommodated social 'unfairness'. Substituted was another system, just as coercive, but working in the opposite direction.

The effect is best appreciated comparatively. In the 1850's, after the breakdown of the organised working-class, there was a rapid expansion of Orange lodges; in 1861 serious Anglo-Irish riots; and from then on mass politics in Oldham largely hinged on the existence of two racial communities.[35] Again, broadening the comparison, marriages between the families of labourers and high-paid craftsmen were far more frequent in Oldham than in Shields (which had no class conflict) and slightly more frequent than in Northampton (where it was very partial).[36] The other side of the social distance coin tells the same story. Shields possessed a highly-developed hierarchy of occupational neighbourhoods; in Oldham this segregation and sub-grouping does not appear to have existed at all.[37] For more than a generation, the social structure of Oldham's very diversified labour force—clerks, labourers, engineers, schoolteachers, spinners, and small shopkeepers—seems to have remained significantly open.

2. Northampton

At the beginning of the century the town had two functions: supplying fine living for the county's landowner aristocracy, and an interim market

[33] Butterworth, 27 March 1834.
[34] Butterworth, 21 February 1833.
[35] *Oldham Chronicle*, 15 July 1854; 8 June 1861; 13 July 1861.
[36] Marriage certificate analysis: all marriages taking place within the registration districts of Oldham, Northampton, and South Shields between 1846 and 1856.
[37] Reply to Royal Commission on Health of Towns (1842) questionnaire (draft at back of South Shields Improvement Act Letter Book 1829–48—Town Clerk's Office, South Shields).

for farm produce. By 1830 a third function had been added. The crisis of rural overpopulation flooded the town with cheap labour (the population jumped from 10,000 to 26,000 between 1821 and 1851) and provided the basis for an industrial sector. By 1851 almost half the labour force was in the shoe industry. Production, requiring no fixed capital, was organised on garret-sweatshop lines, and London merchants mostly supplied the credit and made the profits.

As a community, therefore, Northampton had none of the tight completeness of Oldham: ultimately almost everyone's boss lived over the horizon. Nor had it the simplicity. The three sectors produced tory hoteliers and lawyers (together the pre-1835 corporation); whig-dissenter corn and wool dealers; and radical garret-masters. Along these lines élite politics were set rigid. The lack of a real bourgeoisie and the three-way split in the town economy also had its effect on class. Northampton was not without poverty: the proportion in primary poverty was, if anything, higher than in Oldham; the death rate from TB almost as bad, and from typhus and scrofula worse; life expectation for males at the age of five was identical. But class formation was slight, and what there was had a tame, sheet-lightning quality about it.

'Working-class' leaders there were—duly in contact with a succession of the national associations: London Working Men's Association, the Charter Association, the Reform Legaue; then, right a bit, to Bradlaugh; and finally back left to the Social Democratic Federation. But their influence was restricted to one ward: the West. This had the lowest proportion of households with votes or servants, and the highest proportion of shoemakers, multi-generation families and country immigrants. Even here, the population was by no means solid, and there was never any attempt to practise exclusive dealing.

The language of this 'working-class' reflects its unfortunate background. There was no critique of capital; many leaders were garret-masters and small employers. Targets were the aristocracy, the establishment, and the Church; or, when the mob broke out of the West ward slums, just the rich. In a sense, Northampton's 'working-class' politics remained those of an occupational sub-group—not of labour as a whole. The ruling-class never lost its grip (the town had a barracks and the surrounding countryside was thick with aristocrats); as a result the 'status' system held up. Workers in the other two sectors—shopmen, coachwrights, furniture-makers, and brewery workers (mostly better-paid anyway)—remained deferent, anglican, and hostile.

And even within the shoemaker sub-group it would certainly be arguable that the politics were largely irrelevant to the immediate situation.

Most shoemakers had come in from the surrounding countryside—forced out by unemployment and poverty. Here, in the closed, authoritarian villages, the realities of the class situation bit deep (1830 and the burnings and killings of 1843–4 were one answer). The men that ran the system were clergymen—many doubling the job with landowning; and, not surprisingly, most Northampton shoemakers clenched their fists when they saw a priest.

All these problems and pre-occupations are conveniently summed up in a note from the secretary of the Northampton WMA to the 1839 Chartist convention:

> 'We are struggling hard against many obstacles from the combined influence of whigs, tories, sham radicals aided by all the power of the priests who . . . have hung the terrors of the world to come before the view of their deluded votaries to prevent them co-operating with us.'[38]

3. *South Shields*

As in Northampton, the men who commissioned the work lived outside. Half the labour force was organised round shifting coal to London for the profit of Durham landowners: a quarter were seamen; 10 per cent. shipbuilders; and as many again keelmen, dockers, provisioners, and sailmakers. But there were two important differences. First, there was no permanent economic split in the town élite; largely as a result of the way the shipping was owned. There were two-hundred ships (mostly 300-tonners carrying crews of six or so) distributed among 150 owners: small men—tradesmen, provisioners, shipbuilders—who had invested their savings. This, for a start, gave almost all Shields' trade a common overlap. But interests were tied even closer by the half-a-dozen interlocking insurance and broking clubs that formed a kind of unofficial town senate. This background effectively prevented the rigidity that marked Northampton's élite politics; and political, and even religious, allegiances were notoriously short-term. The structure of shipping ownership also meant that admission to the town's élite (small-time and threadbare though it was) was comparatively easy.

The second big difference (taking in Oldham as well as Northampton) was the absence of work for women and children. In the other towns additions to family income from this source largely made up for pay differentials between men. In Shields the difference between the way a

---

[38] James Robertson, 9 April 1839. Chartist Convention Minutes, Vol. I, f. 225 (BM Add MSS 34, 245A).

shipwright and a labourer could afford to live stood out sharply—in fact, labourers' families had little chance of ever rising above the poverty line (with all that this meant in terms of total pauperisation).

Class formation had, therefore, small scope in Shields. There was no resident bourgeoisie, admission to the town élite seemed easy and the labour force was socially fragmented. There were certainly bad strikes (keelmen, shipwrights, seamen); but the conflict remained strictly economic. Neither delegate nor national rent was sent to the 1839 Chartist convention. During 1839, '42 and '48 Shields, in contrast to the surrounding mining areas, remained quiet. What 'working-class' activity there was took two forms: Chartist rallies organised from Newcastle which brought out the whole town (including the shopkeeper-shipowners)—and to which O'Connor predictably talked about the union of the middle and working classes.[39] Or the sectarian activities of a small group meeting in a waterside pub, and never getting much more for their pains that a couple of inches in the *Northern Star*.[40]

SOME LOCAL VARIABLES AND THEIR MEASUREMENT

The three communities just examined all formed part of the same capitalist society; and did so in roughly the same way—as medium-size industrial towns. Yet their 'social structures' were strikingly different: extreme class consciousness in Oldham; extreme fragmentation in Shields; with Northampton somewhere in between. The previous section was intended as descriptive—sketching in the contexts of these different responses. But the business of description inevitably also involved some degree of explanation, and two general factors have already emerged: the structure of the élite; and the occupational make-up of labour. This section will attempt to pinpoint these factors more precisely; explain why they, particularly, should be important; and suggest methods of measurement. To do this, it is first necessary to make a rough examination of how capitalism in general maintained its social equilibrium, and the ways in which this equilibrium could be disturbed.

1. *Capitalist equilibrium: authority and crisis*

As a social system, capitalism ultimately rested on the military power of the state: the defence of property and the enforcement of contract. In addition, capitalism could also claim the more immediate sanction of being the going economic concern on which everyone depended. Together these gave capitalism its apparent dead-weight permanence. But there

[39] *Northern Star*, 26 June 1839.
[40] *Northern Star*, 20 November 1841.

were also powerful factors working the other way. Socially, capitalism contradicted itself: it operated to the long-term benefit of only a minute proportion of the population, and denied the rest meaningful social existence. Economically as well, capitalism had its contradictions—the most important probably being its imperialist dependence on other economies, and its consequent vulnerability to military defeat. What was the precise *social* manifestation of these conflicting forces? How did the ruling-class sustain its authority within the community? What was the nature of the working-class challenge?

First, ruling-class authority. The most important instrument of mass control seems to have been provided by the sub-grouping process itself. Sub-grouping was, in essence, the way people accommodated social 'unfairness'—by creating small-scale success systems of their own. From the angle of social control, sub-grouping also had a more strictly political side. Sub-groups, to start with, had to define themselves within the existing order—partly in terms of economic function and partly by how far their members could afford to imitate ruling-class spending and behaviour. Sub-groups, in addition, had institutions and leaders, and the men with authority held it fairly directly from the ruling-class: either directly by legal or political arrangement, or because they could claim successful bargaining 'influence'. The sub-group leaders acted, then, as link-men in the overall political system; and the sub-grouping process, besides allowing people to accommodate deprivation, functioned as an authority system by which labour could be tied politically to the ruling-class.

The working-class challenge also derived structurally from capitalism's social contradictions—but more directly. Some people experienced social 'unfairness' in a way that made accommodation impossible: men who had suffered long unemployment; men whose families had suffered class injustice; men who had succeeded within the 'peer system' at school, and then found themselves irrevocably classed as labour in a capitalist economy. Men like this would remain inescapably class conscious, and would find it very difficult to acquiesce in the acceptance of ruling-class values which sub-grouping involved. For them, to use Merton's terminology, the only meaningful social existence would be 'rebellion' or 'realistic conflict'—not 'ritualism' or 'withdrawal'.[41] This group formed the social base of the 'working-class challenge'. So long, however, as capitalism seemed secure and permanent (and the mass social relevance of sub-grouping remained), the political position of this working-class could

[41] Merton, *loc. cit.*

only be marginal. In favourable circumstances, they might hope to direct mass economic conflict in which the interests of capital and labour were visibly opposed—but overall their influence would remain strictly industrial. *Socially*, they were committed to spotlight precisely those social contradictions that people generally were trying to avoid; and *politically* to a policy demanding some sort of class confrontation that was mmediately unrealistic.

The real threat to ruling-class authority came from outside the social structure—though not from outside the system as a whole. Economically, capitalism was prone to instability and crisis. Long-term instability concentrated attention on economic issues in which the conflict between capital and labour was obvious, and gave 'working-class' leaders the chance to seize initiative within labour sub-cultures. Crisis (economic collapse or military defeat) could bring even more dramatic change. On the one hand, defeat or collapse discredited the ruling-class (and, with it, the sub-group proxies); and, on the other, broke the "inevitability" spell of the whole system. At such times, class unity might replace sub-grouping (or labour fragmentation) as the socially relevant mass response—producing a 'revolutionary situation'.[42]

Socially, then, this was the pattern of conflict. There was the 'normal' equilibrium in which the working-class group was insulated from mass influence by the sub-group authority system. Against this, there was the historical dimension of economic change and crisis that could produce a meaningful context for working-class action. With this rough model of capitalist equilibrium in mind, it may be easier to talk about the purely local factors in the equation. Why did class consciousness develop in some English towns and not in others? What factors in a town's economic make-up could prevent working-class leaders taking full advantage of a particular historical situation?

2. *Local context: labour's occupational make-up*

From the earlier descriptions of the three towns it seemed that the differences in occupational make-up had considerable impact on 'working-class' influence. This purely occupational factor seems to have been given its political relevance by the way it affected a town's sub-group structure—by whether or not it made for one or more than one labour sub-culture. A 'single sub-culture' town might develop in a number of situations: where there was only one basic occupation (the isolated mining town, for instance); where the overall differential between male earnings was small;

---

[42] Cp. for a dynamic relation of politics and social structure J. H. Goldthorpe & D. Lockwood, 'Affluence and the British class structure', *Sociological Review* (July 1963).

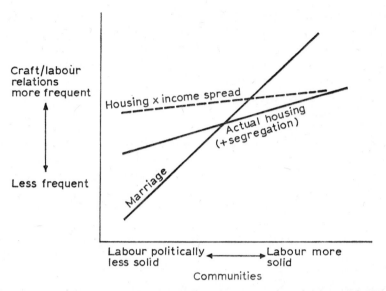

FIG. 16. *Marriage and neighbouring relations between craft and labourer families.* Graph of postulated association between two types of relationship within more and less class-conscious communities.

or where (when there was a larger differential) there was also work for women and children—which allowed semi-skilled and labourer families to level up their incomes. Communities like this presented one way in which a 'working-class' group might acquire *social* influence. With just one sub-culture covering the whole labour force, it was much easier to identify it on some issues *against* capital, and give the working-class critique a social (and not just industrial) foothold. When, on the other hand, the community had a number of labour sub-groups—each defining itself against the others—it would be very difficult to identify one sub-culture in particular with conflict phrased in terms of labour as a whole. In this way, a town's occupational make-up could partially predetermine the political success of its working-class leaders.[43]

What methods are available for measuring this? The first step might be to compare differences in life experience among the general spread of labour families: family structure; housing; poverty—which can fairly easily be done by a punched card sample of census schedules (used in

[43] Erik Allardt, 'Patterns of class conflict', *Trans. Westermarck Soc.* (1964). N. Dennis, F. Henriques, and C. Slaughter, *Coal is our Life* (1957). K. Newton, 'British Communism: sociology of a radical political party', Cambridge Ph.D. dissertation, 1965 (on Welsh mining towns).

conjunction, if possible, with rate-books, and wage and employment data). This, taken comparatively with results from other towns, should show which towns were most *likely* to have an unfragmented labour sub-culture. A census sample, however, cannot show whether a town did, in fact have a socially less fragmented labour force than its neighbours; nor whether this was the result of occupational make-up or of purely political factors.

Luckily, complete information survives for all English towns from the 1840's on the two most important aspects of social distance: who married whom; and who lived next to whom (this potentially very exciting material has so far hardly been used at all). The marriage frequencies between occupations provide a way of discovering whether labour was, in fact, socially fragmented. Marriage within stable capitalist societies takes place within sub-groups. If a town's labour force was split (by occupation) into a number of sub-groups, the town would show up by having a lower frequency of marriages between 'top' and 'bottom' occupations (e.g. between craft and labour) than one where this was not so.[44]

The big problem, however, is the second one. How far was sub-group structure, at a particular historical moment, the simple result of occupational make-up, and how far is one also measuring (as one very probably is in Oldham) the social results of political solidarity—the effect of class consciousness itself? The most helpful solution here is to compare the frequency of *marriage* between occupation with the frequency with which these occupations lived together as *neighbours*. Housing-neighbour frequencies (conditioned by the spread of housing rents) would take into account family income differences. Thus, in a politically class conscious, non-sub-grouped community (where there was no additional element of segregation) the neighbour frequencies would stand for the absolute rock-bottom economic basis to labour's social structure. An inter-town survey would then show whether marriages between labour occupations were, or were not, more frequent than neighbouring relations where labour was politically solid.[45] This, in effect, would make it possible to see if mass class consciousness did have actual *social* results (at least locally); and thus make it possible to isolate the social contribution of a town's occupational makeup (see diagram opposite).

[44] The calculation follows (in reverse) the procedure used by J. Berent in D. V. Glass (ed.), *Social Mobility in Britain* (1954), pp. 321 *et seq.* For the three towns the index of association between craft and labouring occupations stands at 80 in Oldham (5,500 marriages used); 77 in Northampton (3,100 marriages); and 69 in Shields (3,100 marriages) (100 = unity). Similar use of marriage material has been made by T. Geiger, 'Soziale Umschichtungen', *Acta Jutlandica*, 1951; and by Charles Tilly, *The Vendée* (1964), pp. 93-9.

[45] For the relation of marriage and housing see J. M. Beshers, *Urban Social Structure* (New York, 1962).

3. Local context: élite structure

Elite structure, like occupational make-up, also takes its political relevance from the impact it had on the 'working-class' bid for mass support. Elite structure could, it seems, increase or diminish the local plausibility of the working-class social critique—simply because social 'unfairness' was less obvious in some towns than others. The usual reason was that the people who owned the capital and made the profit lived out of sight. Engels developed his concept of a 'resident bourgeoisie' to account (in part) for the differing reactions of workers in Manchester and Birmingham: militant in the former and passive in the latter. Manchester had a resident bourgeoisie because the social distribution of wealth was a fair reflection of the distribution for the economic nation; in Birmingham it was not.[46] Of the three towns examined, the two with the strongest sub-grouping and the least labour solidarity seem also to have had the most primary poverty. But while mid-century Shields and Northampton each had less than a dozen men who would leave more than £25,000 personalty, Oldham had over seventy; and many of these would leave a great deal more than £25,000. In Shields and Northampton several men who passed as influential at mid-century had started out in a small way; in contemporary Oldham none. If a town's top people were not 'well-bred' men of property but garret-masters who started out (and remained) working-men, then a man's picture of his own chance would not be so unfavourable (to society or himself) as it might be otherwise.

The distinction between élite and bourgeoisie (comprehending as it does the incompleteness of the local community and its relation to the larger structure of the national economy) is plainly very important. By itself, of course, the presence or absence of a bourgeoisie could not make the difference between labour fragmentation or solidarity. But where the bourgeoisie was absent the logic of sub-grouping could be made much more credible: 'success' *within* the community plainly could not derive directly from the critical capital-inheritance contradiction of capitalist society. Still more important possibly, the absence of a bourgeoisie broke the immediate, visible dependence of wealth on labour.

Finding out whether a town possessed a 'resident bourgeoisie' (or just a holding company for somebody else) presents its problems. And there seems no easier solution than a fairly intensive study of the ownership, markets and profits of the main industries and a sample of the town élite running to several hundred individuals. The sample is especially difficult.

In the absence of any census of wealth, the only sure way of getting all

[46] *On Britain*, p. 233.

the wealthy families is to spread the net very wide: industrial and merchant firms, professional men, tradesmen, magistrates, and guardians—even, perhaps, every census household with two or more resident servants. Once the sample has been set up, there remains the still more painful task of collecting the facts. The first thing, probably, is to identify the rich and the not-so-rich: probate, rates, and company records; then to examine social mobility to see precisely how industrial structure affected life-chance; and then social distance (frequency of marriage between élite occupations) to see whether or not there actually existed a capital-owning group that cut itself off from the rest of the community. This, given the facts, should be enough to establish the existence or non-existence of a bourgeoisie.

After all this, however, the proof of the pudding must still be in the eating. Did the people show themselves conscious of their class interests? Was the town, like Oldham, unable 'to do without a military force'? Or did it show all the signs of 'accommodated deprivation': race riots, 'model' unionists, and poverty churches? Here, the evidence can only be documentary: home office papers, poll books and pamphlets, the working-class press, diocesan visitations, trade-union, and local government records.[47]

Together, analysis and plain description should make it possible to put most towns somewhere on the class dimension. But it ought to be remembered that the causal factors can vary in time within towns as much as between towns, and that towns can change their characters. In the early 1790s, while Oldham employers could still hire thugs to break up working-class meetings, the people of Shields were planting the Liberty Tree. And at the beginning of the twentieth century, when the tory-imperialist Churchill was MP for Oldham, the SDF were winning local elections in Northampton.

---

[47] The relation between relative deprivation and ethnic conflict is examined, among others, by J. H. Robb, *Working-class Anti-Semite* (1954). Marx's analysis of the ethnic split in the English working-class can be found in Marx-Meyer, 9 April 1870 (and following letters) *On Britain*, pp. 550 *et seq.* Relevant studies of ethnic sub-culture are made by John Dollard, *Caste and Class in a Southern Town* (Yale, 1937) and elsewhere. For labour sub-culture, there are interesting descriptions of modern American textile communities in Liston Pope, *Millhands and Preachers* (Yale, 1942); J. K. Morland, *Millways of Kent* (New York, 1958); and Robert Blauner, *Alienation and Freedom* (Chicago, 1965).

Society and Politics in Exeter, 1837–1914[1]

R. Newton

Victorian Exeter in many respects was not a Victorian city. It scarcely experienced the 'pressure of rapidly increasing numbers of people' and 'the social consequences of new industrial techniques and new ways of organising work'.[2] That the city had missed the economic tides was recognised in Exeter itself. In 1881 a local newspaper regretted that 'we do not grow, simply because the process of growth, as a city, ceased many generations back'.[3] Exeter's surge of urban growth on something approaching the Victorian scale had in fact ceased before the Queen came to the throne. Leicester and Exeter each started the nineteenth century with a population of some 17,000. By the end of the period the population of Leicester was over 200,000, that of Exeter just over 40,000.

Exeter's Victorian history is the record of the survival of a society which still clung to the habits and traditions of provincial, pre-industrial, and unurbanised England. Social standards were derived from the County, from the gentry and clergy, the professional men and cultured tradesmen who could write articles on local history, archaeology, and science. The city's last major buildings denoting faith in progress and civic pride were erected in the closing years of the old unreformed corporation—the Chamber.

It was inevitable, therefore, that throughout the Victorian era, as the Liberal *Western Times* put it in 1868, 'The respectability of the city (was)

---

1 This paper is based on material which has been included in my *Victorian Exeter, 1837–1914*, since published (1968) by Leicester University Press.
2 Asa Briggs, *Victorian Cities* (1963), p. 18.
3 *Flying Post*, 27 April 1881.

undoubtedly Tory.'[4] And in reporting for the Royal Commission on Secondary Education, of 1895, an assistant commissioner commented caustically on the need to enlist the support of individuals of 'aristocratic or quasi-aristocratic position' before new ideas could be accepted.[5] There were signs of belated economic growth and social change in the early years of the twentieth century; but in general Exeter was a small, compact, deferential society where, as an artisan complained in 1871 'a man could not express his feeling . . . as he could in large towns; if he did he became a marked man.'[6] This remains broadly true today.

The population consisted of retired people and professional men, clergy, bankers and merchants, shopkeepers and artisans. Exeter lived on the business brought by its position as a county capital and a cathedral city, as a centre of communications and distribution and as the gateway to the West. There was no opportunity for fortunes on the grand scale. Estates over £100,000 were derived from private banking, the only apparent exception being a brick and tile manufacturer who died in 1906 leaving £120,000 in personal estate. According to the local probate records moderate fortunes of between £30,000 and £80,000 in personal estate were accumulated by a select group which included lawyers, brewers, licensed victuallers and hotel proprietors, goldsmiths and silversmiths; a doctor, church furnisher, horse-dealer, auctioneer and valuer; tea, coffee, and spice merchants; and a draper.

The essential conservatism of a compact and small society is demonstrated by, amid much else, the political history of the city. The city council was firmly divided on political lines from the outset and was controlled by the Conservatives for sixty-four years out of seventy-seven between 1837 and 1914. The Municipal Corporations Act itself aroused no strong opposition. The leading Conservative newspaper urged that the opportunity should be taken to ensure 'a practical and good system of municipal government'.[7] The Liberals acquired a tenuous control of the council from 1837 to 1840, their programme being largely one of 'purity' of government, economy, and staunch opposition to what they termed 'The Odious Impost of a Borough Rate'.[8] The Conservatives' domination began in 1840. In 1881 discontent with what was described as 'the band of political jobbers who (had) for so long controlled the municipality,'[9] and objections to rising expenditure, secured another fleeting period of

---

[4] *Western Times*, 20 November 1868.
[5] *Royal Commission on Secondary Education* 1895, vi, p. 88, report by Mrs. Armitage.
[6] *Western Times*, 24 February 1871.
[7] *Exeter and Plymouth Gazette*, 12 September 1835.
[8] *Western Times*, 17 February 1838.
[9] *Western Times*, 30 July 1880.

Liberal rule. In 1883 the Conservatives regained control, which they maintained till 1900.

In 1900 the whole council retired following the inclusion within the municipal boundaries of outlying areas and the consequent rearrangement of the wards. At the ensuing elections the Conservatives were virtually annihilated, only ten being returned out of forty-two councillors. The Liberals came in once more on a programme of economy and as a protest against a party which had ruled Exeter overlong. The rates continued to rise. In 1908 Exeter returned to its normal Conservative equilibrium.

In the field of parliamentary politics the two-member system which applied to Exeter until 1885 normally ensured the representation of the strong Liberal minority whose core was Nonconformity. In the ten parliamentary elections between 1832 and 1880, excluding by-elections, ten Conservative and ten Liberal members were returned. Eight elections returned one member of each party. Two Liberals were returned in 1868 and two Conservatives in 1874 by small margins of thirty and sixty-six votes respectively. In 1885 Exeter was demoted from two members to one; and in the eight parliamentary elections between 1885 and 1910 Conservatives were returned on seven occasions. Exeter went Liberal in 1906 by a small majority which was in part due to the fact that the Liberal candidate was an aberrant member, politically speaking, of a neighbouring Conservative County family. The second election of 1910 resulted in a dubious Unionist victory after an electoral petition.

Viewed from the outside Exeter appeared a homogeneous society. The city was small and neighbourly. Seen from within, it was deeply divided by religion and by the more subtle distinctions of social and economic status. These were the divisions of the small market town rather than of the 'Two Nations' of *Sybil*. None the less these divisions assumed abiding political form. Socially and economically the city consisted of circles which sometimes touched and sometimes overlapped. Each circle had distinct social values. It was never quite respectable to be a Liberal or a Nonconformist. In contrast, conservatism and membership of the Church of England conferred respectability on men whose claims were at times somewhat dubious. Merchants and shopkeepers, lawyers and medical men, the bankers and the clergy formed exclusive groups.

In 1857 the social division between trade on the one hand and the gentry and the professions on the other caused a revolt within the local Conservative party. In that year a businessman came forward because, he claimed, 'a great number of constituencies were seeking to be represented by gentlemen who were acquainted with commercial pursuits.'[10]

10 *Western Times*, 14 March 1857.

He received the backing of the Conservative political boss, the builder Henry Hooper (1794–1868), who was mayor at the time. The citizens of Exeter were exhorted to refuse dictation 'by a few proud gentry' in the choice of their representatives.[11] The new candidate was in due course elected without, as one newspaper accurately explained, 'the assistance of the respectable members of the party. Squires, bankers, and doctors kept aloof from him.'[12]

This was a revolt against that section of the Conservative party which moved on the fringes of the County. The new member was distinguished largely by wealth and mediocrity and in due course the higher social circles of the party re-established remote control. But the incident was an indication of usually suppressed social jealousies which became evident again in 1889, significantly enough over the election of a banker as mayor. On that occasion the Liberal spokesman in the council was moved to charge the Conservatives with hostility to the 'trading classes' who, it was alleged, were 'held up to derision, scorn, ridicule, and scoffed at'.[13]

The Municipal Corporations Act of 1835 was followed by the gradual withdrawal of 'the respectable members' of city society from activity in local political life, a withdrawal which did not involve a surrender of political influence. Before the Act, social position and membership of the Chamber were in great measure coterminous. For a few years they continued to be so; the two circles then drifted apart even though individuals, especially lawyers, formed a connecting link.

This assessment of social and political forces is supported by the local sources which provide a detailed picture of the interplay of politics and social and economic status. Until 1868, they are sufficient to provide a detailed analysis of the political expression of status. These records include

(1) Local reports of the elections of July, 1831, and December, 1832, immediately before and after the Reform Bill, and of the elections of 1835, 1864, and 1868. These reports give the name, occupation, and vote of each elector.[14]

(2) The city council's minute books.

[11] Election poster in Sheriff's Records: Exeter City Archives, Box 2.
[12] *Western Times*, 28 March 1857.
[13] *Flying Post*, 9 November 1889.
[14] Details of the elections of 1831, 1832, and 1835 are to be found in the *Exeter Itinerary and General Directory* (1831); H. Besley, *Exeter Directory, 1833*; H. Besley, *Exeter Directory, 1835*. The election details for 1864 and 1868 are in *The List of Persons in the Borough of the City of Exeter who voted or were entitled to vote at the Election of a Member to serve in Parliament to fill the vacancy caused by the death of Edward Divett Esq.* (1864) and *A Complete List of Persons in the Borough of the City of Exeter who voted or were entitled to vote at the General Parliamentary Election* (1868). All are in Exeter City Archives.

(3) The declaration books of aldermen, councillors, auditors, and assessors.

(4) Guides and directories, particularly the *Exeter Pocket Journal* from 1791 to 1877 and Besley's *Exeter Directory* from 1828 onwards.

(5) The contemporary newspapers, i.e., the *Exeter and Plymouth Gazette*, Conservative, orthodox Anglican and for long priding itself on its treatment of social and educational problems; the *Flying Post*, Conservative, Evangelical and aimed at the farming community; the *Western Times*, Liberal, sometimes Radical, and consequentially sympathetic towards Nonconformists.

By using these sources it has been possible to analyse the occupations of members of the Chamber in 1835, the last year of its existence, and of the council in 1837, 1848, 1868, 1899, and 1900. An analysis was also made of occupations during three representative periods 1837–46, 1868–77, and 1896–1905 involving 91, 96, and 105 individuals respectively. The local reports do not always give the occupation of the elector. In 1831, for example, the occupations of 31 out of 1,125 electors were unspecified; in 1868, 1,186 out of 4,917. The directories are not always helpful and it is not always easy to be sure which of several identical names is the one required. Formal council records often lack precision, as in the description 'merchant'.

A further pitfall lies in the description 'gentleman'. Gentlemen or gentry in the restricted sense acceptable to Jane Austen's Sir Walter Eliot of Kellynch were few, mostly retired people or members of County families who were also freemen. Inclusion in the 'Nobility, Gentry, and Clergy' section of the directories did not necessarily imply gentility by the standards of the time. The use of 'Esquire' in place of 'gentleman' sometimes distinguishes between a lawyer or a retired businessman and a member of a County family. But Henry Hooper (1794–1868) who, 'for something like a generation—was an immense influence in the city', appears as builder when voting for the Liberal Edward Divett in 1831. Having acquired wealth and influence he appears under the designation of Esquire in 1868 when voting for the Conservative candidate. The great majority of those described as gentlemen were professional men or 'higher tradesmen', active or retired. The point is of some importance since the votes of two 'Esquires' for a Conservative candidate cannot necessarily be accepted as an example of the Conservative sympathies of the County.

To correct misrepresentation by the directories or electoral reports recourse to the massive volumes of the contemporary Exeter newspapers is essential. The reports of social gatherings and dinner parties, of hospitality at country houses and balls, advertisements and the records of public meetings, the epithets and descriptions applied to individuals, all these present the leading citizens in the round, as figures of vigorous flesh and blood, and assist us to correct the over-simplification of voting lists and directories. The defect of the newspapers lies in their bulk. Nevertheless they provide material which enables certain conclusions to be reached and if there are mistakes in, or omissions of, detail, their general validity is unlikely to be affected.

Religious differences were a decisive dividing line in society and politics with the Nonconformists voting Liberal and the Conservative party wholly composed of Anglicans. It had been an offence to Dissenters that none was admitted to the Chamber despite the repeal of the Test and Corporation Acts. Nonconformists were prominent in the ranks of the Reformers before 1835. Issues such as church rates, educational policy, and the drink question, kept the Nonconformists Liberal: when Liberal parliamentary candidates were unable to satisfy 'tender consciences' the latter were inclined to abstain, to the embarrassment of the Liberal High Churchman, John Duke Coleridge, whose defeat by a narrow margin of twenty-six votes in the by-election of 1864 was ascribed to the abstention of a few leading Nonconformists. The religious aspect of politics in Victorian Exeter can be summarised for the whole period by the election of 1852 when out of thirty-four Anglican clergy who voted only two voted Liberal. These two were denounced in the Conservative press as 'standing in the same ranks as Soccinians, Chartists, Jews, and Baptists'.[15] None of the Nonconformist clergy voted Conservative.

Exeter's Liberalism was not of course exclusively Nonconformist. Its outstanding leader, the solicitor Mark Kennaway (1794–1875), was a member of the Church of England. Kennaway was characteristic of that earnest band of Utilitarian Radicals who, in Professor Finer's words, 'cried out for efficiency, comprehensibility, and uniformity'. In his view church rates were the product of 'the dark hours of superstition and ignorance'. Men like Mark Kennaway had integrity but little vision. Kennaway's last appearance in Exeter's affairs was to protest against the council's assumption of the powers of the Improvement Commissioners under the Local Government Act of 1858.

The newspapers and the local election reports demonstrate that the licensed trade and allied activities such as hotel keeping were predominantly Conservative before 1870, and overwhelmingly so afterwards. Thus in 1864 70 votes were cast by this group for the Conservative candidate and 45 for the Liberal. Some of the most ardent Reformers of

15 *Exeter and Plymouth Gazette*, 6 March 1852.

the 1830s held extensive interests in public houses. Two of the early Nonconformist mayors were wine and spirit merchants.

Professor Hanham has suggested that Sir Robert Ensor's description of the responsibility of the publicans for Gladstone's defeat in 1874 requires qualification.[16] But there can be no doubt that in the seventies and thereafter 'the trade' in Exeter threw its full weight against the Liberal parliamentary candidates. Two partners in one firm of licensed victuallers and brewers were mayors of Exeter at this time and one of these, Joseph Harding (1823–1908), was founder of the Exeter branch of the Licensed Victuallers' Association. A third partner, W. J. Richards (1828–1903), was the reorganiser of the Conservative party machine in 1868. In recommending him unavailingly to Disraeli for recognition Sir Stafford Northcote explained that Richards had 'done wonders in the way of party organisation down here.'[17] Joseph Harding, the senior partner of the firm, was mayor in 1871–1872. In the Exeter by-election of December, 1873, he was present at the Exeter meeting of the Licensed Victuallers' National Defence League which, a trifle ingenuously, 'strongly advised the trade to cast aside all party politics in the present contest and to unite their strength for the purpose of supporting a candidate who has shown himself to be a friend of the trade.'[18] Since the Dean also publicly supported the Conservative candidate in the 'best interests of some of our most sacred institutions',[19] the alliance between 'the Rits and the Vits' was more than an invention of Liberal political journalism. This alliance, which in 1873 secured the seat vacated by the Liberal Coleridge, went on to capture both seats for the Conservatives in February 1874. On Harding's death it was acknowledged that the Conservative Party owed 'a great debt for his lifelong though unobtrusive service.'[20] The service was not always unobtrusive.

The relations of the trade with the Conservative Party in Exeter were fostered during Richard's lifetime and continued after his death by men such as Robert Pople, who came to Exeter from Bridgwater in 1868 to acquire the New London Inn, and become a councillor in the following year. At Bridgwater he had been involved in allegations of electoral malpractices at the election of 1868, which had resulted in the disfranchising of the borough. Throughout his life the New London Inn was the headquarters of Conservative candidates and a centre of social and

---

[16] H. J. Hanham, *Elections and Party Management* (1959), pp. 222–5.
[17] British Museum, Add. MSS. 50,016, Northcote to Disraeli, 11 June 1874.
[18] *Flying Post*, 26 November 1873.
[19] *Flying Post*, 10 December 1873.
[20] *Flying Post*, 29 February 1908.

political activity. Pople's contemporary was Alderman Pring, a well-to-do brewer, president of the Exeter Working Men's Conservative Union, treasurer of the Conservative Association and active in the formation of the Conservative Constitutional Club in 1880.

The licensed trade may have been regarded as of doubtful respectability in a cathedral city, apart from its vigorous Conservatism. But the professions were undoubtedly respectable and were predominantly Conservative. In 1835 46 attorneys and barristers voted providing 29 votes for the Conservative candidate and 14 for the Liberal. In the election of 1864 33 lawyers voted for the Conservative Lord Courtenay and five for Coleridge. Doctors and surgeons on that occasion gave 25 votes for Courtenay and five for Coleridge. This, too, it must be assumed, was a voting pattern which persisted throughout the period.

To reach conclusions about the electorate as a whole is more difficult. The electorate was increased by the Reform Bill from about 1,125 to 2,333 including 586 freemen. The figures are necessarily somewhat loose because then, and for long afterwards, the parliamentary returns reproduced the totals of the local registers which included under different serial numbers individuals eligible in respect of several properties. The electorate was increased from 3,700 registered electors to 6,156 by the Reform Bill of 1867. By 1900 it was 8,700, including 65 freemen.

There was much argument prior to the Reform Bill of 1867 over the extent to which the working classes were represented. The term 'working class' itself lacks precision. John Bright would have excluded beersellers, cart-owners, and tradesmen with assistants. Stafford Northcote, who was well informed on Exeter, sought to refute the Liberal contention that the representation of the working class generally had declined from about 30 per cent to 26 per cent. He informed the House of Commons in 1866 that the number of workers on the register at Exeter was 660 and that there were 167 others who were working men 'to all intents and purposes'.[21]

Analysis of the local election reports of July, 1831, and December, 1832, suggests that in the former year about 365 out of an electorate of 1,125 were artisans (porters, gardeners, masons, carpenters, plasterers, and the like), labourers and small shopkeepers who may or may not have employed assistants. Labourers described as such numbered fourteen. In December, 1832, the working class electors may have numbered about 421 in an electorate of 2,333. Thirty-two labourers, seven of whom were freemen, voted in the Exeter election of 1835, providing 20 votes for the

21 *Hansard*, 3rd Series, clxxxii, 1827, 20 April 1866.

Conservative candidate and 20 for the Liberal. The labourer-freemen provided seven Conservative votes and four Liberal. Examination of the election of 1864 suggests that in that year the working class element numbered about 520—or close on 21 per cent—in an electorate of 2,486, a figure which, perhaps fortuitously, agrees closely with the 512 in the Parliamentary Returns of 1855–66.

The Reform Bill of 1867 undoubtedly substantially increased the working class element in the Exeter electorate. Labourers, for example, rose from the four of 1864 to 230; porters from three to 86. It was such men as these whose vote was successfully captured by the organisation of the Exeter Working Mens' Conservative Union in 1868.

By 1868 bakers, boot and shoemakers, carpenters, masons, gardeners, plasterers, smiths, and tailors numbered some 900. From these middle ranks of the electorate Exeter's Liberalism derived its basic support. In the election of 1864 the deferential vote of servants and waiters was Conservative; but bakers, boot and shoemakers, brushmakers, carpenters, smiths, tailors, hairdressers, grocers, and druggists were predominantly Liberal. The commercial travellers voted Liberal by 23 to three. The margins were usually small but so too were the majorities by which elections were decided.

With the introduction of the secret ballot the election reports so useful to the historian were no longer possible. Since, however, Exeter was stereotyped in its politics, it seems reasonable to assume that voting patterns remained the same till 1914.

If respectability ensured that the parliamentary expression of Exeter was largely Conservative, the same influence ensured the Conservative colour of the council without at the same time maintaining its social status. Both parties throughout the period deplored a fall in the quality of members of the council. The Conservatives ascribed this to the allegedly time-wasting practices of the Liberal opposition, the Liberals to corrupt practices and jobbery. More objective was the comment of the Conservative *Flying Post* in 1882: 'Years ago men of position, wealth, and leisure were proud to serve the public offices of the city, and the city was well served by them. But now the difficulty is to find men of position to have anything to do with public work.'[22] The *Flying Post*, however, offered no reason for this changed attitude.

In 1835, the last year of the old Chamber, eight out of 25 members were surgeons, including the mayor. Three were merchants. One was the actuary of the Devon and Exeter Savings Bank. There were one attorney

22 *Flying Post*, 8 November 1882.

and one banker; and one newspaper proprietor whose family history was considered worthy of comment in the *Gentleman's Magazine*. Five others had claims to be classed as gentlemen. The balance was made up of the postmaster, a former mayor, a leather dresser and glove manufacturer, and a hop merchant. All were Anglicans.

A fundamental consequence of the Municipal Corporations Act was the introduction into the council of Nonconformists. There were three Nonconformist Liberal mayors between 1836 and 1840. Significantly the first mayor of the new régime was a Unitarian ironmonger. The Act also enlarged the opportunities for lawyers. In 1837 five out of 48 members of the council were lawyers. There were 11—out of 66 lawyers in the city— in 1848; eight in 1868 and ten in 1899. The licensed trade, including wine and spirit merchants, brewers and hop merchants, numbered eight in 1837. Surgeons were on the other hand reduced to four. There were two bankers and two newspaper proprietors, one who had been mayor in the days before Reform and was to be mayor again. One newspaper proprietor was specifically mentioned by *The Athenaeum* in 1869 with the comment that Exeter press had been 'a credit to literature'.[23] The bulk of the council of 48 members was composed of boot and shoe makers, druggists, merchants and dealers in timber, candles and soap, grocers and ironmongers, builders, and watch-makers.

By 1848 four members of the Hooper family were on the council. Henry Hooper contrived to have a share in most of the important building contracts of his day. A rough, vigorous self-made man, called by his opponents 'the prince of jobbers', Hooper was the first since the Municipal Corporations Act to be elected twice as mayor. He ended his second term of office, in 1857, amid a storm of colloquy and was the only mayor who was not thanked, even perfunctorily, for his services. A vivid account of the Hoopers at work in 1847 was accompanied by the telling comment in the *Western Times* that 'It is well known that the self-styled aristocracy of the city grin and bear the Harry Hooperite rough-riding.'[24] He was virtually the Conservative boss of the city for the best part of a generation.

The withdrawal of the local 'aristocracy' began under the Hooper régime and was virtually complete by 1870. Hooper himself died in 1868. His régime was linked with that of the licensed trade, which followed from the fact that the founder of the Conservative Working Men's Union married the daughter of a Conservative councillor who had been jobbed into the position of city treasurer during Hooper's second mayoralty.

Throughout the whole of the nineteenth century the largest single

[23] *Athenaeum*, No. 2181 (14 August 1869), p. 203.
[24] *Western Times*, 6 November 1847.

occupational group on the council was that of the licensed trade, including wine and spirit merchants, hotel proprietors, innkeepers, and maltsters. These numbered 16 out of 91 members of the council in the period 1837–47 though they did not then provide leadership. In the period 1868–77 'the trade' numbered 15 out of 96 councillors and politically formed the dominant group on the council, a position which in general was retained till 1900. Lawyers took second place with 15 representatives in the first period and 12 in the second. Builders, auctioneers, surveyors and timber merchants numbered nine and 11. The lawyers maintained their traditional position into the new era. The council of 1899–1900 included eleven lawyers and there were still seven after the election for 'greater Exeter' in 1900. Sixteen out of 105 members of the council between 1896–1905 were lawyers. The representation of 'the trade' markedly declined after 1900. Builders, house agents and the like increased to 12 during this period when for the first time Exeter showed signs of relatively vigorous economic growth in terms of building activity.

The elections of 1900 were correctly regarded by contemporary opinion as a social revolution. Council meetings were henceforward held in the evenings for 'the men of the new class', men, complained the *Flying Post*, 'to whom the majority of the citizens would scarcely give a moment's thought in ordinary times. Faddists, extremists of all sorts, and men of parochial minds'.[25] The new mayor was a solicitor. His colleagues included a brass-caster, the first artisan to be elected to the council, a game dealer and poulterer, a pawnbroker, professor of music, and a railway official. The medical profession was reduced to one, the Conservative leader. With the revival of economic growth and the spreading streets constructed for artisans Exeter was moving into a new era. By 1913 there were two railwaymen on the council, one of whom was destined to be the city's first Labour mayor (in 1935).

Denunciations of the 'Junta' and 'Tory monopolists' formed the Liberal theme, with variations, from the 1840s until 1900. Builders, licensed victuallers, hotel proprietors and their friends managed the council when it was necessary to do so. But though they were admitted on occasion to the higher ranks of Conservative society they did not 'belong'. 'Some innocents without political guile,' remarked the *Flying Post*, 'might imagine that all business of the city is, or ought to be, conducted within the walls of the council chamber, but every man and woman of the world is aware that there must be informal discussion and consideration of various matters.'[26] Such discussions inevitably leave little or no

[25] *Flying Post*, 2 November 1900.
[26] *Flying Post*, 20 October 1900.

evidence. There are good grounds, however, for the belief that control at the top, and the intimate contacts with county society which were involved, were exercised through the banker Edward Sanders and his family.

Edward Sanders (1813–1905), a descendent of Sir Edward Courtenay of Powderham, Harrow and Oxford, county cricketer and keen rider to hounds, and devout churchman, was chairman of most of the committees of Conservative candidates for 60 years. He was also chairman of the directors of the *Exeter and Plymouth Gazette*, Treasurer of the Devon and Exeter Savings Bank and, among other duties, for 66 years a member of the Exeter School Trust. He nominated Sir William Follett as Conservative member in 1837 and more than 60 years later he was thanked for his services to the party when Sir Edgar Vincent was elected in 1899. When Exeter required a suitable mayor to entertain the ambassadors and aristocracy who visited the city for the agricultural show of 1850, Sanders was elected. Sanders and a fellow private banker were among those invited 'among noblemen and gentlemen' to stay with Lord Poltimore to meet the Duke of Beaufort in 1858.

The position of a private banker was assured in the social hierarchy. More equivocal, but as vital in the Exeter context, was that of the lawyers. The first lawyer to be mayor of Exeter, John Carew was, however, indubitably County. He was the nephew of Sir Henry Carew of Bickleigh, one of the oldest families in Devon. Carew presided over the Conservative 'Restoration' of 1840. The Iddesleigh Papers in the British Museum[27] reveal the world of the political attorney when John Daw (1803–84) of Exeter, mayor from 1853–55, Richard Brembridge of Barnstaple, and Riccard of South Molton, managed the politics of half Devon. Daw in his time was election agent for Sir Ralph Lopes, Lord Courtenay and Sir Lawrence Palk. His father had been in the service of the Tory magnate Lord Rolle. There was usually at least one lawyer on the city council with the social standing requisite for a link between city politics and the more withdrawn world of county politics.

The Conservative *Gazette* remarked with approval on the 'integrity, respectability, and habits of business' of the new council of 1836.[28] No such approval appears to have been bestowed on the council as a whole in subsequent years. After the enactment of the Municipal Corporations Ordinance the *Western Times* commented that 'it now behoves the people to reflect on the use which they intend to make of a measure which will confer so much power on them.'[29] A few years later the same paper

[27] British Museum, Add. MSS. 50,013–64.
[28] *Exeter and Plymouth Gazette*, 2 January 1836.
[29] *Western Times*, 12 September 1835.

was reporting on the voters at a municipal election who were brought 'in a state of beastly intoxication' to the poll.

In 1914 Exeter was still a survivor from pre-Victorian England. But as early as the 1840s the old pre-Victorian upper classes were withdrawing from open activity in the management of local politics and the process was complete when the generation who had held authority in the days before reform died in the 1860s. The realities of local politics were unattractive and remain so. The prestige once conferred by office in a virtually independent provincial capital dwindled before the assumption that 'all intelligence and honesty is centralised in London' as the Exeter council put it in a resolution of protest on 13 January 1859. By the last year of the nineteenth century the composition of the council suggests that it was composed in great measure of those whose business interests or involvement in the day-to-day work of politics required their membership, and of those few who carried into the twentieth century the Reformers' faith in economy and 'pure municipal government'.

Neither group represented what was described in 1857 as 'the self-styled aristocracy of the city'. The circles of social respectability and the council, almost exactly superimposed in 1837, now moved in different planes. Voting patterns, in so far as they can be surmised, were broadly the same, in the years before the first world war, as they had always been; but now that Exeter had at length been touched by the economic growth usually associated with Victorian England, there came signs of change. The first Labour candidates for the council stood unsuccessfully for election in 1892. Independent candidates were nominated, again unsuccessfully, by working men for the acknowledged genteel ward of St. Leonards in 1895. It was noted at the time that artisans' housing was being developed in the ward. The railways, fulfilling to some extent by 1900 something of the apocalyptic hopes they had inspired 60 years earlier, and the political organisation of the railwaymen, finally dissolved the habits and conventions that had survived from the time of William IV.

The Social Compositions of Borough Councils in Two Large Cities, 1835–1914[1]

E. P. Hennock

This study of local government in nineteenth-century cities is concerned with an aspect that has also recently become the subject of contemporary political inquiries. It is the problem of recruitment posed by the traditional system of local government in England, dependent as it is on the part-time service of unpaid and technically unqualified administrators, drawn from the inhabitants at large.[2]

For many centuries the chief burdens of local administration had fallen on the county. A system of appointment from above had confined the work to the economic and social leaders of the county community. The assured status of the position, no less than the power it conferred, had made the office of J.P. attractive to the leisured and educated class, without whose willingness to assume onerous duties the system would have broken down, as it did break down in eighteenth-century Middlesex.[3]

In the corporate towns the position of alderman and councillor had been even more explicitly associated with power and privilege, in the regulation of such things as tolls and markets, and had originally been occupied by the economic and social leaders of the community. In

[1] The material for the section on Birmingham was compiled with the help of Mr. J. D. Sykes, M.A. The author also wishes to thank the Leverhulme Trustees for the grant which made this work possible.

[2] L. J. Sharpe, 'Elected representatives in local government', *Brit. Journ. Sociology*, xiii (1962); A. M. Rees and Trevor Smith, *Town Councillors, a Study of Barking* (Acton Society Trust, 1964).

[3] For the Trading Justices of Middlesex and the problems of that county see S. and B. Webb, *The Parish and the County* (1906), Bk. II, Chap. II (b) and (c), Chap. VI (a).

numerous cases, however, where the means of appointment were closely controlled by the corporate body itself, there had grown up by the second quarter of the nineteenth century a rather different relationship between the Corporation and the economic and social leadership of the town, important sections of the latter being unrepresented in the former. The Municipal Corporations Act of 1835 introduced election by ratepayers into this situation as a new factor. Election is not in itself an obstacle to the recruitment of the leading citizens for the tasks of urban government. On the contrary, it was intended to produce a more complete representation of wealth and talent. We know that in the case of Parliament this was achieved and the economic and social leadership of the nation was represented, even if the various sections of it unequally so. Ever since the sixteenth century the attraction of a seat in Parliament had been such as easily to outweigh for those who could afford it the expenses of time and money, not to mention the inconvenience associated with the process of election itself. It cannot be taken for granted that the same was true of a seat on the municipal body of corporate towns. To what extent were municipal corporations in the age between the Act of 1835 and the outbreak of the First World War able to draw on the services of those most prominent in the economic and social life of the town? That is the question which I have attempted to answer for two of them. It is a question that does not lend itself to generalisation over the country as a whole. Even a superficial acquaintance with the history of local government shows that the answer has varied considerably from time to time and from place to place.

In the light of the contemporary debate over the inadequate recruitment of talent into elected local government bodies, it might have been better had I taken my studies up to the present day.[4] The scale of the task deterred me. There are also reasons for thinking that the subject had had an importance in the nineteenth century that it has subsequently lost, and that a concentration on the period 1835–1914 was therefore historically justified. This is due to two developments which are closely connected: the growing willingness of Parliament to impose compulsory duties on local authorities, and the growing power of Whitehall to determine and to enforce nation-wide standards of administration. The reliance, first on Local Acts initiated by and applying only to one locality, and subsequently

[4] 'I do not think that enough really able people are interested to-day in taking part in local government. I do not think that enough people from business, from industry, from agriculture and the professions are going into it. . . . Most people engaged or interested in local government agree . . . that the calibre of local government is not equal all round to its responsibilities.' Dame Evelyn Sharp, Permanent Secretary of the Ministry of Housing and Local Government, speaking at the Annual Conference of the Association of Municipal Corporations, 1960.

also on general legislation of an optional kind, had left the *initiative* in the struggle with the new urban environment with the localities themselves. In addition, prior to the creation of means whereby the central government could impose minimum standards on backward communities, the *determination of such standards* was almost entirely in local hands, for the courts were clumsy instruments of enforcement. This point is given additional force by the fact that the sphere in which the means of central control were given their earliest elaboration, i.e. the Poor Law, does not fall within the scope of this study. For these two reasons, i.e. initiative and the determination of standards, local authorities with the possible exception of Boards of Guardians played a rôle in the nineteenth century, which they have lost in the twentieth for all the multitude of their new duties.

One further point requires attention. It might be argued that, if the initiative and the standards of administration depended upon the personnel of local government, attention should be directed rather towards the salaried officials than towards the elected members. Again, such an argument carries more weight for the present day than it would have done for the earlier period. The employment of the salaried official by local authorities, which was still a rare and recent practice at the beginning of the nineteenth century, had become normal by the eighteen-sixties. But the distinction between the officials' responsibility for administration and the Council's responsibility for policy, which is nowadays endangered rather from the side of the officials, was then more likely to be infringed in the other direction. For instance, despite the appointment of a few inspectors of nuisances it was still assumed in the eighteen-sixties and early eighteen-seventies both in Birmingham and Leeds that the members of the Sanitary Committee had a duty personally to inspect the town for nuisances. One particularly zealous Birmingham Councillor died from an illness contracted during the course of duty. The growth of the occupation of town clerk, municipal treasurer, borough engineer, etc., as organised professions able to make their standards felt in relation to backward authorities was a much later development. As for the individual official, the extent to which he was an independent force in setting standards and laying down policy must have varied a great deal. Few towns would have been as much dominated by their Town Clerk as Manchester during Joseph Heron's exceptionally long incumbency from 1838 to 1887.[5] Since the choice of the official and his dismissal was in the hands of the Council, and the salaries that they were prepared to pay seem to have differed

5 Arthur Redford and Ina Russell, *The History of Local Government in Manchester* (1939–40), Vol. II, *passim*.

widely, it can be assumed that they frequently got the official they deserved. In 1857 Birmingham Corporation dismissed the ambitious surveyor, whom they had taken over on the winding up of the Street Commission, and replaced him at half the salary.[6]

Therefore, even when we take the rôle of the officials into account, it is clear that the elected personnel of urban local government played a crucial role in the period under review. The social changes that were turning England during the course of the nineteenth century into an urbanised society pushed those who chose to govern the large towns into the forefront of policy-making. The decisions made at the growing-points of this society were to affect for good or ill the physical and social environment of an ever-increasing proportion of the population. Such are the reasons for concentrating on the process of recruitment to local government in the largest towns of nineteenth-century England, and on the qualification of those who were elected.[7]

In studying the social composition of town councils I have paid particular attention to the occupation from which the personnel was drawn. In the first place I have tried to identify the owners, or directors, of businesses which in terms of the local economy at that time would be classed among the largest in the town. No one single criterion could be used to identify size, for none would have done justice to the diversity of conditions. Nor was it possible to take them all into account, for the information was too fragmentary for such a counsel of perfection. In many cases the numbers of employed were taken, in others the area of the works, in others the capital employed or the rateable value of the premises, where this was the only source of information, e.g. for a shop. Secondly I have looked for those at the other extreme of the scale, the small businessmen, whether shopkeepers, manufacturers, publicans, or small traders. By concentrating on the extremes and leaving a large undifferentiated middle it has been possible greatly to reduce the difficulty of classification. Inevitably there have been many borderline-cases, and these have for the purpose of this paper been added without comment either to the large or to the small category (except in Fig. 19). Thirdly I have looked for certain occupational groups, which either had a particular expertise to contribute or could be regarded as special interest groups— medical men, the drink interest, builders, and working-class representatives being the most important.

It is true of course that the remarks with which this paper has been

6 See below, pp. 321–2.

7 For a study of English County Government from a very similar point of view see J. M. Lee, *Social Leaders and Public Persons* (1963).

introduced point to the calibre of the Councillors as being the really important consideration. I am well aware that this is not really pinned down by means of an occupational survey. There are intangibles in this matter which are bound to escape the meshes of this procedure. As a writer on the contemporary situation has put it,

> 'such qualities as integrity, political nous, will power, judgement, local knowledge and so on—all would need to be taken into account in any realistic assessment of a councillor's calibre.'

But he adds,

> 'there are certain qualities which are clearly relevant to a councillor's functions and which are measurable. It may be reasonably argued . . . that a man who holds a position of executive responsibility in private life, or is used to making administrative decisions, or has had professional training, would on the whole be better equipped as a councillor than someone who wholly lacked this kind of experience, notwithstanding the fact that other less tangible qualities are important and that these are not the prerogative of any one occupation.'[8]

To this there should be added a more specifically historical point. I have argued elsewhere that before the introduction of massive Treasury grants the precarious financial basis of English local government meant that in the growing towns successful administration required among other things a marked flair for business, and that it was essential in order to achieve anything to be able to think *adventurously* about finance.[9] Hence the importance of certain kinds of business experience.

The rest of this paper will present in a highly condensed form the principal results of a study made of Birmingham and Leeds from the introduction of a reformed municipal corporation to the outbreak of the first world war. The statistical information on the composition of the Town Council is drawn from 12 samples. Eight of these were taken at decennial intervals, showing the Council in the January after the census year. Municipal elections were held at the beginning of November, and by the following January the election of Aldermen had been completed and bye-elections held to fill up the vacancies created thereby among the Councillors. The remaining four samples show the Council in mid-decade at 20-year intervals, i.e. in January 1836, 1856, 1876, and 1896. The first of these dates represents the first Council elected under the provisions of

---

[8] L. J. Sharpe, p. 204.
[9] E. P. Hennock, 'Finance and politics in urban local government in England, 1835–1900', *Hist. Journ.*, vi, No. 2 (1963), pp. 212–25.

the Municipal Corporation Act. (For Birmingham, whose charter was not granted until 1838, the equivalent date used is 1839.) Each of the samples for Leeds consists of 64 persons, while those for Birmingham rise from 64 to 72, except for the final year, when the creation of Greater Birmingham pushed the total up to 120. In addition there is a sample of 38 persons, being the unreformed Corporation of Leeds in 1835, the year of its abolition.

For both towns the ample material contained in the local historical collection has been used, supplemented by information drawn from Parliamentary Papers. In assembling the information on the economic status of the Birmingham Councillors I am heavily indebted to Mrs. Barbara Smith of the Faculty of Economics and Commerce in the University of Birmingham, who was compiling a detailed bibliography of the industrial history of Birmingham and placed her card index and her unrivalled knowledge of Birmingham firms unstintingly at my disposal. In consequence the statistical information on the size of firms there is fuller than anything that I was able to assemble for Leeds.

1. BIRMINGHAM

Birmingham did not possess a municipal corporation prior to 1838. The parish had been served by a Street Commission, and there were five similar *ad hoc* bodies for the outlying parts of the parliamentary borough. The petition for the grant of a municipal charter had been a controversial step taken by the politically dominant Radical Birmingham Political Union under the leadership of Thomas Attwood, banker and Radical MP for Birmingham since 1832.[10] The enthusiasm for it had been primarily enthusiasm for a representative institution as such, a voice to speak on behalf of the people and especially to petition Parliament. The charter did not lead to the abolition of the Street Commission or the other *ad hoc* bodies, which survived until 1851. The Birmingham Street Commission as the most prominent of the six, a body with rating powers but no system of election by ratepayers, continued to affront the instincts of the Radicals, who dominated the Council. Certainly until 1842, when doubts about the legal status of the Corporation were finally removed, it was the Street Commission which was generally regarded as the leading institution, representing the respectability of the town irrespective of party. The Town Council, on the other hand, at its inception mirrored faithfully the Radical party in the town, led by a few respectable bankers and merchants and consisting of the bulk of the small manufacturers and tradesmen, who gave

[10] Conrad Gill and Asa Briggs, *History of Birmingham*, 2 vols. (1952), and J. T. Bunce, *History of the Corporation of Birmingham*, Vol. I (1878), Vol. II (1885) are the standard works.

to Birmingham that peculiar social structure that since the days of Cobden
has been frequently remarked upon. There were no professional men on
the first Council, unless one counts a retired naval Captain as such, but
one banker and seven fairly large merchants, some of whom were respected
Whigs who had allowed themselves to be nominated by their Radical allies.
At the other end of the scale there were 35 owners of small businesses
making up about 55 per cent of the Council, of whom 24 (37·5 per cent)
were manufacturers.

In 1842 the position was hardly changed, but by 1852 the winding-up
of the Street Commission, and the transference of its important functions
in providing the environmental services of the town to the Council, had
had an effect on the composition of that body. The large businessmen,
both merchants and manufacturers, now numbered 10 (15·6 per cent) and
solicitors had made their first appearance, three of them. These two
elements between them made up 20 per cent of the Council compared
with 14 per cent in 1839, and there was a marked carry-over in personnel
from the Street Commission to the Council. The small businessmen
provided 37·5 per cent.

The years that immediately followed were dramatic ones in the municipal history of Birmingham. The 1851 Improvement Act had given the
Corporation extensive powers to provide the system of drainage and road

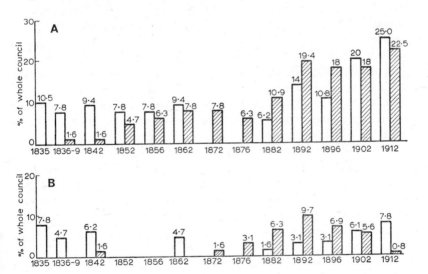

FIG. 17. *Representation of professional men on the town council, 1835–1912* (Leeds—
white; Birmingham—hatched). A All professions. B Medical and Dental Practitioners
only.

paving that the independent inquiries of the previous years had shown to be urgently required. Under its new borough surveyor the Corporation went vigorously ahead, only to run into trouble. The cost of the new schemes had been grossly underestimated. By 1853 there was a deficit in the Improvement Account and in 1855 the Council decided to go to Parliament for powers to raise additional loans. The consent of the rate-payers was required before this could be done, and the ratepayers refused. Representative government, it was held, ought to be cheaper than the régime of the irresponsible Street Commission. The rates had been reduced below the combined rates in the parish of Birmingham before 1851, but the town had no intention of seeing them rise again. A Rate-payers Protection Society had been formed with several of its spokesmen already on the Council. It now asserted itself at the municipal elections and swept out of office those—many of them former Street Commissioners —who wished to see the original scheme completed. The leaders of the economy movement forced the mass resignation of both the Finance and the Public Works Committee and took control.[11]

The effect of these events was visible in the Council of 1856 and continued to 1862. The number of big businessmen fell from ten to seven in 1856 and five in 1862 with particularly important losses among the merchants who had led the Council during the preceding years. The number of small men rose again to 27 in 1856 after the fall in the previous sample (*see* Fig. 19, p. 326. This included a particularly marked rise in the number of licensed victuallers. The drink trade increased its representation in 1856 to eight, i.e. 12·5 per cent of the Council (*see* Fig. 18). If we look at the leadership of the economy movement the contrast with the defeated merchants is even clearer. Joseph Allday, the dominant figure from 1855–9, ran an eating-house, his brother was a small wire-worker and fender manufacturer. The other leaders of the party were a cabinet-maker, a 'High Street' draper, and a solicitor-cum-vestry-clerk.

The implications of the change for the administration of the borough were far-reaching. The borough surveyor was replaced by his assistant at half the salary, the town clerk was driven from office and replaced by a more pliant man. The road-building plans were shelved, and on one occasion the Corporation found itself paying a penalty of £7,500 rather than continue with a project to which their predecessors had pledged themselves.

By the early 1860s the peak of the reaction was over and the complete domination by the Allday party somewhat modified. However, the evil reputation that service on the Council had acquired among the well-to-do

[11] There is a good account of these events in Gill and Briggs, i, Chap. XVIII.

Compositions of Borough Councils

was not overcome until the crusade for the rehabilitation of Birmingham municipal life that formed the background to the municipal career of Joseph Chamberlain in the early 1870s.[12] By 1882 the new régime had been firmly established, and the contrast between the Council in that year and that in 1862 brings out clearly the social, as distinct from the administrative implications of the change.

TABLE II

BIRMINGHAM TOWN COUNCIL, 1862 AND 1882

	1862		1882	
	No.	Per cent	No.	Per cent
Owners of large businesses	5	7·8	14	22·0
Owners of small businesses	21	32·8	12	18·7
Drink interest	5	7·8	1	1·6
Medical men	—	—	4	6·3

It was to the large businessmen that the propagandists of the late 1860s and 1870s had particularly directed their appeal, and in view of the changes in the local economy this now meant manufacturers rather than merchants, as it had done in the first half of the period.[13] The Corporation's purchase of the Gas and Water Companies provided these men with a particularly attractive arena for the display of their talents. Writing in 1914 after 40 years' experience, an observer confirmed that membership

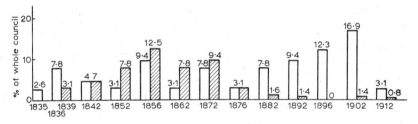

FIG. 18. *Representation of the Drink Interest on the Town Council, 1835–1912* (Leeds—white; Birmingham—hatched).

12 See E. P. Hennock, *The Rôle of Religious Dissent in the Reform of Municipal Government in Birmingham, 1865–76* (unpublished Ph.D. thesis, Cambridge, 1956). Also, Asa Briggs *Victorian Cities* (1963), Chap. VI.

13 V.C.H., *A History of the County of Warwick*, Vol. VII: *The City of Birmingham*, ed. W. B. Stephens (1964), pp. 81–208.

323

of the four trading committees (gas, water, electricity, and tramways) was perhaps more sought after than any other, 'as is natural in a large business community'.[14]

There is no room in this paper to enter into the reasons for the remarkable efflorescence of Birmingham's municipal government in the 1870s. I want rather to ask whether it created a tradition of municipal service among the economic and social leaders of Birmingham that survived into the next generation. With some reservations the answer is 'yes'. The percentage of large businessmen remains just over 20 per cent in the 1890s; that of small men declined even further to a mere 15 per cent in 1896. The representatives of the drink trade to all intents and purposes disappear from the Council. It should not be assumed that this was a normal development towards the end of the nineteenth century. It is in marked contrast to Leeds and Newcastle-under-Lyme among the towns known to me.[15] There were good reasons why brewers and publicans should want to be influential on the Watch Committee. Their failure to do so in Birmingham was the result of deliberate political measures taken against them. The recruitment of medical men, which was related to the heightened awareness in the town since 1874 of the public health aspect of municipal administration, a matter in which Birmingham had previously been distinctly backward, had also not ceased. In 1892 the Council contained seven medical men, a remarkably high number for a profession with so many urgent claims upon its time. At least two of them were men of eminence in their field (see Fig. 17 on p. 321).

After 1896 the trends established in the 1870s lose a little of their momentum. There is a drop in the proportion of big businessmen, to a level close to that of 1882. There is a similar rise in the proportion of small men, again reaching something very near the level of 1882 (see Fig. 19 on p. 326). Professional men as a group show the same phenomenon, a peak in the 1890s with a falling-off, in this case only a very slight one. A similar trend is discernible among such commercial occupations as house-agents, auctioneers, and stockbrokers. We may conclude that despite a certain loss of momentum towards the end, the years from the late 1870s to the creation of Greater Birmingham in 1911 form a single period, as far as the social composition of the Council is concerned.

The greatly enlarged Council of 1912 does not lend itself to straight comparison with earlier ones without distinguishing between those wards

[14] Norman Chamberlain, 'Municipal government in Birmingham', *Pol. Qutly.*, i (February 1914), p. 102.
[15] For Leeds see Fig. 18 on p. 323; for Newcastle-under-Lyme see Frank Bealey,' Municipal politics in Newcastle-under-Lyme, 1872–1914', *North Staffs. Journ. of Field Studies*, v (1965).

TABLE 12

PROFESSIONAL MEN ON
THE BIRMINGHAM
COUNCIL, 1876–1902

Date	No.	Per cent
1876	4	6·3
1882	7	10·9
1892	14	19·4
1896	13	18·0
1902	13	18·0

Cf. also Fig. 17 on page 321.

that had been newly added to the city and the rest. The most striking difference from the previous sample is an increase among the professional men. The numerical total rose from 13 to 27, the percentage from 18 to 22.5, by far the biggest percentage in the history of the Council. It is not due to the medical and dental practitioners, whose numbers dropped to one, but to the addition of nine lawyers (including one lawyer's wife), four accountants, and three teachers in secondary or higher education. The increase was shared evenly between old and new wards with the old wards supplying the larger share of lawyers.[16]

The percentage of big businessmen remained almost the same as in 1902. This together with the increase in the professional element meant that the economic leadership (interpreted fairly generously) furnished in 1912 a greater proportion of the Council than ever before in the history of the Corporation, close on 40 per cent. This should be balanced against the slight decline in the percentage of big businessmen since the 1890s, to which reference has been made. At the same time there was an increase in small businessmen (shopkeepers and the like) at the expense of those connected with medium-sized firms. This latter increase came mainly from the new wards.

As was to be expected, a large proportion of the representatives of the

16 If this reflects, howbeit in exaggerated form, the growing importance of professional men in the community at the turn of the century, as possibly it might, it has nothing to do with anything that can be ascertained from the census figures. The census is concerned with residence, whereas many of those who practised within the city were by then living beyond its boundaries. Thus between 1881 and 1911 the census figures show a rise in the percentage of professional men to the working population in the case of Birmingham and a fall in the case of Leeds. The reason for the difference is almost certain to be that Birmingham experienced a major boundary extension while Leeds did not.

new wards had been members of the previous local authorities (62·5 per cent), so that patterns of representation from authorities unaffected by the history of Birmingham found an expression, though a limited one, on the 1912 Council. Aston sent a brewer, while Aston and Yardley between them sent three building contractors, a group that had hardly been represented before. All four had been on the previous authorities. A final word about organised labour. The year 1912 saw the number of trade union officials increase from two to five, all of them representing the older wards of the city. In addition four skilled manual workers provided the working class with 7·5 per cent compared with 5·6 per cent in 1902.

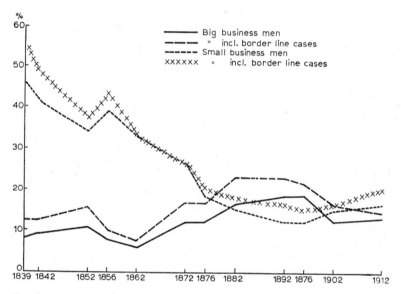

Fig. 19. *Representation of business men on Birmingham Town Council, 1839–1912.*

In the long perspective these slight changes after 1900 are outweighed by the enormous contrast between the whole of the period after 1870 and that which went before.

2. LEEDS

Leeds, although for much of the nineteenth century the fourth largest provincial town in England, has had less attention paid to it by the historians than either Birmingham or Manchester. *A History of the Corporation of Birmingham* in several volumes, published at intervals since 1878, and a *History of Local Government in Manchester*, published in three volumes in 1939–40, proclaim the interest that these authorities have taken in their past.[17] The last municipal history of Leeds was published in 1846.[18] In other words there is none at all for the reformed Corporation, none has ever been commissioned by that body or sponsored by the University, although the material lies plentifully in the archives. Asa Briggs's study of the building of Leeds Town Hall in the 1850s provides a solitary pool of light in the darkness.[19]

There is much the same neglect of the history of the town as such. We shall find nothing comparable to Gill's and Briggs's *History of Birmingham* (again commissioned by the Corporation) or to the respectable town histories that have been appearing for other places. In 1926 the *Yorkshire Post* published a series of newspaper articles to celebrate the tercentenary of the first charter. Subsequently collected between soft covers, they are the nearest that anyone has ever come to writing a general history of the town.[20] Any work on Leeds has to begin by sorting out the elements of its history in a way not necessary for Birmingham. Why was it, one also wonders, that the Corporation of Leeds has at no stage over more than a century expressed civic pride in the manner that has come naturally to so many other municipal bodies?

From the point of view of this study the gaps in the economic history of the town have been the greater obstacle, however. I have leant heavily on the work of W. G. Rimmer and R. G. Wilson,[21] but there is not for Leeds the accumulation of detailed knowledge of its industrial history that had made reasonably accurate comparisons possible for Birmingham between the economic status of Councillors between one period and another. For Leeds the card index is less complete. It has been possible to identify such occupational groupings as the professions, the drink interest, etc., as well as the size of numerous businesses, particularly those of prominent members. But the figures are not complete enough to yield percentages of total numbers in all the cases for which they would have been useful. Hence the rather more impressionistic language of what follows and the greater concentration on the leadership.

In contrast to Birmingham, Leeds possessed an old-established Corporation, dating from 1626. It had been established to enable a small group of woollen merchants exporting overseas to control the market,

[17] Bunce, *op. cit.*, and succeeding volumes; Redford and Russell, *op. cit.*

[18] James Wardell, *Municipal History of the Borough of Leeds*, (1846).

[19] Asa Briggs, *Victorian Cities* (1963), Chap. IV.

[20] *Leeds and its History* (*Yorkshire Post*, 1926).

[21] W. G. Rimmer, *Marshalls of Leeds, Flax Spinners, 1788–1886* (1960) and numerous articles in the *Publications of the Thoresby Society* and *Leeds Journ.*; R. G. Wilson, *Leeds Woollen Merchants, 1700–1830* (unpublished Ph.D. thesis, Leeds, 1964).

standard of quality, etc. From 1626 to the early nineteenth century Leeds was dominated economically, socially, and politically by this oligarchy of woollen merchants, who were wealthy men charging apprenticeship fees of £300 and over.[22] They were closely connected with the local landed gentry, from whose younger sons they were in part recruited, and with whom they intermarried. The most successful of them in turn became gentry or even peers. They furnish a classic instance of that cooperation between landed and mercantile wealth on which eighteenth-century English society rested.

The prosperity of eighteenth-century Leeds was due to its function as a marketing centre for much of the West Riding. It depended on the improved navigation of the rivers Aire and Calder, which linked it to the North Sea ports. Among the Undertakers of the Navigation, who drew substantial revenues from its tolls, the Leeds merchants were strongly represented. The clothiers, who sold their woollen cloth in the Leeds Cloth Halls, normally came from beyond the town, for Leeds itself was a centre of the finishing trades, and displayed in addition the diversity of trades normally to be found in a prosperous market centre.[23] Between 1806 and 1835 this oligarchy came under both economic and political pressure. They lost their hold over the worsted industry of the Bradford–Halifax–Huddersfield region, as that industry became mechanised and a new class of large manufacturers took over the marketing of their own wares. In addition the drying up of the older channels of trade in Europe made it necessary to open up new areas elsewhere. This provided opportunities for newer men willing to work hard, but the returns were less certain and the life less gentlemanly than in the past. In contrast the status and financial rewards of lawyers and doctors were rising. In that generation the sons of merchants were more frequently apprenticed to the professions than had been the case before.

The corporation, which was recruited by co-option, was even in 1835 still predominantly composed of cloth merchants (or wool staplers) and professional men. Out of 38 there were 20 cloth merchants (including one linen merchant), four bankers, four professional men, and one gentleman, comprising over 75 per cent of the total. Those admitted since 1827 showed, however, that the corporation had begun to open its ranks to the owners of wealth created in newer ways. They included two flaxspinners (the factory industry *par excellence* in Leeds), an ironfounder, a dyer, a timber merchant, and a glass merchant.

22 For the following three paragraphs, see Wilson.
23 W. G. Rimmer, 'The industrial profile of Leeds, 1740–1840', *Publications of the Thoresby Society: Miscellany*, xiv, Pt. 2 (1967), pp. 130–57.

Politically the hold of the corporation on the town had been complete. Until 1819 it controlled the vestry, the administration of the Poor Law through the Workhouse Board, and the Street Commission. Between 1819 and 1822 the corporation lost its hold on these three bodies,[24] a prelude to the loss of control over the corporation itself, which this group of men suffered in December 1835 as a result of the elections under the Municipal Corporations Act. They lost it to the Reforming Party led by the *Leeds Mercury*, which under the editorship of Edward Baines had created a new kind of power in Leeds, the power of opinion and of open debate.

Unlike that of Nottingham for instance, the Corporation of Leeds had been a Tory body exclusively composed of members of the Established Church, as by law it ought to have been, certainly until 1828. It had been in close accord with Henry Lascelles, Pittite MP for Yorkshire, and with the dominant opinion in the county during the Pitt ascendancy. The Whig cause was, however, never entirely crushed in Yorkshire. In 1801 the *Leeds Mercury* was launched as a Whig organ and gained rapidly in influence during the two stormy county-elections of 1806–7. The Whig cause triumphed, while the Corporation of Leeds retained its close identification with Lascelles and the Tory cause.[25] In 1832 Leeds returned two Reformers to Parliament as its first Borough MPs. In 1835 after an equally hard-fought election the first Town Council under the Municipal Corporation Act comprised 52 Liberals and 12 Tories. Only six of these had been members of the old Corporation. It was a defeat, not an abdication. Among the unsuccessful candidates were another eight of the former rulers of the town.

In social terms this *bouleversement* should not be regarded as a defeat of the merchants at the hands of the newly emergent manufacturers. To identify the leaders of the Reformers with the new manufacturers, as has been done by some historians, is to go counter to the evidence.[26] Among the 11 men who provided the capital for the *Leeds Mercury* in 1801 were two manufacturers, six cloth merchants, a physician, a spirit merchant, and a gentleman. More to the point is that seven of them were Dissenters, and all of them supporters of Walter Fawkes of Farnley, the 'independent Whig' who was to contest the county in 1806.[27] Much the same is true of the leaders of the Reform agitation in the town from 1806–32. They included members of important merchant houses and leading professional

---

[24] S. and B. Webb, *The Parish and the County*, pp. 94–8.
[25] Wilson, *op. cit.*
[26] Donald Read, *Press and People* (1961), p. 76; Wilson, *op. cit.*
[27] The list of names is given in Edward Baines, *Life of Edward Baines* (1851), p. 47. For religious affiliations see Read, p. 76, for political affiliations see Wilson, p. 375.

men as well as manufacturers.[28] The two flaxspinners among the leaders of the Reformers can be balanced by two flaxspinners on the old Corporation. Between them they owned the largest factories in Leeds. What distinguished them from each other was that the two Reformers, like the vast majority of the party leadership, were Dissenters. The political divisions of the 1830s were the result of genuine disagreement about the nature of authority. To this disagreement the distinction between a Churchman and a Dissenter had some relevance in Leeds; that between a merchant and a manufacturer did not.

If we examine the overwhelmingly Liberal Council of 1836, we shall find the numerical strength of the traditional occupations greater than ever, though in view of the increase in total numbers the percentage showed a drop.

TABLE 13

LEEDS CORPORATION, 1835–6. TRADITIONAL OCCUPATIONS

	Old Corporation 1835	New Corporation 1836
Cloth merchants or wool staplers	16	15
Cloth merchants-cum-manufacturers	4	8
Bankers	4	5
Lawyers	1	2
Doctors	3	3
Gentlemen	1	1
Total	29	34
Liberals	—	26
Tories	29	8

For the occupations, which had already been accepted by the Tory oligarchy in 1835, see Table 14 opposite. They too are now more strongly represented than before. Curiously enough, as can be seen from a comparison of these two tables, it was the relatively recently accepted occupations, not the traditional ones, that provided the higher proportion of Tories on the 1836 Council. Between them these occupations accounted for exactly three quarters of the first elected Council. The rest were drawn mainly from manufacturers and maltsters, but included the odd grocer, hatter and bootmaker.

The old corporation had been controlled by leading merchants and professional men of the town with an admixture of outstanding manu-

---

[28] Names cited in Baines; A. S. Turberville and F. Beckwith, 'Leeds and parliamentary reform 1820–1832', *Thoresby Miscellany*, xii (1954).

TABLE 14

LEEDS CORPORATION, 1835–6

	Old Corporation 1835	New Corporation 1836
Flax and silk spinners	2	4
Dyers	1	3
Timber merchants	1	2
Ironfounders or machine makers	1	3
Total	5	12
Liberals	—	8
Tories	5	4

facturers. The same was true of the new. The more we concentrate on those who actually provided the leadership, the more striking the parallel becomes. It is as if the opposing team had gone in to play. The rival merchants, the rival bankers, lawyers and doctors, even the rival flax-spinners, are now in charge. In 1833 the *Leeds Mercury* had proclaimed its confidence that under a representative régime 'men of character and station would be sought for'. It rejected with contempt and every appearance of justice the claim of the Conservatives to monopolise 'all the respectability of the place'.[29] The really striking change that had taken place in the composition of the Council, apart from its party complexion, was not social, it was religious. According to the *Mercury*, out of the first 51 men elected no more than 20 were Churchmen.[30] Even more remarkable is the fact that during the first 12 years of its history the new corporation elected only two mayors who were members of the Church of England.

Among the doctors on the Leeds Council in the period between 1836 and 1842 had been two men, who were particularly conscious of the threat to health that came from urban conditions. Indeed up to 1842 Leeds was in the van of the movement for the investigation of the sanitary conditions of great towns. The Leeds Improvement Act of that year, which was the work of a group of men who served on all three of important public bodies of the town, the Bench of Magistrates, the Town Council and the Street Commission, was one of the pioneering measures in that age of private-bill legislation. It did much to shape subsequent legislation elsewhere.

[29] *Leeds Mercury*, 20 April 1833; 23 January 1836.
[30] *Leeds Mercury*, 2 January 1836. The bye-election to fill vacancies caused by promotion to aldermen had at that date not taken place: hence the incomplete total.

However, as in other places later, bold plans led to political nemesis. This may have been made worse by the fact that the two medical men most concerned moved away from Leeds at this time. However, even before he left, Robert Baker, who more than anyone else provided the force behind the public health movement, had begun to be obstructed on the Council. The economic climate was changing and by the later months of 1842 the opposition to any further expenditure had begun to render futile any attempts to put the powers of the Improvement Act into effect. Men pledged to economy began to be elected. By 1852 there was not a single doctor on the Council and Leeds had long ceased to be in the van of the sanitary reform movement in England. In the 1860s investigations undertaken by the Medical Inspectorate of the Privy Council held up its sanitary administration to obloquy.[31]

Between 1842 and 1852 the number of small businessmen on the Council rose sharply, swollen among others by the shopkeepers, etc., who made up the group of Chartist Councillors.[32] The number of large businessmen fell. The bankers had gone by 1842. The large cloth merchants dropped off more slowly, but there were important losses during the late 1840s. The two eminent solicitors, T. W. Tottie and J. Hope Shaw, who led the Council on most occasions and were obviously able men, left in 1850 and 1855 respectively. The former had escaped defeat by only the narrowest margin at the aldermanic elections of 1847; the latter resigned in protest against a short-sighted water-scheme. However, the professional men as a group were still as strongly represented in 1862 as ever. There was even a reappearance of doctors, but it did not last. After the shake-up of the 1840s there were no spectacular changes in the social composition of the Council until the early seventies.

In terms of administration Leeds had experienced an outburst of municipal activity in 1851–6, followed by inertia. The 1860s saw a certain amount of street improvement and by 1867 the rates levied by the Corporation had reached the highest figure yet. The following year saw the beginning of a ratepayers' movement. Elections were fought on the issue of economy and the successful new Councillors tended to be shopkeepers. Their share of seats increased rapidly during these years. The general mediocrity of the Council in this period led them to save on the salaries of their officials and yet to squander money through sheer incompetence. It was characteristic of the contrast with contemporary Birmingham that after the Leeds Corporation had acquired the local

[31] *Eighth Report of the Medical Officer of the Privy Council, Parl. Papers*, 1866, xxxiii.
[32] See J. F. C. Harrison, 'Chartism in Leeds' in *Chartist Studies*, ed. Asa Briggs (1959), for Leeds municipal Chartism between 1843 and around 1853.

TABLE 15

RETAILERS ON THE LEEDS TOWN COUNCIL, 1862–76

1862	5	7·8 per cent
1872	11	17·2 per cent
1876	12	18·7 per cent

gasworks in 1870, it was found that they had bought a heap of worn-out equipment, which ran at a loss and in 1873–4 had to be subsidised out of the rates to the tune of £14,000.[33] In Birmingham the gas account contributed a regular £25–30,000 per annum to the borough fund from the first year onwards.[34]

With the retirement in the early 1880s of the older generation of aldermen, those who had been recruited during the 1870s took complete control. The guiding spirit of the Council during these years was Archie Scarr, fruit and general merchant, the 'King of the Market', where he had begun as a boy with a handcart and where by the eighties he employed 30 assistants. Scarr was convinced that he owed his prosperity not to what he had earned but to what he had saved, and he carried his passion for thrift into the Council Chamber.[35] An ardent Temperance orator on Woodhouse Moor, it was difficult to tell from his discourses which of the two causes meant more to him. Between them they formed his philosophy of life. He was a lovable character and to the surprise of the deeply offended 'respectability' of Leeds made not at all a bad mayor. Every good Council can afford to carry an Archie Scarr and is better for having him. The real trouble with the municipal Liberalism of Leeds in the eighties was that he dominated it and represented, though by caricature, the character of those in charge.

From the 1830s to the 1880s the development of municipal government in Birmingham and Leeds had run in opposite directions. The kind of situation that had characterised Leeds in the early years was now to be found in Birmingham, where it had once been markedly absent. In contrast, the later developments in Leeds had reduced the standing of the Council to a position like that of the first two decades in Birmingham.

The 1890s were to witness a transformation, which for the first time broke the hold of the Liberals on the municipal government of Leeds,

---

33 *Leeds Mercury*, 1 October 1873; 1 October, 1874.
34 Bunce, ii, p. 393.
35 Herbert Yorke, *A Mayor of the Masses. History and Anecdotes of A. W. Scarr* (1904).

and also drastically altered the social composition of the Council. It can only be lightly sketched at this stage in the paper. Two incidents provided the occasion for this reaction against the régime. The first was an outbreak of typhoid fever in 1889, which was needlessly allowed to spread through the negligence of the Medical Officer of Health. There was a public outcry, which was not stilled on the dismissal of the Medical Officer but focussed on the sanitary administration of the town in general. The second event was a dispute at the Corporation gas works in consequence of the formation there of a branch of Will Thorne's Gas Workers' and General Labourers' Union.[36] The Gas Committee imported blackleg labour, which provoked a riot but failed in its objective. The cause of the gas workers was taken up by the Conservatives, and the incident probably lost the Liberals support among the working-class electors. The Conservatives then moved into the attack, criticising the majority on the Council, not as in the past from the point of view of economy, but from that of good government. From 1891 onwards municipal policies obtained a thorough airing at elections, which had previously been fought on party cries alone. The Liberals fought back with a municipal programme, which was far removed from the practice of only a few years ago. Even so the Conservatives obtained a majority and in 1895 were able to elect the mayor and aldermen for the first time since 1835. They brought in some of the most prominent names in Leeds industrial circles, and the following year, so as to underline that the issues were not primarily party ones, invited Sir James Kitson, a prominent Liberal and head of the biggest engineering works in Leeds, to be mayor. The Conservative control of the Council lasted until 1904, long enough to clear out the dead wood and to lead to the reshaping of Liberal concepts.

In the field of administration the nineties saw the beginning of new activities and interests—in public health, housing, and slum-clearance, in municipally operated tramways and the provision of wash-houses. In social terms the transformation of the Council is best seen in Table 16 on p. 335. The contrast between 1892 and 1902 is seen in the figure for large businessmen, especially from engineering which was then, for Leeds, big business *par excellence*. The rise in the number of professional men continued after the Liberal come-back, and by climbing much more sharply than in Birmingham reached a very similar percentage for both cities in 1912 (see Fig. 17, p. 321). The similarity extends to the percentage of large businessmen and several other significant indices. The rapid

---

[36] The dispute and its background are described in E. P. Thompson, 'Homage to Tom Maguire' in *Essays in Labour History*, ed. Asa Briggs and John Saville (1960).

TABLE 16

LEEDS CITY COUNCIL, 1892–1912. SELECTED OCCUPATIONS

	1892		1902		1912	
	Nos.	Per cent	Nos.	Per cent	Nos.	Per cent
Professions generally	9	14·0	13	20·0	16	25·0
Doctors	2	3·1	4	6·1	5	7·8
Large businessmen generally	6	9·4	14	21·5	9	13·9
Large businessmen in engineering	1	1·6	6	9·2	3	4·7
Manual workers and T.U. organisers	—	—	5	7·7	6	9·4

transformation of local government in Leeds during the last twenty years of the period is comparable to what had happened in Birmingham twenty years before and led to very similar situations in the two cities. It had its administrative counterpart, as I have already indicated. The resemblance is not mere accident; it was a deliberate move on the part of Leeds to imitate a famous example, and is comparable in this respect with the similar efforts then being made by the London County Council under the Progressives.

CONCLUSION

The similarity at the end should not lead us to disregard the marked differences over the period as a whole. A study of other towns would strengthen the impression of variety. Not all the Councils which had inherited a tradition of municipal service from pre-Reform days lost it by a process of attrition, as was the case with Leeds. Nottingham in the 1870s appears to have been governed still by a business élite drawn from the two main local industries, hosiery and lace.[37]

Although it may be impossible to generalise about the course that events have taken in different towns, it is possible to recognise the pressures which, in different combinations and in different ways, helped to shape that course. I have dealt with some of these in detail in an earlier article,[38] others have been touched upon in passing in this paper. Yet others have to do with the interplay of political organisations or the economic structure of the town. These are factors that have been played down on this occasion far more than they should have been, but for the

[37] R. A. Church, *Economic and Social Change in a Midland Town: Victorian Nottingham 1815–1900* (1966).

[38] E. P. Hennock, in *Hist. Journ.*, see p. 319, note 9.

need to make the subject fit into the limits of a conference paper. Nor should it be forgotten that we are dealing here with the history of ideas and of obligations, generated in social groups or maintained alive in them sometimes by the example and ability of individuals, sometimes by the ethos of an institution.

Discussion

As the papers of Dr. Newton on Exeter and of Dr. Hennock on Leeds and Birmingham fitted so closely together in their chronology and substance, and Mr. Foster's paper on Oldham was so distinctive in treatment and approach, the CHAIRMAN opened the discussion by taking the first two papers together and reserved Mr. Foster's until the second half of the proceedings.

He pointed out that the studies of Exeter, Birmingham, and Leeds dealt with very contrasting types of towns. Exeter, an old cathedral city, had nearly ceased to grow by the opening of the nineteenth century; Leeds and Birmingham were two bursting industrial towns, one of which (Birmingham) was not incorporated until 1838. In some respects the methods of attack were identical in both papers, notably in the analyses of the personnel of the town councils by occupation and to some extent by class, with a view to discovering what changes, if any, were taking place in councils and council attitudes at different periods.

This immediately raised the old question that had never been satisfactorily answered: has the quality of town councillors deteriorated since the Municipal Corporations Act of 1835, and if so when did this happen, and how and why? Closely related to these questions, was how far the Municipal Corporations Act itself had really made any effective changes in the personnel and outlook of town councils. How big were the political changes in 1835–6 and did they have any lasting effect? Who made the decisions on the new councils, or failed to make them? The chairman also suggested with some force that Council records themselves could be quite baffling or misleading on the whole question of the formation of local oligarchies and their use of power.

Dr. SHEPPARD was 'rather surprised to hear quite so much emphasis placed [by the chairman] on political aspects.' As a town councillor himself he thought this could be exaggerated and that 'the basic problem really seems to be one of personalities;' and he added, 'I don't see how you can ever get around that in the past where the persons are dead; the only sources you ever have are literary ones.' He also suggested that the birthplace and education of town councillors were perhaps more significant than their politics in local affairs. Dr. NEWTON disputed the latter point, observing that 'the control or dominance of the city [of Exeter] by the licensed trade in the latter half of the nineteenth century was exercised by people who had been born outside the city.'

Dr. THOMPSON wondered whether one could have a fruitful discussion about the personal quality of councillors since 'quality' was a word with different meanings for different people, and was being considered in an historical context

337

in which more general influences were important. Dr. HENNOCK accepted that this was a real difficulty and that he had concentrated upon the occupational structure of the Leeds and Birmingham councils in order to study something a little less elusive than 'quality'. It seemed to be accepted that the varying quality of town councillors since the 1830's could not be measured satisfactorily, and at one point Professor CHECKLAND went so far as to suggest that the widespread belief that the quality of local councillors had deteriorated was 'a kind of folk-view we have'—a view that in itself justified more research.

A more fruitful argument developed about Dr. HENNOCK's view that the new councils in 1836 had much more initiative in policy-making than councils have today. They had much more say in the determination of standards in combating the vast new problems of population pressure and rapid industrialisation. He thought that local government was much more in purely local hands; and since salaried officials were relatively unimportant until the 1860's this meant that councillors themselves took the decisions, however mistaken these might have been. Dr. THOMPSON did not agree that councils to-day had relatively less initiative and power in decision-making than those of a hundred years ago. He instanced the 'enormous powers' of modern councils over education, town planning, and housing. Professor ASHWORTH pointed out that if one were going to analyse the personnel of town councils, it was equally important to look at the personnel of the Poor Law Guardians, the Local Board of Health, the Police Commission, and other local bodies.

It seemed to be agreed that councils in the Victorian period had wide potential powers arising from the vast amount of permissive legislation of the time, and that part of the problem lay in finding out the reasons why certain councils, or certain groups upon them, responded to this legislation, and why other councils and groups neglected the challenge. Professor CHECKLAND stressed this when he observed 'the relationship between what was done and what it was possible to do seems to me to be the way to try to approach this rather than try to penetrate through public minutes and so on.' The problem was analogous to one in business history, 'and the only way to fill in some of the major gaps is to try to set the opportunity parameters and then to see how the business behaves.' He later instanced among other things the 'great water enterprise' in the 1860's in Glasgow. 'Some chaps saw what that meant for the future and some chaps didn't. I don't think any of us have yet sorted out the origins and the background of the two attitudes.' Dr. MARTIN suggested that one reason for Victorian councils responding to the mass of permissive legislation or ignoring it was purely financial. 'The reformed councillors after 1835 were put in in order to check the spending of money, not to encourage it.' That was why 'this great act of reform produced so little effect: it was precisely the negative effect that contemporaries wanted.'

The CHAIRMAN drew attention to the changing rôle of local government officials. If there were a wider range of powers to-day than in Victorian councils, he suggested that 'the salaried officers are in fact doing nearly all the determining and most of the initiating' and that Victorian councillors were perhaps more important as policy-makers in relation to officers. Dr. SUTCLIFFE took up this point from his researches into the municipal history of Paris. Here there was 'a definite restriction on the initiative of the council as a whole and of individual councillors in the late nineteenth century.' After a brief revolt by the newly-elected council in 1871 against the power of the professional administrators in municipal affairs, they were obliged within a few years to admit defeat. They had to accept the administrators' professional advice in such matters as the construction of great avenues through the town. 'In fact, it was quite easy for the administration to pull the wool over the eyes of the council by the information and advice they gave them, so as pretty well to force the council to vote in the way which they considered best.' The Parisian experience even in the last quarter of the nineteenth century showed that 'it is impossible for the council to establish its own authority over the administration . . . it's not impossible but it is extremely difficult.' Those members of the conference who had had personal experience of English town councils appeared to know only too well how true this is of the mid-twentieth century.

Dr. EVERSLEY reinforced this view of Paris local government from his personal knowledge of the Birmingham council in recent years. The 'Old Guard', members of the great Chamberlain generation, a few of whom still survived at least until fairly recently, and who had had 'a tremendous grip on the essentials of governing the city', treated their chief officers as their servants, though they were distinguished in their own professions. But this was the last phase of the Strong Councillor Era, for by the 'late 1940s and early 1950s the technical complexities of finance, for instance, were really even beyond the detailed grasp of a good businessman,' and no councillor could argue on equal terms with the professional officer. Whereas 'town-planning was created in Birmingham by city councillors' in the nineteenth century, now it was the work of the chief officers. The complexity of modern legislation had led to the disappearance of the dominant councillor.

Professor BARKER saw part of the explanation of differences between local councils in sheer ineptitude and mentioned the attitude of local councils towards the beginnings of electric tramways in the 1890s. There were pressure groups who did not want electric tramways because they could compete with existing interests, but the story was mostly of an inability by councils to make up their minds between the merits of different systems. The subject of pressure groups was regrettably not followed up. Professor CHECKLAND finished off this particular discussion by observing with characteristic realism that over a period of time the same councillor or the same group might well take up different attitudes towards a long-term municipal scheme, depending on the vicissitudes of the local or even national economy.

Professor ASHWORTH opened a new issue by asking how the authors of the two papers envisaged their work in relation to the larger themes of the conference: it had been suggested earlier that there were other things besides urbanisation. Dr. HENNOCK saw his work on Leeds and Birmingham 'very much in relation to the whole problem of urbanisation . . . I am constantly going round nudging economic historians' elbows saying "For Heaven's sake can't you tell me a little more about the economic structure of the city", and they say they can't.' No economic historian in the room was prepared to accept the challenge. Dr. NEWTON wondered 'whether you can talk about the city of Exeter as an urban study at all'. He explained that 'it was embedded in a rural England, and I think it has to be looked at from the point of view of the whole development of an increasingly obsolete society.' To understand Exeter properly one had to go into a wide variety of matters such as religious problems and policies, and the landed interest and so forth, matters which had not been touched upon at all by the conference 'but they do affect Exeter as a community and I think it is extremely difficult to narrow it down to a study of urban history as such.'

The CHAIRMAN thought that Dr. Newton was being rather too modest about his aims, that the conference had possibly become bemused by mere size, by big industrial cities. He thought the smaller city of the Exeter type was by no means unique and was worth studying for itself, whether or not it contributed to the general study of urbanisation. He also hoped that urban studies would not become too sociological. 'There must be case-studies of carefully chosen places ... before you can start immense sociological generalisations.' Dr. PAHL thought that we already had the hypotheses and generalisations. 'What we want to do is to test them.' The chairman was not convinced that this was the whole story. He felt alarmed at the view that one should only study a town because of some contribution it might be able to make to sociological theory in general.

The Conference then turned its attention to Mr. Foster's study of Oldham politics and society in the first half of the nineteenth century, which concentrated mainly on the 1840's. In opening the discussion, Professor HOSKINS said he regarded himself as an historian who had always asked sociological questions, but he wished at the same time that sociologists would learn to ask more historical questions than they usually did. He agreed with Mr. Foster that 'local studies can be quite barren and parochial unless they are related to the class structure of the country as a whole ... it is useless to study any town without relation to the massive statements of the sociologists,' though sometimes their use of words left one in a considerable fog. It transpired for example, that when Mr. Foster talked of 'class formation' he meant, 'working-class formation'. At this, Mr. FOSTER explained more specifically that 'it means the formation of a mass group orientated to conflict in a system of inequality.' The CHAIRMAN had a different hypothesis in mind and illustrated it by reference to a late medieval document at King's Lynn which defined the three classes of that town as the *potentiores*, the *mediocres*, and the *inferiores*. He thought this could be a useful classification for study in more recent periods. Who were the *potentiores* in any given town and how were they constituted? He thought they were as worthy of close study as the *inferiores* who formed the main theme of Mr. Foster's paper. The chairman also wondered whether Mr. Foster's method was applicable to towns other than the new industrial towns. If not, then it was a limited technique. He also suggested that someone might usefully discuss the political importance of the Drink Trade, which had been referred to in the first two papers and was implicit in the Oldham paper. How did the Drink Interest operate *in practice* in local politics?

The discussion opened with a vigorous attack by Dr. CHALONER on some of Mr. Foster's facts and conclusions. He thought that the lack of capital among the working-class was often too heavily stressed, and that it was not so difficult as had been made out for men of working-class origin to rise to the status of mayor of Oldham in the nineteenth century. Mr. FOSTER disputed Dr. Chaloner's use of a particular local brochure and asserted that it was largely irrelevant and useless as an historical source and he produced some contrary evidence taken from manuscript sources in the local record office. The rest of the Conference had to leave this battle over intensely local details to the two protagonists. Neither seemed able to make the other move his position by an inch. Among other points, Dr. CHALONER also said that he regarded Mr. Foster's postulation of a ruling class of seventy capitalist families in Victorian Oldham as a myth comparable with that of the two hundred capitalist families who were supposed to govern France secretly in the days of the Popular Front in the 1930's. He thought, too, that the working-class radical element in local government was purely negative, that 'they were a bunch of anarchists' with few constructive ideas about local government, opposing for example the introduction of the county police in order to maintain the rule of riot so common in England from the early eighteenth century.

Replying, Mr. FOSTER said that Dr. Chaloner had minimised the effects of the poverty life-cycle in Oldham, that in fact until 1865 all the mayors of the town had been drawn from the seventy capitalist families, and that it was not until after 1865 when these families had moved away to their estates elsewhere, that they left the mayoralty open to a different class. He insisted that these seventy families did 'form a group cut off from the rest of the community by social distance, by marriage, by their degree of interaction with the rest of the élite.' They owned perhaps 80 per cent of the means of production, and they ruled the town down to 1850–60 when the very structure of the cotton industry began to change, and they began to disappear to pleasanter places than industrial Oldham. After that engineering became the staple industry of the town. Mr. FOSTER concluded that 'class formation disintegrates in Oldham in the second half of the century and the disappearance of a real *bourgeoisie* left a threadbare élite of managerial people looking after the companies of the big families.'

After some further discussion about the incomes and wealth of the seventy ruling families—during which Mr. Foster described his sources, including the census books, probate records, marriage registers, business archives, and the Home Office papers—Professor CHECKLAND opened up the political side of the paper. How did the working-class compile a list of likely men willing to act in the interests of their class? Mr. FOSTER replied there was no town council at this date, but that in parliamentary elections the working-class politicians exercised a very strong control over candidates and members. In local affairs, they exercised a powerful control through the downright intimidation of shop-keepers who 'didn't toe the line on the Police Commission' by methods which ranged from blacklisting shops to acid attacks. The net result was to prevent the formation of a real police force at all.

Dr. TILLOTT inquired whether there was any biographical information on the working-class leaders? Mr. FOSTER replied that he had listed 200 leaders mainly drawn from Home Office papers over the space of 20 years or 30 years. He had also supplemented this source with reports in the local newspapers. In some cases, these leaders took over trade unions especially in the 1816–20 period, and again later.

Dr. DYOS asked Mr. Foster how he saw his paper fitting into the general pattern of urbanisation in England, and how far his picture of the class-struggle compared or contrasted with what was happening in the villages? Mr. FOSTER replied that he had done far more work on towns such as Oldham, South Shields and Northampton than on villages, though he hoped to do more on the rural class structure. In the meantime he was certain that it was profitable to study towns in the way he had done, that it was possible to measure a number of key factors in the formation of class structure (e.g. through an analysis of marriage certificates). One could also construct a contingency table of the 'neighbouring relations' of people (presumably from the census schedules of 1841 and 1851?). One could also get 'a contingency table of the inter-relationships between all the occupational groups of the town; one can also measure social distance between the bottom level and the top of the labour force.'

Dr. PAHL thought that Mr. Foster's work exemplified the point made by Mr. Westergaard in the morning session that class dimension and urbanisation took different forms in different places, and that one should beware of working upon a single idea of how urbanisation and industrialisation operated. Mr. FOSTER agreed: the class struggle did not exist at all in South Shields but it plainly did in Oldham. Professor CHECKLAND wondered whether the 'class confrontation' operated randomly. Some discussion followed about the relative weight of national and local factors in such 'confrontations' but, understandably enough, no clear answers emerged.

There were further questions about how Mr. Foster had carried out his 'poverty survey' which he answered in some considerable detail; and Dr. CHALONER continued to probe with a view to showing that the 'seventy families' were not united in their political outlook and that the radical movement was also divided and did not form a coherent group. Mr. FOSTER conceded some slight measure of divided outlook but gave little ground and the discussion ended as it had begun with himself and Dr. Chaloner boxing vigorously but hardly touching each other.

W. G. HOSKINS

VII

Toward a Definition of Urban History

S. G. Checkland

Having survived 16 papers and their associated discussions over this week-end we are all feeling much better informed than when we first met. May I say how much I have admired the work of these craftsmen whose closely-argued papers dealing with real problems and real situations we have so much enjoyed. But I am also annoyed with them, for they have lowered your tolerance for the kind of anti-climax that a methodological summing-up such as mine must provide.

You all know the permanent dilemma of definition as it confronts the historian. There is, on the one hand, the danger of sterility and error; if we don't understand what we are doing we won't get results, or we will probably get false ones. On the other hand, once historians have eaten of the apple of 'discipline' they know they are naked, expelled from their innocent Eden of subjectivity into the cold world of definition and aggregates and systematic relationships. To these new methods there are reservations, some of which are justified and some of which are due to laziness and a failure to develop the necessary skills.

May I begin with some general thoughts about the historian and his vocational problems as they relate to urban history?

One approach to definition, that which derives from the fulfilment of urban functions, is precluded to us. Paradoxically, if our concern was indeed with policy problems, life would be much easier. If we were asked to advise about traffic access, or financial administration, or the provision of housing, or crime, or any other such challenge, we could use the tools of the engineers, the economists, the administrators, and so on. We could do a kind of economic and social cost-benefit analysis, and, justified by the inescapable need to decide, make such a 'definition' of the urban past as would seem to serve. This would very likely mean truncating some aspects of the phenomena to be observed as they were fitted to the procrustean bed of policy, relegating others to secondary importance, and dropping others entirely. But the historian cannot properly assume this functional rôle and the methodological simplifications it permits—although some of us, I am afraid, are rather inclined to do so.

Does scholarly specialisation solve the problem of method for us? As you know, there is a resistance among us to the idea that urban history should become a separate study, and even more strongly, to the notion that a further sub-division should develop so that there would appear scholars labelled as urban social historians, urban economic historians, and so on. This would certainly be to go too far. Professor Schnore mentioned last evening the possibility that, in addition to this kind of fragmentation of historical study, there are very likely to be groups of quasi- or pseudo-historians coming from each of the major disciplines—scholars who, starting from a contemporary discipline, are seeking a time perspective. Now, I myself am not too worried about this, especially if what is fashionably called 'dialogue' can take place, as has indeed been the case over the last few days. Indeed this commerce has been two-way; sociology, for example, has certainly benefited from historical inquiries into the social structure of cities and the effects on many aspects of life.

Fundamentally, however, we must come back to this: the historian's job is that of synthesis. It is rather grand to put it this way—but it is his task to try to put the components of human experience together. However wide the differences in disciplinary approach may become, the characteristic role of the historian is to seek always to assimilate the results to a single unified account.

Synthesis is never complete; moreover there is always the question of judging when the moment for attempting it has come. How long should the historian stand aside waiting until the many necessary monographs from the many points of view are written, before he attempts to compose them into a single picture? For example, should he wait until Mr. Armstrong and the computers can really tell us what happened to social Class III in a particular context, and then address himself to the questions why, and with what consequences? The historian might then try, with Mr. Jones, to explain 'The Aesthetic of the Industrial Town' by relating social Class III to social custom—the varnishing of window-sills, the variegated colouring of bricks, and the scrubbing of thresholds. Indeed, should the historian, having decided that, for example, social class is a fundamental concept, become himself an expert in its definition and measurements? If he does he will find that when he writes up his synthesis, he cannot give all the apparatus upon which his monograph rests, with the result that in one sense he is invulnerable to his readers, because, without reworking the ground, his conclusions cannot be tested. This may well suit him, but it means that he must learn to take others on faith, just as he expects to be taken, to a degree which the older schools of history would think improper.

Urban history also presents a pedagogic problem; this derives from the methodological one. One of the tests of the nature and meaning of history that those of us who are university teachers should always have in our minds derives from the teaching aspect. The traditional view in Britain has long been that a post-graduate student chooses a subject of such a kind as will test his historical grasp, that he then studies a wide range of varied sources, and from these he poses the problems to be solved, turns again with great intensity to his materials, and then arrives at his conclusions. Compare this approach with that which might be made by, say, one of Mr. Armstrong's students or one of Professor Schnore's. In these cases the student is provided with a much narrower range of sources, although, of course, as we have learned to our cost at this conference, they are very challenging. The student will probably walk pretty closely in his master's footsteps, for much of the methodology will have been established. In this way the degree of originality demanded of him in carrying out his research programme, which is really a projection of something much larger, thought out by someone else, is much reduced. The question arises as to whether this is an adequate mind-training and whether it can be used as a basis for judging scholarly competence. This, of course, is not a new problem, nor is it confined to the history of cities, but it is being posed with ever increasing insistence in this field as in so many others.

If we look at the efforts to understand urban phenomena made by British historians, they tend to take three principal forms.

The first of these is what, for the sake of convenience, I would call 'secular trend'. It is concerned with the very long-term course of urban experience—the town and the city are considered as part of the evolution of man and society, from nomadism to the present state. What ought the historian to do—what can he do—about this very long-term perspective? Secondly, there is the question of the thematic elements which appear in the evolution of urban life. What aspects can be isolated in the experience of cities that lend themselves to valid and useful comparative studies? Thirdly, there is the very diffuse problem which aroused much discussion on our first evening. What was the nature of urban experience, seen as some kind of totality, in a given context, over a given period of time? What was the quality of life in, say, the Britain of the High Victorian Age, the 1860s to the 1890s?

Some historians think mainly about secular trend, some about themes, and some about context. All the papers we have heard fit into one or other of these three types of approach. I think we have all learned by now that to be effective at any one of these three levels you must do some thinking about the other two. With respect to each of the three, there is the very difficult set of problems, the articulation of the parts. What are the components of trend, theme or context? How do you relate such components to each other? In short, there is a challenge of model-building at each of these three levels. So far the explicit setting out of assumptions and methods is a very genteel affair among historians, and is indeed often painfully amateurish.

Trend has been implicit rather than explicit as far as our discussions at this conference have been concerned; no doubt this reflects something in the British historians' way of thinking.

You know the general ways in which trend history may be presented. It may be couched in largely evolutionary terms, stressing increasing environmental control and the city as a component in this.[1] Thinking in this way we find that the particular city vanishes from our thoughts: the appearance of cities is shown on world maps where the river civilisations of Asia, Egypt, and China, and of Mesomerica are shown, and on a time scale, from Mesopotamia, through Egypt, the Indus Valley, Mediterranean Europe and China, and the New World. We learn of Gordon Childe's 'Urban revolution', of a significance equal to that of the agricultural revolution of neolithic times. We ponder the 'relations between the life-span of cities and the formation and decline of empires'. Such history is indeed, in a sense scientific, for it is the work of archaeologists, social anthropologists, geographers, and historians of culture and of science. The city is seen as the cradle of the scientific attitude itself, the place of the active experimental approach, the key to the control of the forces of nature. We feel that we are seeing the city as a universalised human creation. If we follow the story into modern times with Mumford we have a sense of ghastly, relentlessly cumulative error leading to social corruption and impotence. Moreover we are provided with many ideas that historians

---

[1] An excellent recent example is Gideon Sjoberg, 'The origin and evolution of cities', *Scientific American* (September 1965).

might well distrust as historical abstractions, the product not of observation and analysis, but of a sense of the dramatic.

Is it possible to go further than this, constructing a system of generalised phases or a system of chronological stages?

In spatial terms there have been many attempts at morphological schema that show the shape of the city through successive phases. In spite of serious limitations, of which historians are very conscious, this spatial approach would seem the most successful application to urban phenomena of this kind of trend thinking. Professor Conzen's fascinating paper on 'The Use of Town Plans in the Study of Urban History' contained in implied form the dichotomy that is always present in the mind of the true scholar: there was the insistence upon the need to scrutinise real situations in all their diversity, but it was counter-posed by the urge to discover 'a more effective body of general concepts' and 'a clue to distinct stages in town growth'. Listening to Professor Schnore's impressive paper 'Problems in the Quantitative Study of Urban History', I confess that I thought he shared the urge to conceive of the city as going through defined general phases of spatial experience, following an identifiable universal path of evolution. But when Mr. Bédarida argued in discussion that the continental city was fundamentally different from the classic American type, Schnore accepted this right away. This seemed to be leaving things hanging a little bit in the air. It meant that cities within a particular culture may follow an identifiable path, but those in another culture might follow a different one. We arrive at a kind of culturally conditioned historicism.

All historians have mild flirtations with historicism from time to time: it is not surprising that it affects urban history. Indeed it is proper and fruitful that it should, at least as a hypothesis.

In one form or another evolutionary historicism has been with us for a long time now; it has recently been restated by Rostow and others. Increasingly those concerned with the great changes involved in industrialisation are making a conceptual distinction between the traditional society in which no cumulative change is possible, and the society that has undergone those critical minimal changes that carry it into continuous renovation. Somehow this kind of thinking, if it is to be tenable, must assimilate the city. Is the city, for example, the place in which all kinds of new insights and techniques are developing, almost imperceptibly, so that either by the cumulative effect of these or by some external impact that gives them new relevance, the conditions for rupturing the traditional, agrarian, society are met?

If you cannot stomach evolutionary historicism, there is dialectic, that is to say the idea of an internal mechanism that works through tensions or conflicts between classes that in resolving themselves carry society onward. Most forms of dialectic operate in terms of whole societies, e.g. the nation state. How does such thinking relate to individual cities as components of societies, is there anything in particular you must in consistency hold about urban history and the evolution of towns? Mr. Foster's stimulating paper, 'Nineteenth-Century Towns—A Class Dimension', infused with an uncompromising Marxism, provided our best opportunity to think in these terms. I am afraid we did not really do the occasion justice, having been rather taken aback by its implications. Mr. Foster has produced a fascinating study of three middle-sized towns, in one of which, Oldham, class formation is demonstrated. In the other two, class formation had small scope. If class dialectic is to be our leading clue, we cannot, however, tolerate too much divergence. Is it not the case that with all the very large towns, say those with a population of half a million or more, the basic phenomena of class confrontation must be appearing in all of them, or there must be a serious hole in this way of thinking?

Another form of trend thinking which has a rather stronger hold, and which has been mentioned in this conference, is the idea of taking a single element in the situation and making it more or less determine everything else. There is, for example, the frontier thesis, an application to cities of the way Turner thought or is thought to have thought. The city is regarded as deriving its characteristic form and flavour from some very general circumstance that is basically environmental, like that of the continuous occupation of new lands. This is very attractive, of course, because if you can convince yourself that thinking in this vein is legitimate, you have found a great simplifier. The great clue to differences between cities becomes their proximity to the frontier in both time and space. But this is a very limited form of trend thinking, for, by the nature of things the frontier is eventually closed, at least in the simple geographical sense implied in Turner.

There is also the socio-ecological approach which has appeared in the highly stimulating writings of Professor Lampard. Now this is very difficult to assess. He refers to 'the community structure as the outcome of a changing balance between population and environment (including habitat and other populations) mediated by technology and organization'.[2] I think we all feel, in a way, that we know what he is saying, but it is a hard saying for historians because instinctively they tend to reject concepts and thinking of this kind. They do not feel that reifications like technology

[2] American historians and the study of urbanization', *The American Historical Review*, lxvii (1961), p. 30.

and social organisation are safe, or even respectable, guides, especially when used in this generalised way, as mediating variables. This way of thinking would seem to confine the dynamic role to technology and social organisation, and therefore to imply that the chronology of change is determined by them. It is, of course, grossly unfair to speak this way about Professor Lampard's ideas in his absence (it is very much to be regretted that he is not here) and without quoting him in full. But I do so to indicate what I think is an important element in the reaction of many historians. They feel that this kind of sociology-ecology is rather frightening and may be unmanageable. Some of them are aware that it is used by philosophically-minded development economists and others in attempts to generalise the processes of economic and social growth as a whole; such economists find that when they descend to the level of investigation and the giving of advice, such a formulation is not very useful.

In attempts to deal with this question of trend we continually find in the literature the dichotomy between the city as an independent variable, and as a dependent one. Treating the city as an independent variable means, of course, conceiving of it as containing within itself, at least in certain aspects, the major determinants of its own experience. By contrast, to conceive of the city as a dependent variable is to regard it as the resultant of the interaction of forces that are very much wider than it, that embrace the entire economy and the entire society, and indeed, it may be, the whole comity of societies. It would seem to be clear that all societies, as they improve their control of environment, produce towns and cities where the more concentrated activities may take place. These are thus an intrinsic component of any society capable of more than the simplest cultivation or mineral exploitation. Once created, however, the city becomes a phenomenon in its own right, within which new relationships arise that could not otherwise exist. The urban and rural dichotomy is, therefore, a reality, in spite of the existence of many intermediate or hybrid forms. In this respect urban history poses but one form of a general problem: how do we dissever from the generalised interaction of forces within a society, from which trend derives, those sub-components, like the city, so as to achieve valid and useful results? The business firm and the civil bureaucracy raise the same question; the city is, however, unique in at least two senses. It has a spatial dimension that reacts upon all other aspects, for within the city there is always contention for site, and, secondly, it is a composite, containing not only firms and bureaucracies, but large populations, some members of which, when they have will and opportunity, are in continuous adjustment to their urban context, and some of whom are the passive impotent folk for whom neither economy

349

nor city can find a function worthy of reward, and who must in consequence, be the human residuals of the urban scene, following a locational pattern that is, in part at least, predictable, and which may well have political significance.

It is clear, however, in spite of all the difficulties, that trend thinking is a useful setter of perspective, a kind of historical callisthenic that we ought to indulge in for the sake of our general grasp of human experience. It is a corrective to which we all ought to turn after periods of concentration on the particular and the local.

Thematic history, if it is to be useful, must make possible comparative history. It must therefore consist in detecting the operation of a given factor, or constellation of factors, within situations separate from one another in time or space or both. Dr. Dyos and Mr. Bédarida, in their papers on the scope and development of urban history, were quite rightly concerned in our first session that if a theme is investigated in one urban context it should be treated in such a way that comparability of its operation in others is possible.

But there are general problems here also which the conscientious historian cannot escape. There is the dichotomy which appears in other aspects of history, between the internalist and the externalist ways of thinking. That is to say, in the history of science, for example, you can study the evolution of a scientific idea, tracing how one discovery concerning it arose out of another, thinking purely in terms of the scientific problem that successive men were seeking to solve. But how much further should you go? How far is it necessary to elaborate the economic, social, philosophical, legal, etc., context within which the evolution of the idea has taken place? So it is with our themes in urban history (or indeed any other aspect of history). By the time the discussion has extended far enough to make the thematic treatment appear reasonable, with the terms of comparability of examples fully and precisely established, the limits of the debate may have become very wide indeed. Moreover the phenomenon that is the subject of the theme and comparison will manifest different characteristics in different situations. Does it remain the same phenomenon? If it is social class in the sense of Mr. Armstrong, using the Registrar General's Classification of Occupations, without other implications about behaviour, outlook or aspirations, it probably is; if it is social class in Mr. Foster's sense the concept is much more difficult to deal with. ('The class dimension . . . encompasses the immediate context that moulded a man's behaviour, and involves not just his politics in the narrow sense but who he married, where he lived, how he worked, and what he hoped for.')

The main disciplinary headings under which the significant themes can be grouped would seem to be the economic, social, spatial, ideological, and political. Of these the economic and the social, especially the latter, have rather dominated our thoughts. After listening to the sociologists I have come to respect sociology much more than formerly, but rather in the frame of mind of Mark Twain who once remarked that good music is a hell of a lot better than it sounds.

Ideology has been touched upon fairly frequently in our discussions. How far did the shape of this city or that depend upon the views that its inhabitants, at least those responsible for policy, have taken of their city? Are the politics and ideas of the city (and those of society as a whole), mere derivatives, or do they have their own validity? It seems to me that in this age of advanced science, technology and materialism, there has been, at least to some degree, a retreat from the simple 'epiphenomenal' notion, and an increasing tendency to wonder whether significant limitations to economic growth and social fulfilment do not lie in the mind. For the more confident we become of our scientific skills, the greater, it would seem, is the implication that we do not improve our cities, not because of the lack of means, but because of the inhibiting attitudes that prevail. Certainly historical observers cannot fail to be struck by the difficulties men have always had in accepting the demands that the good urban life has made upon their ability to understand and to control or at least modify their context. This is true of both politicians and planners. The latter are deeply conditioned by experience. In Europe, history has had a long run and has suffered less discontinuity: many, perhaps most, European planners on the whole favour the nucleated city, focused upon, organised around and radiating from a core that is historically determined and which in some way contains the elements of urban fulfilment. American planners entertain and often favour other possibilities including polycentric cities comprising metropolitan regions. The Japanese in this as in so much else are the most advanced pragmatics, for their urban explosion, as part of a great historical discontinuity, makes them so.

It is, of course, the theme treatment that produces the monograph, single or comparative. A glance at the *Urban History Newsletter* edited by Dr. Dyos from Leicester University, which has now reached its seventh number, shows how numerous and diverse these are. They include: housing, building, land use, land tenure, transportation, administration, finance, politics, health, sanitation, food supplies, population, family, social class, élites, power-structures, sub-cultures, crime, conflict, protest, philanthropy, welfare, architecture, spatial planning, the demands of terrain, the aesthetics of the city, locational advantage, the industrial mix, the commercial facilities of the central business district. It seems to me that the historian, professional or amateur, provided that he does a reasonably conscientious job and provided he has looked at the general secondary sources cannot go very far wrong with such monographic themes. For the minute books, the correspondence, the town plans, the reports, will keep him on the rails. He may not go very far in establishing new frames of reference, but he may well put others in a position to do so. It is an invaluable exercise to immerse oneself in the day-to-day records of a public body or a business, trying always to rise above the particular, seeking the meaning of what was done and some criteria for judging it. I think this remains true, in spite of the difficulties so properly raised by Professor Hoskins this afternoon. I don't think that in stressing the limitations of the surviving records as illuminants of what has happened in the Council Chamber he meant to frighten people off looking into the records of a city; rather he sought to imbue a proper modesty and caution.

Indeed, the monographic theme is probably the best starting point, and the best initial training for the beginner in urban history. Of course, some of us tend to remain beginners; there is too often an emotional resistance to trying to extend the monograph to the making of effective comparisons, and so toward some degree of generality. Some of the economic historians here will perhaps remember how Professor Postan once replied to an adverse review: 'Historians are of two kinds, those who go to the facts hoping to find a pattern, and those who go hoping to lose it'. This kind of unwillingness to leave the safety of the particular—unfortunately it is a function of age, among other things—does afflict quite a few of us and it has to be resisted, ladies and gentlemen, although I think I have more sympathy with the historical ditherers than with those who can see with obsessional clarity.

Coming to urban history from economics, it seemed to me, until enlightened by this conference, that if we have to choose one thematic element as being primary in determining the course of experience of a city, it would have to be the economic; if, in fact, there is time and scope for only one discipline to be applied to the historical problem, economics was it. I am inclined now to wonder whether it would be closer to the truth to say that in the phase of founding, growth and expansion of a city, it is economic factors that constitute the basic theme, for the city is the creation of the business initiatives of those who make new job opportunities; when, however the complex is developed to comprise a major city, with all kinds of physical and cultural elements built into it that have their own patterns of relationship and mutual reinforcement, it may well be that, for the city to be made responsive to the future, it is its sociology that should receive the greater attention. If one considers the large British industrial cities there is an identifiable syndrome of growth and prosperity, and conversely, there is one of decline, depression, and contraction. If the economy of the city is thriving, incomes and employment are rising, tax revenues are high, city amenity continuously improves, crime and indigence are moderate, the atmosphere of the place brings new enterprises, shopping, and general service facilities are good, school teachers are plentiful so that classes are small and the stresses of classroom are less. Conversely, if the economic base of the town is failing, there will be high unemployment, low incomes, poor housing, obsolescence running ahead of renewal, social deterioration, high crime rates, a bad educational situation, new enterprises will go elsewhere. The politics of the city will relate to these two conditions. In the phase of decline there will almost certainly in a British city be a Labour council, concerned, quite naturally, with social amelioration rather than with economic growth. It will be largely elected by the denizens of the decayed inner ring (unless they have been strategically dispersed in peripheral housing estates). The middle class will increasingly opt out of the life of the city, taking their homes to independent suburbs and sending their children to independent schools; perhaps they will do this even when there is prosperity. As Professor Court has said of Britain in the inter-war years, 'The sociology of a country in which the observer could pass within the day from the men without work of the stricken mining towns of County Durham to the life of the new featureless suburbs of a thriving engineering centre like Birmingham was strange.'[3]

Whether economics or sociology is primary in this sense or not, we certainly need to know the conditions of viability of a city, how they arise, and how they may diminish. To understand them we must certainly do some thematic thinking, but we must be sure that we do not do it in any exclusive frame of mind. Further questions of course follow, affecting those who are responsible for taking decisions, both in city government and in the city's business firms. What is the form and the strength of their response to the challenges of the viability, in both social and economic terms, of the city? As the example of the city of Calcutta to-day demonstrates, effective government is a condition of urban redemption that is very difficult to supply, and may, indeed, require historical roots. To

[3] W. H. B. Court, *A Concise Economic History of Britain* (Cambridge, 1954), p. 295.

manage the post-industrial city there is need for will, for steadfastness, and for discipline: it may be that in Britain this came as one of the many results of puritanism, in its authoritarian form, manifesting itself in Victorian times.

It may be that the historian is in a position to give guidance on the problem that arises in the disseverance of themes so that they may be separately considered, bearing in mind always his other responsibility, to guard against the false completeness of the monograph the limits of which may have been arbitrarily, and so wrongly, defined. In particular, it may be that in dealing with themes that cut right across the older disciplinary framework the historian has a special rôle. For example, the suburb, as Dr. Dyos has so ably shown, is a valuable theme, but one which cannot be treated adequately without much inter-disciplinary, and perhaps some non-disciplinary, thought. So too with attempts at urban renewal, like those of Glasgow and Birmingham in the later nineteenth century; their study may well show significant aspects and inter-relationships that might otherwise be lost.

Thirdly, we can try to view the city in contextual terms, attempting to conceive all urban experience, in a chosen place over a defined period of time, as some kind of totality. This way of thinking and writing worried Dr. Harris and others a good deal in our first discussion.

How valid are attempts at such a synoptic view? In many cases those who have written this way have done so not as the outcome of systematic thought, but rather in an inspired and intuitive way. What place is there in urban history, or indeed in general urban thought, for this kind of intuitive perception? How far is it possible to identify the 'persona' of a city? Is its generalised essence capable of fairly summary statement? How far is it sound to ask questions like this: 'Is Moscow a city in the same sense as the western European cities: does it have the same feel of city life as Paris?'[4] The archetypal practitioners of this approach, people like G. M. Young, Sir John Summerson, Lewis Mumford, Frank Lloyd Wright, and Asa Briggs, can sometimes produce insights which are highly provocative and which later plodders may use to try to build models on. Young, for example, could conjecture about the relationships between towns and their cultural-historical background in a way that might well escape a social scientist of high professional discipline but low cultural sensibility. In the course of musing on the subtle effects that may be

[4] Asa Briggs, *New Society* (3 March 1966), p. 23.

produced by the projection of basic cultural values into town building, he writes: 'Marlborough, a Puritan stronghold, was destroyed by fire in 1653, and rebuilt with the help of a national subscription headed by Cromwell. The result is one of the loveliest things in England. It is a little town: it has not the amusing metropolitan air of Cirencester, for example, which always seems to be murmuring, "Of course you know, my mother was a Roman colony".'[5] He remarked upon the differences between the English and the American view of the city in Victorian times: 'Very rarely in English writing of the nineteenth century do we come upon the idea of a great town as an entity, as a thing in itself. The idea had to be built up by slow degrees. In America it was there from the first. The best society of Philadelphia was trying to improve and glorify Philadelphia. The best society of Manchester was trying to get out of it. Liverpool alone of English towns had, I think, some trace of the civic self-consciousness of a Nuremberg or a Venice. . . .' As Dr. Eversley indicated this morning, a man not blinkered nor disciplined could sometimes see things that could be the beginning of new understanding. One is tempted to see that, just as science needs metaphysics, so history needs the intuitive writer. The great danger of such an approach is, of course, that the writer will allow his preconceptions to dominate his mind. This is especially likely to happen with respect to the theory held of human nature: anyone who believes, for example, in the adjustability of humans to new situations can always find evidence of this happening, so that even slum life can be shown to have its cosy joys.

Context thinking, by its very nature, is the least organised approach to the city. Perhaps it can be aided by the device mentioned somewhat apologetically in our discussion on Friday night, namely that of a check-list. I thought I detected a feeling that it was disreputable to have notes on your cuff about what you ought for the sake of completeness to bring into your thinking. But surely there is nothing wrong with such a list, derived from the various disciplines here represented. At least it could be used by the intuitive writer in an *ex post* way to check whether what he has perceived is consistent with the humbler observations of others.

It is over this matter of the contextual view that the urban historian encounters a lot of scholars, some of whom are not represented in this room. There is, for example, the student of literature. Should the lecturer in Victorian English Literature give a picture of London, as a preliminary to the consideration of works set within it? If so, in what should such a picture consist? Should the urban historian help him in this? Or, indeed, does the *littérateur* create, of his own motion, new perceptions of urban

[5] G. M. Young, *Victorian Essays*, ed. W. D. Handcock (Oxford, 1962), p. 67.

life, derived from the words of fiction that he is studying? Certainly, he will be seeking some sort of understanding of the urban ambience that is contextual in the sense that I am using that term. Similarly in studying the history of politics. The three papers we considered this afternoon, J. Foster, 'Nineteenth-Century Towns—A Class Dimension', R. Newton, 'Society and Politics in Exeter 1837-1914', and E. P. Hennock 'The Social Composition of Borough Councils in some Large Cities, 1835-1914', indicated how the urban historian makes his contribution to the study of politics by presenting the urban situation in which such processes took place. Most urban historians, I would guess, would like to feel that if they were approached by the student of literature, of politics, or bio-graphy, they could give some sort of generalised account of a given city that, by drawing both upon disciplines and intuitions, would have validity.

Such context thinking leads us to what our American colleagues call city biography. It is in writing the history of a single city that contextual history really presents its challenge. Consider the difficulties that confront Dr. Sutcliffe in his project of carrying the history of Birmingham down to the present. Authors in his position know that if their history of this city or that has any circulation at all, all sorts of people will look at it and will rummage in it for what they think important. Until now, many a bland city historian has quietly ignored those gaps that he could not fill. How honest should the urban historian be in pointing out such voids in his knowledge; how frank should he be, having gone over his check-list, in confessing the extent and nature of his omissions? In the present state of play I should think that the history of Birmingham over the past thirty years or so, if measured against the multi-disciplinary terms of this con-ference, would have more holes than substance. This would certainly be true of the case I know best, that of Glasgow. Professor Briggs wrote his much admired Birmingham volume in an incredibly short period of time. How did he do it? I suspect that it was partly by sheer vitality, and partly by setting up in his own mind what he thought was important and then driving shafts and galleries through the mountain of material. I think that this kind of judgement-based operation will still have to be done if we are to get a reasonable crop of histories of large cities within the next decade or so. Writers of civic histories must form their own judgement of what is important. They must take their own total view of the city, and then bear down on the sources at those points which they have chosen as having a high order of significance.

The closer we get to the present the more complicated the city as a totality becomes. One suspects from conversations with Professor Hoskins and others that there is a belief that life was just as complicated, or at least, just as difficult of historical understanding, if you go back to the sixteenth century or earlier. I find this improbable. For one thing, the sources are so much more numerous now than they have been before; the complexities of urban life have assumed a new intractability. Dr. Pahl, this morning, in discussing urbanism and ruralism illustrated the difficulties by showing the enormous range of social, political, and economic forms that are now possible. We must accept this challenge. This is especially true for those historians who believe that they have something to contribute to policy making, if only in the sense of helping to establish perspective.

*

There remains the question of articulating the parts of the model when thinking at each of the three levels of trend, theme, and context.

To be explicit to the degree demanded by really comprehensive model-building is very difficult indeed. If you are going to do it properly you must, of course, do three things. You must choose the operative concepts and reduce them to categories so defined that they are both unambiguous and measurable. You must have a technique of measurement for each of the components of your problem such as to make possible the demonstration of a generalised pattern of systematic concomitance. Finally, you have to establish the logical relationships between the parts into which you have divided the whole.

Professor Chevalier, as has already been said in this conference, has mounted an all-out assault on this sort of thing in a brave article in the *Times Literary Supplement* of September 1966 entitled, 'A Reactionary View of Urban History'. He tells us that the intrusion into history of disciplines that are alien to history, especially those involving quantification, is generally accompanied by a pseudo-scientific presentation, using poorly understood concepts borrowed from elsewhere. I don't think many urban historians would go all the way with Professor Chevalier; in fact, on balance, I think we would probably reject his point of view. (Economic historians, indeed who are at present challenged so strongly by the 'Cliometrists' have become rather self-conscious and apologetic about their failures in formal presentation.) On the other hand, there is a strong feeling that we must be careful not to succumb entirely to the formalists. We must insist on bringing to bear all the non-quantitative forms of judgement that are available to us. Those who have taken part in discussions based upon a paper containing a cost-benefit analysis will know how easy it is to lose sight of the qualifications that the author of the paper has made as he has listed factors that are important but imponderable, and to argue as though the analysis is definitive. Professor Kabk in the same issue of the *T.L.S.* ('Mathematics and Complexity', p. 804) remarks that computers now make it possible for a group of research workers or even a single individual, to grasp and analyse the entire available material, going into the most minute detail, over a very wide field of historical events. Mr. Armstrong, Dr. Dyos and Mrs. Baker gave us valuable insights into this kind of operation; we have learned a good deal from them about both the scope and limitations of historical quantification.

If you will forgive a personal reference, may I say that my own thoughts on the problems of model-building as a means of interpreting urban experience have been much affected by membership of the Development Corporation for the new town of East Kilbride in Scotland. Watching the new town develop under a public agency armed with statutory powers that allow of a very far-reaching control of environment and of the relationships between the parts, I often wonder as I sit there at the Corporation meetings, how far even our highly talented and highly informed body of officials really understand the totality of the town. It is in this sort of situation that you begin to understand how multiple the interrelations that compose the town really are, and how subtle the patterns they form can often be. For example, in considering rental policy, the Corporation, in the interests of making the town meet economic criteria (which are also incidentally shot through with value judgements) might well decide that rents should be raised. But rents are in fact a complicated schedule depending on the size of houses, the costs of their construction, location, the terms of amortisation and other factors, all of which must be seen in the light of the many social considerations, taking account of the relationship between need and income and so embodying an involved structure of rebates. Any change in rents brings you up against social and economic considerations in intimate interactions; behind these always lie questions of political feasibility. Again, consider what happens if, in response to the unforeseen needs of the society as a whole, the overall dimensions of the partly built town are altered, raising the target population from, say 40,000 to 70,000. At once the total plan will become, to some degree at least, incoherent. Some of its components will be subject to new strains because it is difficult to increase their scale, in proportion to that of the town as a whole, not least because the areal elements now limit one another on the ground. I must say that an acquaintance with the problems of creating a town *de novo*, as a planned artifact, makes one a good deal more sympathetic toward those who built our nineteenth-century cities. It also warns us against judging their performance against ideal, and so false, criteria. So far as historical method is concerned, new town planning certainly emphasises the need for a sound formal logic in establishing patterns of inter-dependence, but, no less, it makes clear how dangerous a false sense of scientific validity can be. Just as the business historian does well to have some experience of business, or at the least should try out his ideas on those who have, so, too, the modern urban historian should have contacts with the politicians and planners who know how things really get done or do not get done.

By way of summary and conclusion, may I pose a question. How should one plan an urban history research programme? All urban historians should be concerned with trend, and theme, and context. But for progress to be made there is need for some degree of concentration of effort. My personal view, as affecting British urban historians is as follows. As I have said elsewhere, it seems to me that the most profitable course for the urban historian is to start his thinking with a significant family of cities, and with a particular one within the family, rather than to talk about urbanisation as a generalised phenomenon.[6] Indeed, in the present state of affairs, those who make thumping generalisations about what happened, even within a particular group of this kind, for example British industrial cities, are likely to find themselves highly vulnerable.

May I say a word or two about our programme at Glasgow: perhaps it will give some degree of concreteness to our discussion of the nature and objects of urban history. We have chosen the British industrial city as the type for study. For very close exemplification we have taken our own city in its many complex aspects. From it we seek to derive the themes and contextual sense that we will test in the wider context. My colleague, William Forsyth, is concerned with the spatial aspect of the city. He is producing a suite of maps intended, in the first instance, to be spatial snapshots at standard intervals of twenty-five years. He then considers the changes that have occurred in each interval. But while trying to be dynamic in this sense, between any two of his master-maps, he has found that all kinds of themes have presented themselves. Now he seems to be building up another suite of maps which are theme-bent, as it were, but which relate to his master-maps. We started in this spatial way because it seemed, in spite of many difficulties, to be manageable, and because it would give definition to many situations. For example, having done this, we will be in a better position to consider economic development and social change. He is struggling with the problem—is Glasgow's spatial evolution consistent with any of the existing morphological schema?

6 *Urban Studies*, i (1964), pp. 34-54.

John Kellett has worked on two main themes. He began with property speculators, including the terms upon which, over time, land became available for building. He has now, as a natural development, turned to the railways, one of the great land-users, and their impact upon the city. In the course of doing this his interest in railways has gone beyond Glasgow and now he is concerned to see what the effects of railways have been on all the major British industrial cities of the nineteenth century. Another colleague, Tom Hart, started with local government (what might be called the 'supervising intelligence' of Glasgow though sometimes it hardly merited that description). He has found the Glasgow situation very interesting, but Hart was not satisfied with seeing Glasgow standing by itself. He has widened out to take in Scotland as a whole; he is rummaging about trying to see what the scope for local government in Scottish cities was in terms of economic development and social initiative, and how effectively it was used. We have for a long time condemned our forebears for the urban messes that they created; it is time to try to assess more precisely the forces with which they had to deal and the means they had available. The middle class has rather fascinated us; Michael Simpson has been looking at the rise of the West End of Glasgow. This, I may say, was to some extent a borrowing of ideas from Dr. Reeder's work from which Simpson has gained a great deal. Charles Allen has made a study of the work of the Glasgow Improvement Commissioners, the authors of the first British attempts to perform a surgical operation on the heart of a mature city. Finally, John MacCaffrey is looking at the politics of Glasgow in the last quarter of the nineteenth century, relating them to social and economic factors. At the moment he is mostly concerned with the national politics, partly because these are easier to deal with in terms of electoral returns and the like, but I am hopeful that he will turn to local politics as well because in this regard the Glasgow story is a significant one. Some of the graduate students in our newly-founded Department of Town and Regional Planning may opt, for their dissertation work, for a topic based upon the evolution of the city.

So that's our agenda. It seems to have arisen—to use a cant word—organically out of the Glasgow context. I suppose you could say that it is positivistic and pragmatic. It owes something to our parallel interest in business history.[7] It might be taken to be parochial, for its basis is indeed within our own city. But we feel that this is the right starting point, from which a more general perspective should begin. We are certainly weak on the sociological side, a fault which, stimulated by this conference, and by work currently going on at Cambridge, we hope to remedy.

7 See P. L. Payne (ed.), *Studies in Scottish Business History* (1967).

Professor Burchard, in summing up the American conference on urban history in 1961, remarked that the floor for the formal papers was given to the thinkers rather than to the doers.[8] In this conference it is the doers who have been dominant. But perhaps this dichotomy is deceptive. For on this occasion most of the thinking in the methodological sense has been done, not by the metaphysicians or impressionists of the subject, but by doers.

It was of set purpose that this was so. The conference has obliged us to face up to the techniques of documentation, quantification (including computerising), visual interpretation, mapping, social structuring, and many others. Most of us will go away no longer conjuring in our minds those notions that are so comforting and which make for easy exposition, but appalled at our ignorance and naïveté, even in matters on which, before this week-end, we thought ourselves worth listening to. The definition of urban history that we require should not be that of the grammarian, who seeks a precision that is permanent, but should rather be an operational one, with all the adaptability that this implies.

---

[8] Oscar Handlin and John Burchard (eds.), *The Historian and the City* (1963), p. 251.

Discussion

There was no doubt that the conference thought it worthwhile to try to define urban history. At the outset the chairman reminded everyone of a suggestion, made at the opening session, that he goes furthest who does not know where he is going. Few speakers took up this suggestion, and Dr. MANN obviously carried the meeting with him when he said, 'We *want* to go the furthest. Surely, the man who doesn't know where he is going walks in circles or disappears in a puff of smoke.'

The utility of the subject having been accepted, the discussion concentrated on two topics. One was the effect which some of the new methods of investigation might have in discouraging originality among research students. The other was an examination of the rôles of the general and the particular in urban history. Two related disputes were at the heart of the latter topic, and speakers moved from one to the other and back again with a sometimes bewildering ease. There was first the question whether the local or the national should have primacy in settling the choice of theme and the distribution of emphasis; and then there was the contest between empiricism and general hypothesis as determinants of the methods and purposes of investigation, a contest that, for much of the time, looked like History *versus* Sociology. But this second topic embraced more than methodological jousting, for it led some contributors to consider and describe their own practices, and it produced a collective effort to see how the general and the particular were involved in some specific examples of investigation.

Discussion of research students and their training came as a pendant to the main debate, from which it was quite distinct. In his paper Prof. CHECKLAND had suggested that research students concentrating on analysis by the methods which Mr. Armstrong and Prof. Schnore had formalised would encounter two dangers: they would not be doing original work in the commonly accepted sense, and they would not get a broad experience of working with varied materials. Mr. ARMSTRONG sought to refute this by pointing out that there was nothing new in carrying on historical research by following other people's models. He also denied that students working on his lines would examine a narrower range of materials than other students. They would begin with a statistical framework but would go on to write a total social survey of a mid-nineteenth century community. A brief dialogue brought out the essentials:

CHECKLAND: You yourself have done 1851. Would you say to a Ph.D. candidate, 'Now, you do 1861 or any subsequent censuses following roughly the methodology I, Armstrong, have developed'?

ARMSTRONG: I wouldn't ask him to do 1861 in quite that narrow sense. Even

362

if he used the categories and classifications that I employed, he would be running into a whole new range of problems involving interpretations that would be new to him. In that sense, I submit that he would be doing original work.

When Prof. SCHNORE added that, though a master's thesis might involve deliberate replication, a Ph.D. student must be more original, and Mr. ARMSTRONG gave an illustration of what was being done by one of his Ph.D. students, Prof. CHECKLAND was satisfied and no other doubts arose on this topic. It was clear that the elaborate examinations of census material involve much more than just measuring the distribution of the people into social categories.

The debate on the general and the particular ranged more widely and produced many more cross-currents. Prof. KÖLLMANN started it all by saying that the whole conference had concentrated on *local* rather than *urban* history, whereas urban history should be a branch of national history. He went on: 'There is first a process of industrialisation. It is a national theme, but we find in Germany (and it may fit only the German case) it is specifically in the beginning, and later as well, an urban process. The second theme would be the development of industrial society. Then you can go to politics, even the development of a labour movement, which is partly a special urban development. . . . If I do a case study, I do not ask, "What are the special questions of *this* community?" (I do ask it too, but this is by the way.) I *do* ask how it is developing from such processes of national history in a community. . . . I ask how national history *influences* the special ways of urban history.'

Others supported him with assurances that Germany was not the only relevant case. Prof. SCHNORE pointed to the tension in American urban history between those who wanted to use cities for the investigation of such themes as Populism or the New Deal and those who advocated the city biography and tried to deal with the city as a whole. Dr. HENNOCK noted that nearly everybody present was British and observed that the conference had been able to take for granted a lot of things that a more international body, or a group more engaged in comparative work, would have had to make explicit. When this last word had been introduced, 'explicit' and 'implicit' were pressed into heavy service. Most speakers were ready to recognise that wider influences are implicitly assumed in detailed urban studies, and some of them were prepared to say what they are or ought to be, and some to say that what is implicit should be made explicit.

But the argument did not all go to one side. At another extreme, Dr. MARTIN claimed that in England it was difficult to approach a town with a question relating to the whole pattern of national history, because in England there was nothing that could be regarded as a typical urban institution. At the beginning of heavy industrialisation, Liverpool, Manchester, and Sheffield each had quite a different form of government and different relations with its land-owning aristocracy. Prof. ASHWORTH gave a reminder that in any specific situation, with a mixture of national and local influences, there could be no presumption that national influences always have the greater weight. Mr. FOSTER, however, going furthest of all for general influences, looked for a conceptual framework that would take in the entire society. He found a possible approach in the contrasting of the very simple rôles in a rural society and the very complex rôles in an urban or industrialised society. But even he had to recognise that some general concepts could be used for only one type of society or one aspect of different societies. He thought that a Marxist conceptual framework could be used in relation to status reactions only within a socialist society. The qualifications to his generalisations got so complicated that he broke off with the remark, 'Probably nobody understands what I am saying, anyway.' But Prof. CHECKLAND showed understanding plus repayment with interest. His immediate riposte was that Mr. Foster's own paper had shown that the way to draw out general contrasts was to do what he had done, get down to understanding three specific cases.

None of this sway of the argument led Prof. KÖLLMANN to alter his views. His last contribution was to ask, 'Where do I get my questions?' And he answered, 'Out of national history', adding an illustration which enabled him to say, 'I took this question and went with it to the sources I had in the city, and when I asked my sources I not only got answers referring to the city alone, but answers referring to explanations of this process in national history.' Those on the other side never went more than part of the way to meet him. The most typical concession came from Prof. CHECKLAND in the middle of the discussion. He was prepared to agree that in studying urban processes we can see in them processes of history in a larger context. But he added a warning that we must not read into the local context a general thesis evolved by earlier scholars on some specific aspect. 'We are trying,' he said, 'to empty out pre-conceptions. Of course, that makes us a bit frightened of what Prof. Köllmann would regard as urban history.'

This was a new provocation which brought another major strand into the argument. There was immediate questioning of the wisdom of those who are suspicious of general ideas, a group apparently equated with the empirical historians who stick to the sources and nothing but the sources. Dr. PAHL was the first to suggest that the conference had revealed this timidity. He thought historians were afraid that other disciplines were supplying the concepts and making history their handmaiden, whereas historians ought to have more confidence and take and use the concepts for themselves. Not put off by Dr. KELLETT's retort that historians were just being practical and were refusing to try 'in an amateurish way to rephrase the professional jargon of the sociologist with a few inadequate illustrations derived at second hand', he renewed the attack. 'It may be,' said Dr. PAHL, 'that sociologists put up the idea before they get the facts, that historians are much more cautious; but because of this caution that historians have developed for their sources, they have an even more excessive caution in launching forth, once they have done the work, on the interpretation of the theories, on the hypothesis, and so on.' He welcomed the approach made by Mr. Foster, who not only adopted openly a general conceptual framework—Marxist in his case—but within it concentrated locally on a problem which had national interest. Without general concepts it could not be clear that there was any general significance in what emerged from local studies. Dr. Pahl's plea was for historians who would continue with the same kind of investigations as at present, but who would make explicit the concepts of process that they used, and who would thus find a new purpose and orientation. His most extreme support came from Dr. P. R. THOMPSON, who was less patient of historians and found the creativity coming all from the sociologists. 'Sociology has supplied some theory which needs testing, and I think this is very exciting for the historians here. But also it makes one ask a lot of questions one would never have asked and it supplies a whole series of explanations which one would never have dreamt of . . . . Historians are not at the moment asking these questions.'

History at this point certainly seemed likely to be claimed as somebody's handmaiden, but the claim did not go unchallenged. Prof. ASHWORTH said that the historians would not be content with the pursuit of theory for its own sake, but only for the sake of discovering something directly about human life. If they were told that the purpose of historical investigation is to prove a theory, they would think the cart and the horse were the wrong way round. More than one later speaker rejected any suggestion that sociologists seek to prove theories and claimed that their purpose was to test hypotheses. But this modification hardly lessened the difference of approach.

The most determined defence of empiricism came from Dr. KELLETT, who insisted that 'whatever we do *must* be founded upon an adequate block of promising source material . . . and this is what every historian *must* start from, no matter what instructions or thoughts may have been put into his mind. . . . We must not think that because historians do the digging they do not know where the gold is. They are just being practical in saying that we must all know what we are working upon.' At first, he seemed to be suggesting that historians start only with a body of source material, which itself gradually reveals the questions to be pursued. He went on, however, to admit that the historian starts with an idea as well, though the sources might lead him to change the questions he wants to answer. But he never abandoned his basic position, which Prof. ASHWORTH interpreted as a reminder that 'whether we are doing urban history or any other kind of history, what we want is the history of the real world, and not to be lured into writing the history of Never-Never Land.'

Other contributors gradually softened the sharp lines of difference. Dr. DYOS denied that historians normally begin with the documents. 'It is true,' he remarked, 'that they say so, . . . but normally they are judicious in their selection and they only pick up certain bundles of documents because they have implicit in their minds certain kinds of question.' This was what he called 'putting Dr. Kellett's position differently from the way he suspects he thinks', a small pressure to which Dr. Kellett apparently yielded. But Dr. Dyos went further and insisted that 'it is crucial *to remain absolutely stuck with the problems and the questions*' even though the sources for a long time fail to answer them. By sticking to the questions he believed that the historian usually found himself led to sources which had the answers.

From the sociologists, too, there were modifying contributions. Dr. MANN said that sociologists might have better techniques than historians but shared some common problems and were no better placed to solve them. He made it plain that the main difficulty in defining urban history was that of defining urban anything. He said that many studies were called urban sociology just because they were about things that happened to be in towns, and it was difficult to make a case for urban sociology as against sociology of an industrialised society. Urban sociology could easily be talked out by those who wanted to, and so could urban history in the same way. Dr. PAHL agreed about the confusion and, as a remedy, turned to a purely practical justification for sociologists to look at the past: 'I am very hopeful that I will understand more about the essential nature of urbanism from England in the nineteenth century than I ever could from Britain in the twentieth century.' And Mr. C. HARRIS put in a late reminder that sociologists who specialise in community studies are just as much attacked for parochialism as urban historians are. So this aspect of the wide debate on the general and the particular, having submerged its original simplicities with complexities of more mixed allegiance, proceeded to something like a truce without a resolution of the differences.

Incidentally it had elicited some useful remarks on the practical business of writing urban history. Prof. KÖLLMANN's 'Where do I get my questions?' and the exchange between Dr. KELLETT and Dr. DYOS about what is practical both provided a stimulus. Dr. KELLETT was not readily convinced by Dr. Dyos's insistence that one must stick to the questions even when the sources are unpromising, and told him, 'You must look for what is practical, and I am sure that you did this, in fact, in spite of what you say.'

'No,' replied Dr. DYOS, 'there were lots of things, especially when I was writing *Victorian Suburb*, which *did* seem impossible. . . . One has a hypothesis, one looks for evidence with which to develop it, or to contradict it, and simply is disappointed after a search that there is nothing. But if one is adamant and importunate in knocking at the doors where it is said that there are no documents, you find then, in the end, something comes into your hands.'

Dr. Dyos also tackled the problem of deciding how he got his questions. His answer was to begin with demography, which would immediately lead to the phenomenon called concentration or village or town or city, and this would pose supplementary questions about how people reacted to each other, and how fertility and mortality rates changed. Prof. CHECKLAND would not have this at all and maintained that the questions, 'Why are people accumulating, what sustains them there?' are prior to anything demographic and demand an economic approach. He was unconvinced and conceded only that there might be a pragmatic case for starting with demography, simply because we have better population figures than income figures, but never because it is logically sounder.

Only when everyone concentrated on one specific case was there much sign of agreement about the way to use alternative and complementary approaches.

Curiously, it was Swansea that showed most resemblance to a Vale of Harmony. Prof. CHECKLAND recalled the part of Mr. C. HARRIS's paper, which had presented Swansea as a kind of non-town, and he wondered whether this was because it had not grown enough. Mr. HARRIS thought probably not. He argued that a solid mass of people close together was not necessarily any different from a series of dispersed nuclear villages focusing on a central point and that here lay the difficulty of deciding whether a continuous mass of bricks and mortar was urban. Speculation then began about the answer to the riddle, 'When is a town not a town?' Did the answer depend on its own social structure or on the limitations of the person studying the town? Prof. BEST thought that an economic historian, looking at Swansea, would conclude that it *was* a town in the same sense as another unit of similar size somewhere else. Thus he would find Swansea to be almost a different entity from what the sociologist had found. This led Prof. BARKER to say, 'The ideal thing would be to have a sociologist and an historian going to the same place. The next best thing would be for the historian, with his preconceptions, to talk to some sociologists before he started and keep on talking to sociologists as he goes on.' But Dr. HENNOCK thought the need was rather for two different kinds of historian, one asking questions about social structure, the other asking questions about economic development, and both going with these questions to the relevant documents.

Mr. C. HARRIS spoke favourably of these ways of approaching the problem he had raised. He suggested that such an investigation would present the town as a series of interlocking systems, cultural, social, and economic, and that ideally this ought also to be sought as a process. He argued that all the various systems were in mutual interaction, none of them dependent or independent, but each imposing limits on the movement of the others at any given time. Together they would contribute to a process of development so complicated as to require a whole set of studies, made in close co-operation, no approach being primary and none being ruled out. Even a local study could be done only in the context of all our knowledge and all we could bring to bear about changes in the local society of which the particular sub-system was a part. Dr. HENNOCK summed it up by saying, 'Mr. Harris and I have thrown out of the window the notion that there is a primary factor and we have replaced it by mutual interdependence, the mutual limitation of all factors by each other.'

Nobody quarrelled with this. It was a common front made by a sociologist and a historian when the former extended more elaborately the views expressed by the latter; and, as the CHAIRMAN remarked, Mr. Harris's speeches came very near to making the historians happy by re-stating something which they know by the name of 'the seamless robe'. But, valuable as this measure of agreement may be, reflexion suggests that its use may be limited, for it is agreement about something very difficult that ought to be done, but as yet without much guidance in the practical business of getting it done.

It was not to be expected, however, that one evening would uncover a solution for all the problems of defining urban history. The value of the discussion was not determined by the extent to which differences were resolved and final solutions achieved. The CHAIRMAN suggested, in his concluding remarks, that this was true not only of the final session, but of the whole conference. He said: 'I think it is pretty clear that in this question of defining urban history we have not solved our problems. What we have done is to establish the value of a continuing dialogue between people who come to this subject from a variety of different origins and bring to it a variety of different experiences and different preconceived notions. And I think we have done a service in clearing our minds where we have cluttered them up with things which we have been taking for granted and using implicitly and failing to make explicit; failing also, perhaps, to question whether we ought to be using them at all. I think we have also benefited from coming and opening our minds to things which we had not really considered seriously before. This must have happened to all of us; and this is perhaps the most useful immediate thing that has come out of this conference.'

W. ASHWORTH

Notes on Contributors

W. A. ARMSTRONG, B.A., Ph.D., is a Lecturer in Economic and Social History in the University of Nottingham whose research is in the field of historical demography. He has contributed to *Annales de Demographie Historique* and to E. A. Wrigley (ed.), *An Introduction to English Historical Demography* (1966). In 1967 he completed a doctoral thesis entitled *The Social Structure of York, 1841–51*, which he is now preparing for publication.

W. ASHWORTH, B.Sc.(Econ.), Ph.D., has been Professor of Economic and Social History in the University of Bristol since 1958 and was before that Reader in Economic History at the London School of Economics. His major publications include *A Short History of the International Economy* (1952 and 1962), *Contracts and Finance* [History of the Second World War: United Kingdom Civil Series] (1953), *The Genesis of Modern British Town Planning* (1954), *An Economic History of England, 1870–1939* (1960), and 'Metropolitan Essex since 1850' in the *Victoria History of the County of Essex*, Vol. V (1966). His current research concerns the economics of British defence policy between 1870 and 1914.

(Mrs.) A. B. M. BAKER, B.A., M.Sc.(Econ.), is a Tutorial Assistant in Economics in the University of Leicester who was at the time of the conference Research Assistant to Dr. H. J. Dyos. She is a graduate of Bryn Mawr and the London School of Economics and is now engaged on a study of foreign investment in Latin America.

T. C. BARKER, M.A., Ph.D., became Professor of Economic and Social History in the University of Kent at Canterbury in 1964 and taught for eleven years before that at the London School of Economics. He has published numerous articles on business and transport history and has written *A Merseyside Town in the Industrial Revolution* [with J. R. Harris] (1954 and 1959), *The Girdlers' Company: A Second History* (1957), *Pilkington Brothers and the Glass Industry* (1960), and *A History of London Transport*, Vol. I (1963). He is at present engaged on second volumes in the history of London transport and of Pilkington's and, in association with Professor J. Yudkin, is preparing a history of diet in the nineteenth century.

F. BEDARIDA, M.A., Agrégé de l'Université, is Director of the Maison Française at Oxford and was at the time of the conference a Lecturer at the Sorbonne. He has written for *Revue Historique*, *Annales*, and *Le Mouvement Social*, and has contributed to L. H. Parias (ed.) *Histoire Générale du Travail et des*

Travailleurs, Vol. III, 1875–1914 (1960) and to L. H. Parias (ed.) *Histoire du Peuple Français*, Vol. V, 1914–31 (1963). He has long been interested in urban development and in the social history of London, 1880–1900, which is occupying him now.

H. CARTER, M.A., is Senior Lecturer in Geography in the University College of Wales at Aberystwyth and is spending the session 1967–8 as Visiting Professor of Geography at the University of Cincinnati. His major work has been *The Towns of Wales: a Study in Urban Geography* (1965), and he is now working on the Welsh towns of the mid-nineteenth century and the development of the whole urban system in Wales.

W. H. CHALONER, M.A., Ph.D., has spent all his academic career in the University of Manchester and is now Reader in Modern Economic History there. He has written very extensively for a wide range of journals, mainly in the fields of local, industrial, and business history, and has published *The Social and Economic Development of Crewe, 1780–1923* (1950), *Industry and Technology* [with A. E. Musson] (1963), *People and Industries* (1963); he has, with W. O. Henderson, translated and edited W. Schlote, *British Overseas Trade from 1700 to the 1930s* (1952), W. G. Hoffmann, *British Industry, 1700–1950* (1955), F. Engels, *The Condition of the Working Class in England* (1958); he has also edited a number of reprints, notably W. T. Jackman, *The Development of Transportation in Modern England* (1962) and *The Autiobiography of Samuel Bamford* (1967).

S. G. CHECKLAND, M.A., M.Com., Ph.D., has been Professor of Economic History of the University of Glasgow since 1957 and was formerly a Lecturer in History in the University of Cambridge and Senior Lecturer in Economic Science in the University of Liverpool. He has written *The Rise of Industrial Society in England, 1815–1885* (1964) and *The Mines of Tharsis: Roman, French and British Enterprise in Spain* (1967). He has also contributed a number of articles to the learned journals, primarily on the history of economic thought and commercial activity, and on urban history. He is working now on a study of the elder Gladstone and his family, the development of banking in the Scottish economy since the seventeenth century, and on various aspects of urban development. He is a member of the East Kilbride Development Corporation.

M. R. G. CONZEN, M.A., Dr. phil., has been Professor of Human Geography in the University of Newcastle upon Tyne since 1965. He is spending the whole of 1968 in New Zealand at the University of Christchurch. His major research has been in the field covered by his paper to the conference, and he has made contributions in it to the publications of the Institute of British Geographers, to *Lund Studies in Urban Geography* (1962), and to G. H. J. Daysh (ed.), *The Growth and Character of Whitby* (1958). His study of the urban morphology of British towns is now being extended to the historical geography of towns in the rest of Europe.

Notes on the Contributors

H. J. DYOS, B.Sc.(Econ.), Ph.D., has spent all his academic career in the University of Leicester, where he has been Reader in Economic History since 1964 and is currently Dean of the Faculty of the Social Sciences. His main field of research has been the history of London in the nineteenth century on which he has written numerous articles, mainly in the *Journal of Transport History* and *Victorian Studies*, and the first volume of a history of one of its suburbs, *Victorian Suburb: A Study of the Growth of Camberwell* (1961 and 1966). He is now working on a second volume concerning its social structure and is planning a general history of London in the years 1870–1914. He has recently completed, with Dr. D. H. Aldcroft, a general introduction to the economic history of British transport.

D. E. C. EVERSLEY, B.Sc.(Econ.), Ph.D., was Reader in Economic History in the University of Birmingham until 1966, and is now Reader in Population Studies in the University of Sussex. He has long taken both a practical and a scholarly interest in town planning and has also contributed to a wide range of journals. His major academic work has been in the field of historical demography, in which his chief contributions have been *Social Theories of Fertility and the Malthusian Debate* (1959), *Population in History* [ed.] (1965), *Population Growth and Planning Policy* (1965), and to E. A. Wrigley (ed.), *Introduction to English Historical Demography* (1966); he has also co-edited and provided with much additional material, a new edition of Charles Creighton's *A History of Epidemics in Britain*, 2 vols. (1965). He now has in hand three major undertakings: the historical demography of the Quakers; a study of women's activity rates; an analysis of the determinants of household formation and the overall demand for houses.

J. FOSTER, M.A., Ph.D., is a Research Fellow of St. Catharine's College, Cambridge, and has recently completed the doctoral thesis, *Capitalism and Class Consciousness in Earlier Nineteenth-century Oldham*, which embodies a more extensive analysis of the paper read to the conference. He is continuing to work on the working-class movement in early nineteenth-century England.

E. P. HENNOCK, M.A., Ph.D., has been a Senior Lecturer in History in the University of Sussex since 1963, and before that taught at the University College of North Staffordshire; he spent part of the session 1966–7 as a Visiting Fellow of All Souls' College, Oxford. He has published papers on the history of sanitary and municipal reform and on the scope of urban history. He is now engaged in completing a book on the subject of the paper which was read to the conference.

W. G. HOSKINS, M.Sc.(Econ.), M.A., Ph.D., is the Hatton Professor of English History and Head of the Department of English Local History in the University of Leicester, from which he is retiring in 1968. From 1951 to 1965 he was Reader in Economic History in the University of Oxford and a Fellow of All Souls', and before that Reader in English Local History at University College, Leicester. He held a Leverhulme Research Fellowship in 1961–3.

371

He was a member of the Royal Commission on Common Land (1955–8) and author of the Historical Appendix to its Report; he also served on the Ministry of Housing and Local Government's Advisory Committee on Buildings of Historical and Architectural Interest (1955–64). He has written and broadcast extensively on local history. His major writings include: *Industry, Trade, and People in Exeter, 1688–1800* (1935), *Essays in Leicestershire History* (1950), *Devonshire Studies* [with H. P. R. Finberg] (1952), *Devon* (1954), *The Making of the English Landscape* (1955), *The Midland Peasant* (1957), *Local History in England* (1959), *The Common Lands of England and Wales* [with the late Sir Dudley Stamp] (1963), *Provincial England* (1965), *Fieldwork in Local History* (1967). He is now working on the social and economic history of England in the sixteenth century and on English harvests from 1086 to 1900.

F. M. JONES, B.Arch., A.R.I.B.A., is Director of the Housing Research Group in the School of Architecture at the University of Liverpool. He has written on industrial archaeology, and his current research concerns human motivation and attitudes in relation to technical innovations in housing.

J. R. KELLETT, M.A., Ph.D., is Senior Lecturer in Economic History in the University of Glasgow. He has published several articles on various aspects of urban history in the *Economic History Review*, the *Journal of Transport History*, and the *Scottish Journal of Political Economy*. He has written a small textbook on the urban history of Glasgow and has recently completed a major study, *The Impact of Railways on Victorian Cities*, which is to be published in the Autumn, 1968. He is now engaged in the study of estate development, landownership and land values, and the Municipal Boundaries question.

J. D. MARSHALL, B.Sc.(Econ.), Ph.D., is Senior Lecturer in the Regional History of North-west England in the University of Lancaster. He has for some years been making a detailed study of this area and has published an important study, *Furness and the Industrial Revolution* (1958). He is continuing his researches into the industrial, social and urban development of Lancashire and Cumberland.

G. H. MARTIN, M.A., D.Phil., F.R.Hist.S., is Reader in History in the University of Leicester. He is spending the session 1967–8 as Visiting Professor of Medieval History in Carleton University, Ottawa. Among his publications are *The Story of Colchester from Roman Times to the Present Day* (1959), *The Town* (1961), *The Royal Charters of Grantham, 1463–1688* (1963), and an edition of Gross's *Bibliography of British Municipal History* (1966). He has written two important papers on the English borough in the Middle Ages, a subject which occupies him still. He is now preparing a critical bibliography of British and Irish municipal history.

R. NEWTON, C.M.G., M.A., Ph.D., is a retired civil servant, who has used his retirement since 1961 to undertake some research into the history of Exeter in the nineteenth century. This has had its outcome in a doctoral thesis, of which the paper presented to the conference is a synopsis. The whole work has now been published as *Victorian Exeter* (1968).

D. A. REEDER, B.A., B.Sc.(Econ.), M.A., Ph.D., is Head of the Department of Education at the Garnett College of Education and holds a University Research Fellowship in Economic History at the University of Leicester in the session 1967–8. He has completed a major piece of research on the development of west London and written a paper on leasehold enfranchisement for the *International Review of Social History*. He is contributing to a new history of Fulham, to be published in 1968, and is now working on a comparative study of suburban development in large English cities between 1841 and 1871. He is also occupied with the history of technical education since 1851.

L. F. SCHNORE, B.A., M.A., Ph.D., is Professor of Sociology in the University of Wisconsin at Madison. He has been a member of numerous public and academic bodies, including the National Research Council, National Academy of Sciences, Committee on Urban Measurements, Highway Research Board, Committee on Urbanization of the Social Sciences Research Council, Population Association of America. He has written *The Urban Scene: Human Ecology and Demography* (1965) and an extremely large number of articles on various aspects of urbanisation and its ecological features, especially in the *American Journal of Sociology* and *American Sociological Review*; he has also contributed to *Encyclopaedia Britannica* and *International Encyclopedia of the Social Sciences*, and acted as co-editor of *The Study of Urbanization* (1965) and *Urban Research and Policy Planning* (1967). His present commitment, which is being supported by the National Science Foundation, is an extensive quantitative study of the ecological patterns in American urban history.

F. H. W. SHEPPARD, B.A., Ph.D., has been the General Editor of the *Survey of London* since 1954 and has been responsible for the nine volumes that have appeared in the series between 1956 and 1966. He has made a number of other contributions to the history of London, including *Local Government in St. Marylebone, 1688–1835* (1958), and is now writing a general history of the making of early Victorian London.

Sir JOHN SUMMERSON, C.B.E., F.B.A., F.S.A., A.R.I.B.A., B.A.(Arch.), M.A., Hon.D.Litt., has been Curator of Sir John Soane's Museum since 1945, and is currently a Lecturer in the Department of the History of Art in Birkbeck College, London, and for the session 1967–8 Slade Professor of Fine Art in the University of Cambridge. He has for some years been a member of the Royal Commission on Historical Monuments, the Historical Manuscripts Commission, and the Historic Buildings Committee of what is now the Ministry of Public Building and Works. He spent over 20 years, many of them as Chairman, of the Listed Buildings Committee of the Ministry of Housing and Local Government. His publications include: *John Nash* (1935 and 1949), *Georgian London* (1945 and 1962), *Heavenly Mansions* (1949), *Sir John Soane* (1952), *Sir Christopher Wren* (1953), *Architecture in Britain, 1530–1830* (1953, 4th ed. 1963), *The Classical Language of Architecture* (1964), and *Inigo Jones* (1966). He is now engaged on the study of the architecture of Victorian London.

INDEX

Aberaeron, 241, 242 *map*, 273
Aberamman, 244–5
Aberdeen, 20*n*
Aberystwyth, 240, 242, 243 *map*
Abram, Wm. Alexander, 21*n*
Accrington, *plate 33*
Adams, R. M., 10*n*
Adburgham, Alison, 264*n*
Age of Great Cities, The, 3
Aigues Mortes, 235
Ainsworth, Harrison, 175
Ainsworth, John, 224*n*
Albuquerque, 206
Algeria, study of urban history in, 49*n*
Allan, C. M., 38*n*
Allardt, Erik, 296
Allday, Joseph, 322
Allen, Charles, 360
Allen, G. C., 22, 24*n*
Allison, J. E., 26*n*
Alnwick, 113*n*, 117*n*, 124, 151
Alsace, 50
Alston Moor, 221
American Cities in Perspective, 9
American Sociological Association, 199
Amsterdam, 213
Anápolis, 203
Anderson, N., 1*n*, 9*n*
Annales d'Histoire Economique et Sociale, 54, 55
Anti-urban bias, 46
  anti-urbanisation, 278
Arbos, P., 49*n*
Archaeology, vii
  archaeological societies, 21
  identification of Maerdrefi, 235
  identification of monastic cells, 234–5
  identification of pre-urban nuclei, 234
  see also Medieval towns
Architecture, 51–2, 171–2, 174, 274
  architectural history, 40, 43*n*, 137

as a total human experience, 171–2
as 'civic design', 174
Classical revival, 166
design of factories, 180–2
echoes of Renaissance, 241
Ministry of Housing's lists, 133–4
Archives du Ministère de la Guerre, 56
Armstrong, W. A., 36, 45, 65, **67–85**, 87*n*, 88, 97, 100, 101, 102, 109, 146, 148, 150, 344, 350, 358, 362, 363
Artisans', Labourers' and General Dwellings Company, 265
Arts and Crafts Movement, 131, 182
Ashbee, C. R., 131, 133, 143
Ashley, Percy, 29*n*
Ashton, T. S., 5*n*, 13, 30
Ashworth, William, 39, 183, 185, 253, 338, 339, 363, 365, 367, 368
Askam-in-Furness, 217
Athenaeum, The, 310
Atlanta, 205, 206
Attwood, Thomas, 320
Auzelle, Robert, 43
Aydelotte, William O., 89, 90, 107, 208*n*
Axon, William E. A., 22*n*

Babbage, B. H., 226*n*
Bailey, F. A., 29*n*
Baines, Edward, 329, 350
Baines, Thomas, 20*n*
Baker, Mrs. A. B. M., 36, **87–112**, 146, 148, 358
Baker, Robert, 332
Baltimore, 206
Balzac, Honoré de, 13
Banbury, 32, 38*n*
Bankers, in local politics, 310, 312, 330, 332
Banks, Paul, 41*n*
Barcelona, 213

375

Index

Index

384

Keith-Lucas, B., 33*n*
Kellett, J. R., 34*n*, 37*n*, 41*n*, 45, 63, 64,
  151, 152, 153, 210, 212, 213, 276,
  360, 364, 365, 366
Kendal, 164, *plates 17, 18, 19*
Kennaway, Mark, 306
Kennedy, William, 20*n*
Keyser, Erik, 16*n*, 114*n*, 120*n*, 124
King Baker, W., 259*n*
Kings Lynn, 20*n*, 162, 163; *plate 16*
Kirkland, Edward C., 17
Kitson, Sir James, 334
Kohn, C. F., 25*n*
Köllmann, W., 148, 272, 273, 274, 275,
  276, 277, 278, 363, 364, 366
Korn, A., 18*n*
Kraeling, G. H., 10*n*
Krausz, Ernest, 31*n*
Kuczynski, R. R., 18

Labour, effect of rural over-population
  on, 291
  employment data, 297
  localising tendencies in labour markets,
    42, 45
  reactions to unemployment, 285
  social fragmentation of, 297
  solidarity of, 283, 290
  structure of labour force, 8, 295–6
  surveys of unemployment, 25*n*
  unemployment for women and chil-
    dren, 292
  see also Northampton; Oldham
Labourers
  classification as skilled and unskilled,
    101, 104, 105–6, 146–9
  use of incomes-earnings differential, 149
Labrousse, C. E., 55
Lacemakers, 74–5
Lambert, Richard S., 264*n*
Lambert, Royston, 29*n*
Lampard, Eric E., 2*n*, 7, 10, 16*n*, 189*n*,
  197–8, 198*n*, 348, 349
Lancashire Witches, The, 175
Lancaster, 26*n*
Land
  Central Land Registry, 139
  Land Tax books, 142

ownership in relation to urban develop-
  ment, 50, 53, 152
ownership revealed in town plans, 117
  118
registration of title to, 136, 137
speculators in, 202, 262, 263, 266, 269,
  275
values, 4
see also Building
Landecker, Werner S., 193*n*
Langford, J. A., 21*n*
Lascelles, Henry, 329
Laski, Harold J., 27
Laski, Neville, 31*n*
Laslett, Peter, 56*n*, 69, 70, 149, 198*n*
Latimer, John, 22*n*
Latin America *see* Urban development
Lavedan, Pierre, 17, 51, 52, 113*n*, 241
Lawton, R., 36, 37*n*
Lawyers *see* Solicitors
Laycock, T., 76*n*
Lazarus, Henry, 265*n*
Lee, J. M., 318*n*
Leech, John, 267
Leed, Jacob, 90
Leeds, 20*n*, 24*n*, 30*n*, 31*n*, 37, 38, 64, 151,
  337
  composition of town council, 317, 319,
    327–35
  declining power of corporation, 329
  history of, 326–7
  occupations in, 330, 331 *tables*
  ratepayers' movement, 332
  retailers on council, 333 *table*
  Street Commission, 329
  Workhouse Board, 329
  worsted industry, 328
  plate 42A
Leeds Mercury, 329, 331
Lees, Mrs Lynn, 91*n*
Legoyt, Alfred, 18, 49
Leicester, 20*n*, 25*n*, 301
  centre of, 159
  unreformed corporation of, 157
  plates 1, 2
Lennard, R. V., 29*n*
Leroy, Maxime, 57
Lespés, R., 49*n*
Levainville, J., 49*n*

27

Index

Police forces (*contd.*)
  Parish Constables Act (1842), 287
  working class intimidation of, 286, 341–2
Polismetrics, 6
Politics, local
  and licensed trade, 306–8, 310, 322, 323, 327, 337, 340
  and social structure, 15, 35*n*, 45, 303, 311–2, 321
  influence of industrial colonies on, 226, 228
  influence of migration to suburbs on, 92
  influence of religious groups on, 219
  intimidation as a force in, 227, 286, 341–2
  religious aspects of, 306, 310, 331
  study of, 34, 35*n*, 45–6, 337
  withdrawal of upper classes from, 312
  working class movements in, 46, 283, 291, 293, 308–9, 342
  see also Oldham; Exeter; Northampton; Town Councils
Pollard, A., 167
Pollard, Sidney, 32, 34*n*, 39*n*, 215
Pollins, H., 32*n*, 254*n*
Poor
  pockets of poverty, 270–1
  primary poverty, 284, 291, 293, 342
  reception area for the, 267
  research on legislative history of the, 46, 149
Pope, Liston, 299*n*
Popenoe, D., 1*n*
Pople, Robert, 307
Population *see* Demography
Population, 54
Port Sunlight, 230
Portman, D., 31*n*
Postan, M. M., 352
Postgate, R. W., 37*n*
Potts, W., 38*n*
Powell, W., 33*n*
Prentice, Archibald, 21*n*
Preston, 21*n*, 225, 229
Prince, Hugh C., 41, 253*n*, 254*n*
Pritchard, M. F., 38*n*
Pritchett, V. S., 43*n*

Privy Council, Medical Inspectorate of, 332
Probate records, 299
Provincial cities
  English, 19
  French, 56
Prudential Assurance Company, 139
Public Health, 57, 173, 331–2, 334
  and social class, in York, 75
  and town plan analysis, 118
  inspectors of nuisances, 317
  research on, 33, 46
  see also Drainage
Public Health Act (1875), 243, 247
Public houses
  as meeting-places, 175
  dates of establishment, 142
Public Record Office
  Chancery Proceedings at, 134–6
  Close Rolls at, 138
  Court of Bankruptcy records at, 141
  Home Office Papers, 341
Pudney, John, 31*n*
Pudsey, 22*n*
Pugh, R. B., 6*n*
Pwellheli, 235

Quantitative analysis, 88–9, 107
Quigby, H., 38
Quinn, James A., 191*n*

Radford, 70, 146
  family sizes in, 74–5
  household composition, 71–2
Radical Leicester, 1780–1850, 35
Railways
  influence on cities and towns, 45, 217, 235, 254, 275–6, 313
  influence on growth of suburbs, 258–9, 260, 265, 267, 268, 276
  underground, 260
  workmen's trains, 260
Ramsbottom, *plates 43, 45, 46, 47*
Rasmussen, S. E., 41, 254*n*
Ratebooks, 136, 137, 142, 271, 297
  difficulties in interpretation of, 137
Raumer, F. von, 21*n*